Executive Summary

As part of a larger study of the strategic arms competition which developed after World War II between the United States and the U.S.S.R., this study of the two countries' strategies for air and ballistic missile defense addresses two broad subjects:

(1) How did each country approach the problem of defense against the threat from the air?
(2) Why did each country accent particular elements of an air defense strategy at various periods between 1945 and 1972?

The first question concerns the means that leaders chose for defense against an increasingly sophisticated offensive threat. For the most part, the history of that sequential selection of defenses from available technology and budgetary resources is a matter of evidential fact. In Chapters IV and V and several appendices of chronologies, tables, charts, maps and notes, this volume provides a distillation of those facts for the 1945–1955 period.

The second question, by far the more difficult of the two, concerns elite perceptions and motivations—the calculus of costs and returns whereby leaders assessed threats, risks and capabilities and devised strategy. The evidence provided by research on the first question offers only partial explanations for the second; observable weapons systems do not explain but only manifest prior decisions. Chapters I to III offer judgments about the relative importance of those decisions between 1945 and 1955 and about internal versus external factors that sustained the allocation of enormous Soviet and American resources to homeland defense against enemy bomber and missile threats.

For purposes of description and analysis, the post–World War II decade is logically split by the watershed outbreak of the Korean War in June 1950. Before 1950, American deployment of resources for air defense reflected the severe budget ceilings imposed on military planners, who generally sympathized with the post war emphasis on economic growth for civilian consumption. After 1950, all aspects of American air defense were expanded.

During the pre-1950 period, constrained by limited budgetary resources, military planners concerned with civil defense succeeded in transferring responsibility for that element of air and missile defense to a civilian planning agency, dependent for execution of plans on state and local civil defense volunteers. By 1950, increasing civilian scientist concern with possible Soviet nuclear attack had sensitized public opinion to the problem. The Federal Civil Defense Act of 1950 established a civil defense operating agency; but Congress then appropriated only token budgets for what was clearly perceived to be a "mobilization," not a peacetime institution.

Although the desirability of a nationally unified and integrated air defense command and control system was recognized early, limited resources helped delay the evolution from the Army Air Forces' impoverished Air Defense Command, established in March 1946, through the Continental Air Command (December 1948) to a Continental Air Defense Command in September 1954. Within the Air Force after 1950, competition among differing functions (interceptor; penetration; tactical fighter) encouraged the conversion of older jets to the interceptor role (e.g., the F-88 which became the F-101). Still, the need for a "1954 interceptor" and the 1950–1951 competition yielded the XF-92 (later the F-102).

It was also limited budgets which constrained military planners from demanding expensive jet interceptors before 1950, although aircraft industry designers responded to defense requests for designs with a clear preference for jets and may be credited with providing the F-80 to units in time for the Korean War.

Lacking adequate air defense interceptor aircraft between 1945 and 1950, the Air Force sought to integrate most antiaircraft artillery into the Army Air Forces between 1944 and 1946; they sought operational control of all U.S. air defenses between 1946 and 1949. Within the limits of defense budgets, initial development activity for surface-to-air missiles proceeded in both the Army (Project Nike) and the Air Force (Bomarc) before the Korean War. This interservice competition for control of both antiaircraft artillery and the surface-to-air missiles was catalyzed by the appearance of a Soviet jet bomber in 1954.

Constrained budgets also confined the development of an effective early warning system to a succession of enormously expensive plans for a distant early warning (DEW) line, first conceived—and rejected—in 1946. It was not until 1950 that interim plans such as the Air Force's "Supremacy," "Lashup," and "Interim Program" could be consolidated in initial construction of a Canadian "Pinetree" line. An M.I.T. study of 1951 argued for extending early warning further away from the U.S., stimulating Canadian 1952 plans for a mid-Canada line, American 1953 final plans for the DEW line and a 1955 DEW-line extension into the Pacific Ocean with radar picket ships and airborne radar.

In the first post war decade, Soviet air defense was dominated by a concerted program to equip fighter forces with jet aircraft. A major commitment was made early in 1946 to focus on advanced jet engine development while using foreign technology to support intermediate aircraft development. The plan breaks down into three stages:

(1) The development of interim aircraft based on captured German engines. This stage resulted in the YAK-15 and MiG-9 aircraft which were first flown on April 24, 1947. These were produced in limited quantities—some 800 MiG-9's and 265 YAK-15's and 610 YAK-17's (an improved version of the YAK-15).

(2) The development of combat capabilities based on imported British technology, namely the Rolls Royce Nene and Derwent engines. This stage was to result in the YAK-23, the La-15, and the ubiquitous MiG-15. Altogether some 120 Lavochkin and 930 YAK-23 aircraft would be produced. Ultimately, approximately 12,500 MiG-15's would be produced in four variants: a day interceptor, an improved performance day interceptor, a limited all-weather interceptor, and a reconnaissance attack version.

(3) The development of advanced interceptors on the basis of native engine technology derived from the efforts of the Klimov, Lyulka, Mikhulin, and Zumansky engine design bureaus: Of the development efforts Klimov's V K-1 engine was the first and was used to power the MiG-15 bis the improved day interceptor.

As the 1946 plan was nearing fruition, the pattern of hectic development slowed. Instead of three or four prototypes being constructed in response to each established requirement, a strategy which focused on modification of the MiG-15 evolved. This strategy coincided with the Fifth Five-Year Plan which extended from 1951–1955. Only the MiG-17, a major redesign of the MiG-15, was committed to series production between 1950 and 1954.

In 1948, a requirement for an all-weather interceptor resulted in development of three different two-engine, radar-equipped prototypes—the Su-15, the La 200A, and the MiG-310. These were awkward designs which attempted to incorporate two centrifugal flow engines and a radar in the same fuselage. They were dropped in favor of a radar modification of the MiG-15—a short-range interim expedient. It was not until 1951, with the development of the Mikhulin AM-5 small, efficient, axial-flow engine that a long-range, all-weather interceptor became technically convenient. Such an engine made practical an alternate aircraft configuration which would accommodate the large radome associated with Soviet air intercept radars of that era. There is sufficient evidence to believe that the aircraft which would eventually accommodate the "requirement" for an all-weather area interceptor, the YAK-25, arose outside of the normal process of Soviet research and development decision-making. The YAK-25 appears to have been the result of an initiative of the designer taken up directly with Stalin. Thus, the aircraft that was wanted concurrently with the formation of PVO in 1948 was not available until 1954.

As was the case in jet technology, the Soviet's post war SAM program was based on German technology. Unlike their well-developed aircraft design capabilities, however, the Soviets had carried on no practical work in guided missiles. Thus, while jet aircraft developed rapidly, SAMs developed at a slower pace with a much greater reliance on German technicians. At the end of the war, the Soviets found themselves with four candidate German systems for development: the Schmetterling, the Wasserfall, the Rheintochter III, and the Enzian. Of these, the only supersonic prototype, the Wasserfall, was ultimately chosen as the focus of development activity.

As the program was relatively more dependent on German technology than the jet aircraft program, so it was more dependent on German technicians. In 1946, a number of German technical teams were transported to the Soviet Union. By 1949, these teams had developed experimental designs for semi-active guidance, for computational equipment, and for a production version of the Wasserfall. In 1951, however, an improved design, about guidance details, was submitted by a German group located at Gorodlomlya. It is believed that this is the design which evolved to the SA-1 system which achieved operational capability in 1954. The SA-1 was deployed in 56 sites, each with 60 fixed launchers in two concentric circles around Moscow, and it appears the system was intended for deployment around Leningrad although construction ceased at an early stage. A more practical weapon, the SA-2, was apparently under way at that time.

Contrary to the trend in western development which shifted attention from guns to surface-to-air missiles, the Soviets maintained a strong AAA development effort. That the program was one of continued emphasis is evidenced by the pace of development: a 100-mm. gun in 1949, a 57-mm. weapon in 1950, and a 130-mm. gun in 1954. Associated with the new weapons were complementary systems of radar and optical fire control. The 100-mm. system was deployed around Moscow in 1950 and 1951 in numbers which, by one estimate, reached 720 while similar, but smaller deployments were undertaken around Warsaw Pact capitals. While it is evident that the Soviets continued a massive production and deployment effort for these and earlier weapons, at this point in the research it is impossible to validate data to a sufficient degree to draw well-founded conclusions. Detailed analysis of trends in AAA deployment and relations to the overall Soviet strategic defense effort will be deferred until subsequent volumes of this report.

Soviet early warning systems during World War II had relied primarily on visual and sound methods, although some radar equipment was apparently used. Still, the technology was available. During the later years of the war, the Soviets received samples and/or significant information on nearly all of the major U.S. and British radars which were in operation. This included the U.S. SCR-584 fire control radar, the British searchlight control radar "Elsie," and a series of others. Possession or knowledge of these radars enabled the Soviets to produce similar models of their own.

From their experience in World War II, the Soviets determined that they would need an integrated, radar-based early warning system. This led to the fielding of an extensive radar early warning system by 1950. Soviet research, after a period of ample time to assimilate foreign technology and as a response to the increasing bomber threat, showed a marked increase in new or improved radar systems from 1952 to 1955. By 1955, the system afforded continuous coverage in fair depth for the entire country with the exception of the least vulnerable portions of the national frontier. It also encompassed Eastern Europe.

The air warning system had the following characteristics at this stage:

(1) Performance was still unimpressive by Western standards;
(2) Limited range necessitated the use of greater numbers of radars to give continuous coverage;
(3) The Soviet Union's great size, as further extended by the East European countries, permitted radar positioning far in advance of the area to be defended;
(4) The system was built for simplicity and relatively maintenance-free operation;
(5) Most of the equipment was mobile and extremely easy to conceal.

By 1948, Soviet civil defense programs had received increased attention in a variety of ways, including shelter construction in new buildings, mandatory study circles and instructor training programs, and periodic endorsements by the media. DOSAAF, a paramilitary organization which assumed responsibility for civil defense training and instruction, was established in 1951. Although few military personnel were previously involved in civil defense, less than two years later an antiaircraft general became chairman of DOSAAF, indicating the growing importance of its defense-related functions. The evolution of DOSAAF and civil defense was further marked by two events in 1955:

(1) The new DOSAAF commander, below, advocated the use of reserve or demobilized soldiers for training and instruction, and
(2) The first compulsory civil defense training, a 10-hour program, was initiated for the adult population of the Soviet Union.

These milestone events, which began the transition from a civilian-directed, local, voluntary civil defense structure to a military-directed nationwide, mandatory program were prefaced the preceding year by the first civil defense literature mentioning nuclear weapons. This public acknowledgement symbolized the beginning of a new civil defense orientation, one in which "weapons of mass destruction" had to be recognized as an inevitable part of defensive measures. Future civil defense developments, spurred by military-political debates over the outdated procedures of old programs, were a result of this changing strategic situation. Thus, civil defense maintained an important position in the defense branches of the Soviet military and eventually gained recognition by the political leaders of the U.S.S.R.

During the first decade after World War II, the contrasts between the two air defense systems of the world's greatest continental powers were striking. In the U.S.S.R., the defense clearly dominated Soviet development and deployment of an obsolescent but nationally integrated early warning system, supported by a diversity of improved antiaircraft artillery, high-speed (limited range) jet interceptors and surface-to-air missiles (to ring Moscow), all under a single national air defense agency aiming at the military integration of all national air defense resources, including civil defense.

Executive Summary

In contrast, the United States (supported by Canada) was attempting to buy time with distance. After the Korean War began, forward deployment of American forces to the Western Pacific and Western Europe gradually provided a base structure for an American deterrent offensive capability. By 1955, homeland air defense, while not entirely neglected, had barely reached a consensus about nationally integrated command and control over limited antiaircraft, interceptor and surface-to-air missile defense systems. Early warning system construction was only beginning and civil defense was largely divorced from military influence.

Why were these contrasts so pronounced? Some of the reasons are so obvious as to require no extensive elucidation. The traditional political "style" of decision and administration in the two societies encouraged noisy controversy, debate and competition for control over decentralized centers of power, on the one hand, and an autocratic and highly centralized approach to problem-solving, on the other. Those historical distinctions in the political and decision process were reinforced by marked differences in economic capability. Impoverished after the war, the U.S.S.R. was in no position to waste resources—a fact which encouraged careful planning of both defense and non-defense resource allocations. Conversely, the United States emerged from the war as the wealthiest country on earth, facing an enormous demand by an impatient population for consumer goods, not more and more defense.

Deeply influenced by those traditional non-military considerations, the approach to air defense by each country's leaders was inevitably driven by a distinctive military heritage. For American leaders, the war confirmed the importance of keeping and fighting enemies at a distance, preferably thousands of miles across two oceans. The experience of the war further validated a continuing American faith in the offense, then (in 1945) translated in precedent and practice to a global stage. Finally, the tradition of competition between the Army and the Navy for resources and roles was a prevailing manifestation of American competitive political, economic, and administrative style.

In contrast, the war confirmed Soviet military planners' historic concern with surprise attack, probably from Europe, directed at the heart of the homeland. Unlike the Americans, who had the tradition and the capability of mobilizing and projecting offensive air and naval power over vast distances, the Soviets needed reliable defensive military power, principally ground forces supported by airpower, immediately available since time-distance factors precluded a lengthy mobilization process.

In the context of their distinctive military heritage, 1945 found the Soviets sensitized to the urgency of defense against a probable threat from Europe, where American and British airpower would be the most likely immediate threat. Air defense was, therefore, a matter of priority for the U.S.S.R. The Americans, confident of their doctrine, their capabilities and their prestige, facing no plausible threat from the air and sensitized in any case, to the foreign war (probably in Europe) instead of homeland defense, awarded air defense a secondary role in the priority of defense issues. Homeland defense was in Europe and Asia.

From the start-point in 1945 of differing priorities assigned to air defense, for reasons of long-term political, economic, and military ingredients in the security environment, American and Soviet strategies of response to perceived threats were largely the result of domestic political and economic considerations before 1950. Given the available technology (British and German, bought or captured) in the U.S.S.R., the Soviet focus on the application of that technology to improved antiaircraft artillery and the jet interceptor reflected the urgency and single-minded Stalinist decision-style of the period. Given their attitude plus a shortage of budgets for military purposes and their competition decision-style, Americans experimented with a variety of air-defense-relevant technologies without building an effective system.

After 1950, the availability of more budgetary resources permitted American defense planners to embark on an enormously expensive early warning system. That system reflected the logic of the American military ethic—to buy time with distance, a logic that erected concentric rings of defense and potential-military warning around the American heartland, first and foremost to the outer reaches of the European peninsula and the Western Pacific, then to early-warning radar lines in Canada and off the American coast. The Soviet (and Chinese) threats in Korea thus gave focus to a new sense of urgency and substance to pre-1950 concepts for American defense policy. The appearance of a Soviet H-bomb in 1953 and a Soviet jet bomber in 1954 plus rising tensions in Europe reinforced a burgeoning pace of strategic interaction after 1950 and encouraged the American development of both supersonic jet aircraft and surface-to-air ballistic missiles.

Initially constrained by their indigenous technology, the Soviets after 1950 urged advanced interceptor and SAM development while making-do with an improved version of the MiG-15 and passive nationally integrated civil defense system. By 1955, the increasing speed of high-altitude, American jet bombers and a coming generation of nuclear-tipped ballistic missiles had seriously eroded the defense utility of the East European buffer and underscored the need for a shift in Soviet emphasis from area and even point defense (whether with AAA, interceptors, or SAMs) to a deterrent offensive capability. The stage was set for a global strategic interaction dialogue in which technology and research and development would become the critical ingredients.

Chapter I

American and Soviet Strategy: A Comparison

A. Factors Influencing Air Defense Development and Deployment, 1945–1950

1. Perspectives of the Threat and Strategic Realities

Differing perspectives and heritages influenced the Soviet and American decision makers and strategists in initial post war security policy and action. Increasingly these would concern air defense, but it was late in the period before substantial commitments resulted. Soviet action bespoke a coherent, deliberate, and central strategy; the American effort appeared more expedient and diffuse.

Seeing the war to have destroyed the existing power balance in Europe and Asia, America thought it would take years before nations—particularly the Soviet Union—would recover from the damage and losses suffered during World War II. Fundamentally, the belief was general that the peoples of Europe and Asia could not possibly face another war. With the early breakdown of former colonial empires and the emergence of independent states, the post war period witnessed the removal of a major cause for war.

Sole possession by the United States of the atomic bomb made a large-scale war very unlikely. The judgment was general that it would be foolhardy for a power lacking nuclear weapons to engage in war against one that had the bomb and could deliver it. To the extent that the American public saw the Communists to be a military threat, the U.S. atomic monopoly provided a simple, solid answer. Basically, Americans thought that Communist resort to military force would result in full-scale war and, in such a war the United States would win with air/atomic power. A significant opinion thought it essential to control atomic arms. Future nuclear developments could produce even more powerful weapons. Countermeasures were unlikely and active defense difficult, even unrealistic. Retaliation capabilities would provide the principal security for the United States according to other sources.

In the immediate post war period within official Washington, the issue of a future atomic war seemed remote. In November 1945, the United States, Britain, and Canada agreed to give up atomic weapons and all other major weapons of mass destruction. One month later, at a meeting of the "Big Three" in Moscow, the Soviet Union agreed to the same terms. While the demobilization of U.S. military forces continued through the spring of 1946, Bernard Baruch, in a speech at the U.N., rejected the idea of making rules for a next war; announced the U.S. purpose as getting rid of war; and claimed disarmament was the way of stopping war. In October 1946, Soviet Foreign Minister Molotov proposed general disarmament.

Within the Soviet Union, however, the successful U.S. nuclear test and immediate employment in war of atomic weapons through strategic air strikes had shocked the leadership. Henry Kissinger described the impact of these events:

> The end of World War II confronted the Soviet leadership with a fearful/challenge. At the precise moment when Soviet armies stood in the center of a war-wrecked Europe and Lenin's prophecies of the doom of capitalism seemed on the verge of being fulfilled, a new weapon appeared, far transcending in power anything previously known. . . . Was this to be the result of twenty years of brutal repression and deprivation and of four years of cataclysmic war that at its end the capitalist enemy should emerge with a weapon which could imperil the Soviet state as never before?[1]

The U.S. nuclear monopoly underscored a fundamental strategic reality: America could obliterate Soviet cities but the Soviet Union had no capacity to attack the American homeland. The Soviets soon would reason that another strategic reality stemmed from the U.S. monopoly; in the near future, as a result of U.S. assistance, western nations could, with relative impunity, engage in actions against Soviet-controlled areas with the American nuclear shield to deter possible Soviet retaliation. Being vulnerable, the U.S.S.R. could not afford to challenge the West, especially the United States directly.

2. Impetus for Decisions

Such factors conditioned the long-standing Soviet disposition for defense. They also helped to put the Soviet atomic program into high gear. The U.S. Smythe Report, which provided a great volume of information on the U.S. atomic effort, was published in Moscow with an initial printing of 30,000 copies. An enforced development of the Soviet atomic bomb and the obvious priority assigned to the effort makes it clear that the Soviet leadership quickly recognized the strategic challenge in a U.S. nuclear monopoly. Unwilling to concede to the West the strategic power position thought to have been won through enormous Soviet sacrifice in the war against Germany, Stalin personally involved himself, along with other principals, in efforts to close the technological gaps that could influence the Soviet strategic position.

In the United States, the atomic bomb and the appearance of jets and missiles caused a lot of rethinking in the military and naval services. The facts of the bomb caused airpower enthusiasts to emphasize the need for a force in being to fill the basic strategic role of providing a first line of defense. While the ocean barriers remained, intercontinental warfare was approaching.

In keeping with the American hope for peace and security, however, many U.S. leaders became convinced that atomic power must be directed to the prevention of war. Before the summer-scheduled atomic tests of 1946, scientists "invaded" Washington and stormed Capitol Hill, urging Congress to cancel those tests with a zeal that put professional lobbyists and pressure groups to shame.[2] The Soviet Union claimed the tests were meant as "intimidation" and protested their being carried out. Concurrently, the Canadian Government released details of an extensive Soviet atomic espionage effort directed from the Ottawa Embassy of the U.S.S.R. The Soviet strategy appeared from these seemingly incidental events to be clear: all-out pursuit of an atomic capability while inhibiting further U.S. development in the nuclear field.

3. Influence of Intelligence and Some Economic Limitations

America judged the Soviets would take considerable time if they were to develop atomic weapons, comparing the tremendous U.S. effort and capacity with the war-damaged Soviet industrial base and limited technology.

---

[1] Kissinger, *Nuclear Weapons and Foreign Policy*, p. 262.
[2] Strikland, *Scientists in Politics*, p. 2; Lapp, *The New Priesthood*, pp. 95–100.

Chapter I: American and Soviet Strategy: A Comparison

In the fall of 1945 an official U.S. estimate deprecated the Soviet ability to develop "trans-ocean missiles" and "B-29 type" bombers, putting that possibility beyond 1950 while at the same time it projected the likelihood of later Soviet capabilities for attack against the United States.[3] A more immediate, even imminent, Soviet attack threat was acknowledged about three years later, however, in an early NSC paper which credited the Soviet TU-4—a "B-29 type" aircraft by then operational in the Soviet Air Force—as capable of attack against the United States. Among its conclusions, NSC 20/4 saw the U.S.S.R. also to be capable "by 1955" of "serious air attacks" against the United States.[4]

An immediate defense against mid-term potentials for air attack on the United States was not needed, it appeared, although U.S. air defense thinking anticipated the future; official positions were that active defenses could be mobilized when required. There was insufficient urgency to gain support for a USAF proposal for developing an early warning system; economy came first.

In the fall of 1947, soon after establishment as a separate service, the U.S. Air Force had developed a plan for an extensive aircraft control and warning system to provide a framework for what could be a functioning air defense system. Congress failed to act on legislation required to support the proposed system. More than a year would pass before required approval of a lesser program came about. This delay resulted in expedient action in 1948 to begin work on a temporary and limited program using available World War II equipment. While U.S. policy recognized growing Soviet hostility and improving military capabilities, air defense support was limited.

Implicitly, estimates at the time demonstrated the simple fact: the United States did not know what the Soviets were doing or had decided to do about strategic force development. Nor were these estimates the evident, direct cause of specific measures for the air defense of the United States. Current concepts inclined to a strategy to:

(1) Deny enemy bases close to America,
(2) Establish good warning,
(3) Improve AAA and fighters, and for the future,
(4) Design missiles to meet long-term offensive air and missile developments.

The 1947–1948 Air Force programs to develop radar warning for the United States, however, felt the pinch of economy; U.S. active military strength also declined through continued demobilization. Overall defense support was only about four percent of the U.S. gross national product. At the same time, however, the United States began an increasing involvement in questions of European security. U.S. views of the strategic situation there were mixed, although a consensus did develop in the face of apparent Soviet aggressiveness. In contrast, from the start of the Cold War, the Soviet leadership had a clear view of strategic purpose in Europe. Various measures were fused to further the security of the Soviet state. The military and technical requirements and priorities necessary to realize that goal rated strong support. The Tupolev copy of the U.S. B-29 illustrated that fact.

The TU-4 had come along more rapidly than anticipated, only one of a number of accelerated developments to confound the United States which were achieved through Soviet programs of enforced technical effort. Derived from three U.S. B-29's which had landed in the Soviet Union in 1944, this Soviet aircraft

---

[3] Joint Intelligence Committee, OJCS, "Strategic Vulnerability of the U.S.S.R. to Limited Air Attack," (JIC 329), 3 November 1945.
[4] NSC 20/4, 24 November 1948.

began to appear in production numbers in 1947, one year following establishment of Long Range Aviation as part of the Soviet Air Forces. U.S. intelligence saw the TU-4 as a B-29 and, therefore, ascribed to it a comparable role. Whatever its role as actually conceived and planned by Soviet leaders, early development of this aircraft was a noteworthy technical achievement. It gave clear evidence of growing Soviet capabilities, in an operational military sense and as a development milestone. Taken together with the deliberate, known Soviet programs for the systematic exploitation of German scientists and other western technology, U.S. intelligence needs concerning Soviet military capabilities seemed to be underscored.

While U.S. intelligence saw the TU-4 as a threat to the United States, the Soviet leaders looked to their developing strike force as a means of defending the homeland, since the TU-4 and the atomic weapon would allow attack of the forward bases needed to launch strikes against the U.S.S.R. Soviet naval capabilities would help against carriers. Protection of the homeland would be carried out by active, coordinated air defense. Growth of Soviet strategic power, therefore, generated intelligence requirements which soon became more acute and difficult when the Soviet Council of Ministers tightened security laws of the U.S.S.R. by issuing in the summer of 1947, a wide-ranging list of items constituting "state secrets."

From the beginning of the Cold War, the U.S. felt an increasing need for good intelligence and information concerning Soviet capabilities and actions. This requirement grew while demobilization caused continuing reductions in military intelligence organizations. That fact and the exclusive jurisdiction given to CIA in certain collection activity made for an increased dependence on CIA. As the Soviet military threat appeared to grow while military intelligence capabilities contracted, there was a tendency to attribute to CIA blame for all inadequacies in intelligence concerning the Soviet Union.

With U.S. official diplomatic representation to Moscow increasingly isolated as the Cold War developed, the Soviet atomic explosion in August 1949 made the COMINFORM's professed intention of "defeating" the West and "crushing" the imperialist camp more ominous. The Soviet pattern of action leading up to the atomic achievement appeared to many Americans as aggressive, sinister expansionism. The Soviet/Communist post war hard line was increasingly hostile; the growth in Soviet military capabilities seemingly backed aggressive intent.

4. Increasing Focus on Europe

The United States saw Soviet aggression in Europe to be growing in likelihood and soon became a conviction. The Soviets, aware of their vulnerability and conscious of the potentials of the atomic bomb quickly sought to ensure their territorial security, looking for a safe, secure protective belt of countries to cover their Western frontier. Initially, the effort attempted to gain Communist political control in areas occupied by Soviet military forces, particularly those countries along its frontiers.

By the winter of 1946–1947, the Soviet leadership decided that the United States would use its strength to define the "capitalist" system in Europe. Specific evidence was seen in Secretary of State James Byrnes' major speech in Stuttgart in September 1946 indicating that America would help reconstruct Germany and that U.S. troops would remain in Europe. The apparent U.S. generosity in helping European recovery and the Marshall Plan's call for "positions of strength," however, seemed to the Soviets to represent a coming threat.

It would be several years later before the United States officially recognized the hostile intent of the Soviet Union and not until 1950 did the NSC declare that U.S. policy would seek openly to reduce Soviet power and influence. In contrast, Stalin quickly had judged the U.S. intent in Europe to be threatening. In early April, 1946, Stalin told the U.S. Ambassador, Bedell Smith, that the "United States of America has definitely aligned itself against the U.S.S.R."[5]

Soviet defensive concepts built on the view that the European area was the primary source of military threat. The Marshall Plan fed Soviet suspicions of U.S. motives because Moscow feared it represented a U.S. calculation that it was cheaper to buy Europeans as soldiers than to equip American forces. This explained U.S. reasons for demobilizing and the fact that the United States had no large, standing Army. Building "positions of strength" would allow successful local wars against Socialist states while retaining the capability for major war with strategic air and naval forces.

Soviet efforts to exploit post war advantages, gained through the Allied victory, involved attempts at expansion while the West demobilized military forces and attempted to rehabilitate Western Europe. However, initial Soviet moves were not made as reactions to specific U.S. or Western threats. Unwillingness to leave Azerbaijan, violations of the Yalta Agreement in Europe, pressures on Turkey, support of Greek guerrillas, an apparent takeover of Czechoslovakia, and support of Asian revolutionary forces were obviously Soviet efforts to expand. Coupled with a continued and increasingly hard line in dealing with the Western Allies, Soviet actions were taken to be dangerous. To the Americans, therefore, the growth in Soviet military capabilities appeared to back aggressive intent.

5. Strategic Concepts

With the resulting declaration of a containment doctrine in 1947, the need for more U.S. military strength grew. Containment required U.S. military strength to back the policy and to be prepared for war if it came although the basic concept also entailed promoting the strength of allies through economic and military assistance, primarily in Europe. The form U.S. military strength should assume became a debate. Air power issues began surfacing in the Pentagon where Secretary Forrestal was urging the development of air power to take place over a span of years. In the newly created Defense Department, he looked to the JCS to provide a "strategic plan" for the military establishment to bring into better "balance" the components of that establishment.

The President's Air Policy Commission, appointed in late 1947 and headed by Thomas K. Finletter, studied air power issues based principally on economic concern for the U.S. aviation industry. The Finletter report, however, stated that security would be found only in a policy of arming the United States strongly enough to deter attack. The Commission had tried to establish the date when an enemy action might have nuclear weapons in quantity but settled on 1 January 1953 through its own judgment. Above all, the report emphasized the need for: "A counter offensive air force in being which will be so powerful that if an aggressor does attack we will be able to attack with the utmost violence."[6] This accorded with the popular view and built upon existing capabilities and the extensive U.S. experience of the war.

Concurrently, the Republican Congress had organized a "Joint Congressional Aviation Policy Board," which also examined issues involved in providing well-balanced military and naval air forces. In a March 1948 report, this Board criticized the JCS for inability to develop a unified plan for defense of the United States and claimed that the only defense against modern war "will be swift and more devastating retaliatory

---

[5] Smith, *Moscow Mission*, p. 40.
[6] Survival in the Air Age: Report of the President's Air Policy Commission, p. 23.

attack."[7] These reports settled little; the B-36 versus the carrier arguments were ahead. That controversy marked the first really substantive post war examination of U.S. military policy and strategy and ritualized "strategic warfare." Prestige and boasts became mixed with convictions and experience. To Americans, military opinions and proposals were fractionated and confused. The bickering about the worth of sea power versus air power, carriers versus battleships, and the strength of the Navy and the Air Force confounded them.

The core of the Air Force–Navy conflict developed over the merits of the B-36. A specific consideration concerned the capability of bombers to penetrate Soviet air defenses. Questions came up about daylight penetration capabilities, expected attrition, and B-36 vulnerability due to slow speed. Soviet jet fighter developments and guided missiles being developed were recognized to improve defensive capabilities. The consideration of Soviet air defense capabilities, however, leaned substantially on U.S. Navy and Air Force operational experience during World War II more than on hard, current intelligence concerning those capabilities. Thus, important U.S. deliberations about security policy and strategy were marked by considerable bitterness and at least some ignorance.

Soviet political objectives were supported by exploitation of immediate opportunities in the post war period. While sensitive to a basic vulnerability in light of the U.S. nuclear monopoly, U.S. capabilities evidently did not bar early Soviet attempts at expansion. The Soviet strategy sought to discourage attacks on the homeland and reflected prudence and caution. Conditioned by events in China and other parts of Asia, however, the Soviets pursued aggressive actions against the West in Central Europe before having achieved atomic capabilities and in the face of significant residual resistance and ferment in the Eastern Europe region. By 1948, hardening Western attitudes, the growth and forward deployments of the U.S. Strategic Air Command accelerated Soviet efforts for defense.

6. Domestic Political Considerations

In Washington, Congress had, since the Republican victory in 1946, pressured the Administration for economies and pledged to reduce taxes. The Truman Doctrine and economic commitments for foreign rehabilitation represented substantial, growing expenditures. New or additional expenditures were resisted. Active opponents of the containment doctrine suggested Europe go it alone with a halt to U.S. economic support or held that reduced U.S. grants should suffice to aid Europe. Some argued that Asia, rather than Europe, rated priority in terms of the U.S. political and strategic focus. This view was given currency as the founding congress of the COMINFORM in 1947 witnessed Zhdenov's call for concerted, intensified activity in Asia as a means of putting the "rear of capitalist system in jeopardy."[8]

Republicans claimed that the Democratic administration had failed to secure U.S. strategic interests in the Far East. Concentration on Europe left Asia, with its vast territories and great populations, prey to Communist expansionism. In terms of world domination, Asia offered the Communists special opportunity. They were already supporting revolutionary activity in Burma, India, Indo-China, Malaya, China, and the Philippines.

Significant reserve about official American strategy perspectives for Europe existed and were later stated by Senator Taft: "Before the Russian threat, I was very dubious about the policy of advancing money

---

[7] National Aviation Policy, Report of the Congressional Aviation Policy Board, pp. 7–8.
[8] Ulam, Expansion and Coexistence: The History of Soviet Foreign Policy 1917–1967.

Chapter I: American and Soviet Strategy: A Comparison

to Europe in such large amounts . . . All of this aid has been extended to Western Europe out of all proportion to our aid to the rest of the world. . . ."[9]

Seeing America as "the citadel of the free world," Senator Taft thought that Americans should give first consideration to defense of their own country, for its destruction would mean "an end to liberty everywhere . . . ."[10]

Political considerations showed in other ways. There was a sharp contest for control of atomic development; the McMahon bill appeared to be an effort to keep it from military hands with a new all-civilian Atomic Energy Commission to control future nuclear production. With military backing, an alternative appeared in the May-Johnson bill. The provisions of the May-Johnson bill differed only slightly from the McMahon bill. There would be a powerful AEC to control all phases of atomic energy research, development, and industrial uses. Stiff penalties for unauthorized disclosure of information would be enacted and military officers could serve on the Commission. Many scientists opposed this last provision and that provision did not appear in the McMahon Act, which was passed and signed into law. That appeared to limit U.S. military intelligence on defense policy.

Thus, the nation witnessed a number of split views about security and was a direct party to an official denial to the U.S. military establishment of the authority to develop the most potent weapon known. Senator Vandenberg, leader of the bi-partisan foreign policy, who agreed to the transfer of control over atomic energy to peacetime civilian control, wrote: "I do not agree that in the present world affairs the Army and the Navy should be totally excluded from consultation when they deem national security involved."[11] Yet, the President personally was active in denying the armed forces custody over atomic weapons and representation on the AEC. Mr. Truman believed the basic post war issue about nuclear weapons was linked to control. He later wrote: "I strongly emphasized the peacetime uses of atomic energy, and for that reason I felt it should not be controlled by the military."[12]

Even in 1948, at the time of the Berlin crisis, the President rejected a request of the Secretary of Defense, James Forrestal, for custody of atomic weapons on the grounds that he did not want "to have some dashing lieutenant colonel decide when it would be proper to drop one."[13]

In the Soviet Union, the U.S. nuclear monopoly limited the capacity for action because a direct challenge to the West entailed substantial risk. To undertake the development of an atomic program in the face of domestic demands for reconstruction theoretically entailed considerable political risk, but firm controls of Stalin and the Party leadership supported and facilitated defense planning. Defense priorities could be and were determined quickly and at the top.

---

[9] Taft, *A Foreign Policy for Americans*, p. 85.
[10] Ibid., pp. 74–75.
[11] Vandenberg, *The Private Papers of Senator Vandenberg*, p. 256.
[12] Truman, *Memoirs II: Years of Trial and Hope*, p. 2.
[13] Millis, *The Forrestal Diaries*, p. 458. (The issue of custody would come up again. By 1949, when the possibility of a surprise atomic attack by the Soviets was more a reality after successful detonation of an atomic device and the TU-4 became operational in the Soviet Air Force, it was argued that to be instantly ready to retaliate it was necessary for the USAF to have atomic weapons ready and to maintain continuing control over them. President Truman ruled that the AEC would keep custody. In July 1950, after the outbreak of the Korean War, a decision was made to stockpile non-nuclear components of atomic bombs in Britain and, in April 1951, President Truman decided to transfer nuclear components to the armed forces. A significant part of the inventory was not transferred until after a special committee of the NSC recommended this action in September 1952. Hewlett and Duncan, *Atomic Shield*, pp. 521, 537–539, 585.)

The American process of strategic decision making was more tortured. Prestigious committees, commissions, and boards often invested energy and attention in becoming informed on national security issues; many became sounding boards; others eventuated as conduits for skillful, partisan pleaders. While Americans looked to the Washington leadership for ways to realize peace and security in the early post war period, there was no single focal point in the government for development of coherent policies to secure the peace.

7. Decision Style

Calls for firmness with the face of early Soviet moves lacked real definition and brought little action. Only gradually did U.S. policy take shape. Containment checked demobilization however and, from 1947, U.S. military capabilities in strategic striking power improved.

The U.S. decision-making process was more structured following enactment of the National Security Act. Changes in emphasis and procedures also followed but while machinery existed for handling important national security matters, playing by ear and ad hoc arrangements seemed a regular resort.

Apart from the lack of acceptance of a credible Soviet general war threat, U.S. security policy frequently lacked "national" perspectives; lack of general agreement on fundamental defense questions and basic strategic concepts tended to fragment and inhibit the evolution of U.S. security policy. The concept of "balance"—something for everyone—and consideration for "Allies'" sensitivities complicated policy making. While the NCS was proposed as a "policy forming" body to assist the President, the lack of a single decision point for security/defense matters was notable. Within the Defense Department, internal decisions, made in the post war period or derived from earlier practice carried over in the years that followed as precedents to govern in the allocation of roles and missions done by the general realignment of the National Military Establishment. Various boards and committees examined issues and made recommendations on the basis of merit, environment, and perceived interest.

Emphasizing a limited role for the NSC, President Truman, in the period from inception of the Council in September 1947 to late June 1950, attended only 11 of 56 meetings. As the Council functioned during the period, members of the NSC inevitably began to circumvent the established structure and procedures and to submit their recommendations directly to the Council or the President. More and more recommendations come to rest in ad hoc committees.

Following explosion of a Soviet atomic device in late 1949, President Truman directed that all major national security policies be "coordinated" through the NSC and its staff and he began to attend regularly the meetings of the Council. Soon, he directed a reorganization of the staff and greatly restricted attendance at NSC meetings. While the reorganization tightened the structure and limited attendance enhanced the role of the NSC, Walter Millis stated in 1950 that in the pre–Korean War period: "The effect of NSC is not prominent: NSC no doubt considered the staff papers, debated policy and arrived at recommendations, but every glimpse we have been given of the actual policy making process . . . shows Defense, State, the Budget Bureau, the White House making independent determinations—usually on a hasty if not extemporaneous basis—which really counted."[14]

---

[14] Millis, op. cit., pp. 454–455. As one illustration of ad hoc arrangements, General Bradley reported details of U.S. deliberations following the 25 June 1950 invasion of South Korea during the Congressional hearings on the relief of General McArthur held the following year. General Bradley reported that the President scheduled a 7:45 PM dinner on 25 June 1950 at Blair House to which Secretaries of State and Defense, together with Secretaries of the Armed Forces, General Bradley and the Joint Chiefs of Staff and certain State Department officials were invited. There was not enough time for prior JCS meetings or conferences by the Armed

But the NSC did develop and formally considered in early years basic studies dealing with the likelihood of Soviet threats to U.S. security which influenced planning and action for the strategic air defense of the United States. Approved by the President on 24 November 1948, NSC 20/4 concluded that the gravest threat to the United States stemmed from the "hostile designs" of the Soviet Union.

In April 1950, the NSC published a basic policy statement against the backdrop of an incident over the Baltic Sea the same week when a U.S. patrol plane was shot down by Soviet fighters and the Soviet Union officially protested to the United States an alleged violation of Soviet territory by the U.S. aircraft. U.S. policy, thereafter, would seek to reduce the power and influence of the U.S.S.R. which—in the view of the Joint Chiefs of Staff expressed in the NSC paper—could, if war should occur, overrun Western Europe, attack the British Isles by air and attack selected targets in North America with atomic weapons. After setting 1954 as the "critical date" when the Soviets would possess 200 atomic bombs, NSC 68 declared: "The United States must increase . . . air and civilian defenses to deter war and to provide reasonable assurance in event of war that it could survive the first blow."

While positive in its recognition of the need for an improved U.S. air defense, the primary threat foreseen in NSC 68 was a massive ground attack against a hostage Europe. It would take the partial mobilization following the outbreak of war in Korea to provide the real impetus for an improved U.S. continental air defense.

8. Significant Initial Air Defense Decisions

Soviet decision making built on the proven wartime arrangements and procedures of the combined political and military leadership under Stalin. While the problem of strategic air defense was new to the Soviets, they set out to analyze and utilize experience of World War II. Systematically they examined the feasibility of various air defense measures and attempted to determine the requirements for systems.

Extrapolating from known actions early Soviet decisions concerning air defense included:

(1) Closing the technological gap;
(2) Developing and deploying an early warning and surveillance system;
(3) Developing, producing, and deploying large numbers of clear weather jet interceptors; and
(4) Developing guided missile technology.

The precise times and circumstances relating to these decisions is difficult to affirm. Some appear to be the product of a continuing momentum; some may be linked with external factors. On balance, none taken in the initial post war period appear to be specific reaction to U.S. developments.

The Soviet strategic position, preferred strategy, experience of failure and success, ambitions, and personality of different principals in the decision-making process and internal competition for resources all impinged on how decisions were made. Contrasted with the United States, the Soviet Union obviously made decisions on the basis of Moscow's perception of goals and objectives. Top level direction and authority underwrote the decisions. Actions taken were in keeping with a hard, dogmatic line and in the face of the

---

Forces Policy Council. The guests included some, but not all, NSC members. "A major portion of the evening was taken in the individual, unrehearsed, and unprepared statements of the several Chiefs and Secretaries"; this appears to constitute ad hoc arrangements (cf. General Bradley, *MacArthur Hearings* Part II, p. 1049; Ibid., Part IV, p. 2580).

U.S. nuclear monopoly at the beginning of the post war period. The U.S. monopoly did not impel Soviet air defense measures but may have emphasized their importance.

While the Soviet Union reduced and reorganized its Armed Forces and watched a growing "capitalist encirclement," actions were put in motion to have ready a balanced, integrated operational air defense force. Steps to this end were gradual, but accelerated in the late 1940's. With the Korean War, the Soviets made an increased commitment to the air defense of the homeland.

U.S. decisions for post war air defense were substantially influenced by the recommendations of the Patch and Simpson Boards which brought about a general reorganization of the Army in early 1946 and realigned research and development and procurement functions. Both boards also gave attention to an Army Air Force proposal that a large antiaircraft artillery component (118,610 personnel) be established in the post war Air Force. (See Appendix A for details of similar AAF proposals during World War II.) The Patch Board recommended the several artilleries—Coast, Field, Antiaircraft—be combined under the Army Ground Forces believing that transfer to the Air Force of AAA would have the Army/OSE AAA fire support useful against ground targets.[15] The Simpson Board treated the transfer question in more detail, stating:

(a) The Air Force is charged with the mission of air defense and will require antiaircraft artillery under its command to carry out this mission. However, the Board believes that for the immediate future, at least, antiaircraft artillery can be trained with and attached to Air Force units from time to time in order that the necessary coordination can be developed to enable the Air Force to carry out its mission of air defense.

(b) The Board also considered the enormous task the Air Force will have in carrying out the many additional duties that will devolve upon it when it becomes a separate Service. It is doubtful if the organization and training of antiaircraft units should be added to these new duties at present. At a later date when we have a Single Department of the Armed Forces, it may be found desirable to organize a common Antiaircraft Artillery Arm to serve the air, land and sea forces.

(c) The Board further believes that to transfer the antiaircraft artillery to the Air Forces because some of it is needed to operate with fighter aircraft in air defense would, in effect, constitute an admission that every Service must be completely self-contained. This is contrary to the best principles of organization.

(d) In view of the above, the Board believes that the recommendation of the Patch Board is sound and that the Antiaircraft Artillery should not be transferred to the Army Air Forces at present.[16]

The issue of control of AAA, then internal to the Army, would continue as a factor in the basic roles and missions allocation to occur as part of the realignment of the National Military Establishment under the National Security Set of 1947. A decision on the issue would establish a precedent, however, to guide or govern that later role and mission allocation.

The War Department, in early 1946, assigned responsibility for Continental defense to the Commanding General, Army Ground Forces. Following reaction by the Army Air Forces, the War Department published Circular 138 in May 1946 specifying that the recently established Air Defense Command of the Army Air Force would provide for the air defense of the United States.

In June 1946, AAF staff and the "Air Board"—a group of distinguished civilians, retired Air Force generals, principal Air Force commanders, and including the Commanding General, AAF—met in Washington

---

[15] War Department, "Reorganization of the War Department," Lieutenant General Patch.
[16] War Department, "Report of Board of Officers on Organization of the War Department," Lieutenant General W. H. Simpson, President.

to consider the antiaircraft question as developed by the Simpson Board. As a result, the AAF formulated ten proposals for presentation to the War Department which substantively urged integration of AAA into the Air Force. This elicited a reaction from the AGF and General Devers soon sent General Spaatz a study, "Security from Enemy Action," which took the basic position that defense against air attack by AA guns, within their range, was a ground force responsibility. In September 1946, the War Department decided that the AAF would control AA units with an operational air defense mission while AGF would provide technical training to AA units.

These judgments reflected World War II experiences and built upon retrospect. References to "assigned missions" and "unity of command" were frequent. Although some appreciation for the potential growth and importance of AAA was evident in the AAF position, its central concern was to control AAA to avoid the hazard of possible friendly fire against aircraft. A particular problem was identification.

The AAF believed the problem was insoluble. Positive identification was required more than ever. Visual identification was impracticable at greater ranges and generally unreliable. No system had been devised to assure positive identification. Since various elements of the Army were then engaged in development of guided missiles for air defense, the likelihood was that the greater ranges of such weapons and the increasing speed of aircraft and missiles would further complicate the identification problem.

B. Systems Developments

1. Unilateral Efforts, Service Concepts, and Continuing Momentum in a Context of Challenge and Change

During the initial post war period, U.S. air defense system developments progressed in various stages and at differing paces. There was no agreed master plan specifically to guide development of new air defense systems by the services (primarily Army and Air Force) to meet scheduled, required dates for having operational air defense capabilities deployed, manned, and ready.

The essence of most of the high-level plans and policy papers which addressed "requirements" for U.S. air defense was to point up a year of need when a significant threshold for Soviet atomic capabilities was expected. Implicitly, this indicated when U.S. forces and programs should be ready to help face that eventuality. NSC 68, the first comprehensive statement of a U.S. national strategy since the formation of the NSC, called for a great U.S. military build-up in the hopes of averting an all-out war with the Soviet Union. Prepared subsequent to the Soviet atomic explosion of 1949 and following the bitter debates about Service roles and missions and the U.S. H-bomb program, it appeared to confirm the U.S. strategy of retaliation. President Truman, however, had not approved the NSC 68 policy statement when Korean hostilities began and U.S. programs for air defense development continued on the basis of earlier, essentially unilateral, Service planning.

The debate preceding the H-bomb decision appears significant to historical consideration of air defense systems developments because strong support for a thermonuclear program gradually increased among the military services and, by bringing them together on that issue, not only helped to unify military concepts on strategic bombing but brought them in concert with the thinking of Secretary of Defense Louis Johnson who took a strong stand on the issue. At the same time, it appeared to put some distance between the military family and prominent, previously unchallenged political and scientific opinion which had become so significant in national security questions concerning the Soviet Union. That stand was in step with American public opinion and the Congress, restive and apprehensive over the early Soviet atomic success and communist espionage, and apparently ill-disposed toward a proposal to delay further U.S. nuclear research.

Scientific advice on the H-bomb issue was split and, in the State Department, a strong difference of opinion existed between George Kennan, head of Policy Planning, and Paul Nitze who replaced him and who headed the joint ad-hoc State-Defense study group which developed the paper later designated NSC 68.[17] Kennan, the premier U.S. political expert on the Soviet Union, opposed the H-bomb because it could not conceivably have a purely military employment. He believed that current U.S. programs were sufficient to deter the Soviets. He regarded Soviet atomic attack on the United States as unlikely and impractical.[18]

Scientific opinion post war on any military development was significant. Prominent scientists like Vannevar Bush and Robert Oppenheimer, by their wartime roles and well-established reputations, became increasingly important because their views on military programs had consequences for other fields of military development. Vannevar Bush left a record of opposition to new missile ventures and as early as December 1945 he testified before a Congressional Committee that he considered a 3,000 mile missile "impossible" because, he added, "technically I don't think anybody in the world knows how to do such a thing. We can leave that out of our thinking."[19] A statement of that kind had to have effect on any concept for an antimissile development.

Bush didn't believe Soviet science and technology were to be feared because scientific progress depended upon political freedom. Reacting to questions about German development of the V-2 he asked if it had paid off and then answered that from a "strict damage and cost basis the answer is no."[20] Bush mocked military opinion on weapon developments and emphasized their great problems and costs.[21] Military experience did not provide senior officers who had significant influence with an authoritative basis for challenge of such views. General Eisenhower had said of the V-2 that, "if the Germans had succeeded in perfecting and using these new weapons six months earlier than he did, our invasion of Europe would have proved exceedingly difficult, perhaps impossible."[22] Discounting weapons on the basis of cost, despite risks, appeared easy at a time when economy was a watch word. Besides, other influential senior military officers, with significant credentials, provided apparently confirming predictions. General W. Bedell Smith, U.S. Ambassador at Moscow, later Director of Central Intelligence and Under Secretary of State, told Secretary Forrestal in July 1948 that the Soviets did not, in his opinion, have the industrial competence to develop the atomic bomb in quantity for five or even ten years.[23] General Leslie R. Groves, who supervised the Manhattan Project and

---

[17] Acheson, *Present at the Creation*, pp. 346–347.
[18] Futrell, op. cit., p. 221.
[19] U.S. Senate, Inquiry Into Satellite and Missile Programs, p. 823.
[20] Bush, *Modern Arms and Free Men*, pp. 203–210.
[21] Ibid. (Bush maintained that long-range missiles had no foreseeable future in war; jibing the military and their concepts he said: "We are decidedly interested in the question of whether there are soon to be high-trajectory guided missiles of this sort spanning thousands of miles and precisely hitting chosen targets. The question is particularly pertinent because some eminent military men, exhilarated perhaps by a short immersion in matters scientific, have publicly assented that there are. We have been regaled by scary articles, complete with maps and diagrams, implying that soon we are thus all to be exterminated or that we are to employ these devices to exterminate someone else. We even have the exposition of missiles fired so fast that they leave the earth and proceed about it indefinitely as satellites, like the moon, for some vaguely specified military purpose." Bush then went on to point out the great problems and costs involved in making intercontinental rockets.)
[22] Eisenhower, *Crusade in Europe*, p. 294.
[23] Futrell, op. cit., p. 222.

Chapter I: American and Soviet Strategy: A Comparison

who knew the enormous problems of producing an atomic bomb, reportedly advised the U.S. Government that "the Soviets would need fifteen or twenty years to build the atomic bomb."[24]

How important scientific views like those Vannevar Bush advanced in the post war period cannot be stated precisely. There seems to be little question that his attitude made missiles and rockets look ridiculous to U.S. senior officials. When proposals for large missile programs went the route required for approval and authorization, the words and thoughts of scientific opinion—like Bush's—would be in the minds of various senior officials, particularly budget officials. Oppenheimer, as Chairman of the General Advisory Committee of the AEC, opposed the H-bomb and, during the four years after the war, led its opponents in advancing the case against its development largely on moral grounds.

These scientists had similar views of the world, the same belief in the dominance of American science, and shared a basic reluctance to promote significant new programs for military application. Bush felt the Communists could not advance science effectively. America would dominate the Soviet Union technologically; because it was free, the United States had little to fear from Soviet technology. Oppenheimer thought America should lead by example; since American science was so respected its actions would determine whether any nation would develop the H-bomb. Oppenheimer and Bush both thought America would lead and then Soviets would follow. Both opposed expensive new projects. In opposing military application of nuclear power and missiles, each would question technical feasibility and implied that all that was needed for war had already been developed.

Such perspectives had helped give rise to a national perspective that the Soviets were behind the United States in weapons technology. For five years after the war relatively little was done in the nuclear and missile fields even as the movement to link these weapons was under way, which would strip away America's traditional protection and leave the nation open to the threat of instant destruction. Those years were being used by the Soviets to close the technological gap. Not only did they develop their own technology but they also engaged in a major intelligence effort to gather technical and industrial know-how from the West. From individual agents to local native communists and direct open purchase, the Soviets gathered and exploited technical literature published in the West. By the fall of 1946, German missile components and a variety of test equipment were sent to the U.S.S.R. and German scientists worked there for about five years thereafter. By early 1947, a high-level coordinating group monitored Soviet missile developments and separate design teams began work on various missile projects, starting from German technology. While U.S. programs were opposed on various grounds, the Soviets were driving ahead in development of various projects having military application, including a high-priority effort for air defense, directed and supported by the top Soviet leadership. The technological gap which existed in 1945 vanished in some critical areas within a relatively few years. The myth of American scientific technical omniscience continued.

2. Air Defense Systems Components

a. Command and Control

Budgetary constraints, limited forces, and split views on roles and missions constrained effective arrangements for a centralized, unified U.S. air defense while the Soviets moved to develop an integrated organization built initially on the existing territorial jurisdiction and assigned responsibility of military

---
[24] Shepley and Blair, "The Hydrogen Bomb," p. 13.

district commanders for security of the Soviet state using available capabilities. By 1947 the concept of an integrated, national air defense organization emerged and an ordered progression to realize it begun.

b. Early Warning and GCI

Against the backdrop of directed economies, USAF planning for early warning generated a substantial program Supremacy, which was rejected in favor of a more limited eventual system. By the time of Korea, Lashup—an effort which began in late 1948—had 44 radar stations in operation. Stations were undermanned, personnel lacked training, and repair and maintenance were difficult. This stop-gap system later would be replaced by a 75-station, permanent net authorized by Congress and approved by the President in 1949.

Financial limitations affected the radar system development; in addition, however, priorities for SAC and the concept that attack would come over the polar area were great influences on this development. In turn, the Pearl Harbor investigation provided a compelling lesson not to be caught again by surprise air attack and that lesson impressed itself on Air Force commanders who had air defense responsibilities. The initial post war civil defense studies anticipating surprise attack against the United States also appear as significant influences on early warning developments. (The U.S. Civil Defense planning actions of the first five years represented a systematic and progressive development which culminated in the Federal Civil Defense Act of 1950 and the activation of a civil defense operating administration. The Act came into law in the crisis situation of the Korean War, however, and under the circumstances of the recent bitter debate about a U.S. thermonuclear program. As a result, it developed as an expedient, lacked substantial Federal fiscal support, and put responsibility for civil defense to State and local levels of government.)

The Soviets quickly recognized their technological lag in radar as early as 1945 when they obtained through lend-lease the U.S. SCR-584 and, through wartime aid from the United States and Britain, gained a ready base of radar technology. Based upon that and in recognition of their wartime experience and other operations (surprise attack and V-2 rockets) they quickly determined a need for effective early warning. Before 1950, they developed and fielded a Soviet-produced acquisition radar—Dumbo—and followed that soon thereafter with a product of native design, Token, which quickly spread across the country in the early 1950's.

c. Interceptor Development

At the end of the war, a U.S. decision to produce a jet interceptor resulted in the F-89. Decided on in August 1945, and originally envisaged as a propeller-driven aircraft—not because of a lack of appreciation of jet technology or budget constraints—the effort looked for a quick and reliable development. Most manufacturers' designs proposed jet-powered planes. A jet design became acceptable to the Air Force when some of the manufacturers' proposals were recognized as providing the desired, specified characteristics more easily through a jet-powered aircraft.

Appearance of the Soviet TU-4, however, found the United States facing a new threat. This tended to intensify U.S. concern for air defense but did not directly affect U.S. interceptor development. Operational deployments of available fighter capabilities stepped up. These tactical fighters served as interceptors for several years thereafter. Soon a replacement for the P-61 became critical and the T-33 was programmed for conversion to the F-94 largely because of crippling difficulty with the desired all-weather aircraft, the F-89. Concurrently, in order to have all-weather aircraft, the Air Force programmed a rapid conversion of the F-86.

Chapter I: American and Soviet Strategy: A Comparison

Soviet aircraft development in the immediate post war period quickly sought a jet fighter responsive to Stalin's reported injunction to the Soviet aircraft industry to build aircraft that would fly higher, faster and further than any in the world. With a high priority, three or four competing programs were established to meet interceptor requirements. Stalin personally was interested and, twenty months after the first Soviet jet fighters, the MiG-15 was displayed and quickly put into production. It is noteworthy that this decision took place soon after the establishment of a national air defense component in 1948.

The context of Soviet immediate post war interceptor development indicates that the aircraft were not specifically designed against the early U.S. bomber threat. The prime impression of the development effort is that it appears to have been viewed as a technological competition with foreign fighters.

d. Surface-to-Air Missiles

Development of the Army's Nike family began in 1945, weathering reductions from an overall missile funding cut the following year and a more limited budget in 1947 and maintaining steady progress thereafter. By March 1950, the Nike development was projected to become an operational weapon system and received continued support after the Korean War.

Three months later, the product of two long-standing feasibility study projects were brought together to define the characteristics of another, but long-range air defense missile or pilotless interceptor for the Air Force, which was dubbed Bomarc.

The service rivalries over air defense missiles during the period concerned roles and missions and centered primarily on operational capabilities. As a jurisdictional question, the disputes over roles and missions impacted only obliquely on these technical developments.

German scientists and technicians assisted the Soviets in their early SAM developments. By the fall of 1946 Germans were engaged in missile projects which by 1948 included the conduct of electronic experiments for development of the guidance subsystem of what eventuated as the SA-1 weapon system.[25] By November 1950, they were tasked to develop the guidance system for the SA-1.[26] Available information makes it appear that this system was the principal air defense missile weapon under development at the time. As developed—with a capacity for simultaneous engagement of significant numbers of aircraft—and later deployed at Moscow, it was intended to counter large, massed bomber raids comparable to World War II operational activity. It is not evident that it was designed to counter any specific U.S. aircraft threat.

e. Ballistic Missile Defense

In the United States (and, inferred from available evidence, also in the Soviet Union) there was a recognition in the immediate post war period that the war had uncovered the remarkable demonstration of the nuclear weapon and a long-range missile. Their appearance and potentials would require consideration of possible defensive measures. This engendered a number of studies following the war, but these efforts must be characterized as early research. Their results inclined to the view that practical steps to develop defenses against missiles would have to await significant advances in various technologies. As one seeming contrast, however, it is noteworthy that in the Soviet Union, Stalin and Malenkov are

---

[25] DIA-ST-CS-14-1-68-INT, "Soviet SA-1 SAM Systems."
[26] Ibid.

reported personally to have encouraged the development of long-range, intercontinental missiles soon after the war. This stands apart from the perspective of a principal U.S. scientific advisor, Vannevar Bush, at about the same time.

f. Summary

Postwar, both the U.S. and U.S.S.R. faced challenges for national air and missile defense. These challenges were both technical and strategic. The basic technical requirements were driven largely by the demonstrated or potential advances in offensive capabilities, both air and missile.

Each nation recognized and responded to the challenge and quickly put in motion new weapon system developments for defense. Neither acted on the basis of a "master" air defense plan nor to generate a specific counter to the other's offensive capabilities or developments, during the initial post war period. Nonetheless, threat assessments, on a worst-case basis, conditioned by World War II thinking and experience, were reflected by later operational deployments.

Soviet judgments and actions regarding national air defense requirements were conditioned by and coordinated with integrated political military strategy. Soviet actions show an early, high-level commitment to strategic air defense measures and the establishment of an organization to protect the homeland. Based upon the record, there was a priority and willing support given to post war air defense in the U.S.S.R. A variety of difficulties and problems developed and substantial resources were required.

Before the successful Soviet atomic test, the United States saw no early and credible threat to the security of the continental United States. Initial organizing steps and developmental activities were faced with disparate, competing demands and proposals, budgetary constraints, limited resources, and considerable inertia. Air defense concepts at the time included an acceptance of the strategic realities existing in the U.S. nuclear monopoly and the proven American capacity for strategic bombardment. Active air defense would rely on mobilization of reserve and National Guard units and there would be time enough to recognize the need for their call to active service.

C. Factors Influencing Development and Deployment, 1950–1955

The Korean War permitted U.S. military strength to be rebuilt, neither exclusively nor primarily to fight in the Far East theater but to counter the growing threat, visualized by NSC 68 earlier in 1950, of increased Soviet strength and to build the mobilization base in the United States in readiness for a possible general war. In Washington in the fall and winter of 1950–1951, U.S. leaders seriously feared the war in Korea was a Soviet ruse, designed to cause U.S. forces to be committed to what General Bradley, Chairman of the Joint Chiefs of Staff, called "the wrong war in the wrong place," while the Soviets attacked in Europe. The JCS thought war in Europe was close.

In the period of the Korean War, a basic debate took hold in America arguing the choices of "containment" versus "liberation"—holding the line against further Communist expansion or attempting to roll back the extensive Soviet controls in Europe. In Europe and America at the time there was growing talk and action to set up a multi-national force (EDF) under a European Defense Community. Indications pointed to the likelihood that a West German force would be included in the EDF or become part of the NATO forces. Together with the rapid expansion and deployments of U.S. armed forces to the European area as well as to the Far East, these developments appeared to confirm prior Soviet perspectives on

Chapter I: American and Soviet Strategy: A Comparison

U.S. motives in Europe, i.e., the real purpose of the U.S. rehabilitation effort was to develop military forces in order to threaten the U.S.S.R. From a meeting of Soviet and East European foreign ministers at Prague in 1950 there came a combined proposal to forbid German militarization while holding out a prospect for a unified Germany. Soviet moves seemed apprehensive. "Capitalist encirclement" seemed to be a reality.

Air defense requirements became larger as Western air offensive capabilities to threaten the U.S.S.R. grew. SAC had begun a regular system in 1948 to rotate bomber groups to England, Germany, and the Far East. Following the Korean War, a crash program to develop overseas bomber bases lengthened runways in England and Guam; opened French Moroccan bases in 1951; and in 1954, SAC aircraft began basing in Spain. Air refueling techniques pre-dated Korea but when the KC97 (tanker) fleet became operational in late 1951 the B-47s that were deploying that year became more significant pending the arrival of the B-52 on the operational scene in 1955.

Apart from those physical realities, the U.S. leadership confronted the issues of the on-going war against the backdrop of a rising concern about the 1952 general election. "Roll-back" advocates saw a significant shift in U.S. policy in 1951 because up until that time American post war support of Western Europe had emphasized economic rehabilitation. In the Mutual Security Act of 1951, that emphasis shifted to military aid. (Included in the Act was a provision authorizing $100 million to the President, whenever he deemed it to be in the U.S. national interest, to form military units of escaped Iron Curtain nationals or "for other purposes"; this provision immediately demonstrated Soviet sensitivities to possible subversive action or increased overt resistance in Eastern Europe. Vishinsky berated the U.S. motives and action in developing the Act at the U.N. General Assembly meeting in Paris in December 1951, two months after the Act became law. For several years thereafter this provision of the MSA of 1951—PL165, 82nd Congress—known as the Kersten Amendment, caused the Soviets to condemn U.S. intentions in various international forums and in their propaganda.)

To the Soviets it appeared easy to find confirmation of their worst fears. A long-standing belief seemed validated; militarists dominated the U.S. leadership—from Clay in Germany; Bedell Smith in Moscow; CIA and the State Department; Marshall in China, Defense, and State; MacArthur in Japan and later a Presidential hopeful; to Eisenhower in NATO and later the President. A genuine Soviet apprehensiveness may have caused fear that extremists were gaining power in America. This may have been a basis for Stalin's 1952 call for peaceful coexistence. The Soviets obviously were sensitive to U.S. aircraft operating near the homeland; in addition to the violent reaction in the Baltic in April 1950, a U.S. Navy aircraft was shot down in November 1951 and within two weeks, Soviet fighters forced a USAF C-47 to land in Hungary.

Following Stalin's death in 1953, Moscow surely had reason to be concerned about possible Western efforts to exploit political realignment in the transition. The basic vulnerability of the Soviet Union was especially great if, lacking a definite, secure Soviet hierarchy, the conditions giving rise to the Berlin riots of June 1953 and concurrent unrest in Poland and Czechoslovakia, were exploited by the U.S. "roll-back" extremists. What if that were coupled with air strikes against the U.S.S.R. on the theory that the advantageous time for an attack on the Soviet Union would be when the Kremlin leadership was disorganized? By this time, U.S. naval aviation, including nuclear strike aircraft, had been based in the Mediterranean region about two years and Soviet air defense now faced various air threats.

History of Strategic Air and Ballistic Missile Defense, 1945–1955: Volume I

1. Air Defense Requirements and Related Actions

U.S. continental air defense began to grow with the mobilization effort of the Korean War. The pattern of action was erratic and moved forward primarily because of the war. Based upon an initial ADC plan of 1949, 37 vital industrial areas required defenses. In March 1950, a revised plan called for defense of 60 "critical" localities; 23 would be provided AAA defenses—3 atomic energy installations, 7 SAC bases, and 13 urban industrial centers. Sixty-six AAA battalions were required for this plan. At the time, 15 AAA battalions were available for continental air defense. Forty-four radar stations of the Lashup net were completed and operational but limited by use of World War II equipment. Nonetheless, some operational capability existed and, in April 1950, armed intercept of hostile aircraft was authorized in certain areas of the United States.

In the following year, the air defense system continued its gradual build-up, but the component elements faced difficulty. There was competition for priorities; the Air Force, as a service, faced the formidable tasks of building up SAC, fighting the war in Korea, and meeting the demands for tactical air forces to serve with augmented army forces in Europe. The Army devoted a fraction of its resources to continental air defense being heavily burdened by global commitments. Thus, calls for increased air defense by various congressional leaders in the Korean War period were generally unrealistic because they looked for immediately ready forces even though they were qualified by the caveat "as soon as possible."

When they surveyed national requirements and capabilities in 1951, the Joint Chiefs of Staff were evidently impressed by the growth of Soviet air capabilities as compared with those of the United States. The notion that the U.S. could easily and cheaply achieve qualitative and technical superiority over a backward enemy was dispelled by the MiG-15 in Korea.[27] The Air Force pointed out that the Soviet Union had engaged in an accelerated development program and emphasized the rapid conversion of its sizeable air forces to jets. General Twining reportedly stated that the Soviets had several hundred TU-4s available, and the fact of a rapid growth in radars and AAA defenses in the Soviet Union was noted.

Following a long review, the JCS recognized the air defense mission of the Air Force to be an essential "D-Day task." Giving it high priority, the JCS then said: "We place such high priority on this task because we know that our continental air defense system . . . could not stop all the bombers that might be sent against us hence, our long range atomic counterattack against enemy air forces must of necessity provide the principal means of our air defense of American cities and centers of production."[28]

The JCS thus recommended to the Secretary of Defense in the fall of 1951 that the Air Force structure be increased from 95 to 143 wings. President Truman approved the increase and provided the authorization for the Air Force to reach that level, not through FY 1953, but, as suggested by his economic advisors, in the FY 1954 budget. Thus, the target date would be 30 June 1955 and, under the FY 1953 and proposed FY 1954 budgets, the Air Force received substantially greater support than the Army and Navy. With the new Administration, Secretary of Defense Charles Wilson moved to change the FY 1954 budget, taking $5.0 billion from the Air Force, $1.7 billion from the Navy, and increasing the Army's share by $1.5 billion.

Wilson was trying to narrow the Korean War mobilization base. He questioned the basis for planning requirements and the practice of aiming at a "critical" date chosen more by guess than by knowledge when

---
[27] Futrell, op. cit., p. 295.
[28] Ibid., p. 296.

Chapter I: American and Soviet Strategy: A Comparison

the Soviet threat supposedly would reach its peak. He asked proponents of a "counterattack" bombing strategy concerning:

(1) The need for a full intercontinental bomber force as well as full system of overseas bases to use for medium bombers and short-range aircraft;
(2) The need for so many bombers if three of them could carry the force of destruction it took 2,700 aircraft to lift for support of the St. Lo breakout in World War II;
(3) The need for 143 wings; he asked, if that total was irreducible, why was it when the number of aircraft per group had doubled since the concept and need for 143 wings developed.

Change was under way in the Defense Department. Both the Munitions Board and the Research and Development Board were abolished and more responsibility became vested in the Secretary of Defense, who sought to return the Joint Chiefs of Staff to "strategic planning." Appointment of Admiral Radford as the Chairman alarmed the Air Force, who recalled his prominent role in the B-36 controversy. The Air Force resisted the move to cut back the 143 wings, arguing against the concept of "balanced" forces. The question involved priorities. At issue was the minimum level of "air atomic" power needed to provide a *large margin of superiority* over the Soviets. That issue impacted air defense planning because other pressure had been building to improve continental air defense. The Air Force, responsible for air defense, argued for SAC to have an overwhelming force-in-being.

2. The Summer Study Group—Other Air Defense Views

In the summer of 1952 a group of scientists came together informally in Cambridge, Massachusetts, to discuss civil and military defenses. They were entirely an unsponsored and unofficial group, later known collectively as the Summer Study Group. They wrote a report based on their deliberations that concluded:

(1) The Soviet Union would be capable of crippling the United States by a surprise attack in two or three years by long-range bombers carrying atomic weapons;
(2) U.S. in-being and planned military and civil defenses were inadequate and capable of achieving no more than a 20 percent kill rate; and
(3) Foreseeable new technology (specifically "forward scatter" radar) would make it feasible to develop an air defense system capable of achieving a kill rate over enemy attackers of 60 percent to 70 percent.

They recommended establishing a distant early warning radar line across Canada to provide three to six hours of warning of approaching jet aircraft and establishment of a northward defense in depth. They also recommended a communications system capable of rapid transmission of air defense data through the use of automatic and integrated equipment, as well as new and improved interceptors, and the development of homing missiles for interception and destruction of enemy aircraft. Much of the technology involved in the new developments they visualized was still in the experimental stages, but the scientists had great faith in their ability to provide the hardware they anticipated. At first they estimated about a half-billion dollars to be required; later their estimate approximated $20 billion for the total project, including the computerized air direction centers. The group recommended an all-out effort to be ready by 1954.[29]

---
[29] Lapp and Alsop, "We Can Smash the Red A-Bombers," *Saturday Evening Post* (21 Mar 1953), p. 19.

The Air Force was not very receptive to the Summer Study Group report. Although the Air Force had responsibility for air defense among a number of missions, the leadership of the Air Force was unenthusiastic over the commitment of the several billion dollars required to fund the recommended developments, particularly in the light of the JCS action the year before. Soon, however, a great deal of public attention was given to the matter.

The scientists took their case to the American public by giving their report to the Alsop brothers—reporters and columnists with large reader followings. Articles appeared in the *Saturday Evening Post* and in syndicated newspaper columns telling the American people that American scientists had the answers to improving the inadequate U.S. active air defenses, and ". . . there is a way for us to be sure of destroying 85 percent—even 95 percent—of the attacking force, say the scientists."[30] The scientists did not rely on "leaks" to the public media alone, but by-passed the Air Force and Department of Defense and got their report to Jack Gorrie, Chairman of the National Security Resources Board. Gorrie introduced the report to the NSC with a strong recommendation for immediate construction of an Arctic warning line at a cost of $1 billion during the first three or four years. The Truman Administration deferred the question by a continuing study of air defense requirements. Secretary of Defense Lovett appointed a civilian committee, chaired by the President of the Bell Telephone Laboratories, Mervin Kelly, to study the air defense problem. The committee's findings would not fall due until the new Eisenhower Administration took office. Similarly, another legacy for the new administration, NSC 141, analyzed the implications of the Soviet development of the atomic bomb and included recommendations for more intensive efforts in air defense and civil defense.

The Truman Administration's bequests confronted the new administration with decision requirements for significant improvements (and expenditures) for continental defense, and indicated that the study of the Summer Study Group recommendations was under way.

Thus, the Eisenhower Administration quickly faced the problem of carrying out its campaign promises for reduced military spending aware that continental defenses had carried a low priority and needed extensive renovation to become effective. Another study group, composed of business executives, educators, and assorted labor leaders, publishers, lawyers, and one military officer, was appointed by the new Administration to study air defense from a civilian or "business" viewpoint. They recommended a policy of not rushing action on the air defense recommendations of the Summer Study Group, and did little to solve the President's dilemma.

The Kelly Committee reported in May 1953, and it too rejected the urgency of the Summer Study Group report, while recognizing the need for an improved continental air defense. The Kelly report stressed the need for a powerful SAC to deter attack and deplored the publicity promoting the scientists' misleading claims of capabilities for devising a more effective air defense system.

The Administration appointed yet another air defense study group, this time drawn from within the government, and chaired by President Eisenhower's war-time chief of operations in Europe, Major General "Pinky" Bull. General Bull had given his name to a study report on civil defense in 1948, and was a proven, skilled investigator. In July 1953, General Bull's study group reported in favor of spending $18 to $27 billion on U.S. air defense over the next five years. Another study group analyzing Soviet air-atomic capabilities also reported to the NSC favoring large expenditures on continental defense. The NSC noted the reports

---

[30] Futrell, op. cit., p. 303.

Chapter I: American and Soviet Strategy: A Comparison

but continued its study of a strategy appropriate for the Eisenhower Administration, to be based on the need for a new balance between military and domestic demands.

3. Soviet Perspectives After Stalin

While the Eisenhower Administration's "New Look" strategy was developing, the Soviet leadership was assessing the growth in U.S. military might. The *overt manifestations of policy* under Malenkov appeared to indicate that the Soviet policy of aggressive expansionism would be replaced and Soviet energies given over to developing agricultural and consumer goods. Military requirements remained a reality because of obvious growth in U.S. capabilities and the strong anticommunist line in the West under the U.S. lead. There was distrust; Soviet initiatives about Germany had elicited little Western reaction.

The Soviets had reason to be pleased with their progress in weapons technology. The U.S. nuclear monopoly, which had radically altered the international balance of power, no longer existed; there was progress in the thermonuclear field; and, in missiles, the Soviet arsenal had an edge over the United States and was far advanced over those in Western Europe. Soviet scientists and engineers had developed anything they had been asked to do in the post war period. Approximately two years before the United States decided to undertake an intercontinental missile development program, the Soviet political leadership made the bold decision to build an intercontinental missile. Taken at a time when Soviet policy appeared to be in flux over basic questions of guns or butter, that decision appears remarkable. It represented a giant leap into the unknown; failure could be very costly. But the Soviets were willing to take the risks and gamble on a vision of a possible pay-off. To do so while many problems of Soviet security remained makes that decision seem daring. Apart from NATO's growing strength, the tasks of providing active air defense for the homeland remained to be solved. In this light, the ICBM decision provides a basis for the judgment that the relative effectiveness—and projected, planned development—of the Soviet air defense system was acceptable and proceeding in step with priorities desired and prescribed by the Soviet leadership. Apparently the Kremlin was satisfied.

By 1953, initial post war early warning had been strengthened by wide-scale deployment of the Token radar, a Soviet V-beam equipment inspired by the U.S. AN/CPS-6 V-beam set. This directly complemented the growth of jet fighters as the dominant and most significant part of the Soviet air defense forces. Soviet radars provided warning and made the fighter more effective by facilitating intercept. Later in the decade, a large-scale deployment of surface-to-air missiles would make ground systems the backbone of the PVO. In 1953, their development programs were already actively under way. Initial systems tests of the SA-1 took place in late 1952 and construction began in the Moscow area for the operational deployment of this system to begin by 1954. The SA-2 system began development in 1951.[31] At the same time, the Soviets had developed, produced, and deployed in the post war period two new AAA gun systems and new fire control systems including associated radars. Another, heavy gun system was being developed at the time and would be deployed by 1955. Development, production, and deployment of various jet aircraft, bombers, and fighters had already impressed the West and, while the post-Stalin policy review was going on a medium jet bomber, the TU-16 Badger became operational and the MiG-19, an initial, somewhat limited all-weather interceptor, was deployed with Soviet air defense units.

---

[31] DIA-ST-CS-14-02-70, "Soviet SA-2 Surface-to-Air Missile System," p. 163.

A sweeping reorganization of Soviet industry took place in 1953 and a number of separate production ministries amalgamated into four large "super" ministries to cover overall defense needs. Concurrently, the strength of Soviet armed forces had grown; a new division structure was introduced to give line divisions of the Soviet army increased, improved armor, artillery, mobility, and communications; and improved tactical air defense of the reorganized field forces introduced as part of a general modernization program.

4. Evolution of the "New Look"—NSC 162

A particular concern for U.S. planning, however, was the development of an extensive, sophisticated Soviet long-range bomber force. In 1954 and again in 1955, the Soviets put on an impressive show of aircraft in a Moscow fly-by. Demonstrating new aircraft in 1954 which appeared in considerable numbers in the show put on the following year suggested a three-year lead time advantage for the Soviet Union in development and production of a heavy jet bomber. While this factor was significant in U.S. decisions concerning air defense, principal immediate results were decisions for stepped up B-52 production and development of a U.S. ICBM. These appeared to reflect a changed U.S. judgment about Soviet technological capabilities. In October 1955 the NSC recommended the highest national priority be given to ICBM development and, by December, President Eisenhower had assigned highest priorities to the Atlas and Titan and Jupiter and Thor programs.

Soviet achievements, real or estimated, also impacted on Mr. Wilson's hope of getting away from "crisis" reactions aimed at a critical future date based upon essentially limited knowledge of growing Soviet military capabilities. U.S. rhetoric in the arguments over "containment" versus "liberation" had helped to develop general images of the Soviets and induced certain fears of them through concepts of a "tide of communism" that would "roll on" because of the diabolically clever apparatus of Soviet communism. Since the Communists had demonstrated aggressive expansionism and proved to be an open, difficult enemy in the Korean War, they had become literally, in the American mind-set, "the forces of aggression," and there was a need to be able to retaliate against their moves everywhere. In truth, in perceptions and in weapons systems, a firm foundation for a "strategic interaction" dialogue had been laid by the end of the Korean War.

Soon after the Soviet explosion of a thermonuclear device in August 1953, the National Security Council embodied the "New Look" strategy in NSC 162. Approved by the President in October 1953, the paper identified the threat by the Soviet Union as being "total," gave the Soviet Union the capability of making a nuclear air attack against the United States, concluded that national defense must have the highest priority in national strategy, and recommended that almost all the recommendations made by the Summer Study Group be approved. In effect, the American scientists, with an assist from the Soviet Union, won over the vast majority of the influential members of the new Eisenhower Administration who were primarily economy minded and pro strategic air power. In early 1954, the American and Canadian governments agreed to proceed with the development of the Distant Early Warning (DEW) Line in northern Canada and Alaska. The first construction on the DEW Line began in 1955, together with other measures to improve the air defense of the North American continent.

These developments together with the start of Nike deployments underscored the need for a joint, unified command for U.S. air defense. In 1954 the Joint Chiefs of Staff approved forming a joint command for the air defense of North America. The Continental Defense Command under the command of General Chidlaw, USAF, resulted. It included the Army Antiaircraft Command and Naval Forces assigned to continental defense. Since the new command was superimposed on the Air Force's ADC and responsive to the Chief of Staff of the Air Force acting as Executive Agent for the JCS, complaints against Air Force dominance of continental defense exacerbated a growing inter-service rivalry that concerned missiles.

5. Growing Differences

Basic differences between Army and Air Force concepts of defense surfaced again with the accelerated development of competing technological capabilities. The issues again centered on control of Army weapons. It came to the surface as a disagreement on the range of missile weapons to be developed by the Army. If the Army SAM development could be seen as no more than an extension of the traditional anti-aircraft artillery role it provoked little concern. The AAA role had emphasized localized "point" defenses. In contrast, Air Force interceptors had an "area" air defense role. The initial Nike missile system, Nike Ajax, developed and deployed in 1953 seemed to the Air Force to be in the category of "point defense" weapons but the development of Nike Hercules, with a considerably greater range, bothered the Air Force. Arguments on the merits of "point" versus "area" defense began in this decade, intensifying after 1955.

While fissures appeared in the U.S. efforts to coordinate a national air defense system, Soviet actions seemed to proceed as part of a steady growth with an integrated force. By 1954, the national air defense of the Soviet Union was made the responsibility of PVO Strany. Designated about the same time as CONAD in the United States, PVO Strany was headed by Soviet Army generals who identified fighter aviation as the most important element of Soviet air defense. Inter-service rivalry was not expressed although competition for budget and other resource support must be assumed. PVO Strany obviously enjoyed high priority; allocations for air defense rose rapidly during the Korean War but began to be challenged by requirements for strategic offensive systems and the context of reduced Soviet military budgets in 1953 and 1954. Economic and resource limitations beginning in 1954 appeared to make an impact on Soviet strategic air defense efforts about then.

D. Systems Development

1. An Overview

By the mid-1950's, the sizeable Soviet air defense forces; deployed radar warning and surveillance systems; very large numbers of antiaircraft guns and clear-weather fighters; great effort and high priority for developing defensive missile technologies manifested deliberate effort. By the end of the first post war decade, surface-to-air missiles were part of the active defense of Moscow. Civil defense received a big boost during this period when, in October 1952, the 19th Party Congress decided to develop an all-out defense of the Soviet Union.

U.S. strategic air defense moved from a low priority element in U.S. defense strategy to a high priority element in national security policy. Basic decisions were made to protect America against manned bomber attack with nuclear weapons; programs for early warning systems to provide six hours warning against a propeller-driven bomber and two hours warning for jet bombers began. Backing the early warning system was: an all-weather interceptor force and ground-based AAA and missile units. A variety of development and planned actions to expand and increase their efficiency and effectiveness and to field new, improved systems were under way. But the improvements and systems conceived did not address the on-coming threat; by 1955 it was evident that the Soviets had in motion significant long-range missile programs and were on the verge of testing a 1000-mile missile. Concurrently, however, U.S. air defense programs projected a defense against the air breathing threat. The associated ground environment conceived for control of the U.S. programmed strategic air defense structure would be critically vulnerable to possible missile attack.

The main thrust of U.S. civil defense built on the concept of evacuation which did little to defend the population against fallout. Lacking the specific impetus of the Korean War, attempts to delegate civil defense responsibilities to Federal agencies led to difficulty and confusion because of overlaps in mobilization planning. By the end of the period, U.S. civil defense organization and planning confronted many unresolved problems. The Federal Civil Defense Administration itself moved to Battle Creek, Michigan, during 1954 and, while less vulnerable to an attack against Washington, the agency's relocation from the center of government seemed to downgrade its prestige and effectiveness.

The contrast between the Soviet and U.S. air defense and civil defense programs of the early 1950's appears sharp. American programs slighted air defense in favor of offensive forces; Soviet planners obviously emphasized and sought, as soon as possible, an integrated, national air defense program and supported civil defense. Despite the handicaps of a war-damaged economy; long-standing, unfulfilled promises to the Soviet people of "the fruits of revolution"; and acute technological gaps, the Soviets made substantial progress in the decade after the war to protect the homeland. Stalin dominated the decision-making process and personally set the direction and priority given the effort. The U.S. air defense commitment, however, was gradual and disparate. Requirements derived from different perspectives and built on limited, and sometimes erroneous, information. Individual departments and agencies, both in and out of government conceived air defense weapon systems designs and unilaterally promoted their development. Lack of centralized, authoritative planning and direction, budget constraints despite a greatly superior economic position, and basic strategic disposition to favor the offense were substantive elements influencing the evolution of U.S. air defense.

2. Air Defense System Components

a. Command and Control

Accelerated efforts for integrating U.S. command and control arrangements followed the outbreak of the Korean War. Under an agreement concluded by General Collins, Army Chief of Staff, and General Vandenberg, Chief of Staff, USAF, in August 1950 the Air Force was authorized to determine the basic rules of engagement (ROE) to govern AA fire against an enemy; to draw up the conditions of alert for AA; and direct AA when to open and to hold fire. Covering air defense in the United States, the Collins Vandenberg Agreement gave rise to ADC issuing rules of engagement in February 1951 as active defenses grew in the continental United States. Under ADC's ROE, antiaircraft normally would be in a status of "Release Fire," whereby any aircraft declared to be hostile could be engaged. ADC indicated an order to "Hold Fire" would be given "only when necessary."

About a year later, these ROE changed. Under the new rules, three conditions were set. "Weapons Free" indicated that any target not identified as friendly could be fired on by AAA. "Weapons Tight" meant that only targets identified as hostile could be fired on by AAA and "Hold Fire" would provide an overriding command. "Weapons Tight" would constitute the normal AA status until an attack was imminent.

Chapter I: American and Soviet Strategy: A Comparison

Various efforts to promote a unified air defense command developed during the period. Organizational proposals arose in 1950, again in 1953, and finally in 1954, culminated in CONAD.

The terms of reference establishing CONAD gave "operational control" to CINCONAD of all forces assigned or available. "Operational control" was defined to include:

(1) Direction of the tactical air battle
(2) Control of fighters
(3) Specifying the alert condition
(4) Stationing early warning units
(5) Deploying combat units of the command.

CONAD, after two years, was overhauled. Major problems the initial experience uncovered—apart from interservice difficulties—centered on the growth in the effectiveness of weapons and their impact on command and control (e.g., SAMs replacing guns with vastly superior performance capabilities in terms of range, maneuver, and kill probability). USAF controllers were not taking advantage of, or avoided use of, Army weapon capabilities and tended to rely on the fighter/interceptor. The identification issue plagued the CONAD components. There was a lack of confidence in the existing procedures and system and a mutually satisfactory and understood agreement, and doctrine on identification. These issues became more serious as steps progressed to provide improved capabilities for centralized CONAD control of the air battle. Longer-range ground control intercept equipment and early warning radars promised more effective intercept and held promise for automatic all-weather intercept. Since the speed of aircraft was increasing, the requirements for speedy, reliable identification were apparent; equally demanding were the needs for extensive communications, data link and rapid, continuing interchange of identification information on aircraft within the zone of responsibility of subordinate commanders.

Soviet national air defense forces grew after Korea and, together with preparations for the incorporation of the SA-1 system, growth helped to promote improved command and control of the growing force. In addition to the reorganization of Soviet armed forces in 1950, the establishment of PVO Strany as an operating organizational structure in 1954 and the employment of fighter aircraft with airborne radar from mid-1954 brought out other requirements for modifications in command and control procedures. Use of airborne radar improved the all-weather capabilities of the system and that fact, building on the operational experience derived from the Korean War, must have influenced control procedures. U.S. aircraft in Korea found that coordinated employment by the Communists of searchlights and fighters required significant use of electronic countermeasures, both jamming and chaff, in order to defeat those tactics. Communist AAA in Korea—weak by World War II standards—lacked radar. U.S. employment of ECM against communist air defense systems in Korea as late as 1953 is assumed to have induced some C^2 changes in PVO Strany. A basic concept appeared to have been to have fighter aircraft operate beyond the range of AAA. Soviet actions adhered to the basic operational principle of centralized control of all resources used in air defense. Recognizing such problem areas, Soviet air defense planners sought solutions, and anticipated the introduction of new, improved weapons and the growing needs for the coordination and mutual support of air defense forces deployed as part of PVO Strany.

b. Early Warning and Ground Controlled Intercept

Declared goals for Soviet air defense projected a defense in depth. Evidence of a continuing commitment to "brute force" solutions, high priority to warning, and indicative of the problems faced in protecting vast regions of the U.S.S.R., overlapping air surveillance and early warning networks began to appear in some regions of the Soviet Union during this period. Priority to these regions limited coverage capabilities in others. Large numbers of manned interceptors enabled the employment of barrier patrols to provide some warning and limited engagement capabilities for these regions in good weather. Visual observers also continued active even as overall radar warning capabilities grew.

The experience of the Korean War also showed the Soviets the increased importance of a first attack by jet fighters. In a "majority of cases" they found the first attack was the only possible one. This put a high premium on warning and effective GCI as well as improved pilot training. Thus, as PVO Strany moved to improve the Soviet national air defense system, increased and continuing emphasis was given to GCI equipment.

The Token development and deployment gave evidence of Soviet technological capacity since it marked a modest time lag between appearance of a prototype and the subsequent large-scale deployment. It provided a practical demonstration of the great strides made by the Soviets in mastering Western technology, but in particular, seemed to underscore the sense of urgency and purpose in Soviet air defense developments.

The concept of a DEW Line for U.S. continental defense was furthered by the Summer Study Group although its report ran into stiff opposition which felt the feasibility of the proposal was limited by funds and technology. The Bull report confirmed the Summer Study Group concepts, however, and recommended an expenditure of $18 billion to $25 billion over five years to automate air defense systems and establish the DEW Line. Technical problems and better understanding of costs uncovered when the program moved to operational status in 1957. Despite action to move the Pinetree line north and the stress on the need for warning of attack from 2,000 miles, U.S. programmed activity appeared to contrast sharply with the manifest determination and urgency of the Soviets.

Air defense requirements grew for the U.S.S.R. as the threat of Western strategic air increased. The Soviet actions to plug gaps in the developing air defense system with available capabilities and expedients contrasted with U.S. deliberations about costs and commitment to strategic offensive forces. The Soviet basic concern for warning was evident; less clear is whether it derived its form and dimension because of specific U.S. developments and deployments. As it uncovered, the major portion of the Soviet effort appeared to be directed against strategic attack possibilities. By the early 1950's, U.S. carrier aviation and the growth of NATO tactical capabilities extended the problem. Indicative of Soviet sensitivity and capability, incidents of reaction to U.S. flight activity in peripheral areas included shooting down a U.S. B-29 in October 1952 over the Kuriles, and another, two years later, over Hokkaido. As further evidence of the violence of Soviet reactions, a Navy P2V aircraft was shot down in September 1954 over the Sea of Japan and, earlier that year in Europe, two Navy aircraft were attacked by Soviet aircraft near the German border with Czechoslovakia.

c. Interceptor Development

In the early 1950's the predominant fighter in Soviet air defense was the MiG-15. By mid-1954, a trend had begun to employ fighters with airborne intercept (AI) radar capabilities. This had a marked effect on

Chapter I: American and Soviet Strategy: A Comparison

the character of the air defense system by providing an all-weather capability. Introduction of the YAK-25, MiG-17, and MiG-19 aircraft were evidence of the Soviet effort for improved interceptors with some electronic capability and improved armament.

The day-version of the F-86, which was procured in quantity because it was the best fighter available at the time, remained in service for U.S. continental air defense until 1954. A new generation of supersonic interceptors began development in the early 1950's. The period saw an attempted speed-up of the F-89 program; an effort to plug the existing, perceived gap (F-80 and F-84); and programs to modify other aircraft as interceptors (F-94C and F-86D). The growing pressures of the Soviet Tu-4 force build-up, the Soviet atomic explosion, the outbreak of the war in Korea, and the availability of new technologies contributed to the difficulties of developing an integrated interceptor system. Because planned availability by 1954 of a desired interceptor was seen to be infeasible in late 1951, a planned aircraft (F-102) was expedited to provide an "interim interceptor." This soon ran into trouble; and although the F-102 flew successfully 3 years later, its accelerated development and production included a redesign of the fuselage. (Modifications and retrofitting continued for several years after the aircraft was first operationally deployed.)

By the mid-1950's, the evident need for greater range to meet improving Soviet bomber capabilities had coincided with prospects for an extensive ground environment; a long-range interceptor requirement resulted. To fill the gap until the ultimate aircraft (F-106) would be available, two interim interceptors (F-101 and F-104) with requisite range were adapted for air defense. These aircraft were not fully compatible with the SAGE system and later, difficulty occurred in trying to fit them into that system.

Rapid advances in technology, competing demands within the Air Force for fighter performance, and industrial influence extended and ramified the problems of U.S. interceptor development. By comparison, the progression of developing Soviet bomber capabilities appear less significant to that development.

d. Surface-to-Air Missiles

U.S. operational requirements for air defense missile support—for forces and weapons—derived somewhat after the fact of their technical development. The individual services conceived designs for weapons to meet the perceived needs of that service, not necessarily as a response to the statement of need by an operational commander. The long lead times in development of surface-to-air missiles exceeded operational planning cycles and clearly, therefore, their development was not driven by the specifics of the Soviet threat during this period.

Four months after the outbreak of the Korean War, Mr. K. T. Keller, retired former President and Chairman of the Board of Chrysler Corporation, was brought into the Defense Department as Director of Guided Missiles. Taking his instructions from the President to advance the U.S. missile program, Keller quickly pressed for workable systems. He understood that highest priorities were to be given to development of air defense missiles and he designated Nike, Terrier, and Sparrow for expedited development.[32] By November 1953, the Nike system was ready to begin an extensive deployment for defense of designated localities in U.S. Bomarc began development coincident with the SAGE evolution. By this time both Nike Hercules and HAWK systems were being developed.

CONAD was informed of these developments and operational planning for U.S. air defense increasingly took into account potential improvements and on-coming problems of coordination as these capabilities were

---

[32] Futrell, op. cit., p. 438.

forecasted and scheduled programs of trained forces and standard missile weapons became reality. While missile systems became increasingly significant to U.S. strategic air defense planning, their development did not stem directly from the specific capabilities of the Soviet offensive threat at the time. Defensive missile capabilities were the product of design and their performance characteristics derived essentially from those concepts, guided by service perceptions of need and realized by the available "state of the art" technologies.

Soviet SAM development culminated in the start of a missile defense for Moscow. Representing an extensive and high-priority effort, the Soviet program, however, was primarily devoted to developing required missile and guidance technologies. Preliminary actions were under way on the SA-2 system. German scientific support, significant to the SA-1 program, also backed this development. From the emphasis given the program and the extent of U.S. (and other Western) capabilities for offensive air attack against the Soviet Union, it appears that the Soviet SA-2 program was intended as a specific answer to the threat appreciation of U.S. capabilities held by PVO planners in the 1950's.

e. Ballistic Missile Defense

In the early 1950's, the Army examined critically the feasibility of ballistic missile defense leading to a decision in February 1955 to conduct specific economic and technical feasibility studies for a missile defense. Based upon the resulting assessment, in December 1955 the Army requested $7.7 million in supplemental FY 1956 funds for an antimissile program and called for the assignment of service responsibility in this area.

In 1953 and 1954 increasing intelligence reports of active Soviet missile tests gave rise to establishment of The Technological Capabilities Panel under the NSC. Reviewing these reports in 1955, the Panel recommended stepping up the U.S. missile program. Under the chairmanship of James R. Killian, the Panel projected a rapid rate of Soviet missile progress and predicted that soon the Soviets would be testing 1000-mile missiles which would enable them to threaten Western Europe. That same year U.S. radars based in Turkey to determine the extent of Soviet tests began picking up 750-mile missiles being tested by the Soviets.

This evidence made it clear that the Soviets had made great progress in rocketry. As a direct result, Army, Navy, and Air Force missile programs were accelerated by a crash effort for the development of 1,500-mile missiles. The Atlas priority was increased and Titan authorized. Redstone and Atlas had been in development ten years; these two were joined in 1955 by three more—Thor, Jupiter, and Minuteman. In September 1955, the Secretary of Defense was called on to decide between other intermediate-range missile proposals. They were similar; to choose was difficult; fear of Soviet missile progress a dominant factor. The U.S. was trying to catch up. On 8 November 1955, Mr. Wilson announced his decision to proceed with both programs. In effect, this provided for Polaris which began the following year.

The Wilson decision was based on the recommendations of the JCS which had an Army dissent because, as proposed, they would have excluded the most experienced U.S. missile team, the Army group at Huntsville, from participating in the effort to overtake the Soviet achievements. These facts were influential in the Army's collateral pursuit of Defense Department approval and action to develop an antimissile missile system.

E. Summary Judgments

Soviet strategy and action for air defense of the U.S.S.R. in the first decade following World War II demonstrate greater emphasis, more extensive commitment and higher national priority than the American

Chapter I: American and Soviet Strategy: A Comparison

effort for continental air defense. Rapid, continuing growth within a phased, orderly development marked the Soviet pattern following a relatively slow start.

Technological limitations underlay Soviet moves to provide an effective, integrated national air defense. Qualitative deficiencies and gaps were recognized at the start and intensive effort made thereafter to offset such limitations through relatively large scale, quantitative commitment of resources and systematic wide-scale exploitation of foreign technology. While these conditions induced "crash" actions, progress to achieve an effective national air defense system was steady, consistent, and continuing. The goal of an integrated national system was established and adhered to. During this decade weapon systems for Soviet air defense were in a substantial transition: jet fighters entered the operational inventory quickly and quantity production backed the growing requirements of this component as the primary arm of PVO Strany. The systematic but accelerated development and deployment of a national radar warning and surveillance network was being advanced by a sustained effort and, while AAA guns continued as primary ground-based weapon systems, surface-to-air missile development progressed to the point of beginning an operational deployment. Command and control needed to provide an effective, flexible, coordinated yet centralized direction and employment of the various components developed concurrently with the growth of the overall system.

Soviet emphasis on quantitative solutions to air defense problems and technological limitations probably represented a combination of predisposition and experience. Traditional predilection for defense, World War II experience, and a doctrinal, strategic preference to have a reliable, self-contained capacity for security were in keeping with the work of an effective strategy: concentration. Genuine fear and a sense of inferiority gave impetus to the program, at least under the circumstances of the U.S. nuclear monopoly.

Soviet decisions probably built on a worst-case basis yet obviously were influenced by assessments of conditions of a future war. There is, however, little evidence to reflect Soviet air defense developments during the decade being directly responsive to decisions concerning strategic weapon systems.

The clear and overriding purpose of Soviet air defense during the decade was to "protect the homeland." Along with the growth of a substantial force for the purpose, Soviet air defense at the end of the period had solid acceptability and, in PVO Strany, an able, central institutional advocate for agreed programs to improve the defense of the homeland. In marked contrast to the Americans, the Soviets rarely criticized decisions; open criticism was lacking. The extensive Soviet efforts for air defense became part of the integrated national air defense program and tended to complement other commitments for "protection of the homeland."

U.S. efforts for continental air defense were keyed primarily by official and unofficial perceptions of the threat and continuing official views of fiscal constraints. Basically, U.S. strategy did not recognize an urgent need for active air defense until late in the decade when the Soviet threat was thought to be more real.

A basic issue underlying a seeming delay in progress toward a U.S. strategic air defense program during this decade involved contention over the commitment of resources. The contention centered on the unresolved question of what relative balance was wanted between the U.S. strategic forces and the growing Soviet forces. The U.S. strategy was agreed: the defense of the United States would be provided essentially by strategic air-atomic forces.

U.S. defense efforts showed a continuing concern for roles, functions and missions, repeated appeals for "balanced" forces, and delayed clean-cut decisions on the size of strategic offensive forces. Lacking resolution, that issue became extended and tended further to delay judgments on air defense.

Early Soviet commitment to national air defense represented a basic long-term strategic choice. Military requirements had to be supported because, despite the severe economic strain they entailed, the U.S.S.R. was strategically very vulnerable. The U.S. nuclear monopoly was a central fact influencing the Soviet overall strategy; national air defense complemented their forced-draft nuclear developments and concepts for defense against a threat from Europe.

The nuclear monopoly appeared to obviate choice in the American strategy. With a demonstrated air-atomic capacity, the strategy was nearly patent. Self-imposed post war economic constraints on military spending influenced the U.S. strategy and helped to affirm it but did not drive it. From the start, research and development for U.S. air defense projects had funding support; however, the American strategy inclined to accent strategic air offensive capabilities in basic post war defense policies.

Economic constraints substantially influenced the American strategy because of domestic political considerations. During the initial transition from war to peace and through the period of growing U.S. recognition of inimical Soviet intent, funding for U.S. military programs was limited. While the Korean War provided a specific basis for substantial subsequent support for U.S. military programs, U.S. decision makers were already disposed to a stronger stand against an aggressive communist expansionism.

The following chapters outline U.S. and Soviet strategies in greater detail, accenting factors bearing on decisions during the first decade after World War II relating to the development of capabilities for air defense, civil defense, and ballistic missile defense. Chapters II and III concern the American and Soviet strategies; Chapters IV and V treat U.S. and Soviet systems developments.

Chapter II

American Strategy for Air and Ballistic Missile Defense

A. 1945–1950: Entering the Atomic Era

1. World War II Heritage

a. Strategic Debate

World War II clearly established the strategic and tactical importance of air power, but the debates over the role of air power continued unabated after the war. The debate basically devolved to the question of "Air superiority, or superiority of the air arm?"

There were those who believed that control of the air was a prerequisite so that surface operations could be undertaken, and there were those who believed that the air arm could win unaided. There were equally strong proponents of the superiority of strategic air offensives over air defense forces and of the superiority of the defense over the offense. Each could point to various phases of World War II to support their position.

The introduction of the atomic bomb at the end of the war added a new dimension to the debate, which seemed to tilt in the direction of the strategic offensive advocates. Other new technology introduced late in the war obscured the issue and fed new fuel to the debate and new fire to the debaters. The jet-engine fighter aircraft strengthened the argument for the air defenders, as did the surface-to-air and air-to-air missiles, airborne radars, night fighters, and improved early warning and ground control radars. Since most of the new technology was relatively untested and in primitive states of development, there was no conclusive evidence for either side, and indeed the debate continues to this day.

The introduction of the supersonic V2 rocket by the Germans shortly before the invasion of France, added the problem of missile defense to those of the air defenders, and so the problem and the rhetoric escalated. Not only was there no agreement on very basic points concerning the use of air power, but there was no agreed-upon doctrine for such widely practiced operations as the air defense over ground armies and the tactical or close air support of ground forces. Though air power established itself as a critically important element of warfare, the end of World War II left many important questions on the future of air power unresolved.

b. Continental Defense

During World War II, the continental United States relied chiefly on its two flanking oceans for air defense, but the Army Air Forces did establish some 95 radar sites—65 of which were on the Pacific coast—four interceptor commands and a ground warning network supported by one and a half million volunteers of the Ground Observer Corps. A civilian civil defense organization was also created for the purpose of protecting the civilian population and civilian industry. Perhaps fortunately, neither defense organization was ever really challenged by enemy forces. As the danger of enemy air attack on the United States became slight, the AAF substituted a standby defense system for its active system in September 1943, and inactivated the aircraft warning network in April 1944. President Truman abolished the Office of Civil Defense by Executive Order on 30 June 1945, in the first of many steps to cut the costs of the rapidly winding down war.

Although the defense of the continental United States was relatively unimportant when viewed in light of the other events of World War II, it left a certain legacy for the future. The Army Air Force was recognized and awarded the responsibility for air defense of the United States, supported by a civilian aircraft warning network and Army antiaircraft gun and balloon defenses. The ground defense of the United States was the responsibility of the Army with a tenuous but workable relationship with the civil defense organizations that proliferated across the nation. Both the air defense and the civil defense organizations were mobilized a relatively few months before the attack on Pearl Harbor, and could properly be called mobilization rather than peacetime organizations. Both air defense and civil defense were phased out before the end of the emergency, leaving no residual organizations for future continuity.

c. Lesson of Pearl Harbor

One important legacy of World War II that made a lasting impression on future strategic thought was the lesson of Pearl Harbor. One of the first orders of business after the war was a detailed and highly publicized investigation of the circumstances surrounding the success of the surprise attack on Pearl Harbor. Among the results of the investigations was the fact that radar was successful in detecting the approach of the Japanese air fleet; but administrative failure and break-down had negated the value of that tactical warning. The principal lesson learned was "don't be surprised!" Much of the future thinking about the onset of another war was postulated on a war that would start with a surprise attack on the United States.

d. Strategic Doctrine

As World War II was the most total war in modern history, involving deliberate attacks on civilian populations and industry, the use of atomic weapons, and the doctrine of unconditional surrender imposed on Germany, and to a lesser degree, Japan, it was natural that this aspect was carried over in future planning after the war. Most strategists believed that future wars would probably be total wars with national survival at stake, and that atomic weapons would probably be used in future wars.

World War II confirmed the basic strategic doctrines of the U.S. military. The basis of that doctrine was reliance on the mobilization system for expanding small peacetime military services to whatever forces are required for successful military operations. The civilian industry of the U.S. provides the necessary equipment and supplies by dint of mobilization of the industrial base and diversion to wartime requirements. Using that system, the United States organized, trained, equipped, and supported over twelve million men in uniform (simultaneously) during World War II—the mightiest military force in the history of man. That force was projected overseas on a global basis to carry the offensive to the enemies, wherever they could be reached. The industrial base was so prolific that it provided surplus arms and supplies for the allies of the United States, the British, the French, the Russians, and the Chinese, as well as the means to transport the supplies to them and control the air and the seas between the continental United States and the overseas destinations. The industrial output of the United States was so great that a considerable portion of it was excess to wartime requirements by the beginning of the summer of 1945.

While U.S. military men were indoctrinated with the spirit of the offensive, wartime experiences during World War II impressed them with the importance of providing protection for the vulnerable industrial mobilization base. Britain was successful in staving off concerted efforts by the predominately tactical German Air Force to bomb Britain into submission preparatory to a German invasion. Later attacks by German subsonic V1 rockets, largely directed against English population centers, were unsuccessful due to a combination of interception by British air defenses and the inherent lack of accuracy of the weapons. There were no defenses against the V2 attacks except overrunning the launcher sites with ground forces on the continent. Despite all three forms of air and missile attack, the British were able to maintain and improve their industrial output, principally because British industrial capacity was not targeted by the Germans.

Germany was subjected to devastating air attacks on civilian industry and population centers by British and American strategic bombers. The German air defense of the homeland made a number of basic mistakes, but by the end of 1944 was the most formidable the world had ever seen. Deployed within Germany were some 16,000 heavy antiaircraft guns, 50,000 light and mobile guns, 7,500 searchlights, and some 1,500 barrage balloons. The Germans had both ground and airborne radar, controlled the long ground approaches into their cities, and innovated in defensive fighter tactics in the attempt to inflict unacceptable bomber losses on the allied bombers. Despite Hitler's refusal to give the production of fighter/interceptors and jet aircraft first priority in the defense of the Reich, the German air defense was very nearly successful. Post war surveys determined that German production actually rose during 1944–1945, while still under the massed attacks of the greatest bomber forces mobilized during the war. The German air defense example left the U.S. air defenders with the belief that it was possible to organize an air defense system that could protect the industrial base and inflict unacceptable losses on an attacking strategic force.

The strategic air attack on Japan presented the "worst case" example of just what can happen to a civilian population and an industrial base when an effective air defense is absent. Japan sent its airpower far from the home islands. When the B-29 and naval air strikes took place, they were virtually unopposed in the air. In fact, the leader of B-29 forces stated that the air over Japan was safer than that over training bases in the United States. The air defenders in the United States military forces took the lesson of Japan to heart, much as those who adhered to the belief in the supremacy of air power held up Japan as an example of the ability of air power to win unaided.

World War II then, confirmed U.S. faith in the mobilization system and the mobilization industrial base, encouraged a belief in a global war started by a surprise attack, conclusively proved the virtue of the strategic offensive, and strongly implanted a relatively new belief in the necessity of providing effective defenses for the industrial base in the continental United States.

e. Demobilization

After the surrender of Japan in Tokyo Bay, the vast majority of the American people believed that the wartime emergency was over and that the United States should turn its complete attention to peace and away from the recent war. They had considerable reason to so believe after four long years of war and relative hardship required to overwhelm and subjugate the Axis nations. The United States had a monopoly of atomic weapons and there was no apparent enemy in sight. The United Nations organization was widely heralded as the future guarantor of world order and peace. It followed that the United States no longer had a need for its very large and extremely powerful military forces. On the contrary, the American people wanted its men in uniform *home*, and the men in uniform couldn't wait to get home and out of uniform. The overseas forces were brought home and discharged as fast as shipping could move them, despite a point system designed to provide a system of justice for the returnees while preserving some semblance of occupation forces. Within a year the once-mighty U.S. armies, navies, and air forces had disintegrated, leaving a pale shadow of former military strength. This form of voluntary unilateral disarmament left ill-trained, under-manned, and generally combat-ineffective units deployed overseas to act as occupation forces and to man the overseas bases that supported them. Though total uniformed strength shrank to less than two and a half million men, they were deployed forward with barely enough strength in the continental United States to support a rotation base. Though not entirely by design, U.S. military strategists could not return to prewar isolationism from the rest of the world. The leaders of the U.S. military forces, at any rate, were men who were accustomed to thinking in a global context and being concerned with the global security environment.

2. Immediate Postwar Developments

a. Unification

Long before the final shot of World War II sounded, the military services began reviewing the lessons learned in preparation for the peacetime years to follow. Perhaps the primary lesson learned was the necessity for the integration of the nation's fighting forces into a single unified organization. Many of the major problems generated during the course of the war emanated from the division of the forces into the services of the Army (and Army Air Forces) and the Navy (and Marine Corps).

Although the War Department was opposed to the establishment of a separate air force, it became a strong advocate of a single unified military organization, with subordinate ground, air, and naval forces or services. The Navy, more or less self-contained with its own naval, ground, and air elements, feared that it would lose the Marine Corps and perhaps elements of its air arm in a functional reorganization, and thus fought a rearguard action against unification that continued long after the decision had been made in favor of such a unification. The Army Air Forces saw such a reorganization as its greatest hope to become an independent air arm, and consistently backed unification. From the first discussions of reorganization, it became apparent that there would be many hazy areas caused by a simple functional division, particularly in the boundary areas between ground, air, and sea.

There was little dispute among the services that air defense was a natural function of the air force and should be an assigned mission for a separate air force. There was little problem with the Navy for the senior officers of the Army Air Forces neither expected nor wanted to be assigned the mission of providing air defense for naval forces. The Marine Corps had its own air arm and organic ground air defense elements and was accustomed to close cooperation with the Navy for the air defense of its beachheads.

The heart of the air defense problem lay in the fact that the Army had a deep and abiding interest in retaining organic ground air defense units (antiaircraft, searchlights, barrage balloons, etc.) for the air defense of its deployed ground armies. There was a considerable Army investment in ground air defense equipment, and a portion of the Army's officer strength had specialized in the field of air defense.

Chapter II: American Strategy for Air and Ballistic Missile Defense

Although the Army agreed in principle with the concept of establishing air superiority through centralized direction of all air resources in a theater, in practice they thoroughly disliked operating without air cover and air defense in the presence of an enemy air threat. Considerable acrimony had developed in certain theaters between Army air and ground commanders over the question of who controlled the air defense forces. The problem was generally finessed on a pragmatic basis as each theater commander attempted to resolve the issue without benefit of agreed-upon doctrine. As the Army prepared for the separation of its air arm in anticipation of unification, the problem was finessed once again, hopefully to be resolved by the overall reorganization plan.

b. Inter-Service Rivalry

The development of jet aircraft and the German introduction of V1 and V2 missiles led American air defense planners to conclude that air defense weapons with greater range, accuracy and destructive power were required to counter those specific threats. In 1944, the United States initiated several projects designed to fulfill the requirements for new air defense weapons. (See Chapter V.)

We have noted in Chapter I how the Antiaircraft Artillery Board (January 1944) described the military characteristics for a controlled antiaircraft rocket projectile and recommended that one be developed. Independently, a concept for radar ground guidance of a controlled antiaircraft rocket (using a radar to track the target continuously and a separate radar to track and guide an intercepting missile) was developed and incorporated into the design requirements.

Well before the end of World War II, while development activities for advanced antiaircraft weapons were being initiated, the ground and air defenders within the Army were contending for the control of the new weapons. The Army Air Forces had long wanted to bring all air defense weapons under its control in order to achieve unity of effort in air defense (as the British and German air defense forces were unified under their air arms). The Army Ground Forces resisted transferring Army AAA to the AAF, holding that AAA was an extension of artillery and properly a Ground Force weapon. The Army Ground Forces was investigating the development of the use of guided missiles in conventional ground to ground artillery. To resolve the issue the Army Deputy Chief of Staff, Lieutenant General Joseph McNarney, issued a policy directive to the Army Air Forces, the Army Ground Forces, and the Army Service Forces, allocating responsibility for research and development in the guided missile field.

The air arm did not agree with this directive and was successful in having the directive revoked in October 1946, by a directive which gave the Army Air Forces complete responsibility for all research and development in connection with guided missiles. By that time, however, enough research had been directed toward guided missiles in accordance with the McNarney Letter, so the mold was cast. (See Chapter V.)

Developments begun to counter technological capabilities that were introduced in World War II, at a time when there was no specific enemy threat in sight. The general threat they were designated to counter was the possibility of a yet-unnamed enemy combining the capabilities of the supersonic V2 missile with an atomic payload. The Army Ground Forces started its research early on a guided missile antiaircraft and antimissile projectile, while the Army Air Forces lagged behind with the development of an aerodynamic lift antimissile interceptor. Both branches of the Army turned to civilian industry to develop their concepts.

The two different systems were spawned in an atmosphere of rivalry between the ground and air elements of the Army, and after their development, were the basis of further interservice rivalry between the Army and the then independent U.S. Air Force.

c. Civil Defense

There were a series of civil defense study boards under the military, but no operational civil defense organization was developed until the Korean War took place. (See Chapter V.)

d. Guided Missile Development

ICBM research was not begun early as scientists doubted that an ICBM was feasible. Research concentrated on jet engine propulsion. Requirements were established for air defense guided missiles. (See Chapter V.)

e. Politicization of the Scientists

The atomic weapon was developed during World War II by scientists who worked under military direction in the closely controlled and highly classified Manhattan Project. Many of the scientists were thoughtful men who were able to consider the policy implications of the awesome weapon. By the extremely close-hold nature of their work, they were able to discuss the implications among themselves and develop beliefs and positions which were generally shared by the scientific community that had been marshaled to achieve the atomic breakthrough. These scientists believed that once the feasibility of the atomic weapon was demonstrated, there was no way to prevent other scientists from duplicating their efforts and developing similar atomic weapons. Carrying this logic a step further, they were able to see a very dangerous world emerging—one in which atomic bombs proliferated under military controls, with no possible defense against surprise atomic attacks except passive defenses. This dangerous world would lead to an erosion of the democratic process, the captivity of scientific knowledge by military leaders, and the eventual destruction of civilization.

Faced with conclusions which made a nuclear Armageddon virtually inevitable, the scientists were able to overcome their self-avowed naiveté in political and international matters to make recommendations on future controls for military applications of scientific knowledge, in general, and atomic energy control, in particular. The scientists were generally in agreement that secrecy coupled with scientific developments would contribute to a dangerous international arms race. They also generally agreed that the already developed atomic knowledge and technology should not remain the possession of any one nation (since it *could* not, given their foregone conclusions), but should be brought under some form of international control for the future safety of the world. They believed that nations would act like rational men and share their beliefs; that they had much more to gain from the peaceful exploitation of scientific knowledge than they did from engaging in a suicidal arms race. Some scientists combined the two aspects of the generally held beliefs and advocated providing all nations with full and complete knowledge of the facts about atomic weapons before they could develop those facts themselves in secrecy.

The scientists were realistic enough to believe that any international agreement on the control of atomic energy must be backed by real and effective controls, not just paper promises. They knew that national survival was too important a stake to trust to the unsupported goodwill of other nations. This issue has been

Chapter II: American Strategy for Air and Ballistic Missile Defense

basic to disarmament negotiations to this day—how to establish effective international controls and inspection mechanisms. The scientists, however, reasoned that every nation has an interest in self-preservation and thus is deeply interested in achieving an agreement for control of the weapons of mass destruction. Such an agreement must essentially depend on the intensity and integrity of the nations' intentions and on each nation's readiness to surrender some of its sovereignty, in return for a peaceful future.

Holding such beliefs, it is not surprising that the scientists were opposed to using the atomic bombs on Japan, as that would be clear demonstration that the technology of atomic weaponry had been mastered. President Truman appointed a committee headed by Secretary of War Stimson to advise him on whether or not to use the atomic bomb against Japan, and on the post war disposition of atomic energy. The committee, composed of a number of wartime scientific leaders, weighed the matter carefully and regretfully recommended using the bomb against Japan. Dropping the bomb on Hiroshima and Nagasaki also had the effect of unmuzzling the younger scientists who opposed the decision and were no longer forced to remain silent by security requirements. They were vociferous in their demands for a "one world" policy toward atomic energy, and for establishing a United States Atomic Energy Commission under civilian control. They turned to the forum of public opinion and to politics to make their demands heard.

Having made the decision to use the atomic bomb, President Truman turned his attention to post war policy for the control of nuclear weapons. Secretary Stimson's committee of scientists also favored bringing atomic energy under some system of international control. After consultation with the British and Canadian atomic partners, a decision was announced in the Truman-Attlee-King Declaration of 15 November 1945. It was proposed that the United Nations Organization establish an atomic commission to eliminate the use of nuclear weapons, to promote the peaceful use of atomic energy, and to bring about an open world as far as nuclear energy was concerned. Since the ABC powers had a monopoly on atomic weapons at that time, it was clear that they favored international control of atomic weapons.

President Truman assigned Undersecretary of State Dean Acheson the task of developing detailed policy to implement the ABC Declaration. He, in turn, appointed an advisory panel of high-ranking American scientists, chaired by David Lilienthal, and including Robert Oppenheimer, both leading nuclear physicists. The report of the Lilienthal panel became the basis for the United States plan for the international control of atomic energy. As Bernard Baruch was the senior U.S. representative in the United Nations at the time of the atomic energy negotiations, the U.S. position became known as the Baruch Plan. It proposed an Atomic Development Authority which would be given monopoly control of all the world's dangerous fissionable materials and atomic production plants—in effect the U.S. inventory and production capability. Any attempt by any nation to produce atomic materials or weapons would be subject to such sanctions as the United Nations should determine. From the U.S. viewpoint the Baruch Plan would prevent any future surprise attack by preventing the proliferation of atomic weaponry. Since the United States already enjoyed a substantial advantage in the world as a result of its military-industrial production capacity and relatively remote geographical location, it could readily forego the atomic weapon in order to gain military security and freedom from a large military force in being.

The Soviet Union did not agree with the American position. It is now known that they were hard at work developing their own atomic capability with considerable assistance from their penetration of U.S. atomic secrets by means of their espionage apparatus in the United States. The Russians knew that time was on their side, and the Baruch Plan was defeated.

History of Strategic Air and Ballistic Missile Defense, 1945–1955: Volume I

In effect, the U.S. Government adopted the idealistic beliefs of the U.S. scientists in a "one world" approach to the worldwide control of atomic energy. Though the Baruch Plan failed, many of the scientists retained their beliefs in the need for an open world with an atmosphere of mutual confidence and trust—until the Soviets exploded their first atomic device in August 1949. At that time many of the scientists experienced a change of heart and again turned to public opinion and political channels to influence public policy in quite a different direction, which would have a direct bearing on U.S. air defense strategy.

f. U.S. National Strategy

As a result of renewed faith in the pre-war mobilization system and the huge spasm of spontaneous demobilization after World War II, the United States attempted to return to its pre-war strategy. Although American military forces were substantially larger than in the years between World Wars I and II, military policy was based on relatively small standing forces and the mobilization of industry and the citizen-soldier. The realities of the U.S. support for the United Nations Organization and the worldwide forward deployment of U.S. forces after the war brought about certain modifications to the pre-war strategy. In effect the United States abandoned its traditional isolationism for collective security through the United Nations and continued cooperation with its wartime allies in the occupation of the lands of their former enemies. American military leaders continued their wartime predominance in foreign policy as leaders of the occupations of Germany and Japan, as High Commissioners of American interests in Austria, and as the senior American representatives in such far-flung places as Trieste, Korea, Berlin, and Moscow. It was generally accepted in 1945 that the key elements of future U.S. strategy would be:

(1) Support for the United Nations (to include military forces if required)
(2) Forward deployment in both the Atlantic and Pacific
(3) Relatively strong Air and Naval forces in being
(4) Continuation of the U.S. monopoly of atomic weapons pending an effective system of international controls
(5) A small Regular Army
(6) A large well-organized reserve of citizen soldiers provided by Universal Military Training

This strategy fitted the mood of the American people at that time, and indeed, it is doubtful if any more militant strategy would have been possible in face of the overwhelming desire to buy the cars and build the houses and raise the families that wartime conditions had precluded. There was a widespread feeling among Americans that all the enemies were defeated in World War II, and that the prestige that American military might had accrued in the war would deter any future enemies.

At the national level in the United States the decision makers were hard-headed realists who recognized that the overwhelming concern of the American people was for their own economic and domestic policies. President Truman placed a budget ceiling on the cost of U.S. armed forces and adamantly refused to raise it despite repeated requests by his key national security advisors. He did not concern himself much with the way the military services divided up that budget or what they bought with it, as long as they carried out the strategy and remained within the austere budgetary limitations he imposed.

Chapter II: American Strategy for Air and Ballistic Missile Defense

He did concern himself with reorganizing the war-making structure and capability for fighting a future major war. He consistently fought for Universal Military Training, which was consistently denied by the Congress. The draft laws were not used and were allowed to expire. The military services were "unified" by the Military Security Act of 1947, which created a separate air service, as well as a national intelligence service (the Central Intelligence Group, later the CIA), the National Security Council, and an agency for planning wartime mobilization, the National Security Resources Board.

Due to the austere military budgets and reliance on the mobilization system, there was little thinking or planning for any future war except the "big war." Military planners and leaders were oriented towards a major war in Europe employing strategic airpower with nuclear weapons and a projection of mobilized U.S. military strength overseas to fight another total war. It was not anticipated that the Soviet Union would develop atomic weapons until after 1952, so the post war strategy was believed to be valid for some years. U.S. military forces were not ready for the events they experienced after 1947, though generally the responsibility for that lack of preparedness had been taken out of the hands of U.S. military leaders. President Truman determined both U.S. strategy and the U.S. force level prior to the Korean War.

g. U.S. Foreign Policy

The U.S.S.R. had not proved to be a particularly friendly or cooperative wartime ally, no doubt based on the fairly justifiable belief that she had nearly single-handedly met and bested the German war machine. Soviet casualties and war damages were huge and the feats of Soviet arms and production were formidable by any standards. Though there were very substantial contributions to the Soviet war-making capability by U.S. and British lend lease shipments, the abrupt cessation of that aid at the end of the war did much to negate any goodwill that may have emerged from it.

Though men of goodwill may have hoped for good post war relations between Russia and her wartime forces bedfellows, there was very little real evidence to support that optimistic outlook. Even before the end of World War II, Ambassador Harriman in Moscow cabled the warning: "The Soviet program is the establishment of totalitarianism ending personal liberty and democracy as we know it." The Soviets, he said, were simultaneously pursuing three lines: collaboration with the United States and Great Britain in establishing a world security organization; creation of their own security system by extending their sway over their neighbors; and extension of their influence into other countries through local Communist parties and the opportunities offered by economic chaos and democratic freedoms. Agreeing that the Soviets interpreted the "generous and considerate attitude" of the United States as a sign of weakness, he urged that the United States follow a tough policy and maintain positions that would be hard for the Soviet authorities if they maintained positions hard for us; and that we should hurt them if they hurt us.[1]

There was ample evidence that Harriman was correct in his assessment of the U.S.S.R.: the Russian backing of the Polish Communist group as the future government of Poland did not result in a fully Communist-controlled Polish Government until 1947, but Russian intentions were plain as early as 1945; the forcible installation of the Communist-dominated Groza government in Rumania in March 1945, and the subsequent refusal by the Russians to allow elections appeared to violate the Yalta Agreement. Rightly or wrongly, in Washington a number

---
[1] Huntington, *The Common Defense*, p. 33.

of the President's advisors accepted the Harriman analysis and President Truman himself quickly became disenchanted with the Russians and took an increasingly tough line with them from that time on.

On February 6, 1946, Generalissimo Stalin delivered a speech in which he stated that peaceful international order was "impossible under the present capitalistic development of world economy" and announced a five-year plan for massive industrial expansion.

Shortly thereafter from Moscow George F. Kennan cabled his explanation of Soviet behavior: "The Soviet leaders, he said, had inherited 'the traditional and instinctive Russian sense of insecurity' which reinforced their adherence to Marxist dogma and their view of the inevitability of conflict between the capitalist and communist worlds leading to the victory of the latter. Russia, he warned, would expand its influence through every possible means and attempt to fill every power vacuum. At times, tactical considerations might lead the Soviets to appear more friendly and amenable, but such moves were only temporary maneuvers." To meet this force Kennan urged "cohesion, firmness, and vigor."[2]

For the purpose of this study, it is useless to attempt to resolve the reasons for the onset of what came to be called the "Cold War." It was a real conflict between "East" and "West" and resulted in increasing antagonism at a level below total or nuclear warfare. In the three years after the end of World War II the Cold War expanded and widened the gap between antagonists—in Poland, Bulgaria, Yugoslavia, Albania, Hungary, divided and occupied Germany, Iran, Turkey, and Greece.

In March 1947, President Truman announced, and the Congress legislated, American aid for Greece and Turkey—the so-called Truman Doctrine. The United States had moved beyond diplomacy to throw its own resources into the conflict, after the British were forced to greatly curtail their aid to Greece due to economic conditions at home. The Soviet Union formed the Communist Information Bureau (Cominform) in October 1947, viewed by many as a resurrection of the old Comintern, and a clear indication that the world was divided into two camps—a bi-polar world.

In 1948 the United States introduced the Marshall Plan into Europe (first announced in June 1947); the Communists took over Czechoslovakia in February; Yugoslavia was read out of the Cominform for heresy; and the Soviet Union imposed the blockade on Berlin. The western allies responded with an airlift to supply Berlin and the United States moved several wings of B-29's to England and Germany, as many (including President Truman) believed that war was imminent between Russia and the west. The crisis passed without the expected violent confrontation, but undoubtedly the margin was close as the Soviet Union backed down and lifted the blockade the next year after the allies demonstrated their determination and ability to supply the city of Berlin.

The next year, 1949, 15 nations formed the alliance called the North Atlantic Treaty Organization (NATO), subsequently enlarged to include Greece and Turkey. In China the Chinese Communist Armies overran the entire Chinese mainland, forcing the withdrawal of the Chinese Nationalist forces to the island of Formosa (Taiwan). Shortly thereafter the world learned that the Soviet Union had exploded an atomic device, some years before it was expected. The waves of shock that were felt around the western world probably impacted greatest in the United States, which suddenly found itself no longer in possession of an atomic monopoly, but pursuing an outdated strategy of deliberate military weakness.

---

[2] Ibid., p. 34.

Chapter II: American Strategy for Air and Ballistic Missile Defense

3. Planning and Developing an Air Defense

a. The Watershed Year: Controversy and Decisions in 1946

The first planning for the post war organization of the Armed Forces began in late 1943 in the War Department. Looking forward to unification of the Armed Forces, provisions were planned for a separate air force. General Marshall directed that planning be based on a relatively small standing Regular Army, but with a combat-ready air force capable on "M" Day of repelling an enemy attack or quashing any incipient threat to world peace. After rejection of over-ambitious initial force levels for the air force, Army Air Force planners settled on a minimum peacetime strength of 70 groups with approximately 400,000 personnel.

In November 1945, General Dwight D. Eisenhower became Army Chief of Staff, while General Carl Spaatz began to assume the duties of Commanding General, Army Air Forces, in anticipation of General Arnold's announced retirement. One of General Eisenhower's first actions was to appoint a board of officers, headed by Lieutenant General W. H. Simpson, to prepare a definitive plan for the reorganization of the Army and the Air Force that could be effected without enabling legislation and would provide for the separation of the Air Force from the Army. In January 1946, Generals Eisenhower and Spaatz agreed on an Air Force organization consisting of the following major commands: the Strategic Air Command, the Air Defense Command, the Tactical Air Command, the Air Transport Command and the supporting Air Technical Service Command, Air Training Command, the Air University, and the Air Force Center.

Army Air Forces leaders urged that the Air Defense Command should be the centralized system for controlling all means of air defense: fighter aircraft, radar, and antiaircraft artillery. Further, they wanted all antiaircraft artillery integrated into the Army Air Forces to make centralized control of air defense resources effective. Doctrinally, they were on sound footing for the War Department Field Manual 100-20, *Command and Employment of Air Power*, published in 1943 stated: ". . . [T]he efficient exploitation of the special capabilities of each (i.e., AAA and aviation) and the avoidance of unnecessary losses to friendly aviation demand that all be placed under the command of the air commander responsible for the area. This must be done."

Notwithstanding, the antiaircraft artillery officers in the Army did not want to be separated from the Army and integrated into the new Air Force. There were able to adequately influence the Simpson Board so that it recommended that the antiaircraft artillery should not be transferred to the Army Air Forces, but that antiaircraft artillery units should be trained and attached to Air Force units from time to time.

The Air Defense Command was activated in March 1946, at Mitchel Field, New York, under the command of Lieutenant General George E. Stratemeyer. By that time Army Air Force strength had diminished from 218 effective combat groups on V-J Day to less than 109 groups, many of which were not effective due to the high loss of skilled specialists to keep the aircraft flying. Army antiaircraft artillery strength was demobilized at a rapid rate until by the end of 1946 there were only two gun and two automatic weapons battalions in existence, all at cadre strength with zero combat effectiveness. The question of integrating AAA units into the Air Force became largely academic. By that same date the entire Army Air Forces were down to only 55 groups, of which only two could be counted as combat ready. It quickly became obvious that the Air Defense Command would be relegated to the role of a mobilization measure, to be given effective strength by mobilizing Air National Guard and Air Reserve units.

Despite the realities of the lack of tactical assets, the Army Air Forces assigned General Stratemeyer an air defense mission which assigned ADC control over antiaircraft artillery assigned to the air defense of the

United States. He was instructed to organize and administer the integrated air defense of the Continental United States and exercise direct control of all active measures of air defense. While attempting to carry out his mission, General Stratemeyer discovered that the War Department had previously assigned the Army Ground Forces the mission of: "Under the general plans of the War Department, and in conjunction with designated air, and naval commanders, prepare for, and on order, or in imminent emergency, execute planned operations for the defense of the United States. Coordinate ground plans, including coastal defense and antiaircraft projects, with designated air and naval commanders."

The Army Air Forces brought the ambiguity, or duplicity, to the attention of the War Department. The Commanding General of the Army Ground Forces, however, believed that his directive was doctrinally correct in that air defense could not be separated from national defense, and that any air attack would be accompanied by a ground attack. He felt that a task force composed of all services would be necessary to successfully meet such attacks, and that such a task force should be under the command of the Commanding General of the Army Ground Forces—the traditional defender of the Continental United States.

The War Department issued War Department Circular 138 in May 1946, designed to clarify responsibilities for air defense. The circular instructed the Army Air Forces ADC to provide for the air defense of the United States and to control and train such antiaircraft units as might be assigned to it. Since at that time there were no combat effective antiaircraft units, the Circular probably had air defense *after a mobilization* in mind. The circular also directed the Army Ground Forces and the Army Air Forces to cooperate in developing AAA tactics, in deciding upon the types of weapons required, and in drawing up manning and equipment documents for AAA units assigned to the defense of CONS. The AAF was also charged with recommending to the War Department the required antiaircraft artillery for CONS air defense.

The AGF disagreed with Circular 138 because it assigned control of AAA units to the Air Force. The Air Force was not fully satisfied with the circular because it did not assign AAA units to the ADC, but only provided for control over such units as might be assigned to it. Again, the absence of effective AAA units in the United States emphasizes the doctrinal or theoretical nature of the dispute.

The Army Air Force lost little time in convening a meeting of the Air Board and the Air Staff in early June of 1946, to resolve the problem of antiaircraft artillery. A memorandum was prepared and forwarded to the War Department, entitled "Recommended Policies on Air Defense and Security." The memorandum contained ten recommendations:

(1) To integrate antiaircraft artillery into the Army Air Force.
(2) To give priority to offensive air power and air defense units over all other national defense forces.
(3) To make the Commanding General, AAF, the principal advisor on all matters concerning air defense to include amounts of deployment of antiaircraft artillery, other than that required for local AAA defense of AGF tactical units.
(4) To maintain sufficient air defense units to all types in the regular establishment "to provide a nucleus quickly reinforceable by air to insure a reasonable defense of our overseas bases and to provide a framework for the rapid mobilization of our continental air defense."
(5) To organize all areas subject to air attack in the Zone of the Interior (Continental United States) and overseas into Air Defense Commands, subdivided as necessary, charged with:
    (a) The entire responsibility for air defense
    (b) Overall supervision of passive air defense
    (c) Control of AA fire of naval vessels when in port.

Chapter II: American Strategy for Air and Ballistic Missile Defense

    (6) To charge appropriate overseas Air Force Headquarters with air defense missions, in times of peace, with a deputy commander for air defense and a staff to permit continuity of air defense training and operations when the Air Force Headquarters is moved or engaged in another mission.

    (7) In theaters of operations, air defense of areas forward of Air Defense Commands shall be charged to:

        (a) Army Ground Force Commanders for employment of assigned AAA forward of the AGF rear boundary but subject to AAF authority to restrict fire and illumination against unidentified aerial targets within rules prescribed by supreme commanders.

        (b) AAF Commanders for maintaining communications with AGF antiaircraft major control centers.

        (c) Tactical Air Force Commanders for employment of all air defense means other than antiaircraft artillery, over the entire area and for the employment of all antiaircraft artillery employed in the defense of air installations located in the area and that antiaircraft employed in the area in rear of the Army Ground Forces rear area boundary.

    (8) All units capable of effective employment in air defense and assigned to other than Air Defense Commands would be made available to such commands in emergency and would also be made available to Air Defense Command for training for such emergency.

    (9) Staffs of Air Defense Commands and subdivisions would include officers qualified in all specialties. There should be no parallel organizations such as antiaircraft commands.

    (10) Qualified "ground combat" officers would be equally eligible with flying officers for command of air defense commands.

The Army Air Force air defense specialists wrapped up all of the air arm's disputes, hopes, goals, and aspirations in this one memorandum designed to settle once and for all the major air defense problems that were identified in World War II. As the Service charged with primary responsibility for air defense, they were on sound doctrinal grounds in making these recommendations.

The Army Ground Forces moved equally quickly and simultaneously in producing a study entitled *Security from Enemy Air Action*, which was forwarded to General Carl Spaatz, Commanding General AAF on 14 June 1946. The study concluded:

    (1) Ground action against any adversary is basically a ground responsibility.

    (2) Air power cannot efficiently be tied to the defense of any one point or small area.

    (3) Antiaircraft artillery should be assigned the defense of specific points and small areas against enemy air operations.

    (4) Within its range an adequate antiaircraft artillery defense is the most effective protection against enemy air action directed at the defended point.

    (5) The combining of antiaircraft and fighter aircraft under joint command and control is not desirable tactically because of their differing tactical concepts and spheres of action and is objectionable because it destroys antiaircraft artillery flexibility.

    (6) The problems of identification and recognition can be solved to a degree that will reasonably safeguard friendly aircraft.

    (7) Exchange of information on airborne enemy aircraft among the air warning service, the antiaircraft artillery intelligence service, and the Navy centers should be continued and improved.

    (8) Passive defense measures are inseparable for each unit and installation.

The study recommended that "air defense" remain an air force responsibility, but restricted to defense by air by piloted aircraft, by air launched missiles, and through an aircraft warning service. The purpose of air defense was to deny enemy air access to air space over friendly territory beyond the range of ground-to-air defenses. The study further recommended that antiaircraft defense be a ground force responsibility, and that it be defined as "all ground to air action." Such defenses would include antiaircraft artillery, searchlights, barrage balloons and intelligence service, with the purpose of defending specific objectives against enemy air action within effective range of its weapons.

The study recommended that the air forces be responsible for all operations against enemy air beyond the range of ground defenses, and for continuously advising appropriate ground defenses of the locations of friendly and enemy aircraft in the air. Ground forces would be responsible for the defense of objectives on the ground within the range of their weapons and would continuously advise the air forces of the locations of defended areas. Passive defenses would be the responsibility of each unit and installation commander.

At the heart of the AGF's arguments lay the old unsettled doctrinal dispute raised on many occasions during World War II. The antiaircraft artillerymen did not like to have the air force given the authority to tell the AAA to withhold fire. They believed that the air force did not have adequate faith in AAA to take the necessary precautions with friendly aircraft to enforce known procedures for identification of friendly aircraft. Rather than restrict friendly aircraft from flying over areas assigned AAA, or having them properly identify themselves so the AAA wouldn't fire on them, the air force had a tendency to require the AAA to withhold fire. The AGF believed that friendly aircraft defended best by destroying the enemy on or over its own territory, not by defensively protecting limited friendly areas and points. The AAF, on the other hand, had enough experience with having its own aircraft shot down by "friendly" AAA through lack of adequate coordination procedures, that it had become extremely chary of its own ground-to-air defenses.

The AGF study also addressed other arguments advanced by the air proponents. Among these were the joint use of radar, safety of friendly aircraft, and selection of the most adequate means to meet an attack. While admitting the great utility of the Air Force radars, the study pointed out that AAA had been forced to rely upon its own equipment for target acquisition because of the inadequacy of the Air Force air warning system. As for safeguarding friendly aircraft, "This is considered an avoidance of the problem of recognition and identification," the study stated. It then went on to list the means available to achieve identification and insisted that the identification problem was capable of solution. The AGF study took the firm position that AAA was the best means for air defense of local targets, and should be used to the exclusion of fighter aircraft.

Applying these arguments to continental defense, the Ground Forces proposed that they be given the mission of providing defense of ground targets from aerial attack within the range of their weapons. AGF would perform this mission by allotting AAA weapons to the Continental Armies, establishing priorities for defense upon the basis of directives from higher authority, and informing the Air Forces of the locations of ground defended areas. Within these areas, the friendly aircraft would be permitted to operate provided the defenses were advised of their approach. When attacking aircraft reached the defended area, AAA would open fire and fighter aircraft would break contact to wait until the enemy aircraft emerged from the confines of the ground defended area.

In August 1946, the AAF replied to the AGF memorandum. The principal AAF point was the importance of *unity of command*, long regarded by military men as one of the foremost principles of warfare. For a single mission, air defense, there must be a single commander. The speed and range of modern aircraft, together with the great destructive power they wield, made any attempt to divide the single mission of air defense between two separately operating agencies one that would be fought with disaster. The one air defense commander must have the authority over a wide area, the communications to reach all air defense resources instantaneously, and the power to direct and allocate air defense resources as he determines

Chapter II: American Strategy for Air and Ballistic Missile Defense

proper. The AAF reply pointed out the obvious inefficiencies of split command with duplicate communications facilities, electronic countermeasures, detection systems, and intelligence systems.

The AAF felt that the AGF overly emphasized World War II experiences when the Allies enjoyed overwhelming air superiority. The homeland and the Army rear areas were virtually free from enemy air attack, allowing the AAA the freedom to move on with the ground armies. Further, fighter aircraft were never tied to the defense of fixed points, but carried on operations over fixed points if the tactical situation made such operations sound. The Ground Forces did not seem to recognize that future developments in ground-launched guided missiles might render these weapons far different from gun weapons in range and other characteristics. To limit aircraft to the sphere outside the range of ground-launched weapons when guided missiles reached an advanced state of development would probably be tactically unsound.

With respect to the AGF assertion that an adequate AAA was the best means of local air defense against targets within range, the AAF contended that each weapon had its own role to perform and, according to circumstances, one or the other would be the best weapon to use. As for the AGF position that ground action against any adversary was the responsibility of ground forces, the AAF retorted that the mission of the weapon was more important than the point in space from which it was launched. The recent war, it was asserted, had proved that the mission molded forces. Joint operations under the command of the service chiefly concerned with carrying out the mission was one of the most important lessons learned in the recent war.

Identification, the AAF said, was not a soluble problem. No system had yet been devised whereby identification could be achieved in an acceptable percentage of cases. Furthermore, no defense system could be based upon voluntary exchange of information between the AAA radar system and that of the air warning service. Those agencies must be under one commander.

The recently created Air Defense Command added several other objections to those raised by the AAF. Defense in-depth, ADC asserted, was made necessary by the speed of modern aircraft, and local air defenses as such might very well be eliminated in future air defense arrangements. Air attack might be sudden and without warning, so that in-being forces, under one commander, were requisite in peacetime. While recognizing the need for Ground Defense Zones in addition to Air Defense Zones, ADC felt that these zones should be designed according to weapon capability, and not assigned without qualification to particular commands. ADC did not commit itself to Rules of Engagement for such zones, and made no comment concerning those described by the AGF study. In summary, ADC recommended that the AGF principles be applied only within a single force, and that air defense be defined to embrace all measures designed to prevent or lower the effectiveness of air attack.

In September 1946, the War Department resolved the controversy by accepting the AAF position that the air defense mission was unitary. The AAF would control AAA units with air defense missions.

Decisions as to the future role of guided missiles in air defense were deliberately withheld, in order to "maintain service-wide doctrinal flexibility in the use of this arm . . . ." However, it was believed "neither feasible nor desirable" to change Circular 138, which provided for a single command charged with complete responsibility for carrying out the active defense of the United States against air attack. AAA employed with the ground forces was of primary concern to the Ground Forces, while AAA assigned the mission of CONUS air defense would come under the command of the Air Forces.

The War Department specified that both the AAF and the AGF should submit to the War Department their AAA requirements for the next three to five years. The Air Defense Command was to make its staff an integrated one, incorporating AAA officers, and ensure that AAA assigned to it was trained in combat missions, not to interfere, however, with the fulfillment of the primary air defense responsibility. The Ground Forces, on their part, would continue to provide technical training for all AAA units.

Thus the doctrinal dispute over the control of AAA was settled at a time when there were virtually no air defense resources in being. It would have a major impact in later years when the Korean War emergency caused the mobilization of a CONUS air defense. The Air Force was never again to relinquish the dominant position in air defense.

b. The Early Impact of "Unification"

While the AGF and AAF were exchanging memorandums on air defense, planning for unification of the armed forces moved ahead, spurred by the Bikini Atoll atomic bomb test and the release of the United States Strategic Bombing Survey, both in July 1946. The Bikini test underlined the importance of the air arm in the nation's defenses, and the bombing survey explicitly recommended the establishment of a separate Air Force. The National Security Act of 1947 was passed by the Congress and implemented by the Executive Department in July of 1947. James Forrestal was named the first Secretary of Defense over the National, Military Establishment, unifying the Departments of the Army, Navy, and Air Force. The Joint Chiefs of Staff became a permanent organization, though without provision for a Chairman.

A series of agreements between the Army and Air Force took place to ensure the orderly division of functions and responsibilities as they became separate departments. One of the first agreements was signed in July 1947 between General Devers, Command General Army Ground Force, and General Spaatz, still signing as Commanding General Army Air Forces. The agreement simply stated that the Air Defense Command had responsibility for AGF units participating in air defense of the Zone of the Interior, when AGF AAA units were so designated and assigned. The ADC was to establish communications to the AAA units; the AAA units were to follow ADC standing operating instructions for assignment of targets, opening and ceasing fire, conditions of alert and minimum manning requirements. The extent of participation and the areas to be defended by the AAA units would be determined by joint agreement between Army commanders and corresponding Air Defense commanders. General Devers was not giving anything away that was not already directed, and there were no AAA units in existence to place under ADC control with the exception of antiaircraft school troops at Fort Bliss, Texas.

Chief of Staff of the Army, General Eisenhower, and General Spaatz signed over 200 agreements in separating the functions of the Army and Air Force. One of the Eisenhower-Spaatz agreements specifically confirmed the Devers-Spaatz agreement.

To further clarify the functions of each service, Secretary of Defense Forrestal held a series of conferences with the chiefs of the services in Key West, Florida, in March 1948. The Air Force was assigned responsibility for the defense of the United States against air attack. An Air Force attempt to have AAA units integrated into the Air Force was rejected by Secretary Forrestal. The Army retained the responsibility for organizing, gaining and equipping AAA units and providing them as required for Air Defense.

Despite the reorganization and "unification" of the military services, the budget for fiscal year 1949 was prepared by the individual services unilaterally without reference to the Joint Chiefs of Staff, and together totaled $10 billion—the amount that President Truman had established for total defense requirements. The Air Force piece of the budgetary pie allowed for a maximum of 55 combat groups and 17 separate squad-

Chapter II: American Strategy for Air and Ballistic Missile Defense

rons, providing $700 million for the modernization of active groups by replacing World War II aircraft. The Army and Navy were funded at a level that would keep them in an appropriate balance with the air arm's forces. The small size of the Air Force appropriation made it impossible for the Air Force to do justice to all the missions assigned to it, and forced a priority system in order to do any one mission well. There was consensus among the Air Force leaders that the Strategic Air Command should have first priority. The Air Defense Command was unable to have its plans for an aircraft control and warning (AC&W) system funded in FY 1947, FY 1948, or FY 1949, although such a system was considered a prerequisite for a successful CONUS air defense.

The Air Force had devised an AC&W plan in late 1947, known as Supremacy, that was to be implemented within five years from the time that funds were allocated.[3] The plan called for providing 24-hour operation of Alaska and peripheral continental radar stations, and part-time operation of interior U.S. stations. The plan was to cost $388,000,000 to provide 411 radar stations, 374 of which would be in the continental United States, manned by 25,138 Regular Air Force and 13,788 National Guard troops. The Air Force had let a contract with General Electric for a new improved search radar (jointly funded with the Navy) which was to be in production by 1953. The ADC considered the Supremacy radar network as the minimum that would be acceptable, but wanted it tied in with the Canadian Air Defense Command, the Alaskan Air Command, and a proposed Northeast Air Command. General Stratemeyer also wanted the extension of coastal radar coverage by airborne early warning stations and radar picket ships. The ADC, in November of 1947, decided to go ahead with implementation of the plan with such AC&W assets as the ADC possessed.

The newly designated USAF assigned the ADC a definite mission directive in December 1947.[4] General Stratemeyer was directed to provide for the defense of the United States against air attack, using designated SAC and TAC units, and Air National Guard units in the event of war or an emergency. Although ADC was given very few means to carry out its mission, it had a clear directive to plan the air defense of CONUS. The existence of such an ADC air defense plan was to have major implications for the future.

c. Strategic Interaction: The Threat of War in 1948

In 1948, even while the Joint Chiefs of Staff were sitting with Secretary Forrestal at Key West, the crush of events in Europe brought about a war scare. The Communist coup in Czechoslovakia and German currency reform in the non-Communist zones caused General Clay, American Military Governor in Germany, to cable from Berlin that he believed war might come "with dramatic suddenness" at any moment.[5] Although there was no overall JCS increase in U.S. defense readiness, General Spaatz directed immediate augmentation of the Alaskan air defense system and ordered the Alaskan Air Command to operate its warning radars on a 24-hour basis by 4 April. Headquarters USAF moved fighter squadrons to Alaska and the Northwest, reinforced the Alaskan radar system with several radar sets, and directed ADC to reinforce the radars in the Seattle area and place the radars in 24-hour operation. General Spaatz ordered the ADC to place the air defense system in the Northwestern United States into immediate operation, to be continued for at least the next sixty days. Shortly after 12 April, ADC was given word that the crisis was over, and ten days later the

---

[3] USAF Historical Studies: No. 126, p. 11.
[4] Ibid., p. 12.
[5] Ibid., p. 19.

24-hour operations of the makeshift AC&W system was allowed to return to more normal operations. The short-lived crisis served to emphasize the meagerness of the resources available to General Stratemeyer; he wasted no time submitting his report to Headquarters USAF, recommending that the ADC be given the means for carrying out its mission.[6]

As if in reply, General Stratemeyer was ordered on 23 April 1948 to establish with his current resources AC&W systems in the Northwestern United States, the Northeastern United States, and the Albuquerque, New Mexico, areas, in that priority.[7] No additional funding was available nor were other additional resources available. Within the means available, General Stratemeyer and the ADC, strove to carry out the directive, but necessarily fell far short of minimum acceptable success. As any good commander would, General Stratemeyer protested his lack of readiness and resources to Headquarters USAF. Air defense exercises in May and June in both the Northwestern and Northeastern air defense regions further proved the inability of ADC to defend against hostile air attack. General Stratemeyer reported that he could not provide an effective air defense if he were provided all the resources of the entire USAF, as air defense depended on an effective AC&W system and the Air Force was lacking in those resources.[8]

The Air Force attempted to get its Supremacy plan before Congress in 1948, but could not get it out of JCS channels before Congress adjourned. The Air Force fell back and devised an Interim Program designed to use radar equipment already on hand or under current procurement.[9] This program called for 61 basic radars and 10 control centers to be deployed in 26 months, with an additional ten radars and one control station for Alaska. As the radars would provide only high-altitude coverage, a system of ground observers would be necessary for low-altitude coverage, plus Air National Guard gap fillers and air transportable radars. The Interim Program required supplemental appropriations by Congress in the amount of $44,300,000.

The Air Force position on the Interim Program from the first was that is was not a substitute for the Supremacy plan, but a makeshift substitute to fill the gap until the Supremacy plan network could be approved and constructed. Perhaps it was inevitable that the Department of Defense should seize on the Interim Plan as a less expensive substitute for the larger and more expensive original request. The ADC also planned a First Augmentation to the Interim Plan—the addition of 15 more radars at an additional cost of $41,900,000.[10] The Interim Plan and First Augmentation were eventually put together and placed before the Congress with a request for an appropriation of $85,500,000. The bill passed the Congress in March 1949, and was signed by President Truman, giving the USAF an authorization for an Aircraft Control and Warning System, but some time would elapse before the Congress was to appropriate money for the system, and more time would be required to build the system.

Pending construction of the permanent Modified Plan, the USAF worked out a temporary network to be put together with minimum cost on land already owned by the government, and using on-hand obsolescent radars. The temporary network would serve for training purposes and would provide some measure of defense pending construction of the desired network. The network was named Lashup for obvious reasons

---
[6] Ibid., p. 20.
[7] Ibid.
[8] Ibid., p. 21.
[9] Ibid., p. 23.
[10] Ibid., p. 24.

Chapter II: American Strategy for Air and Ballistic Missile Defense

and would take two years to put together.[11] By the end of 1948 ADC began preliminary work on Lashup. The ADC could expect to see some semblance of an air defense system in 1950—until that time the CONUS was virtually defenseless against hostile air attack.

The Air Force had long believed that 70-group Air Force was the absolute minimum air power necessary for the security of the United States, but had accepted the 55-group Air Force imposed by President Truman's insistence on a $10 billion ceiling for defense spending. During Congressional hearings for the Defense Establishment's fiscal year 1949 budget, in March of 1948, Congress indicated an interest in a 70-group floor under the Air Force. Shortly thereafter the Soviet military blockade of Berlin began, which brought back into sharp focus the importance of airpower. Based on recommendations of the JCS, President Truman forwarded a request to Congress in May 1948, for a supplemental appropriation of $3,068,411,000, to be nearly equally split among the three services. The Air Force decided to attempt to activate additional groups by using many moth-balled airplanes, rather than buying all new aircraft, climbing in its planning almost to the 70-group level it advocated. It also contracted for 2,201 new aircraft from the augmented FY 1949 appropriations.

d. The Problem of Budgets

In mid-1948, an economic recession wiped out an expected budget surplus of $5 billion and caused a budget deficit of $2 billion, persuading President Truman to set a ceiling of $14.4 billion on the National Defense budget for fiscal year 1950. This was done in the summer of 1948 without consulting the National Security Council or the JCS. Air Force planning was forced to *reduce* its combat strength to 48 groups and 10 separate squadrons. To achieve this cutback from the 55-group strength, the Air Force concentrated on building up SAC at the expense of the other missions. In order to make the best use of all air resources in CONUS, rather than dividing them among several commands, the Continental Air Command was established at Mitchel Field on December 1, 1948.[12] ConAC received command of the six air forces formerly assigned to ADC and the Tactical Air Command, reducing both ADC and TAC to the status of operational headquarters. ConAC also assumed responsibility for the Air National Guard and the Air Reserve. This reorganization was completed on February 1, 1949. Lieutenant General Stratemeyer took over as Commanding General of ConAC. This economy measure reduced ADC to the status of a major command with no assigned air defense forces—it was to assume operational control over such forces as would be placed under it whenever an active air defense became necessary.

In March 1949, Louis M. Johnson succeeded Forrestal as Secretary of Defense, whereupon he instituted an economy program which cut all services proportionately in personnel, equipment and facilities. He continued the established concentration on strategic air power and SAC but cut the construction of the Navy supercarrier already under way. The Air Force cancelled orders for some 470 aircraft and concentrated its purchases on 75 additional B-36's for SAC. The Navy staged the so-called "revolt of the admirals" which placed the merits of the B-36 and the supercarrier before the public's eye in a heated controversy. Although the controversy was hailed as a manifestation of service rivalry, more properly it was a manifestation of an honest difference of opinion between members of two services of how the increasingly scarce defense dollar should be allocated for the overall defense of the United States. As the supercarrier was designed to carry Navy air-

---
[11] Ibid., p. 25.
[12] Ibid., p. 28.

craft with atomic weapons, the Navy naturally saw it as adding greater flexibility to the U.S. strategic offensive air capability. The public controversy, however, did nothing to further the cause of national defense.

e. Strategic Interaction Revisited: The Soviet Atomic Bomb, NSC 8, and Korea

At the time that the U.S.S.R. exploded its first experimental atomic device in August 1949, American scientists had not expected the event until 1952. The surprise sent shock waves throughout the United States that had far-reaching impact on the future military posture of the nation. The most immediate result was to stimulate research and development in the field of nuclear weapons development. The scientific community had resisted further atomic developments in general, and the development of a thermonuclear weapon in particular following the Soviet explosion, a public debate on the further development of the United States' atomic program ensued. During that debate, in January 1950, Dr. Klaus Fuchs, a former group leader of the Los Alamos atomic weapons laboratory, confessed that he had passed nuclear secrets to the Russians.[13] President Truman, on 31 January 1950, directed the Atomic Energy Commission to work on all forms of atomic weapons, including the hydrogen bomb. As a result of that directive, the United States developed a family of nuclear weapons, including an efficient atomic bomb capable of being carried by a fighter-type aircraft. The age of tactical nuclear weapons had arrived, and the age of fusion weapons was not far behind.

Concurrent with directing the new atomic program, President Truman directed the Departments of State and Defense to review U.S. foreign and domestic policy in light of the loss of China, the Soviet mastery of the atomic bomb, and the prospect of the hydrogen (fusion) bomb.[14] This directive took the action out of the National Security Council and resulted in an *ad hoc* joint State-Defense study group, chaired by Paul Nitze, director of the State Department Policy Planning Staff. The State Department, which had consistently borne the brunt of the military weakness of the United States in attempting to deal with world affairs, gave its full backing to the study effort.

The Department of Defense backing was confused and disjointed. Secretary Johnson and the Joint Chiefs of Staff had accepted President Truman's insistence on minimum military spending to protect the nation's economy. Since the summer of 1948, a belief had grown that the Soviets were deliberately maneuvering the United States into increasing its defense expenditures beyond that which the economy would safely bear. Military men and civilians alike had come to believe that the economy of the United States was its first line of strength and security, and that to damage it by overspending for defense was tantamount to losing a military war.[15] President Truman had reduced the FY 1951 military budget from $14.5 billion to $13.0 billion to compensate for the military aid sent to Europe to bolster the defenses of NATO allies. Although the military Joint Chiefs believed that the nation's security required expenditures of around $30 to $40 billion for defense, they quietly concurred in the $13 billion ceiling imposed on defense spending. This acquiescence was reflected in their initial attitude toward the directed strategic study.[16]

Under State Department leadership, the study advocated an immediate and large-scale build-up in U.S. military strength and that of U.S. allies to right the power imbalance with the Soviet Union, in the hopes of averting an all-out war with the Soviet Union by forcing a change in the nature of the Soviet system.

---
[13] Hammond, *The Cold War Years*, p. 38.
[14] Huntington, p. 49.
[15] Ibid.
[16] Ibid., p. 50.

Chapter II: American Strategy for Air and Ballistic Missile Defense

Underlying that conclusion was the implicit belief that the Soviet Union only respected strength and would only change from its aggressive policies if faced with equal or greater strength.

The study group estimated that the Soviet Union would be adequately armed with nuclear weapons by 1954 to launch an all-out attack on the United States. The United States and its allies also faced the prospect of piecemeal aggression subversion, disunity in the NATO alliance, and loss of American will. President Truman referred the study to the NSC after it had received the concurrence of the four Joint Chiefs, the three service secretaries, a reluctant Secretary Johnson and the enthusiastic Secretary of State Acheson. The NSC assigned the number 68 to the study.[17] NSC 68 was the first comprehensive statement of a national strategy for the United States since the formation of the National Security Council. It meant tripling the budget, increasing taxes at a time when the Congress was reducing taxes, and arming in peacetime without the support of an aroused public. NSC 68 lay on President Truman's desk throughout the spring of 1950, with no approval from the President. The communist invasion of June 25, 1950, of South Korea resolved the issue. From the viewpoint of a rather lopsided international strategic arms competition, the Communist timing couldn't possibly have been better for the United States or worse for the Soviet Union.

4. Summary: 1945–1950

The period from the end of World War II until the outbreak of the Korean War saw the development of the Cold War with Russia which split the world into two hostile groups. The United States concentrated on the development of its economy and its monopoly of the atomic weapon, at the expense of military strength. Due to the deliberately low military expenditures, the military services had to skimp to meet their overseas deployment commitments, and neglect air defenses and civil defense except as planning activities. The military services turned to civilian industry for further development of the advanced technologies first demonstrated in World War II. Despite the development of a "unified" military department, the individual services controlled their own research and development programs which were in competition with one another. Due to budgetary limitations, and their own planning premises of a "big war," the U.S. military forces were not ready for the "limited" challenges of the Berlin Blockade and Korea. Instead they were planning the resolution of potential problems in mobilizing civilian industry and military reserve forces to meet the challenges of a "big war." The 1949 Soviet atomic explosion caught the U.S. by surprise and triggered off actions to greatly increase U.S. military strength. However, even with the scare effect of the Russian atomic bomb, it is doubtful if the American public would have supported the increased taxes and spending that such an increase would demand. That public reluctance was significantly reduced after the Communists committed open aggression against South Korea. The Korean invasion provided the event that U.S. national leaders needed to raise U.S. armaments to the level that the world situation required.

B. 1950–1955: Defense Against the World War II Threat

1. Strategic Interaction: Impact of the Korean War

a. Perceptions and Budgets

The well-prepared invasion by the North Korean armed forces of the Republic of Korea on June 25, 1950, was taken as another example of militant Communism on the move. The Communist takeover of

---
[17] Ibid.

China and the explosion of the Soviet atomic device thoroughly alerted U.S. policy makers to the lack of military preparedness of U.S. forces. Korea left no doubt that the Communists would use force to accomplish foreign policy objectives unless opposed by substantial military strength. It also provided a clear-cut provocation for response by U.S. military force, taking place as it did under the nose of the largest concentration of American military power outside the United States. The American response through the United Nations organization was measured and limited. President Truman was keenly aware of the Korean conflict having the potential to spread into a third world war, and was adamant that the conflict be limited to the borders of Korea. The United States was not prepared for a full-scale all-out war with Russia, and its allies in Europe were in an even more dangerous position. The major effort of U.S. policy toward the Korean War was to limit the conflict and prevent war. Certain of the President's subordinates did not comprehend that fact and were summarily relieved or allowed to resign.

The Korean War created a clear and present danger that the American public could rally behind. As a result the lid was raised on defense expenditures and tax revision was rewritten to raise individual and corporate income taxes. The money voted for rearmament totaled $22.3 billion in FY 1951, rose to $44.0 billion in FY 1952, and peaked at $50.4 billion in FY 1953.

b. The New Strategic Vision

From President Truman's viewpoint, the limited war in Korea made rearmament possible, but he made no bones of the fact that rearmament was not directed primarily at fighting the Korean War. The Administration was rearming to counterbalance the threat of increased Soviet strength and building the mobilization base of the United States up to a point where it greatly increased the readiness of American industry for full mobilization for the expected general war. General George Marshall replaced Secretary Johnson as Secretary of Defense in September 1950, and steadily built up U.S. military strength to act as a long-term deterrent to Soviet aggression, while preparing to fight a general war if deterrence failed.

The costs of the Korean War were thus a relatively minor portion of the increased Department of Defense budgets throughout all three years of the Korean War. The other measures that were taken to mobilize the nation's resources for war must be viewed in the light of an overall preparation for a much greater conflict than the relatively small and limited war in Korea, even after the Chinese forces entered the battle and temporarily tipped the scales in favor of the Communist forces. The enemy was clearly identified as the Soviet Union; the atomic threat posed by the Russians was revised from the 1954 estimate to 1952; and the fear on the part of U.S. policymakers was that Europe was the real target of Soviet aggression.[18] To meet that threat SAC was to be substantially expanded to the point where it would be able to absorb a Soviet surprise attack and still retaliate effectively against the U.S.S.R. The ground forces would be built up with strong ground reinforcements dispatched to bolster the ground defenses of NATO against the Red Army. Allied forces would be strengthened from the rearmament production effort to bolster collective security and insure the maintenance of bases overseas for U.S. projection of its military power overseas. July 1952 was conceived to be the target time of maximum danger.[19]

To strengthen the U.S. armed forces for that time of maximum danger, the planned strength of the armed forces included 20 Army division and 18 regimental combat teams; 1,130 ships in the Navy; 3 Marine divi-

---
[18] Ibid., p. 80.
[19] Ibid.

Chapter II: American Strategy for Air and Ballistic Missile Defense

sions and 3 Marine air wings; 95 Air Force wings; and a total military strength of 3,636,000 men. The Air Force was projected to build to an over-all strength of 143 wings (first set for 1954 then stretched to 1955 to spread the cost more acceptably).

c. Organizational Changes for Air Defense

As the Korean War was the excuse for partial mobilization and rearmament to prepare to fight "the war" against the Soviet Union, a series of executive orders created emergency offices in the Executive Office of the President to handle the mobilization of the U.S. economy, the stockpiling of strategic resources, and the management of defense production. Due in part to the arousal of the U.S. public to the increased dangers of attack of the continental United States and in part as a "mobilization event" which had been planned for in peacetime, President Truman created the Federal Civil Defense Administration in December 1950.[20] At the same time he forwarded draft legislation to the Congress and asked them to expedite a bill which would provide legislative basis for the civil defense agency. Congress passed and the President signed the Federal Civil Defense Act of 1950, in January 1951, which satisfied the public clamor for and the mobilization requirement for an organization to provide for the defense of the civilian population and civilian industry. The Federal Civil Defense Administration was placed outside of the White House Executive Office and outside of any existing Federal department or agency. The legislation placed the responsibility for civil defense on State and local governments and gave the Civil Defense Administrator only token authority to coordinate the efforts of the several states. The civil defense legislation was designed only to respond to the current threat, and was not suitable for a long-term peacetime civil defense effort extending past the Korean emergency. The Congress voted only nominal appropriations for the FCDA, despite the formulation of a $2 billion Federal plan for the development of a shelter program, to be matched dollar for dollar by State and local governments. The first Civil Defense Administrator was a man whose name was virtually unknown on the national scene and who lacked any prestige to throw behind the program. Neither President Truman nor the Congress intended the civil defense effort to become effective except as a token effort.

Like civil defense, the mobilization and activation of an in-being active air defense of the continental United States was just another "mobilization event" in preparation for a general war with the Soviet Union. With the front pages of the newspapers filled with the news from Korea, and the mobilization of dozens of Army and Air Force units to meet force requirements for the buildup for deterrence, the activation of CONUS air defense went virtually unnoticed.

After the formation of ConAC in December 1948, the ADC was reduced to a planning headquarters while awaiting the assignment of air defense units by ConAC. The Army's air defense effort consisted of two regular AA battalions located at the Antiaircraft Artillery school at Fort Bliss, Texas. The ADC called a series of conferences on air defense which resulted in an air defense plan for the defense of CONUS. The plan was almost totally dependent on mobilization of Army and Air Force National Guard and Reserve units for implementation. In the initial plan in 1949, the ADC and Army planners decided on the protection of thirty-seven vital industrial areas with AA defenses, requiring 95 AA gun battalions and 127 AA automatic weapons battalions. For area defense, planners estimated that twelve groups of interceptors were required, totaling 900 interceptor aircraft. The Army planners felt the lack of an Army air defense command similar

---

[20] Executive Order 10186, Dec. 1, 1950.

to the Air Force's ADC, as each Zone of the Interior Army was charged with negotiating agreements for Air Force operational control of the AA units.

The Army Ground Forces was renamed the Army Field Forces in March 1948, with responsibility only for training, while the six continental armies were placed directly under the Army Chief of Staff. As an interim solution, the Army created an Antiaircraft Artillery staff section at ConAC, and started planning for the creation of an Army Antiaircraft Command to command AA units passed to the operational control of the ADC.

In March 1950, the Army and Air Defense Command revised the air defense plans, now agreeing that the sixty localities in the country which were judged critical for air defense, twenty-three would be provided with AA defenses.[21] These consisted of three atomic energy installations, seven Strategic Air Command bases and thirteen major industrial and population centers. A total of sixty-six AA battalions were required to man the defenses. By early 1950, the Army had started to build up the AA strength in the Active army. During 1949, fifteen battalions had been organized for CONUS defense.

Prior to the invasion of Korea, ConAC had recommended a reorganization of its many functions to assign all air defense responsibilities to the subordinate Eastern and Western Air Defense Forces, eliminating Headquarters, ADC.[22] It was almost an irony of fate that the recommendation was approved on 1 July 1950, at the very time that the slow build up of air defense forces was about to begin. As the Permanent System radar sites began to become operational and as additional newly organized Air Defense fighter squadrons were being organized, General Whitehead reversed the recommendation and proposed that the Air Defense Command be reactivated separate from ConAC.[23]

The Air Defense Command was redesignated a major USAF command on 10 November 1950, and reestablished on 1 January 1951 at Ent Air Force Base, Colorado Springs, Colorado, with General Whitehead as its commander. In April 1951, ARAACOM also moved to Colorado Springs, leasing space in the downtown Antlers Hotel (where it remained until August 1953, when it co-located with ADC at Ent AFB). On 10 April 1951 ARAACOM assumed command of 23 AA battalions and assorted other headquarters and units assigned to it by the Department of the Army. Most of the AA units were located at Army posts at considerable distances from the locations they were designated to defend.

d. Assets for Air Defense

When the Korean War broke out, the Army had 14 National Guard battalions, ready for employment in the defense of CONUS. Due to the shortfall from the required 66 battalions, San Francisco and four Air Force bases were deleted from the list of localities to be protected by AAA. The Army formed the Army Antiaircraft Command on 29 June 1950, to command the Army units allocated to the air defense of CONUS. ARAACOM was also charged with planning for the tactical deployment of AA units, and for becoming the Army component of a joint continental defense force, if and when the joint force was designated. No AA units were placed under ARAACOM control (and therefore none were placed under ADC operational control), as it slowly built up strength of its headquarters and acted as the AA element on the ConAC staffs. To be closer to ConAC, ARAACOM moved to Mitchel AFB, New York on 1 November 1950.

---

[21] Barnard, *The Gun Era*, p. 49.
[22] USAF Historical Studies: No. 126, p. 35.
[23] Ibid.

Chapter II: American Strategy for Air and Ballistic Missile Defense

When the Korean War broke out, ConAC did not have much in the way of air defense assets to work with. The 44 radar stations of the Lashup radar network were completed and operational, but limited by World War II obsolescent radar equipment. The Air Force had to reallocate $50 million of appropriated funds from other projects to start construction on the high Priority Permanent System of radars in February 1950, with the first 24 radar sites to be constructed by the end of 1950. It would be May of 1952 before the original construction program for the Permanent System would be completed.

In April 1950, Lieutenant General Whitehead, commander of ConAC since April 1949, was authorized to begin armed interceptions over the Atomic Energy Commission installations and on the East Coast.[24] ConAC was authorized to organize a Ground Observer System and the CAA established. Air Defense Identification Zones (ADIZ) in the most vital defense areas. The Lashup AC&W network was placed on 24-hour operations, but it was not organized to handle sustained operations and they were later dropped.

General Whitehead estimated that a total of 61 air defense fighter squadrons were the minimum for an adequate air defense of CONUS.[25] When the Korean War buildup program began it was planned to organize a total of 35 regular air force squadrons for assignment to air defense, to be available by the end of June 1951. After repeatedly being turned down, his request for an additional 15 squadrons of Air National Guard was approved and the squadrons were federalized in early 1951. He further requested that another 23 ANG squadrons be mobilized as soon as adequate housing and operational facilities were available. By 1 March 1951 all but 16 ANG fighter squadrons were federalized, and those squadrons were programmed for air defense when they were made available. The squadrons were equipped with an assortment of propeller-driven and jet aircraft, few of which were all weather interceptors.

e. Summary of the First Year

By the end of the first year of the Korean War, bit by bit and piece by piece, the air defense of the Continental United States was building up. It could not be called a system as there was not a contiguous radar coverage; there were large gaps in the Ground Observer Corps coverage; the assigned fighter aircraft were severely restricted in their capability for around-the-clock coverage; there was not adequate AA artillery to protect targets that were designated as "vital"; and existing AA was still located far from its assigned tactical areas.

Air defense was not given a high priority in the overall defense buildup because few military men believed that an effective air defense was feasible or desirable in light of higher priority military requirements. Priority was afforded the vital industrial mobilization and production base, atomic production facilities, and the strategic air offensive deterrent. There was no concept of attempting to protect the citizens of the nation, except as they contributed to a vital defense function.

Korean War money was being used to fund production of many of the research and development air defense weapons that were developed after World War II, in anticipation of a more pressing need for air defense a few years in the future. The Air Force, which had principal responsibility for continental air defense, simply had its hands full building up SAC, fighting the war in Korea, and providing tactical air forces for the augmented ground forces in Europe. The Army, with similar global commitments in Korea and Europe, devoted only a small fraction of its resources to air defense, and was principally concerned

---
[24] Ibid., p. 31.
[25] Ibid., p. 34.

with keeping up with the Air Force's air defense efforts and providing suitable employment for its AAA units.

f. R&D Strategy: The Relationship Among Early Warning "Adequate" Attrition and Civil Defense

It was at this juncture that the Air Force decided to mobilize the efforts of the American scientific community to assist in tackling the air defense problem. When the Air Force was created as a separate service in 1947, it did not choose to establish the Army's arsenal system for the development of new weapons and equipment. As the Army Air Force had worked closely with the American civilian aircraft industry over the years, it continued that association when it became a separate service, and turned to other civilian industrial firms for the development of other non-aircraft requirements. Early in 1951 the Air Force contracted with the Massachusetts Institute of Technology for a study of the best means of proceeding with the difficult air defense problem. One of the recommendations of the study (Project Charles) was that a permanent laboratory be established with a civilian institution to work on the technical problems of air defense.[26] The laboratory was established at M.I.T., known as the Lincoln Laboratory, in September 1951, on contract with the Air Force. The Lincoln Laboratory immediately went to work on the technical problems of detection of enemy aircraft and their associated interception.

The scientists were working on an entirely different air defense problem from that encountered in World War II. World War II air defenses were designed to inflict an unacceptable attrition rate (probably anything over 10 percent) on enemy bombers making repeated attacks with conventional iron bombs. Even though 90 percent of the bombers made it through the defenses and dropped their bombs, in time the loss rate would be unacceptable by either damaging the morale of bomber crews or by destroying bombers faster than they could be produced. The advent of the atomic bomb with its tremendous destructive power made it imperative that attrition rates be raised drastically upward and as near to 100 percent as feasible, or the air defense would be ineffective. New tactics and new and rapid means of detecting enemy attacks and dispatching highly efficient weapons to destroy them must be developed. Adding additional increments of existing radars, antiaircraft guns, and day fighters just would not do the job.

The American scientific community that had become politicized in the days after Hiroshima and Nagasaki in the effort to bring atomic energy under international control, had become somewhat disillusioned when the Soviet Union exploded its atomic device. The scientists understood better than most Americans the truly terrifying effects of the atomic weapons, for atomic weapons effects was still a highly classified subject. Though the American scientific community was not a unified group, the scientists working on the Lincoln Laboratory air defense study tackled the subject with more than average enthusiasm in the determination to defend America against Russian atomic strikes.

In 1952 another group of scientists belonging to a research institute known as Associated Universities and headed by a President Emeritus of M.I.T., Lloyd Berkner, was awarded a contract by the Department of Defense (acting in behalf of the National Strategic Resources Board and Federal Civil Defense Administration). The contract called for an examination in depth of the civil defense program in the United States. The civil defense project was known by the name "East River" and was a massive investigation of all aspects of the subject. Some of the Associated Universities' scientists who worked on "East River" were

---

[26] Huntington, p. 329.

Chapter II: American Strategy for Air and Ballistic Missile Defense

also members of the Lincoln Laboratories, and many members of the two groups were in close association. The scientists working on "East River" concluded that civil defense could not be effective without adequate warning time to permit the population to take shelter before an enemy attack—something in the nature of four to six hours' warning. As warning time was a function of the active air defense forces, the "East River" scientists prevailed upon the Lincoln Laboratory scientists to examine the question of the military defenses providing adequate warning time for the civil defenses.

In the summer of 1952 a group of Lincoln Laboratory and Associated Universities scientists came together informally in a caucus to discuss civil and military defenses. They were entirely an unsponsored and unofficial group, later known collectively as the Summer Study Group. They wrote a report[27] based on their deliberations that concluded:

(1) the Soviet Union would be capable of crippling the United States by a surprise attack in two or three years by long-range bombers carrying atomic weapons
(2) U.S. in-being and planned military and civil defenses were inadequate and capable of achieving no more than a 20 percent kill rate
(3) foreseeable new technology (specifically "forward scatter" radar) would make it feasible to develop an air defense system capable of achieving a kill rate over enemy attackers of 60 percent to 70 percent.

They recommended establishing a distant early warning radar line across Canada to provide three to six hours of warning of enemy bombers. They also recommended a communications *system* capable of rapid transmission of air defense data through the use of automatic and integrated equipment, as well as new and improved interceptors, and the development of homing missiles for interception and destruction of enemy aircraft. Much of the technology involved in the new developments they recommended was still in the experimental stages, but the scientists had great faith in their ability to provide the hardware they based their hopes for an improved air defense on.

The "East River" report also included a section on active air defenses that echoed the conclusions of the Summer Study Group. The Department of Defense neither expected nor wanted its civil defense study group to advise it on active military air defenses, and coolly brushed off the Associated Universities report with a terse letter of acknowledgement. The Air Force, as the official sponsors of the Lincoln Laboratory, was scarcely more receptive to the Summer Study Group report. Although the Air Force was charged with responsibility for air defense, it was only one of a number of missions and the leadership of the Air Force was unenthusiastic over the commitment of the several billion dollars required to, fund the recommended developments. The Air Force refused to forward the Summer Study Group recommendations to the National Security Council.

The scientists drew on their experience with politicization in the mid-1940's and took their case to the American public by giving their report to the Alsop brothers—reporters and columnists with large reader followings. Articles appeared in the *Saturday Evening Post* and in syndicated newspaper columns telling the American people that American scientists had the answers to improving the inadequate U.S. active air defenses, and ". . . there is a way for us to be sure of destroying 85 percent, even 95 percent, of the attacking force, say the scientists."[28]

---

[27] Ibid.
[28] *Saturday Evening Post*, March 21, 1953, p. 19.

The scientists did not rely on "leaks" to the public media alone, but by-passed the Air Force and Department of Defense and west directly to Jack Gorrie, Chairman of the National Security Resources Board. Gorrie, with a seat on the National Security Council, introduced the report to the NSC with a strong recommendation for immediate construction of an arctic warning line at a cost of $1 billion during the first three or four years. The Truman Administration was in its last days in office and did not choose to approve the recommendations, but deferred the question by continuing to study the needs of air defense. Secretary of Defense Lovett appointed a civilian committee, chaired by the President of the Bell Telephone Laboratories, Mervin Kelly, to study the air defense problem. Since the results of the committee's findings would not fall due until the new Eisenhower Administration took office, the membership and purpose of the Kelly Committee was cleared with prospective members of Eisenhower's new team. Similarly, NSC 141 was prepared and left as a legacy to the new administration.[29] It analyzed the implications of the Soviet development of the atomic bomb and recommended more intensive efforts in air defense and civil defense, among other recommendations. Thus the Truman Administration put the new administration on notice that significant improvements (and expenditures) were required for continental defense, and that a study of the Summer Study Group recommendations was under way.

g. The Eisenhower Administration

By the summer of 1952 the American public was surfeited with the stalemated Korean War and opposed to continued large expenditures for military forces at the expense of domestic needs. Eisenhower won the 1952 election on a platform of ending the Korean War and promised reductions in defense spending, a balanced budget, and reduced taxes. As the Eisenhower Administration assumed the leadership of the government it was faced with the problem of carrying out its campaign promises, yet aware that the continental defenses had been low priority in President Truman's administration and needed extensive renovation to become effective. Eisenhower's principal advisors promptly split on the continental defense issue, though in agreement that military spending overall must be reduced. Another study group, composed of business executives, educators, and assorted labor leaders, publishers, lawyers, and one military officer, was appointed to study air defense from a civilian or "business" viewpoint. As the group was headed by seven prominent businessmen, they were known as the "Seven Wise Men." They recommended a policy of not rushing into the air defense recommendations of the Summer Study Group, and did little to solve the President's dilemma.[30]

The Kelly Committee reported in May 1953.[31] It too rejected the urgency reflected in the Summer Study Group report, while recognizing the need for a much better continental air defense. It emphasized the need for a powerful SAC to deter attack by the Soviet Union, and deplored the publicity being stirred up by the scientists which was misleading the public with the claims for being able to devise an effective air defense system.

The Administration decided on more study of the air defense question and appointed yet another study group, this time drawn from within the government, and chaired by President Eisenhower's war-time chief of operations in Europe, Major General "Pinky" Bull. General Bull had given his name to a study report

---
[29] Huntington, p. 331.
[30] Ibid., p. 334.
[31] Ibid., p. 332.

Chapter II: American Strategy for Air and Ballistic Missile Defense

on civil defense in 1948, and was a proven skilled investigator. In July 1953, General Bull's study group reported in favor of spending $18 to $27 billion on air defense over the next five years.[32]

Yet another study group analyzing Soviet air-atomic capabilities also reported to the NSC in favor of large expenditures on continental defense. The NSC duly noted the reports and continued its study to a strategy appropriate for the Eisenhower Administration throughout the summer of 1953. The strategy was based on the need for a new balance between military and domestic demands, and was to be designed for the "long haul," as opposed to Truman's crash efforts to build military forces to peak in the "year of need" when the Soviets were expected to have a significant atomic capability.

2. Strategic Interaction: The Soviet Thermonuclear Device 1

At that critical point in decision making for continental defense, the Soviets inadvertently contributed the decisive argument when they exploded their first thermonuclear device on 12 August 1953. The Russian hydrogen bomb effectively ended the controversy in favor of going for an effective continental defense system.

a. The "New Look" Strategy

In order to get the best advice from the new incoming Joint Chiefs of Staff, President Eisenhower borrowed a technique from Prime Minister Winston Churchill and sent the Joint Chiefs off without benefit of staff to draft up their views on national strategy (to incorporate military strategy and implications on fiscal policy and other non-military strategy and implications on fiscal policy and other non-military aspects of governmental activity). The Joint Chiefs agreed that strong nuclear strategic retaliatory forces were first priority and that effective continental air defenses were second priority.[33] This was particularly significant because the Joint Chiefs made their conclusions *before* the Soviet nuclear explosion, and this was the first endorsement by the JCS that an effective air defense was both feasible and necessary.

The National Security Council embodied the "New Look" strategy in NSC 162, approved in October 1953.[34] The paper identified the threat by the Soviet Union as being "total"; gave the Soviet Union the capability of making a nuclear air attack against the U.S.; concluded that national defense must have the highest priority in national strategy; and recommended that almost all the recommendations made by the Summer Study Group be approved. In effect, the American scientists, with an assist from the Soviet Union, won over the vast majority of the influential members of the new Eisenhower Administration who were primarily economy-minded and pro strategic air power. The decision to build an effective air defense was not accepted by many of its opponents, and President Eisenhower did not make a point of issuing a comprehensive public statement explaining the administration's new strategy. In light of the fact that NSC 162 proposed spending $20 billion over the next five years on continental defense, the President's decision to keep his hand close to his vest was probably prudent.

b. The DEW Line

President Eisenhower visited Canada and stated that the American and Canadian Chiefs of Staff were in agreement on measures to be taken in matters of joint defense. In early 1954 the American and Canadian

---
[32] Ibid., p. 333.
[33] Ibid.
[34] Ibid., p. 334.

governments agreed to proceed with the development of the Distant Early Warning (DEW) Line in northern Canada and Alaska. The first construction on the DEW Line began in 1955, together with other measures to improve the air defense of the North American continent.

The FY 1954 budget was revised downward by $5.1 billion with very substantial cuts in all the military services, except the Air Force, which was projected to increase to an end-strength of 137 wings over the 1953 strength of 110 wings. The FY 1955 budget was also revised downward, with the exception of approximately $1 billion more for continental defense, spread over all three services, with the bulk going to the Air Force for significant increases in fighter-interceptor wings, radar warning and control, and for communications systems. That amount was certainly not the $4 billion called for in NSC 162, but it did reflect a new commitment to continental defense at a time when other defense outlays were decreasing.

The Eisenhower Administration's emphasis on SAC and continental defense upset the traditional slicing of the defense budget pie approximately equally among the three services. The Air Force ended up with twice the money allocated the other two services. This caused the top leaders in the Air Force to alter their opposition to continental defense as being in competition with SAC. It also set the stage for greater in-fighting between the Army and Air Force as the Army fought to establish a strategic role for itself and thus regain its nearly equal slice of the budgetary pie.

c. Continental Defense Command

In 1954 the Joint Chiefs of Staff voted to form a joint command over the air defense of North America. The Continental Defense Command under the former leader of the Air Defense Command, General Chidlaw, was formed. It included the Army Antiaircraft Command and the naval forces assigned to continental defenses. This did little to mollify the Army's complaints against Air Force dominance of continental defense and exacerbated inter-service rivalry even further.

3. Summary: 1950–1955

By 1955 the air defense of the continental United States had moved from the status of a low priority element of military strategy to a top priority element of national strategy. The Eisenhower Administration made the decision to build an effective air defense system designed to afford protection to every American against attacks by enemy manned bombers carrying nuclear weapons. As Russia was identified as the enemy, the air defense system was planned facing northward in permanent sites. To provide early warning and interception of Russian bomber attacks, a contiguous line of radars across the northern United States and southern Canada (the Pine Tree Line) was planned for joint operation. Another line of radars (the Mid-Canada Line) was to be built by Canada along the 55th parallel to provide early warning for Canadian air defense forces. By 1955 the Distant Early Warning Line was under construction in northern Canada, to be completed in July 1957, to provide six hours warning against a propeller-driven bomber, and two hours for jet bombers and possibly missiles. Backing up the early warning system was a force of over 1,200 all weather interceptors based in 41 locations in the United States and Alaska. The Army provided point defenses with 79 AA battalions, 38 of which were equipped with Nike Ajax missiles, and the remainder of which were being converted as the missiles became available. The Nike Hercules missile was successfully tested in 1955 and was programmed to replace the Nike Ajax as it came off the production lines. Plans were being developed to tip the Nike missiles with atomic warheads. Other new developments in air defense weapons and systems were rapidly being developed to provide rapid and automated command and control facilities, supersonic interceptors, unmanned long-range interceptors (Bomarc), seaward extensions of the radar lines, and new and improved air-to-air weapons. The air defense effort was more or less under unified control with the Air Force as executive agent with control over subordinate Army, Navy, and Air Force elements. Prospects for future expansion, increased efficiency, and greater effectiveness were bright. There seemed to be little doubt that the future combined and joint air defense system for the North American Continent would be the most effective air defense against the World War II manned bomber ever devised.

Unfortunately, the Soviets demonstrated their new jet bombers and the turbo-prop Bear bomber in the 1954 and 1955 May Day parades, thus rendering the American air defense system largely obsolescent. The Soviets' new strategic offensive capability once again caught the U.S. air defenders by surprise and seriously compromised the very extensive effort put forth to defend against the TU-4 Soviet bomber force. This would ultimately prove fatal to the concept of providing the United States with an effective air defense against enemy attack. There had been too much publicity and ballyhoo about building an effective air defense system, which resulted in a great deal of money and effort put into "sunk costs" for a permanent and rigid air defense system that was only marginally effective against advanced enemy aircraft. Against intercontinental ballistic missiles, which followed shortly thereafter, the air defense system was totally ineffective. Even the most rudimentary application of "cost effectiveness" analysis quickly established the lack of efficiency involved in maintaining a $30 billion dollar air defense with annual operating costs of over $2 billion to defend against several hundred obsolete Soviet bombers. For all intents and purposes the U.S. air defense system was dead in 1955, but it would be years before it was dismantled and buried.

4. Evaluation of U.S. Strategic Air Defense 1945–1955

Though the lessons of World War II clearly identified air and civil defense as critically important elements of national military strategy, the United States placed them in low priority in 1945 to 1950. The principal reasons to justify the lack of continental defense were the importance given to the civilian economy over military preparedness, the reliance on a strategy of nuclear deterrence based on an atomic monopoly, and the absence of a credible Soviet general war threat. The Soviet threat was seen to be principally the threat of a massive ground attack against a hostage Europe, and creeping expansionism around the perimeter of the Communist Bloc. The U.S. response was the strategy of containment largely carried out by providing economic and military aid to willing non-communist nations surrounding the Communist Bloc, with particular attention to Europe.

The Soviets severely challenged the U.S. strategy by the early detonation of a fission device in 1949, which provided a strong impetus to U.S. general re-armament against the U.S.S.R. The overthrow of China by the Chinese Red Army was seen as an act of aggression by a protégé of the Soviet Union, and signaled Communism's willingness to use force to achieve its goals. The invasion of South Korea by the North Koreans under the guns of the largest overseas concentration of U.S. military power, provided a provocation for placing U.S. military forces in the path of communist aggression and for massive U.S. re-armament against the Soviet Union.

As a result of a partial mobilization for re-armament under the cover of the Korean emergency, continental defenses were brought into being. U.S. air defenses were gradually built up by organizing new air defense units as a result of an overall mobilization process, and by federalizing National Guard and Reserve units for the Korean emergency. A civil defense administration was activated as a mobilization procedure and response to growing public concern for its own safety. Neither the air nor the civil defense organizations were given a high priority in relation to building up SAC, reinforcing Europe, rearming allies, or fighting the Korean War.

American scientists became vitally interested in continental defense and promised technological developments to make an effective air defense feasible. The U.S. military leaders were not particularly interested in building an expensive air defense system, and were highly skeptical of the effectiveness of such a defense. The American public grew tired of the Korean War and the high costs of re-armament and elected an administration that promised to end the war and cut down on military costs. The Eisenhower Administration took office and halted the Korean War through negotiations backed by a nuclear threat. The U.S. military forces were trimmed down for a long-haul confrontation and Cold War. Public pressure stirred up by the news media and the scientists clamored for effective continental defenses. The explosion of the Soviet fusion device in August 1953 probably tipped the balance in favor of building an effective U.S. air defense of the North American continent. The Eisenhower Administration adopted effective air defense as the number two priority of its national strategy, though it did not publicize the fact. The armed services jumped on the air defense bandwagon and put service money on air defense weapons and systems they had long been developing. The Army and Air Force saw the strategic air defense mission as a source of high-priority support for an expanding piece of the military budget. Though the Air Force had won a clear doctrinal superiority and had a virtual monopoly in the command and control, radar, and interceptor elements of air defense, it had failed to develop true ground-to-air guided missiles. The Army, through an early start and a highly successful research and development effort, emerged with a clear advantage in air defense guided missiles which showed promise for antimissile applications. The Army built up its air defense artillery and equipped it with guided missiles, approaching numerical parity with the Air Force in 1955. The Joint Chiefs of Staff created a joint air defense command with the Air Force in command to create unity of effort and to put an end to inter-service rivalry in the air defense field.

By 1955 the U.S. military was committed to develop an effective air defense to provide protection to the entire North American continent. The Soviets demonstrated a growing capability to penetrate the air defense system with jet bombers and to circumvent it by low-flying long endurance turbo-prop aircraft. The promised technological advances were not adequate to overcome the new threat, and proved to be totally inadequate to meet the missile threat when it appeared. The growing costs of an air defense system that was capable of countering only the obsolescent elements of the growing Soviet threat eventually doomed it to reduction and dismantlement. Never again would the American Government and American people put their money and faith into an air defense system that would be incapable of meeting new technological advances in the enemy strategic offensive forces.

Chapter III

Soviet Strategy for Air and Ballistic Missile Defense

A. The Historical Backdrop

1. Long-Term Factors

The development of Soviet air and missile defense after 1945 must be viewed from the perspective of a series of long-term factors which have conditioned Soviet attitudes toward defense in general, the nature of the primary threat, the pursuit and use of technology, the conduct of debate, and the accomplishment of decisions.

Soviet concern for defense is based on both doctrinal and historical grounds. Lenin identified imperialism as the final stage of capitalism, and domestic communist propaganda has continuously belabored the danger from capitalist encirclement. There was the further worry that the capitalist countries, goaded to action by the threat to their security posed by domestic but Soviet-supported communist parties, might strike at what, between the two world wars, was the world's solitary communist country. At the same time, the Soviets fully appreciated that their own regime was spawned by the shambles stemming from Russian involvement in World War I; that their government was almost toppled by foreign intervention during the Civil War of 1918–1920; that Japanese aggression had to be blunted in 1938; and that they almost succumbed to Nazi Germany in World War II. They also realized that at the end of World War II there was considerable hostility toward communism and thus toward the Soviet Union in both West European countries and the United States and, in fact, that there was some expressed sentiment for the forces of the Western Allies to top off the victory over fascism with a victory over communism.

From the viewpoint of Russian leaders, the traditional source of military threats to Russian security has been the European balance of power system. The rapid rise of Germany under Hitler following the German defeat in World War I was simply another very recent example of the manner in which European countries could quickly forge and project military power. At the end of World War II Europe could still be viewed as the principal source of threat to the Soviet Union, this despite the strategic power which had obviously accrued to the United States. The bulk of the Soviet population and industry was still in basic proximity to Western Europe. Distances across Asiatic Russia were huge. The commitment of U.S. bombers across the pole had not yet jelled as a capability. And finally the threat from theater forces in Western Europe fitted more into past pattern. The new traditions of the air age would have strategic air attack serving as an extension of theater operations. Thus, there was no automatic recognition of the United States as posing the main strategic threat to the Soviet Union, either with respect to military force requirements in general or strategic air defense in particular.

Historically, the early example of Peter the Great's aggressive interests in the fruit of the European industrial evolution established a pattern of Russian search for foreign technology. By 1945, Soviet industry was still very new. Although it had accomplished enormous production feats, the general level of technology was still low. Extensive experience had already been gained during the 1930's in the successful adaptation of foreign technology. The ever-present goal was to catch up with and surpass the leading capitalist countries, and the pursuit of this goal was reinforced by success. In turn, espionage and any other feasible avenues for getting at foreign technology were viewed as legitimate and, indeed, preferable means for improving Soviet technology.

Just as Russian domestic political tradition had accepted authoritarian power in the hands of the Czar, so the conduct of debate within the Soviet government, the Soviet military, and Soviet society as a whole has followed the rules of "democratic centralism." Under this concept, debate and criticism have been allowed but have been kept within generally understood limits. Once a decision was made, strict compliance would be demanded. The purges of the 1930's, including those which devastated the military command structure—3 out of 5 marshals, all 11 Deputy Commissars of Defense, 75 out of 80 members of the Military Soviet, all military district commanders who held that position in June 1937, and 13 out of 15 army commanders all killed[1] left an imprint on attitudes wherein a decision on force structure, relative priorities, etc. would be adhered to without substantial challenge. The weight of that system by 1945 made for considerable inertia once a specific direction had been established.

These factors of military, technological, and political traditions set the stage for what was to be a generally consistent march toward a unified air and missile defense system after 1945. At least until the death of Stalin, there was relatively little discernible debate over roles and missions of different force components (e.g., between representatives of fighter aviation and antiaircraft artillery) and no real opportunity for competition to develop, for example, between the Soviet army and the air force.

2. Soviet Air Defense: The Inter-War Years

Because the Soviet Union was a continental European power, the Soviets had to weigh the need for air defense well before the approach of World War II. In 1930, a special directorate was established within the Headquarters of the Red Army, subsequently becoming the independent Main Air Defense Directorate of the Red Army, with responsibility for general air defense planning on a countrywide scale. M. Ye. Medvedev, the head of this directorate, wrote in a book published in 1932 that: "the air defense of points and objectives had to be in full readiness to ward off an enemy air attack even during peacetime; for this the whole air defense organizational and control system had to be identical in peacetime to what it would be in wartime."[2] Thus these two elements of air defense strategy—countrywide air defense planning and combat readiness in peacetime—which were to become essential in the post–World War II environment had their origin well before the war. Implementation, however, was by no means immediate. At times—to use a favorite Leninist argument—it was necessary to take one step backward in order to take two forward.

As the time for World War II drew near, two principles underlay Soviet air defense organization:

(1) The provision of protection for the important political and industrial-economic objectives and railway communications in the zone threatened by enemy aviation, and

---

[1] Kolkowicz, p. 60.
[2] Batitskiy, *Voyennaya Mysl'*, p. 31.

(2) The decisive massing of forces and means for the defense of the more important centers and objectives of the country, employing the concept of a "circular" or all-around defense to protect the individual objectives.

The country was divided into air defense zones which corresponded territorially with the military districts.³ The zones were divided in turn into air defense regions within which there were individual air defense posts.

The largest administrative-political and industrial centers of the country—Moscow, Leningrad, and Baku—had the most highly developed air defense system, echeloned in-depth with all types of air defense forces. Almost half of all Soviet medium antiaircraft artillery batteries and considerable forces of fighter aircraft defended these centers.⁴

Organizationally, air defense corps were established for the major centers. These corps, in turn, included antiaircraft artillery divisions; antiaircraft searchlight regiments; air warning, observation, and communication regiments; barrage balloon regiments; and machine gun regiments. Certain other centers, such as Kiev, were defended by air defense divisions of similar but scaled-down composition. Thus, by 1941 the bulk of the air defense means had been welded into combined arms commands. The fighter aviation, which was assigned to the air defense of major centers, was still under the command of air forces of the military districts. At the same time, the basing of fighter aviation was accomplished under a common air defense plan. The fighter aviation participated in all joint air defense exercises, and in case of war was to come under operational subordination to air defense large unit commanders for the performance of joint missions.⁵ In another mark of the time, the Higher Military School for Air Defense was established in 1941.⁶

3. World War II Experience

For the Soviet military the taste of victory in World War II was enormously exhilarating and satisfying. The experience shaped Soviet attitudes toward defense for the next 25 years. The initial German attack was one of trauma for Soviet air defense. Some 1,200 airplanes were lost on the first day of the war.⁷ German air capabilities, however, were geared more for support of front operations than for striking deep into the Soviet interior. In turn, as the Germans advanced toward Moscow and then toward Stalingrad, that industry which could be moved to the rear was so moved. That which could not be moved was largely destroyed, either initially by the Soviets as they retreated or later by the Germans as they withdrew back to the west. This pattern meant that after the first year and a half of the war the role of national air defense was substantially diminished. Even at its time of greatest significance, air defense tended to be an extension of tactical front operations.

At the end of 1941, major changes were made in the air defense system in order to improve the coordination and flexibility of the hard-pressed air defense capabilities. A commander of National Air Defense Forces was designated, and corresponding control elements were established, including an Air Defense Fighter Aviation Directorate and Headquarters and an Office of Chief of Air Defense Antiaircraft Artillery.

---

³ Ibid., p. 32.
⁴ Batitskiy, *Voyska Protivovozdurhnoy Oburony Strany*, p. 46.
⁵ Ibid.
⁶ Ibid., p. 50.
⁷ Dzhordzhadze and Shesterin, p. 33.

Air defense forces were removed from the jurisdiction of the military districts and fronts and were placed under the Commander of National Air Defense Forces and his command elements. One exception was the forces under the Leningrad Military District, which were left under the Commander of Troops of the Leningrad Front. At the same time, previously existing air defense zones were redesignated as the Moscow and Leningrad corps and a number of air defense divisional regions.[8]

In June 1943, after the Battle of Stalingrad had swung the strategic balance toward the Soviets, another reorganization was accomplished in the air defense forces. Two air defense fronts—Western and Eastern—were established. The position of Commander of National Air Defense Forces was abolished, and responsibility for supervision of the activities of air defense fronts and zones, weapons planning, and supply was transferred to the Commander of Artillery of the Red Army. The following elements were placed under him: Central Headquarters of Air Defense Forces, Central Headquarters of Air Defense Fighter Aviation, the Main Air Defense Inspectorate, the Air Defense Forces Combat Training Directorate, and the Aircraft Warning Service Center. The fighter aviation defending Moscow was combined into the First Air Defense Fighter Army.[9]

The Western Air Defense Front was moving continuously to the west in the wake of the advancing theater forces. As a result, the forces of the Western Air Defense Front were heavily engaged against enemy aircraft, while those of the Eastern Front were rather idle. This led to another reorganization in the spring of 1944. The Western Front was changed into the Northern Front, while the Eastern Front became the Southern Air Defense Front. At the same time, a Transcaucasian Air Defense Front was also established. Later in the year, in December, another renaming occurred, again reflecting the geographical location of the air defense forces. The Northern and Southern air defense fronts became the Western and Southwestern fronts respectively, while a new, Central Air Defense Front, with headquarters in Moscow, was established to control the forces protecting objectives in the deep rear.[10]

Throughout the war air defense was essentially point defense, this being dictated largely by the technical level of the air defense forces in which the static nature of antiaircraft artillery, the limited range of fighter aviation, and inadequacies in warning, control, and communications limited the flexibility with which resources could be employed. There were some examples of a zone defense concept, although at a rudimentary level. The concentration of fighter aircraft in the Moscow area during the first year of the war, the establishment of a large Moscow Air Defense Zone, and the creation of an extensive warning and control system permitted the interception of German air attacks at some distance from Moscow and also the flexible defense of other cities and objectives in the greater Moscow industrial region.

Thus, Soviet air defense organization and concepts underwent considerable evolution, change, and development throughout the course of the war. Various lessons were perceived which were to influence the subsequent development of Soviet air defense. The importance of surprise—or rather the avoidance of it—received particular emphasis. Success of surprise air attacks was attributed to three things.[11] The first and principal reason was considered to be the failure to comprehend the importance of air power and air defense, with attention still focused predominately on land and sea battles. The second reason was

---

[8] Ibid., p. 35.
[9] Ibid., p. 37.
[10] Ibid., p. 39.
[11] Ibid., p. 34.

Chapter III: Soviet Strategy for Air and Ballistic Missile Defense

inadequate air defenses and a low level of air defense troop combat readiness. The third reason was the inadequate preparedness of command personnel in matters of combat against an air adversary. Other lessons concerned the need to improve integration of air defense to go beyond the point defense philosophy which characterized most of World War II air defense; to improve the technical capabilities of the weapons systems and of warning, command, control, and communications capabilities; to formulate the doctrinal concepts of modern air defense; and to adapt the overall air defense capabilities to the new conditions which followed the war. In some cases the lessons which were cited reflected problems which were soon to pass. In other cases the problems still have not been solved. Mass night attacks was an example of the former. One Soviet writer noted that the next problem on the post–World War II agenda would be the battle against wings and ballistic missiles.[12]

B. The Formative Years, 1945–1950

1. Strategic Context

With national air defense having little relevance during the concluding stages of the war, relatively few air defense forces were retained within the homeland. Nor was there any apparent rush to return active air defense forces from the forward area to stations within the Soviet Union once the war was over. For the air defense forces it appears that inertia prevailed. Since they were in the forward area when the war ended, that is where many remained.

In the meantime, demobilization was occurring. There was a reduction in the number of personnel in the National Air Defense Forces, and a changeover to peacetime staffs was accomplished.

The context for change within the Soviet national air defense system derived from both external and internal conditions and included political, economic, and technological considerations as well as basically military aspects.

Germany, prostrate, divided, and occupied, clearly posed no immediate threat, lacking both the military capability and the control of its destiny to recreate one. The United States and England, however, did possess a strategic air offensive capability and this basic capability had been enormously augmented by U.S. possession of the atomic bomb. There was a further question as to how other countries might augment the capabilities of these two. On the matter of intentions there was no clear-cut evidence of a U.S. or Western intention to initiate hostilities, but the communist takeover in Eastern Europe was clearly exacerbating relations between the Soviet Union and the West.

As time progressed, other sources of tension arose, including the prolonged and reluctantly ended Soviet presence in northern Iran, Soviet pressure on Turkey, Yugoslav pressure along its northwestern border, and finally the Berlin airlift. All of these events contributed to a hardening of Western positions, the formation of NATO in 1949, and with this a demonstration to the Soviets that their pressures had toughened Western resistance rather than undermining it and that military capabilities, including strategic air defense, would have to be strengthened in order to offset any growth of the power of NATO.

Technology was simultaneously posing a threat where it was being exploited by the West for its contribution to military capabilities and was also offering an opportunity to offset the strategic advantage accruing to the United States through its possession of nuclear weapons and strategic delivery means. For Soviet

---

[12] Batitskiy, *Voyska Protivovozdurhnoy Oburony Strany*, p. 341.

air defense the avenues to technological improvement were very evident—the development of jet fighters, surface-to-air missiles, and radar and communication systems—and much of the wherewithal was already in their hands, especially as a result of the capture of German scientists and materiel acquisitions through Land Lease.

Internally the problem was to rebuild the economy which had been enormously disrupted, both by the scorched earth policy followed by the Soviets as they retreated during the initial stages of the war and also by the later destruction which was dealt by the withdrawing Germans. Resource constraints were thus severe. Resources diverted to the military would slow the pace of economic reconstruction.

A further problem, peculiarly Soviet and Stalinist, was to ensure that even mild challenges to the prestige and preeminence of Stalin and the Communist Party be prevented. Consequently, the propaganda apparatus began to minimize the military's contribution to victory and to give all credit to Stalin and the Party. For example, wartime hero Marshal Zhukov was relegated to the command of a remote military district. Essentially this meant that Party dominance over the military was firmly reestablished and any tendency on the part of the military to have real debate over the roles and missions of the military and over the allocation of resources to and among the armed forces was minimized.

2. The Organizational Approach

During the war organizational changes were made as the situation dictated, especially as the line of the fighting front ebbed and flowed, first pushing deeply into the country and then moving away from key political and industrial objectives which had to be protected by national air defense forces. At the end of the war, adjustments were required, both to go to a peacetime situation and also to take into account the lessons of World War II and the new post war conditions.

In February 1946 the post of Commander of National Air Defense Forces was revived, although subordinate to the commander of Artillery of the Armed Forces. This partially corrected what Marshal Batitskiy later identified as a mistake in the organizational structure of the National Air Defense Forces when in 1943 the Commander of Artillery was given the additional responsibility of head of air defense forces. According to Batitskiy, this represented only a partial improvement because of the continuing subordination to the Commander of Artillery.[13] Meanwhile the four air defense fronts—Western, Southwestern, Central, and Transcaucasian—which had been created in 1944 were reorganized into air defense districts.

By 1948 the basic direction for Soviet air defense had been sorted out, and extensive organizational changes were made. The problem of the organizational structure of the National Air Defense Forces was entrusted to the Forces themselves and to the air defense elements of the Ground Forces and of the Navy. The entire country was divided into two sectors: border belts and internal territory. The responsibility for the air defense of the border belts was entrusted to the commanders of the respective military districts with all means of air defense located therein being subordinate to them. Responsibility for air defense of naval bases fell to the air defense forces of the fleets. Then in 1948 it was established for the first time that the National Air Defense Forces were an independent element of the Armed Forces on a par with the Ground Forces, Air Forces, and Navy.[14] In this way they were finally removed from under the Commander of Artillery.

---

[13] Batitskiy, *Voyennaya Mysl'*, p. 36.
[14] Batitskiy, *Voyska Protivovozdurhnoy Oburony Strany*, p. 350.

Chapter III: Soviet Strategy for Air and Ballistic Missile Defense

3. Pursuit of Systems Development

The basic theme which pervaded Soviet Air defense system development was to adapt advanced technology to air defense requirements. The approach which soon took shape was to draw upon technology wherever it could be found—abroad or at home—and to push for early deployment of new capabilities.

This Soviet effort to upgrade air defense capabilities was quickly reflected in the development of fighter aircraft. The Y-15 and M-9 jet fighters were demonstrated already at the Tushino Air Show in August 1946; however, neither of these aircraft met the criteria for mass deployment. A little over a year later, in December 1947, the first test flight was made of the M-15, and its extensive appearance in fighter aviation followed soon thereafter.[15] With the arrival of the MiG-15, the conversion for Soviet fighter aviation from piston aircraft to jets proceeded rapidly and was basically accomplished by 1952.

Although the first Soviet surface-to-air missile was not deployed until 1954, a major effort was begun immediately after the war, utilizing captured German scientists and the work which they had started, in order to create a Soviet SAM capability. At the same time, the improvement of antiaircraft artillery capabilities was also pushed, although it could have been anticipated that the significance of antiaircraft artillery in Soviet national air defense would begin to decline and that the extensive deployment of new AAA guns would be an expensive temporary measure. During the initial post war years, new 57- and 100-mm. guns offered better range and rate of fire. With improved target acquisition and fire control equipment they also had greater accuracy.

It was also clear to the Soviets that the wartime approach to early warning was largely inadequate and that it was necessary to have greatly expanded use of improved early warning radar. The route which was taken was to adapt foreign radar sets as quickly as possible and then proceed to the development of native sets. Work in this area went slowly at first, and it was only after 1950 that radar equipments began to appear in the kinds and amounts which were needed. Reflecting the attitudes of the early post war years, a particular concern of the time was how to combat massed enemy flights at night under conditions of radio and radar interference.[16]

During the initial post war years civil defense received little attention as an adjunct to air defense. A slight pickup occurred in 1948 in the form of shelter construction, mandatory study circles and instructor training programs, and periodic endorsements by the media.

4. Soviet Strategy

During the first post war years basic attention was paid to the elaboration of the theory for the organization and conduct of air defense of the major centers of the country. The principle of the massing of forces and means was put at the basis of air defense organization. The air defense of points, as during the war, was all-around. The focus of the forces was concentrated on the most likely directions of approach of enemy aircraft. It was felt that the air defense of an objective, because of the great speed of the means of air attack, should be deep and should be capable of defeating the attack along the approaches to the objective. Thus fighter aviation was echeloned along the approaches to defended objectives so that the fighters could make

---
[15] Ibid., p. 345.
[16] Ibid., p. 333.

consecutive strikes against the enemy. The gun fire area was also increased significantly with groups of batteries being located along several firing perimeters.[17]

At the same time it was recognized that more had to be done to provide the theoretical elaboration of what was largely a new phenomenon in military art, the concept of air defense operations. Work was begun along these lines in 1948, and since 1949 it has occupied a basic place in the operational training of the command and staff officers of the National Air Defense Forces. The term "air defense operations" was defined as the aggregate of the engagements and battles being carried out according to the unified strategy of the National Air Defense Forces in coordination with the fighter aviation and antiaircraft artillery of theater fronts and fleets for the purpose of stopping air operations undertaken by an enemy against major regions or objectives of the country.[18] It was felt that air defense operations could be conducted both by the forces of one district as well as by those of a group of air defense districts.

All elements of the air defense arms were to participate in operations; however, a decisive role was accorded to fighter aviation which had the following basic missions:

(1) During daytime: the complete destruction of aircraft flying individually or in small groups, particularly at high altitudes, at distant approaches to objectives, and the interception of enemy aviation formations and their destruction prior to their approach to defended regions and objectives
(2) During nighttime: interception and destruction of aircraft with radar or searchlight support
(3) The interception of enemy aircraft on their return flight, their pursuit and destruction
(4) The combating of unmanned air attack weapons by intercepting and destroying the cruise missiles or the parent aircraft from which they may be launched.[19]

Antiaircraft artillery was also named as a basic means of air defense. It was to defend against enemy aircraft and missiles which penetrated to the near approaches of a defended objective. Antiaircraft searchlights were also involved. They were to support night fighter operations when the fighters did not have radar sights and also to support the firing of antiaircraft artillery.

During this period there were no basic changes in the combat employment of fighter aviation. The combat formations of fighter aircraft consisted of several tactical groups. A portion of the fighters was assigned to an attack group for destroying bombers. Groups were also created to provide protective cover and to perform other missions. Group air combat was thus considered to be the basic type of combat.

5. Summary: 1945–1950

The concept which emerged between 1945 and 1950 was thus one which started with World War II experience as a foundation and, lacking other practical experience to the contrary, made only those adjustments which were clearly dictated by improved technology and capabilities of the air defense systems.

The first years after the war was a period of slowly building momentum—stagnant at first, picking up direction by mid-period, and then closing with a rush as new systems were deployed. But the link with the experience of World War II was still very strong.

In their perceptions the Soviets saw that, despite the victory which had been gained over Germany, there was a threat and a challenge posed by U.S. possession of the atomic bomb. The primary threat which existed

---

[17] Yakimanskiy, p. 66.
[18] Ibid., p. 68.
[19] Ibid., p. 69.

Chapter III: Soviet Strategy for Air and Ballistic Missile Defense

was the specter of the projection of "strategic" air power from European bases. This meant that air defense of the homeland had to have high priority. At the same time Soviet theater force capabilities, posing a threat to overrun Europe, represented a degree of deterrence to U.S. and British strategic air attack capabilities.

One basic Soviet response to the strategic air threat was to deploy available World War II aircraft and antiaircraft units around principal cities and industrial complexes and to increase the centralized control and integration of air defense capabilities. The second response was to pursue the exploitation of new technology, launching a conversion of fighter aviation to jet aircraft, improving the capabilities of AAA defense, creating a national radar early warning system, generally pushing the incorporation of electronics in air defense, and also pushing the development of both ground-to-air and air-to-air missiles. The net result was a pattern for future Soviet air and ballistic missile defense systems. Although many obsolescent and outmoded concepts still persisted, the direction had been firmly set.

C. The System Established, 1950–1955

1. The Strategic Context

The Korean War represented a watershed event in that it spurred both the United States and the Soviet Union to push the development of their strategic offensive and defensive capabilities. This in turn meant that an ever-escalating striving to achieve technological superiority became institutionalized and that the outmoded concepts of World War II were soon to be discarded.

With the onset of the Korean War, the U.S. attitudes which had hardened politically during the late 1940's were now reflected in a new approach to force deployment and operations. The increased range and speed of U.S. aircraft, their forward deployment, and the aggressive efforts to learn about Soviet air defense capabilities placed much greater stress on the Soviet system which then had to contend with a U.S. strategic bomber threat coming from all directions, not just the European Theater.

Meanwhile, the western offensive threat was institutionalized as the capabilities of NATO forces began to develop. This development led the Soviets to formalize their military arrangements with East European countries through the formation of the Warsaw Pact in 1955. While helping to rationalize Soviet military presence in Eastern Europe, the pact facilitated the accomplishment of combined military goals. The net result was to give added substance to the depth of the air defense system along the western approaches to the Soviet Union.

During the 1950–1955 period, the continuing advance of technology, reflected in the improvement of U.S. strategic attack capabilities, meant that the Soviet national air defense system, despite its extensive deployment and continuing improvement, lagged substantially in its ability to cope with the real offensive threat.

Internally, significant changes were also occurring. The death of Stalin in 1953 ended some of the arbitrariness which had characterized the official policy process and permitted the emergence of new flexibility. But there was no direct evidence during the rest of this period that the opportunity for flexibility was reflected in air defense policy.

2. Organizational Integrity Achieved

The organizational arrangements which were accomplished in 1948 were left unchanged until 1951. At that point, a border air defense line was set up in an effort to tighten the defenses in response to the pattern of U.S. air operations around the periphery of the Soviet Union. These measures were found to be deficient since they complicated the maintenance of unity of command. Therefore, in 1953 the 1948 arrangement was reestablished.[20]

Finally, in 1954 the march toward centralization of the national air defense system reached its culmination with the establishment of the prestigious position of Commander-in-Chief of the National Air Defense Forces and by the comprehensive integration of air defense capabilities.[21] This involved close coordination between the air defense districts and also with the air defense forces of the theater forces and fleets. The new organizational structure permitted the echelonment of air defense forces to a considerable depth. Several echelons were created along approaches to the most important regions of the country. The first echelon consisted of the fighter aviation and antiaircraft artillery of the fronts and fleets. The operational mission of this echelon was to make the first attack against the incoming enemy bombers and also to deal with their fighter escorts.

The second echelon was composed of the forces of the air defense districts directly behind the rear boundaries of the fronts. The forces of this echelon were to continue the attack against the intruding enemy, if possible preventing their penetration any deeper into the country.

The third echelon consisted of the forces of the air defense districts in which the objectives of the enemy attack were located. Their objective was to defeat the enemy along the approaches to the objectives.[22]

3. The Systems Mix in Transition

Weapons systems development continued at a steady pace during this period as follow-on jet fighters were introduced; the 130-mm. antiaircraft gun was deployed, and the SA-1 missile was committed to the defense of Moscow. This represented a balanced program of weapons development and deployment in which gaps in capabilities were generally avoided, even when order of magnitude improvements could be anticipated in the near future. Thus, risk-taking was avoided and substantial resources were committed despite the awareness that systems would soon become obsolescent.

The Soviet commitment to MiG fighters continued with the deployment of the MiG-19 in 1953 and the completion of the development of the MiG-19 in 1955. Neither of these aircraft was the answer to the need for an all-weather jet interceptor which had been expressed in 1948. A partial answer was finally provided in 1955 with the appearance of the YAK-25. The thrust of the jet development program was to build on success, and the MiG series represented success. Fitted with a five-nautical-mile air intercept radar, the MiG aircraft had a limited all-weather capability which could be purported to be a solution. In any case, Stalin's profound satisfaction with the MiG fighters made the question of a good all-weather interceptor a non-problem from 1948 to 1951. Finally, in 1951, designer Yakovlev finally reached Stalin with a proposal, and the result was the YAK-25.

The deployment of the 130-mm. antiaircraft gun which had begun by 1955 represented the highest point in the use of antiaircraft artillery in the national air defense system. At the same time its appearance post dated that of the SA-1, and consequently its days of active use were numbered even before deployment began. Still, antiaircraft artillery in the hands of the North Koreans and Chinese had proved its value during

---

[20] Batitskiy, *Voyska Protivovozdurhnoy Oburony Strany*, pp. 352–353.
[21] Batitskiy, *Voyennaya Mysl'*, pp. 38–39.
[22] Batitskiy, *Voyska Protivovozdurhnoy Oburony Strany*, p. 355.

Chapter III: Soviet Strategy for Air and Ballistic Missile Defense

the Korean War, and thus it represented an acceptable interim solution until the SA-2 could be deployed. The SA-1, which began to appear in the defense of Moscow in 1954 served meanwhile to portend a new era in air defense wherein the primary role in air defense would pass from fighter aviation to surface-to-air missile troops.

Changes in the approach to civil defense presaged a greater role for it in the overall national air and missile defense system. DOSAAF was established in 1951 as a paramilitary organization with responsibilities which included civil defense training and instruction. Two years later an antiaircraft general was named chairman of DOSAAF. The new commander pushed the use of reserve and demobilized military personnel in training and instruction and initiated the first compulsory civil defense program which was conducted for the adult population of the Soviet Union. These events marked the beginning of the transition from a civil-directed, local, voluntary civil defense structure to a military-directed, nationwide, mandatory program.

4. The Interim Strategy

The period of the Korean War and its immediate aftermath was clearly transitional. The deployment of the SA-1 introduced a fundamentally new weapons system which was still inadequate for extensive deployment. The strategy therefore was to make full use of an obsolescing system—antiaircraft artillery—while awaiting the availability of more suitable air defense missiles. For example, in the antiaircraft artillery steps were taken to improve the density and effectiveness of the fire from the new 57-, 100-, and 130-mm. systems. Batteries of eight guns were created in place of previous ones with four, and close-set formations were used.

Marshal Batitskiy noted[23] that during this period the point principle of air defense was eliminated and that a new form of conducting battle action—the air defense operation—was established. Air defense operations were to pursue decisive objectives—to destroy the attacking enemy aircraft, to disrupt enemy air operations, and to provide total protection of the defended objectives. It was further intended that the air defense operations of the National Air Defense Forces would be complemented by operations involving Long Range Aviation and other means of attack against the main enemy airfields. At this stage it was felt that air defense operations would involve clashes between large masses of aircraft. Thus the main role in air defense operations was to be played by fighter aviation. Antiaircraft artillery was also considered to be an active arm of the air defense forces with the advantages of possessing strong firepower, being unaffected by weather conditions or the time of day, and being in constant readiness to open fire immediately.

5. The Korean Proving Ground

The Korean War provided the first real opportunity to test Soviet air defense systems and operational concepts. Although it was necessary to employ North Koreans and Chinese to test concepts and equipment under conditions which were strongly different from what would have been expected in defense of the Soviet Union, much was learned. For example, the increased role of the first air defense attack pass by jet interceptors was accepted. It was found that in a majority of cases the first pass was the only possible one. In this regard, there was a sharp rise in the demands placed upon fighter pilots in the areas of piloting technique and aerial gunnery.

---

[23] Ibid., p. 356.

Further experience was gained in attempting to react to U.S. flights along the periphery of the Soviet Union and to U.S. incursions over Soviet territory. These flights served to test the Soviet early warning system and also gave a measure of the responsiveness of Soviet fighter aviation.

6. Summary: 1950–1955

The period from 1950 to 1955 marked a new stage for Soviet air defense in which the primary threat was that of strategic air power encircling the U.S.S.R. Defense predominated in Soviet strategic systems thinking. At the same time, it was linked with the concept of an offensive against NATO as representing a deterrent counterbalance to U.S. strategic capabilities. Those capabilities required that the ever-lagging Soviet air defense be improved still more.

Soviet responses to these developments emphasized the continuing improvement of all systems, leaving primacy with fighter aviation for the moment while awaiting the availability of an air defense missile system which could be given extensive deployment.

D. Decision Making in Soviet Air and Missile Defense

1. The Problem of Data

There is little direct evidence with which to analyze the Soviet decision-making process as it functioned with respect to national air defense during the period from 1945 to 1955. Only Soviet aircraft designers' writings have provided virtually unique insights. Similar insights from the political leadership and from the military are generally lacking, although Khrushchev in his reminiscences does shed some light on the general decision-making process.

For this early period, there are no windows such as existed later with the IRONBARK material. And even the IRONBARK debate should probably be viewed as a unique event in which the only major debate—and a substantially controlled one at that—which occurred during the post war years happened to coincide with the one intelligence window that the U.S. had for viewing a secret debate.

Otherwise, our understanding of decision making in Soviet air defense has been based largely on developments which could be observed physically. This approach carried with it a tendency to see things as being smoother and less controversial than they probably were in actuality. But the two-fold pattern of rapid development and deployment of new systems and the complementary rather than competing nature of those systems suggests a simple and centralized decision-making process.

2. The Major Actors

The major actors in the decision-making process were individuals and groups in the political leadership. Their story is told in greater detail in Chapter V-B, but essentially it is a story of political leaders who had all of the seats of power firmly under control, who ruled in an autocratic and arbitrary style, who had long continuity in office, and who had a strong interest in military force structure and capabilities. The military and industry were supporting actors. They identified requirements and suggested solutions. Until his death, Stalin made the decisions, although key individuals around him also played a role. As is evident from the following statement, even Khrushchev was not one of those key individuals:

Chapter III: Soviet Strategy for Air and Ballistic Missile Defense

> ... While Stalin was alive, he completely monopolized all decisions about our defenses. ... We were sometimes present when such matters were discussed, but we weren't allowed to ask questions. ...
>
> Not too long after Stalin's death, Korolyov (Soviet missile designer) came to a Politbureau meeting to report on his work. I don't want to exaggerate, but I'd say we gawked at what he showed us as if we were a bunch of sheep seeing a new gate for the first time. When he showed us one of his rockets, we thought it looked like nothing but a huge cigar-shaped tube, and we didn't believe it could fly. Korolyov took us on a tour of a launching pad and tried to explain to us how the rocket worked. We were like peasants in a marketplace. We walked around and around the rocket, touching it, tapping it to see if it was sturdy enough—we did everything but lick it to see how it tasted.[24]

The Soviet aircraft designer A.S. Yakovlev, whose writings are available in the West, provided detailed insights into Stalin's manner of functioning and the criteria which were important to him. In 1939, Yakovlev, along with 10 other designers, participated in a competition to produce new fighter designs. Stalin personally indicated what was wanted—the best flight and combat characteristics and the earliest delivery date. The first three available designs, one of which was Yakovlev's YAK-1 fighter, were committed to production before testing was even complete.

In 1946, the first Soviet jet fighters had just been produced and appeared at the Tushino Air Show in August of that year. The day after the air show, Stalin sent instructions that 10 to 15 of these new jets—the MiG-9 and the YAK-15—were to be ready for the October Revolution Parade less than three months away. The airplanes were ready on time.

Stalin's approach produced results, although not always the desirable ones. The requirement for an all-weather interceptor was posed in 1948. Lavochkin, Mikoyan, and Sukhoi had produced such aircraft by 1950, but they were unsatisfactory. Subsequently, it was decided to fit the MiG-15 with an air intercept radar, and an instant all-weather interceptor was the result.

Stalin's acceptance of this modification and his preference for continuing to improve the MiG series stymied the development of a true all-weather area defense interceptor until Yakovlev wrote directly to Stalin suggesting a new design. In meetings with Stalin, Yakovlev found that Beria tried to undercut his design and to put Yakovlev and Aviation Minister Khrunichev in personal jeopardy. Prodded by Beria, Stalin's temper flared, and it was only with great difficulty that he was persuaded to hear Yakovlev's full story. The result of the meeting was approval for Yakovlev to proceed with development of the YAK-25 all-weather interceptor.

The pattern of actor behavior expressed in these sequences and reflected in other examples as well had the following characteristics:

(1) Stalin had a strong degree of personal involvement in decisions on military systems and capabilities and almost totally dominated the decision-making process;

(2) Competition was built into the decision-making process but was controlled from above and was used as a device to increase the tempo of response to the demands of the political leadership;

(3) Preference was given to systems which promised early availability, simplicity of design, and reliability of operation;

(4) The opportunity for organized lobbying by groups or fashions within the military and industrial communities was virtually nonexistent. That lobbying which did exist was primarily from individual members of the design community directly to Stalin or to him through other members of the political hierarchy;

(5) Once they had established themselves, designers had the opportunity to suggest and innovate and gained a degree of continuing influence;

---
[24] Khrushchev, pp. 45–46.

(6) Arbitrary decisions by the political leadership governed the process and were frequently expressed in terms of highly compressed lead times;

(7) The supporting actors, especially the designers, were under extreme pressure to produce results and were gripped by a fear of the consequences of failure or misstep.

3. Influences on Decision Making

The major influences on the decision-making process were embodied in the perceptions and attitudes of the political leadership.

A very basic concern for the defense of the communist homeland evoked a sense of urgency in developing and fielding effective air defense systems. There was an apparent awareness of the inferiority of Soviet strategic offensive systems which in turn necessitated an emphasis on strategic defense coupled with the idea of holding Western Europe hostage to the capabilities of Soviet theater forces.

Technology, in the view of the Soviet leadership, was to be exploited in whatever way it would contribute to the enhancement of political, military, and economic power. Any backwardness of Soviet technology was not a signal for inaction but rather a stimulus to acquire technology by all possible means, but especially from foreign sources.

There was a strong tendency not to relax one's guard. Although the Korean War did not involve the Soviet Union directly, Soviet air defense was greatly strengthened during the war as a consequence of a more than doubling of the resources which were committed to it.

The threat of foreign air power was readily perceived, both because the power was openly displayed and also because the Soviets operated a very comprehensive espionage system.

Because of the absence of significant factional power outside the control of the Party, there was an absence of organized pressures from within the Soviet system. Inter-service rivalry was not permitted. The Soviet legislature was a rubber stamp organ. Industry was state-owned and party-controlled. Any effort on the part of the military, industry, or the legislature to exert organized influence and pressure on the decision-making process would have been viewed as a challenge to the political domination of the Party leadership and had no really opportunity to occur.

4. The Consequences

The decision-making process and the attitudes that went with it had the following consequences:

(1) High importance was attached to national air defense in relation to other force components;
(2) Early emphasis was placed on nationally integrated early warning, command and control, and civil defense;
(3) Early deployment of the first available and effective system was stressed;
(4) Simple, reliable systems were preferred rather than the most advanced possible system;
(5) Frequent incremental improvements were made in established systems;
(6) There was concurrent emphasis on the continuing development of new systems.

E. An Appraisal of the First Decade

1. The Accomplishments of the Period

A review of the entire period from 1945 to 1955 reveals a pattern of steady progress toward the creation of a strong and extensive national air defense system. At the same time, those things which were accom-

Chapter III: Soviet Strategy for Air and Ballistic Missile Defense

plished tended to lag substantially behind the threats which were posed. Thus, while the massiveness of the commitment of resources to air defense suggested enormous power built into the system, a problem of relative effectiveness still persisted.

Soviet attitudes of the period are reflected in the relative importance which they attached to strategic attack and defense systems and to the components within the overall air defense effort. Less clear is the absolute value of what they did and the rationality of their commitment of resources.

2. Relative Values

For the period before 1950, the data on force structure and operations are inadequate to support an analysis of the relative value attached to air defense and to the different elements of air defense. For the period from 1950 to 1955, the data have their inadequacies but are still useful for reflecting relative value and also the pattern of resource commitment.

Looking first at the relative commitment of resources to Soviet strategic attack forces and strategic defense forces (the amounts are in terms of billions of 1964 U.S. dollars), the following emerged[25]:

	1950	1951	1952	1953	1954	1955
Strategic Attack	1.88	1.96	1.94	1.88	2.56	3.93
Strategic Defense	1.95	2.45	3.67	4.24	4.30	4.57

In every case, the amount going to strategic defense was larger. Interestingly, the total for strategic attack remained relatively constant throughout the period of the Korean War, whereas the amount for strategic defense doubled. In 1954 and 1955 a convergence began to appear, reflecting both a slowing of the rate of investment in strategic defense and a dramatic increase in the flow of resources into strategic attack. It should be noted also that, for the remainder of the 1950's, air defense remained slightly ahead at about the same ratio as in 1955.

Looking now within air defense (again the amounts are given in billions of 1964 U.S. dollars), the initial and evolving relative emphases are readily seen[26]:

	1950	1951	1952	1953	1954	1955
Control and Warning	0.46	0.55	0.69	0.80	0.84	0.82
Interceptor Aircraft	0.72	0.93	1.81	2.38	2.13	1.97
SAMs	—	—	—	0.03	0.26	0.73
AAA	0.76	0.98	1.16	1.03	1.05	1.05
TOTAL	1.95	2.45	3.67	4.24	4.30	4.57

All force components increased over their 1950 levels with the greatest increase (three times at one point) being in the case of interceptor aircraft. The amount going to control and warning almost doubled

---
[25] CIA notes.
[26] Ibid.

from 1950 to 1953. Even antiaircraft artillery experienced a 50 percent rise from 1950 to 1952 and then receded slightly. The deployment of the SA-1 is reflected in the 1953 to 1955 expenditures on SAMs.

3. Absolute Values

The "absolute value" of the Soviet air defense system in terms of its ability to prevent unacceptable destruction by nuclear delivery systems is a different matter. Here there is a Soviet tendency to identify or admit deficiencies only after they have been corrected. A basic problem in the estimate of a Soviet notion of absolute value concerns their perception of the need for attrition of an attacking force. If the rates of World War II, or even several times those rates, would fail to cope with the atomic bomb and the hydrogen bomb, then something close to 100 percent might be required. This the Soviets did not discuss, nor did their capabilities suggest that they would be able to approach anywhere near this rate of attrition.

4. Strategic Decisions: Why and How

The factors influencing strategic decisions and the manner of reaching them can be summarized as follows:

(1) A fundamental Soviet preoccupation with the defense of the homeland, a general concern for defense in the context of European great power rivalries, and new awareness of the threat posed by Western strategic attack capabilities, especially U.S. nuclear delivery capabilities set the stage for Soviet decisions on strategic air defense;

(2) A basic tendency to centralize institutions in the Soviet society and the rationality of an integrated air defense system in light of World War II experience and evolving post war condition set the stage for a steady Soviet march toward an integrated system;

(3) Reorganizations of the Soviet Armed Forces did not noticeably hamper air defense programs but rather appeared to facilitate them;

(4) Service rivalries were sufficiently well contained so that they had no discernible effect on Soviet strategic air and missile defense doctrine, development, and deployments. In fact, Soviet air defense during the first post war decade was an organization headed by artillery generals which gave primary to fighter aviation;

(5) The availability of technology and the striving for its application had a strong influence on the continuing upgrading of Soviet air defense capabilities;

(6) Intelligence on the potential enemy was so readily available that intelligence misperceptions could have had little impact on decisions, unless it was in the sense of ascribing more aggressive intentions to the West than actually existed;

(7) There was an implicit competition for resources both between the civil and military sectors and between the military services; however, the competition did not prevent the channeling of massive resources into air defense;

(8) Finally, the key factor in Soviet decision making was the total domination of the society by the Communist Party leadership and, in particular, by Stalin personally.

Chapter IV

American Systems

A. Introduction

This chapter separately analyzes six general categories—or *streams*—of U.S. strategic air defense decision-making during the first post-WWII decade. In reality, these six streams are confluent; they comprise the entire set of air defense decisions made during the period. Yet, there is considerable heuristic value in the admittedly artificial separation of these *streams*.

The six streams are labeled: Civil Defense; Surface-to-Air Missiles; Ballistic Missile Defense; Interceptor Aircraft; Early Warning Systems; and Command, Control, Roles and Missions. Obviously, there is some overlap attending this scheme of separation, but the overlap is useful. For example, it will be seen that decision making in the area of Command, Control, Roles, and Missions (CCRM) is of one character when undertaken apart from any specific force-building context, but of a different character entirely when caught up in, say, the surface-to-air missile (SAM) rivalry. It is instructive to view CCRM decision making in both contexts—as an isolated issue and as a central issue in the SAM debate; because decisions which shaped CCRM were themselves made in both, as well as other, contexts.

Similarly, our discussion of ABM developments might have been subsumed in the analysis of SAM decision making. Instead, we have treated the ABM separately—for two reasons. First, ABM decision making was qualitatively different from the general body of SAM decision making. Second, and perhaps more important, ballistic missile defense (BMD) will be the central concept in our analysis of strategic air defense from 1956 to 1972; the reader is best served by the separate attention given the germination of the BMD concept and its associated technologies during the 1945–1955 period.

Our six-stream approach is primarily valuable because it illustrates six different kinds of decision making; each stream has its own unique pattern and intensity. The implications of this may be unsettling to those who search for a single best model of U.S. decision making; we admit to having been mildly unsettled ourselves, given our hope that we might uncover "the" pattern. The fact is, however, that the following pages confirm an almost irreducible complexity in the U.S. decision-making process.

The history of civil defense is a study in deferring a decision until an emergency provides the necessity to act, by continuously seeking another opinion. When the time came to organize a civil defense operational agency, the studies and plans were largely ignored and a weak, impotent organization was spawned.

In contrast, SAM decision making is illustrative of the most intense interservice rivalry to be found in any of the six streams. The brutal competition between ground and air forces for control of SAM RED and for control of operational systems was the driving force in the SAM programs. As in the case of a few other streams, external (i.e., Soviet) stimuli were secondary. The Nike's threat was the Bomarc, an unworthy adversary that was overwhelmed in the technological and bureaucratic arenas.

ABM decisions, however, did not much resemble this larger body of SAM decisions. Throughout this decade, ABM decisions focused on the definition of requirements and the conduct of feasibility studies. The field of endeavor was constrained by the fact that technology had not yet caught up to the idea of an antimissile missile system during these years.

Decisions regarding interceptor aircraft were of yet another genre. Service rivalries played only a limited role, and budgetary constraints, while inevitably impacting upon procurement, has a minimal effect upon the limiting factor of attaining sufficiently high interceptor *quality*. The primary force shaping interceptor decisions were: initial difficulty in determining the nature of the Soviet threat and of the appropriate response to it; technological bottlenecks resulting from the ever-increasing complexity of weapon requirements and the uneven development of different branches of relevant technology; and the need for haste that resulted from the unexpectedly rapid development of Soviet offensive capabilities.

Decisions regarding early warning (EW) and AC&W systems in many ways resembled those regarding civil defense. Radar nets were small potatoes, compared with missile or aircraft programs; and EW-AC&W decisions were small decisions. The intensity in this stream was low, decisions seeming at times to make themselves. This self-sustaining progression which characterized EW-AC&W decision making derived in large part from the relatively high level of external (Soviet) stimulus to this particular decision stream. No one seems to have questioned the *need* for EW; and, within the limits imposed by rather impecunious budget allocations, our warning lines advanced northward and incorporated increasingly sophisticated technology essentially apace with the development of the Soviet strategic bomber threat.

The sixth stream, CCRM, is characterized by continuing interservice disagreement over roles and missions. The basic problem stemmed from the desire of the field commander, be he air or ground, to have operational control over both tactical air and AAA assets in his area of operations. The problem evolved from War Department indecision when faced by AAF and AGF contentions, to relatively succinct role and mission statements by the Department of Defense. Constrained by austere budgets in the pre-1950 years, CCRM took on an increasing Air Force flavor by the end of the time period with the creation of the USAF-executed CONAD.

B. History of Civil Defense

1. World War II Background

Civil Defense in the United States dates back to 1916, prior to the U.S. entry into World War I, when Congress established the Council of National Defense for the purpose of mobilizing the resources of the nation for use in time of "need." The same month the United States entered World War I (April 1917), all States established a State Council Section to coordinate mobilization at the State levels. The participation by the various governments of the States in wartime measures has been a trademark of Civil Defense since that time.

Though the end of World War I quickly brought about the demise of Civil Defense, the legislation passed during war time lingered on to provide a foundation for the post–World War II Civil Defense program.

Again, the onset of World War II saw the creation of the National Defense Advisory Commission in May 1940, for the purpose of establishing administrative machinery for partial industrial mobilization. A year later the Office of Civil Defense was created by Executive Order from a branch of the National

Chapter IV: American Systems

Defense Advisory Commission—that branch which dealt with State and local cooperation. Mayor Fiorello La Guardia of New York City was appointed the first Director, operating directly under the President for the purpose of protecting civilian industry and the civilian population. OCD, in carrying out its role of protecting the civilian population, relied heavily on an organization of civilian volunteers in a highly decentralized structure based on regional offices.

Fortunately the Civil Defense organization was never given a real challenge by enemy forces during World War II. The only known bombing of the continental United States by manned enemy aircraft was conducted by a lone Japanese seaplane operating from a submarine off the coast of the State of California, early in the war. The pilot dropped incendiaries in a heavily timbered area (well known to Japanese pre-war lumber buyers) but failed to ignite the massive forest fires he was targeted to cause, due to an unseasonal heavy rainfall the day prior to the incident. The Japanese were also known to have launched several thousand balloons carrying antipersonnel bomblets into the jet stream, but succeeded only in killing six picnickers who apparently found and examined a grounded balloon. As it was difficult to sustain civilian volunteer interest in the face of an ever-decreasing threat, by the end of World War II the civilian leadership of U.S. Civil Defense has been replaced by the assignment of an Army Lieutenant General.

United States Civil Defense in World War II suffered from a number of shortfalls. First and foremost, it came into being "under the gun," some 20 months after hostilities began in Europe and less than 6 months before Pearl Harbor brought the country into the war. Before the appointment of a Federal Civil Defense, there were large numbers of citizens at the State and local levels who observed the British civil defense and realized that, unless we followed the British example, we would be exposed to similar losses and damage. Thus local communities anticipated U.S. involvement in the European War and organized numerous volunteer organizations to limit damage and save lives. When the Federal Civil Defense was created, it was given large responsibilities without commensurate authority over State and local civil defense entities. The result was a loosely coordinated effort among dissimilar organizations which depended heavily on "volunteerism" and cooperation for the limited successes that were achieved. Even that responsibility which was assigned was divided with the military, which had both responsibility and authority for the military security of the civilian population.

Large numbers of volunteers joined the various civil defense organizations immediately after Pearl Harbor, until by the end of January 1942, nearly 8,500 communities had enrolled more than 5,000,000 persons. Unfortunately, the activities of these volunteers were diverted from the primary objective of civil defense, resulting in protracted involvement in programs selling war bonds and stamps, child care, housing for war workers, family security, nutrition service, ballet dancing, consumer programs, race relations, and library service.

The third major shortfall was the lack of effective coordination between civilian defense and established Federal, State, and local agencies with overlapping responsibilities. Virtually every aspect of the volunteer Civil Defense program was already covered by an agency which was far better qualified to handle the responsibilities than were the paid and volunteer personnel available to the Office of Civilian Defense. It is difficult to escape the conclusion that if U.S. Civil Defense has been given a severe test by enemy air attacks, the results would have been chaotic, if not catastrophic. On the plus side, it was probably the greatest spontaneous outpouring of volunteer participation in a major cause in the history of any democratic nation.

World War II left a legacy of the awful role of offensive air power against the civilian populations of warring nations. Many observers were convinced that World War III would most certainly begin with a surprise attack on the United States with the purpose of destroying our war-making capacities. The war would be a total war involving both military and civilian targets, probably simultaneously. The United States would be without allies, since the initial devastation of the attack on the United States would be certain to deter less powerful potential allies. The civilian population of the United States would bear the brunt of the enemy attack for at least the first year of the war, as the forces for mobilization and counter-attack would take time to muster and prepare. Among other conclusions, given those beliefs, it would be difficult to deny that Civil Defense would play an important, perhaps crucial, role in the outcome of World War III.

It would be logical to assume that the explosion of the U.S. atomic bombs over Hiroshima and Nagasaki in August 1945 would have provided the impetus for post–World War II Civil Defense planning. When President Truman assumed office following the death of President Roosevelt, with the end of the war in sight, he cast about for means to cut the mounting costs of World War II. On 30 June 1945, by Executive Order, he abolished the Office of Civil Defense.[1] Immediately the War Department (Army) submitted a recommendation through staff channels that plans be made for "civilian participation against enemy action directed at civilians including civil installations and communities." The day before the first atomic bomb was exploded over Japan, the Commanding General of the Army Service Forces issued a directive to the Provost Marshal General requesting that his office conduct a study of Civil Defense, to include an evaluation of:

(1) Experiences of the former Office of Civilian Defense
(2) Experiences of comparable agencies in allied and enemy countries
(3) Current surveys by United States Bombing Survey Board
(4) Contribution of State Guards to Civilian defense during World War II.

It was further required that the study develop:

(1) The agency that should be responsible for future study and planning, and
(2) The agency of the government that should be responsible for implementing the plans.[2]

2. Initial Civil Defense Planning

Other writers have speculated on why the War Department should have been the agency to initiate peacetime Civil Defense planning. There was no enemy threat of any detectable magnitude in 1945, once the European members of the Axis surrendered and it was foreseeable that Japan could not long stand alone. The U.S. military had considerable Civil Defense experience during World War II through the participation of selected individual officers in U.S. Civilian Defense. The U.S. military also knew at first hand the significant role that British Civil Defense played in the overall war effort of Great Britain. They had seen the seriousness of the threat posed by German V1 and V2 rockets and knew that guided missile technology would play a major role as a strategic offensive weapon in future major wars. The military knew of the importance of strategic bombing in the campaign to defeat Germany, and also knew of the general ineffectiveness of German Civil Defense efforts in combating the damage to German civilian morale. As World War II wound down, the

---
[1] Office of the White House, Executive Order 9562, 30 June 1945.
[2] U.S. War Department, Army Service Forces, "Civilian Defense Against Enemy Action Directed at Civilians, their Installations and Communities."

Chapter IV: American Systems

War Department General Staff made a concerted effort to preserve the lessons learned from the war and initiated study efforts in many areas before experienced personnel and available records should disappear from the scene. As the War Department had primary responsibility for the ground and air defense of the continental United States, it was logical that it should study Civil Defense as a passive defense against enemy attack. The lack of a clearly identified enemy has never been a deterrent to military planning for "defense."

The Provost Marshal's staff studied civil defense during the period 4 August 1945 to 30 April 1946, and thus had available the World War II experiences of Great Britain, Germany, and Japan, as well as that of the United States.[3] The staff struggled with the dilemma of whether to honestly recommend what *should* be done, or whether to temper the ultimate conclusions to recommend that which public opinion would endure during peacetime.

The study assumed a "worst case" estimate of a future war, based on its examination of past experiences and contemporary concepts of the probable character of future war:

> ... The next war will be a *total* war which may begin at *any* time; it will be fought at least initially, in the United States which will be attacked *first and without warning*; there will be strong undercover enemies from within who perhaps even now are working against us; and the enemy will be at least as competent and as powerful as we are. It logically must be assumed that the enemy will meet with considerable initial success and that millions of casualties—some published estimates run as high as forty million—most of whom will be civilians, possibly could occur during the first hours of a truly "lightning" war. Although it is assumed that we will possess strong existing task forces for counterattack, complete mobilization of our armed services probably will not occur within a year after some future M-Day. We cannot base our plans on having a large ally *at any time* during a future war since any potential ally, presumably being weaker than this country and seeing unprecedented terror and devastation being visited upon it, doubtless will make its own terms, however prejudicial to itself, with the enemy. The penalty for ineffective preparedness, whether or not it resulted in our capitulation to the enemy, would be tremendous and terrible. If we miraculously escaped the probable punishment for our sins of omission—that of going down to early or eventual defeat—the cost in lives, resources, wealth, and culture still would be appalling. If, on the other hand, we were forced to yield, those of our people who survived the ravages of total war would be marked for annihilation or perpetual bondage. An aggressor nation, in the absence of and unchecked by strong democratic allies, would seek nothing less.[4]

The report also hypothesized: "The brunt of an enemy attack, for at least the first year of the next war, will be borne by the civilian population. The ability of the people to withstand that attack will determine the outcome of the war and the future existence of the nation. Their ability to withstand the attack depends on the thoroughness and efficiency of plans prepared by the national government for their organization to resist and survive the attack."[5]

The study group did not hesitate to attack the then-current proposition that the explosion of two atomic bombs in Japan destroyed in that nation the last faint spark of will to resist. After careful examination of on-the-ground investigations by experts, the reports stated: "The will of the people in the two atomic target areas was only slightly affected, and that of the people throughout the rest of Japan, if affected at all, was in the direction of strengthening their resolve to resist and increasing their hatred of the enemy."[6]

While admitting that the atomic bomb in the hands of an enemy is capable of destruction and devastation so extensive that it is "horrible to contemplate," the report stated that it is possible to defend the civilian population against the effects of an atomic bomb with proper warning and by placing a disciplined

---
[3] U.S. War Department, Office of the Provost Marshal General, "Defense Against Enemy Action Directed at Civilians."
[4] Ibid., Par. 3, Exhibit "N."
[5] Ibid., p. 5.
[6] Ibid., p. 4, Par. 7a.

population in proper shelters. The report concluded that there is a defense against atomic bombs, and that is "a grave and fundamental responsibility of our government, and a natural function of its War Department to develop means of protection and to create plans to put those means of protection into effect *without delay*."[7]

After extensive study and deliberation, the Provost Marshal General's study group apparently decided to solve the dilemma of what to recommend by compromising and recommending that which public opinion would endure during peacetime. Their study of all available historical experience dictated that civil defense operating agencies must be formed in peacetime long before the onset of armed hostilities, for civil defense to be effective. The recommendations were directed toward establishing a civil defense *planning agency* in peacetime, to prepare for a declaration of a "limited national emergency." Only then would the skeleton civil defense organizations be mobilized and fully manned under a War Department chain of command. A declaration of full national emergency would be necessary to effect the total mobilization and operation of all civil defense activities. It is difficult to rationalize the recommendation for a three phase or step mobilization with the assumption that the next war will begin with an all-out surprise attack.

Though the study does not purport to go beyond "the category of a purely exploratory analysis," the recommendation was made that a separate permanent Civil Defense Division of the War Department General Staff be authorized and established. Pending the authorization for that separate Civil Defense Division, it was recommended that an interim agency be formed at once to operate under the Plans and Operations Division, War Department General Staff. The Provost Marshal General, Brigadier General Blackshear M. Bryan, in signing the report volunteered the information that his office would continue to study civil defense planning until such time as a new agency was created for that purpose. As the report was classified "Confidential" and was not declassified until 15 February 1965, the concern of the War Department about future wars and the safety of the civilian population was not revealed outside of the War Department.

Despite seeming inconsistencies between assumptions and recommendations, the Provost Marshal's study was notable for several reasons. While the study was being conducted, the United States dropped two atomic bombs on Japan, Japan surrendered, ending the global war, the United States had no known enemies of any significance and possessed a monopoly on atomic power, and the United States rapidly dismantled its military power as quickly as shipping could bring the scattered U.S. forces back to the United States. The first order of business of the United States was the conversion of its economy to a peacetime basis, the occupation and subjugation of its erstwhile enemies, Germany and Japan, and providing support for the new international organizations, the United Nations, the International Monetary Fund, etc. A highly vocal segment of American scientists were pushing very hard to bring the atomic weapon under international control in order to ensure that it would never be used in future wars. President Truman imposed severe budgetary ceilings on military appropriations, thereby reducing military strength to near impotence for the remainder of the decade of the 1940's. Many overseas bases were retained in support of the military occupations of Germany and Japan, thus giving the U.S. a *de facto* strategy of forward deployment, however thin the back-up and reserve military forces in the continental United States. Despite all this, the study group had the breadth of vision to look ahead and visualize a situation where a great power armed with atomic weapons might inflict a surprise attack on the United States. They tackled the awesome question of the effects of the

---

[7] Ibid., p. 3, Par. 4.

Chapter IV: American Systems

atomic weapon squarely, and declared that it was possible to prepare passive defenses which could save millions of lives in the face of an atomic attack. Finally, the study was emphatic that civil defense must be planned and prepared for immediately, and was successful in goading the War Department into establishing a Civil Defense Board.

In August 1946, the Acting Secretary of War informed the Director of the Bureau of the Budget that the War Department considered the subject of civil defense to be a matter of equal and direct interest to the civilian as well as to the military agencies of the government and since major matters of national policy were involved, the subject should be considered in conjunction with the overall study that the Bureau was making for the President with regard to the Reorganization Act of 1945.[8] The Director of the Budget replied that there was no argument that considerable work must be done in civilian defense planning during peace time to be prepared for a future emergency, and that they should move promptly to fix primary responsibility in an appropriate agency. He said:

> My main question is whether this phase of national preparedness planning should be considered by itself or whether the organization of all phases of the broader problem have to be considered together. We are now giving some attention to the whole question of how a National Security Resources Board, as recently endorsed by the President, should be organized. We have tentatively been looking on civilian defense planning as one aspect of the general problem with which that Board should be set up to deal. In any event, you may be sure that we will consider your suggestions carefully in conjunction with our work for the President in carrying out the provisions of the Reorganization Act of 1945.

On 25 November 1946, the Acting Secretary of War established the War Department Civil Defense Board headed by Major General Harold R. Bull, General Eisenhower's wartime operations chief in Europe. The mission assigned the board was:

(1) Allocation of responsibilities for civil defense to existing or new agencies of the Government
(2) The responsibilities which should be handled by the War Department and the allocation thereof to existing or new staff agencies
(3) The structural organization, from the national level down to the operating groups, and the authority which must be vested therein for the adequate discharge of its responsibilities
(4) The action in matters of civil defense which should be undertaken currently by the War Department pending the foregoing determinations.[9]

The Bull Board met with a sense of urgency. The members felt that civil defense was a matter of great national importance that no other agency of the government was planning. Many agencies of the government have direct interests in civil defense, as did almost every state and single city. Informally, the Director of the Bureau of the Budget stated that as part of the overall study for reorganization of the military into a single department, the administration wanted to create a National Security Resources Board which should probably assume overall responsibility for civil defense, but that the subject was sensitive and would require Congressional authorization and support. In the absence, of that authorization, the War Department was the only single Federal agency that could look at civil defense.

The Provost Marshal General's study had recommended the immediate formation of a civil defense agency within the War Department, but the War Department did not want to take that action until a broad

---

[8] U.S. National Military Establishment, Office of the Secretary of Defense. *A Study of Civil Defense*.
[9] Ibid., Par. 2, p. 1.

study by both the military and civilians had so recommended. In addition, the War Department budget and appropriations had been cut so severely that the War Department was reluctant to take on a new unassigned mission unless specifically assigned that responsibility (and by implication, unless it was specifically funded). There was also fear in the War Department that civil defense was so broad a responsibility that it would divert the War Department from its primary mission of "beating the enemy." The American Legion was after the War Department to publish a course of action on civil defense, as it wanted to publish its own plans and views in the forthcoming annual national convention. Also the members of the Board had other assigned duties to perform and wished to finish the study and get it over with in no more than three months' time. The War Department staff was operating on an austere basis and could ill afford the loss of the board members from their primary duties. The all-military board was appointed specifically to preclude the possibility of its being designated as the agency to continue civil defense planning.[10]

The board was entirely military, with senior Major Generals representing the Army Ground Forces, the Army Air Forces, the War Department General Staff, the National Guard Bureau, and the Bureau for Reserve and ROTC Affairs. Brigadier General Bryan, the Provost Marshal General, was also a member, providing continuity from the initial civil defense study. The board contained a representative of the Intelligence Division of the War Department General Staff, and its first order of business was to interview other members of the Intelligence Division. As a result, it reached much more moderate assumptions concerning the future than the Provost Marshal General's study group. In the opinion of the board:

> It may be expected that international agreements and organizations for the maintenance of peace will grow in effectiveness with time. The United States must, however, for the foreseeable future, provide for constant readiness to act to maintain its security.
>
> In the event of war, it is assumed that:
>
> a. Some period of strained relations, with or without declaration of emergency, will precede the outbreak of hostilities.
> b. The enemy may use weapons of mass destruction if he considers it to his advantage.
> c. There can be no guarantee of a specific warning of an attack.
> d. Strategic areas in the United States and its possessions, territories and trusteeship territories may be subjected to initial surprise attacks by air to cripple our industrial effort and destroy the will and ability of the people to resist.
> e. A major war involving the United States will require rapid total national mobilization.
> f. It may logically be anticipated that "Fifth Column" activities will have to be faced in the United States in case of an emergency.
>
> It is assumed that the armed forces will be united under a single department of national defense.[11]

This was an extraordinarily restrained and optimistic view of the future in light of the events that had transpired and were under way while the Bull Board deliberated (November 1946 to February 1947). Ex-Prime Minister Churchill made his famous "Iron Curtain" speech at Fulton, Missouri in March 1946, clearly anticipating the bi-polarization of the world into communist and anticommunist camps. The U.S.S.R. had revealed its expansionist intentions in Iran, Turkey, and Greece, and President Truman was priming himself to appear before Congress to "scare the hell out of the country" and request authority for $400 million assistance to Greece and Turkey—the historic Truman Doctrine. The intelligence community must have made clear to the Bull Board the growing possibilities of war between the United States and U.S.S.R.,

---
[10] Ibid., Annex I, p. 10.
[11] Ibid., Par. 6, p. 3.

Chapter IV: American Systems

as both sides became increasingly hostile and belligerent, and the United Nations was shown to be ineffective in handling the hard facts of the international competition.

During the next three months the Board interviewed 59 witnesses, representing the military, civilian organizations, and academia. In a very thorough and methodical fashion the Board probed in depth, examining wartime members of the Office of Civilian Defense, senior members of the Strategic Bombing Survey, experts from the Provost Marshal General's staff, scientific experts, and senior military commands who had World War II experience with civil defense. The Board also had the Provost Marshal General's study and annexes to assist them.

The conclusions reached by the Board were clear, direct and eminently sensible though it took 15 years before the same conclusions were reached by a "trial and error" process. The main points were:

(1) Civil defense is an essential part of national defense; no effective civil defense organization was in existence and no coordinated planning was being accomplished; and the nation should be organized immediately for civil defense.

(2) Civil defense as organized and directed in the United States during World War II would be inadequate for the future.

(3) A single, permanent, federal Civil Defense Agency should be responsible for planning, organizing, operating, coordinating, and directing civil defense matters at all levels of government. This agency should get its general national policy guidance from a cabinet level group. As civil defense is basically a civilian problem, it should be a separate civilian agency, but within the Department of the Armed Forces (later designated Department of Defense) for maximum guidance and cooperation.

(4) Regional civil defense organizations should be established and made responsible to the Director, Civil Defense Agency, for federal-state and interstate coordination. The States should be charged with responsibility for establishing and operating their necessary civil defense organizations in accordance with the general pattern determined by the Federal Government.

(5) Federal and State legislation is required to establish statutory civil defense organizations, define responsibilities, and allocate authority both in war and peace.

(6) The Secretary of War should recommend to the President that an early decision should be made to establish the Civil Defense Agency, and in the interim the War Department should be charged by the President to develop civil defense plans at once.[12]

The Board recognized that civil defense was part of a larger problem which involved many agencies at different levels. It did not want to burden the Civil Defense Agency with responsibilities for internal security, dispersal of industry, protective building construction, mass evacuation, the development of underground sites, and the many activities of volunteer agencies during wartime. It did base its civil defense concept heavily on Great Britain's model, fully recognizing the vital role played by the national government, while also embodying the principle of "self-help" and the principle of mutual aid. Unfortunately, these points were lost on later civil defense planners who directed civil defense efforts at those very endeavors. In particular, the principal of "self-help" was lifted out of context and used as a rationale for placing the main burden of civil defense on State and local government, not the Federal Government.

The Board did not recommend placing the Civil Defense Agency under the Department of the Armed Forces in order to build up the missions, appropriations or prestige of the armed services, but rather because testimony had fully established that many "States Righters" in a civilian civil defense organization would not take federal direction except from members of the armed services. In fact, the Board was chary that the

---

[12] Ibid., Pars. 20–26, pp. 20–21.

military might be distracted from their primary mission of "defeating the enemy" if overburdened with civil defense responsibilities. The military did not want to assume the responsibility for civil defense, but could not avoid it if it were to assume its rightful place in overall national defense.

The Bull Report was completed in February 1947, classified "Confidential." As a result, it had very little impact on public opinion. The recommendations contained in the report were not carried through, but they did provide a useful basis for further study of civil defense. In retrospect, this is not very surprising. The *verbatim* testimony in the annex to the report stated that the members of the Board knew that civil defense was essentially a civilian subject. They knew that further study of civil defense by a civilian board was necessary, and that the Bull Board was deliberately composed only of generals for the specific purpose of NOT involving them further in civil defense planning. They also knew that the Bureau of the Budget was planning the reorganization of the armed forces and that the National Security Resources Board was planned as the top-level policy-making organization to be charged with responsibility for civil defense. With all the changes in the air, about the best the Bull Board could do was to transmit a sense of urgency together with its truly outstanding recommendations.

Events were moving too quickly to expect a rapid reaction to the Bull Report recommendations. The National Security Act of 1947, creating the National Military Establishment, a separate U.S. Air Force, the National Security Council, the National Security Resources Board, and other means of directing and coordinating national security programs, was approved on 26 July 1947. A strong motivation behind President Truman's advocating a unified military establishment was his central concern with civilian control of the military establishment.[13] The new Secretary of Defense, James Forrestal, established the Office of Civil Defense Planning on March 27, 1948. Mr. Russell J. Hopley of Omaha, Nebraska, was appointed Director of the Office and Deputy to the Secretary of Defense for Civil Defense matters, from the position of President of the Northwestern Bell Telephone Company. He was assigned the mission:

(1) To provide for the development of detailed plans for, and the establishment of, an integrated national program of civil defense;
(2) To secure proper coordination and direction of all civil defense matters affecting the National Military Establishment; and
(3) To provide an effective means of liaison between the National Military Establishment and other governmental and private agencies on questions of civil defense.[14]

The Secretary of Defense Memorandum that established the Office of Civil Defense Planning was a logical extension of the "Bull Report" recommendations, which were abstract and general. Detailed guidance in the Memorandum made it clear that Mr. Hopley's task was to develop detailed plans and recommendations to be implemented by a "permanent federal civil defense agency which, in conjunction with the several States and their subdivisions, can undertake those peacetime preparations which are necessary to assure an adequate civil defense system in the event of a war."[15] The principle of peacetime civil defense planning had been established—the question remained "by whom" and "how."

---

[13] U.S. President (Truman), "Unification of the Armed Forces of the United States," Message from the President of the United States, 19 December 1945, pp. 6–7.
[14] U.S. Office of Civil Defense Planning, *Civil Defense for National Security*, p. 291.
[15] Ibid.

Chapter IV: American Systems

The staff selected for the Office of Civil Defense Planning consisted of 49 other individuals, only six of whom were military, selected from Federal, State, local governments, and industry. In addition, the OCDP was authorized to consult any persons of agencies within the National Military Establishment for information or assistance, and to solicit the help of other individuals or agencies, both governmental and private, it deemed appropriate. It was also authorized to establish such advisory committees as it deemed necessary to carry out its assigned duties.

In just over six months the OCDP produced a 300-page report entitled *Civil Defense for National Security*, published in unclassified form for public consumption on November 13, 1948, and thereafter generally known as the "Hopley Report." Mr. Hopley and his staff did a remarkable job of producing a comprehensive analysis and a detailed organizational outline to accomplish the assigned tasks. It is still viewed as a model textbook on a civil defense program for the United States, with few reservations. The OCDP did not take a strong position on the probability or shape of future wars, except to say that it hoped that ". . . International agreements and organizations for the maintenance of peace will succeed in their objective, and in the conviction that this nation does not want war; yet realistically facing the fact that as long as armies are maintained and war remains even a remote possibility, this country must be prepared for any eventuality."[16] It did give a clue that it thought that another atomic super power might be involved when it wrote: "If attack should come, it might be by bomber squadrons dropping atomic bombs, incendiaries or gas bombs, or super explosives, on one or a score of our major centers. It might come via guided missiles from distant points, or from submarines off the American shores. Or it might come from within the borders of the United States, through saboteurs and fifth columnists."[17] As justification for maintaining an Office of Civil Defense in peacetime, the report stated ". . . if there is a 'next War,' it may start, as did the last, with a surprise attack in force upon this continent."[18]

The program proposed by the report included:

(1) A National Office of Civil Defense, with a small but capable staff to furnish leadership and guidance in organizing and training the people for civil defense tasks
(2) Basic operational responsibility to be placed in States and communities, but with mutual assistance plans and mobile supporting facilities for aid in emergencies
(3) Maximum utilization of loyal volunteers, existing agencies and organizations, and all available skills and experiences
(4) Well organized and trained units in communities throughout the United States, its territories and possessions, prepared and equipped to meet the problems of enemy attack, and to be ready against any weapon that an enemy may use
(5) Intensive planning to meet the particular hazards of atomic or any other modern weapons of warfare
(6) A peacetime organization which should be used in natural disasters even though it may never have to be used in war[19]

On the question of the location of a National Office of Civil Defense in the Executive Branch of the Federal Government, the Hopley Report preferred that it report directly to the Secretary of Defense, but stated that it would be appropriate to have it report directly to the President.[20]

---
[16] Ibid., p. 2.
[17] Ibid.
[18] Ibid., p. 18.
[19] Ibid., p. 2.
[20] Ibid., p. 18.

A major difference from the Bull Report was the stress of the Hopley Report on the use of volunteers to perform all major operational activities. It envisioned as many as fifteen million people involved in all phases of civil defense, and even postulated that virtually every man woman and child would have to be assigned to tasks in a civil defense organization fighting for the nation's life. Concern was expressed, however, that men not be diverted from the Armed Forces to fill civil defense positions. In keeping with its general philosophy of building on existent capabilities, the Hopley Report stated "Full use should, of course, be made of civic, social, fraternal, veterans and other community organizations, including woman's groups, organizations of boys and girls, business, labor, agricultural and professional associations and the like."[21]

A unique aspect of the Hopley Report which placed it years ahead of its time, was its insistence on establishing a useful role for civil defense organizations, people, and equipment in peacetime. Specifically, it stated: "There should clearly be a basic purpose of disaster action in organizing for Civil Defense, for many parts of such an organization would be automatically adaptable to the handling of emergency situations in times of peace as in war."[22]

Perhaps the most unfortunate aspect of the Hopley Report, when viewed in retrospect, was its insistence that the basic principle for civil defense should be ". . . that the primary operating responsibility for civil defense must rest with state and local governments, that they must be the directing force in the protection of their own citizens."[23] When a civil defense operating agency was finally authorized at the Federal Government level, it was based firmly on that principle of the primacy of State and local governments.

By the time the Hopley Report was published, there was considerable interest in organization of local civil defense agencies, as there had been prior to World War II. The Berlin Blockade crisis grew out of a series of events in the Spring of 1948, culminating in Allied monetary reform for Germany in all zones except the Russian Zone. The Russians retaliated by blockading all access routes to Berlin except the air corridors, and cut off the flow of electric power from the Soviet sector of Berlin to the Western sectors. The Allies in turn cut off all trading between Western zones and East Berlin and the whole Soviet zone, denying East German industry the coal from the Ruhr. By the end of June 1948, President Truman had determined that there would be no withdrawal from Berlin. The decision was made to resupply Berlin by a makeshift airlift, assembling every transport aircraft that could be made available. In addition, B-29 aircraft were moved to West Germany and England. It was not announced whether or not they were equipped with atomic bombs, but the inference was clear.

By September, the situation was extremely dangerous so that the Western nations felt that they teetered on the edge of war.[24] The newspapers, of course, duly brought to the attention of the American people all of the implications of the situation. One of the by-products of the first war scare since the end of World War II was an increased interest in civil defense. The Hopley Report was issued at precisely the right time to capitalize on that interest, and it did much to further discussions of governmental organization for civil defense among responsible State and local officials. The 17 organizational charts at the back of the report provided the basis for much of the civil defense organization that ensued. Public reaction to the report was generally favorable, with a minimum of negative or critical comment in the public press. As a result, there

---

[21] Ibid., p. 16.
[22] Ibid., p. 17.
[23] U.S. National Military Establishment, Office of Civil Defense Planning. *Civil Defense for National Security*. "Hopley Report," p. 15.
[24] Truman, *Years of Trial and Hope*, p. 128.

was a great deal of civil defense legislation enacted as civil defense organizations were created by State and local governments.

At the national level, the Hopley Report did not attract comparable attention. By the time that President Truman took further action on civil defense, the crisis of the Berlin Blockade and airlift was passing as a result of successful allied supply of the besieged city. President Truman decided not to create a permanent Office of Civil Defense as recommended in the Hopley Report, but to further civil defense planning instead. He assigned responsibility for civil defense planning to the National Security Resources Board on March 3, 1949, thus removing civil defense from the military establishment.[25] The three civil defense studies compiled by the Department of Defense and the War Department had carried civil defense planning about as far as it could go. The President could not very well ignore the recommendations of those studies and expect the Department of Defense to continue civil defense planning indefinitely. As the National Security Resources Board was already assigned the mission of mobilization planning for the industrial base of war production, it was logical to also assign it the mission of mobilization planning for civil defense.

The NSRB carried out its civil defense mission in three distinct ways:

(1) The coordination of civil defense planning by other federal agencies;
(2) The education of civil defense workers and the public in furtherance of civil defense objectives; and
(3) Planning for a mobilization civil defense operating agency. It was also influential in simulating the continued development of civil defense activities at the State and local levels.

The NSRB expanded the planning initiated by the Hopley group by involving all of the pertinent federal agencies with civil defense functions in planning for mobilization or wartime civil defense operations. This coordination reached down as well as out to budding and existing local level civil defense organizations, greatly encouraging them in their search for federal support and guidance. The NSRB staff compiled numerous educational publications, the most famous of which, *Survival Under Atomic Attack*, was published in October 1950, eventually reaching a distribution of 250,000 copies and a wide readership. It was the first official publication which described the effects of atomic weapons in an unclassified text and layman's language, and elicited tremendous public interest.

3. Civil Defense Operating Agencies, 1951

Once again, the sweep of events overtook deliberate civil defense planning. Simulated by the open display of Russian force which accompanied the Berlin Blockade, the nations of Europe banded together to form the North Atlantic Treaty Organization, joined by the United States in July 1949. On September 23, 1949, President Truman announced that the U.S.S.R. had exploded an atomic device, ending the United States monopoly of the atomic bomb several years before the anticipated date. The psychological impact of that chain of events which reflected great concern with the status of U.S. military forces and defenses. Though this change in U.S. strategy of no longer relying on the monopoly in atomic weapons was not sudden and drastic, it did evolve into a new strategy of building up U.S. military forces to meet the requirements of a far more dangerous world. The takeover of China and the establishment of the People's Republic of China, announced on October 1, 1949, added to the swell of U.S. public opinion and interest in foreign

---
[25] Maxam, William P., *Federal Civil Defense 1946–1963: A Study*, p. 151.

affairs, and concern for U.S. security. Though there were extensive investigations and much acrimony concerning our "loss of China," U.S. public opinion turned from Asia to Europe, much as U.S. foreign policy "wrote off" China and dropped support of the Chinese Nationalists forces had ensconced on Taiwan. The invasion of South Korea by the Russian-sponsored forces of North Korea on 25 June 1950, brought the United Nations and the United States squarely into that conflict. President Truman proclaimed "the existence of a national emergency" on December 16, 1950, and the necessary machinery for wartime mobilization was triggered by a small "police action" on the rim of Asia.[26]

The NSRB submitted its civil defense report, *United States Civil Defense* (NSRD Document 128), to the President on 8 September 1950, and he in turn quickly forwarded it to the Congress for consideration on September 18, 1950. President Truman relieved the National Security Resources Board of the responsibility for civil defense on December 1, 1950, when he issued Executive Order 10186 temporarily establishing a Federal Civil Defense Administration in the Office for Emergency Management. Millard F. Caldwell was sworn in as the Federal Civil Defense Administrator on December 6, 1950.

United States Civil Defense,[27] commonly known as the "Blue Book," was a continuation of the Hopley Report in that it expanded the number of governmental agencies which would be responsible for future planning activities, and delegated more responsibility for program development of State and local agencies. It also expanded on the principle of "self-help" by declaring "civil defense rests upon the principle of self-protection by the individual, extended to include mutual self-protection on the part of groups and communities."[28] It also extended the remarks of the Hopley Report about the use of existing resources when it stated "Plans for civil defense . . . must be made with full recognition of the importance of maximum economy in the use of the available supply of men, money, materials."[29] Though that statement was probably written before the outbreak of the Korean War, it was interpreted after the outbreak of the Korean War and its subsequent demand on scarce resources. In that light, it further lessened any possibility of legislation for a strong civil defense.

The Congress circulated the draft legislation for civil defense among the agencies of the Federal Government that were involved, as well as to the Council of State Governors. The revised draft legislation was reintroduced in the House on November 30, and the Senate on December 1, the same day President Truman created the Federal Civil Defense Administration by Executive Order. The entry of the Chinese Communist forces into the Korean War cast a pall over the country as daily the headlines announced Communist advances and victories and U.N. forces withdrawals and defeats. President Truman addressed a letter to the Congress explaining his Executive Order and requesting rapid passage of the Civil Defense Act.

Congress did hold its hearings with a sense of urgency, but at the same time delved into the proposed legislation vigorously and comprehensively, calling many witnesses from the military services, Federal departments and agencies, State and local governments, professional and public organizations, and some individuals. There was general agreement with the basic thrust of the legislation, that it was both feasible and desirable to protect the civilian population of the United States against atomic bomb

---

[26] Office of the White House, Proclamation No. 2914, 15 F.R. 9029.
[27] Executive Office of the President, National Security Resources Board. *United States Civil Defense.*
[28] Ibid., p. 1.
[29] Ibid.

Chapter IV: American Systems

effects. There were few disagreements on the substance of the legislation and the recommended law. The notable exception came from witnesses representing the American Municipal Association, which represented the mayors of the American cities. The mayors strongly believed that Federal civil defense organization should be under the Department of Defense, if there was to be effective coordination between the civilians in the local municipalities and the military at the national level. All of the three previous reports on civil defense supported the mayors' judgment based on close examination of civil defense in the United States during World War II. At that particular point in time when the hearings were held, the Department of Defense was almost totally occupied with fighting the war in Korea and reinforcing U.S. military forces in Europe, and did not want to undertake civil defense as well. Thus, the mayors failed to get any support from the Department of Defense, which normally would have been strongly in their corner.

The mayors indicated two other major objections. The Blue Book concerned itself with the threat of atomic (or fission) bombs, as the thermonuclear (or fusion) bomb had not yet been developed. The atomic bomb with its limited nuclear yields had been employed only on cities, and was visualized primarily as a threat to the 50 largest American cities. In effect, the entire civil defense problem boiled down to protecting those 50 cities, since blankets of fallout were not envisioned as threatening non-urban areas. Yet, carried away by the concepts of "self-help" and "self-reliance," the legislation proposed funding civil defense by a matching funds provision. The local government (cities) were to put up the first dollar for civil defense, and the Federal Government would match it with the second dollar. Since the hearings were considering the expenditure of two billion dollars over a period of three years, the mayors of only 50 cities were faced with the problem of raising a like amount, though they lacked the tax base and means of the Federal Government. Due to the rapidity with which the legislation was introduced and the Federal Civil Defense Administration brought into being, the American Municipal Association was not prepared to introduce alternative formulas for dividing the funding responsibility between the Federal and local governments.

The mayors' third major objection grew out of the military type chain of command outlined in the Blue Book and proposed legislation, linking the Federal Government through the State governments to the local governments. This direct chain ignored the existing problem of almost uniformly bad relations between big cities and their host states, best exemplified by the long-standing feud between the New York State government in Albany, and the City of New York. The mayors, who were intimately familiar with their own feuds and State assemblies, felt that the chain would seriously impede efforts to develop effective civil defense efforts at their levels.

Despite the mayors' objections, Congress passed the proposed legislation after some reorganization of the act, clarification of some of the provisions, and the addition of some definitions. By January 2, the bill was passed by both houses, to be signed by the President on January 12, 1951, as Public Law 920, 81st Congress, the Federal Civil Defense Act of 1950.

The crisis of the war in Korea clearly provided the occasion for the rapid enactment of the Federal Civil Defense Act of 1950, and the activation of a civil defense operating administration. Growing awareness of vulnerability to atomic weapons delivered by Russian intercontinental bombers provided the cause. The American public was increasingly made aware that President Truman's pre–Korean War military budgets were so austere that they left the North American continent virtually defenseless in the event of a Russian attack.[30] The Korean War "requirements" budget and supplements provided sufficient funds to activate an air defense for the United States by mobilizing National Guard and Reserve interceptor and antiaircraft units, but time was required to modernize and produce new equipment.

The Act of 1950 was passed under crisis conditions with the intent to do something about an existing threat, not as a sound legislative basis for a long-term future program which could build solidly on existing civil defense capabilities in anticipation of the day when the clearly identified enemy, Russia, would possess a truly significant atomic weapons capability. The civil defense program in the United States was launched with a very bad start from which it never entirely recovered.

The first Federal Civil Defense Administrator, Millard Caldwell, one-time Congressman and ex-Governor of Florida, was a political unknown who possessed little of the national prestige that would have gotten civil defense off to a flying start. The Congress, despite talk of appropriating two billion Federal dollars in the first three years, granted only token appropriations far below the level requested by the FCDA. Under the Act of 1950, the FCDA did not have the authority necessary to invoke an effective civil defense program, for the Act placed the responsibility for civil defense at the State and local levels. In redefining the term "civil defense," Congress made it so narrow as to exclude Federal civil defense assistance in countering natural disasters. It also excluded peacetime civil defense preparatory and regulative authorities, concentrating on national civil defense in time of emergency only. Like some other wartime emergency agencies that were created to expedite the prosecution of the Korean War, the FCDA was clearly a wartime emergency measure. The provision for fund splitting between Federal and local governments virtually ensured that civil defense would be funded at a very low level.

The Act of 1950 did not create new Federal instruments and authorizations with which to hammer out an effective civil defense system, but merely created an administration that was outside the Executive Office of the President and the departmental structure of the Executive Branch, with an Administrator who derived his authority from the President. If the Administrator were to become effective, however, he would necessarily need the authority to coordinate and direct (in the name of the President) other Federal departments and agencies, as well as State and local governments. That authority was not forthcoming. It can only be concluded that President Truman did not intend the FCDA to be more than a token emergency move to placate public opinion and concern for the safety of the civilian population in the face of a growing atomic bomb threat.

The main thrust of the FCDA under Governor Caldwell was on providing shelters against the effects of atomic attack. The majority of the talked-about 2 billion Federal dollars for civil defense was planned to go into deep shelters to protect the populations of the most likely targets (fifty cities) from blast, heat, and the initial radiation effects of atomic weapons. When it became obvious that the cities were not about to come up with that level of funding, the Federal program was shifted to surveying the sheltering capabilities of existing shelters in structure. Plans were made to develop and supplement existing capabilities to shelter the citizens of the critical urban areas, but they met with little enthusiasm from either the public or local governments.

In 1952, the Department of Defense contracted for a study of civil defense on behalf of the DOD, the NSRB, and the FCDA. The contractor was Associated Universities, headed by the President Emeritus of

---

[30] Martin, Harold H., "Could We Beat Back an Air Attack on the U.S.," *Saturday Evening Post*.

Chapter IV: American Systems

the Massachusetts Institute of Technology, Lloyd Berkner. President Berkner had been active in the studies of Air Defense of the North American Continent conducted in behalf of the U.S. Air Force by the Lincoln Laboratory, an adjunct of M.I.T. created in 1951 for the specific purpose of furthering the effectiveness of air defense. The civilian scientists of the Lincoln Laboratory had concluded collectively that based on anticipated advances in early warning radar technology, an effective air defense of the North American continent was both feasible and highly necessary. Many of the same civilian scientists who arrived at that conclusion were active in the study of civil defense, which was known by the code name "East River."[31]

The East River report was submitted in ten parts, Part I being the General Report, Part II covering Measures to Make Civil Defense Manageable, and the remainder devoted to CBR Warfare, Urban Vulnerability, the Destructive Threat of Atomic Weapons, Disaster Services and Operations, Warning and Communications for Civil Defense, Civil Defense Health and Welfare, and Information and Training for Civil Defense. The recommendations covered in Part I were general and included the following points[32]:

(1) Civil Defense must be a permanent partner in national defense.[33]
(2) The Civil Defense program must emphasize as a positive goal of first priority, those activities that will improve the individual citizen's chance of survival and minimize his property damage in the case of enemy attack.[34]
(3) A civilian Civil Defense must be developed to the maximum degree possible.[35]
(4) Civil Defense must be organized and operated on the principle that existing agencies and facilities should be used to the greatest extent possible.[36]
(5) Civil Defense must be accomplished, in the main, as an extension of the normal duties of various officials at all levels of government assisted by volunteers and volunteer organizations.[37]
(6) The Civil Defense job must be accurately dimensioned as a prerequisite to dividing it into its component parts.[38]
(7) The Civil Defense job must be delimited by Civil Defense.[39]
(8) Civil Defense functions must be clearly defined and responsibility for each function precisely assigned.[40]
(9) Civil Defense must conform to traditional and accepted methods, means, and organizations in carrying out its program.[41]
(10) Dual use of equipment and facilities for Civil Defense should be encouraged to the maximum practical degree.[42]
(11) All areas of the U.S. are not of equal vulnerability to the several elements of the threat and Civil Defense programs must be adjusted to the requirements of the individual area.[43]
(12) Civil Defense must be effectively organized with priorities for the most critical target and immediate support areas and then extended to other areas.[44]

---

[31] Associated Universities, Inc. *Project East River*, New York, 1952.
[32] Ibid.
[33] Ibid., pp. 9–10.
[34] Ibid., pp. 10–11.
[35] Ibid., p. 11.
[36] Ibid.
[37] Ibid., p. 13.
[38] Ibid.
[39] Ibid.
[40] Ibid., p.14.
[41] Ibid.
[42] Ibid., pp. 14–15.
[43] Ibid., p. 15.
[44] Ibid.

(13) Reduction of target vulnerability is an essential function of Civil Defense.[45]

(14) Because of its complexity and magnitude, the Civil Defense task must be a continuing operation, carefully programmed.[46]

(15) The Civil Defense program must place first reliance on the efforts of the individual and the community to increase chances of survival, to minimize damage, and to recover as quickly as possible in the eventuality of an enemy attack.[47]

The report further spelled out what was meant by the statement that "The Civil Defense job must be delimited by Civil Defense." It stated that the Civil Defense tasks must be delimited through adoption of an effective military defense; and reduction of urban vulnerability.[48]

In Part IIA, the report spelled out those military measures that must be taken precedent to achieving a manageable Civil Defense: the Air Defense Command must provide one-hour warning of the approach of enemy aircraft, an enemy attack must be detected 2,000 miles from critical U.S. targets, interception of enemy aircraft must take place well out from the critical targets, the sea and land approaches of the United States must be covered by early warning radars, means must be developed of detecting low-flying enemy aircraft, electronic counter measures must be developed against enemy aircraft, no unidentified aircraft must be allowed in the Air Defense Identification Zones (ADIZs), an effective system for detecting enemy submarines must be developed, and a Joint Operational Development Force (for air defense) must be created.

The Department of Defense had seen those same recommendations before from the Lincoln Laboratory scientists, who had banded together in an extra-official group known as the "Summer Study Group" and submitted their opinion that an effective air defense was feasible and necessary. The Department of Defense did not agree with those conclusions and had no intention of spending the money, time or effort to make the air defense mobilized by the Korean War effective.

As a result, the East River report had little impact on civil defense through official channels. The scientists who were rebuffed by the lack of interest in their report, turned to unofficial channels and "leaked" their findings to select members of the press to transmit their sense of urgency about air defense to the American public. The net effect of the East River report was to turn the thrust of providing protection to the American civilian population from civil defense to air defense. It was not effective in bringing civil defense and military defense into successful cooperation.

4. The Period from 1952 to 1955

On October 31, 1952, an event took place which was to have a tremendous impact on civil defense—the United States successfully exploded a thermonuclear device at Eniwetok. The United States was in the midst of a Presidential election, which saw General Eisenhower elected on a ticket which promised peace in Korea and a reduction in military expenditures. With an imminent change in administrations, Millard Caldwell resigned as Federal Civil Defense Administrator on November 15, 1952. President Eisenhower appointed another ex-governor to follow him—Val Peterson, the outgoing Governor of Nebraska. Governor Peterson's ambition was to be Ambassador to India, but the opposition of Nebraska's United States Senators precluded that appointment. There was no Senate opposition to his appointment as Federal Civil Defense

---
[45] Ibid., p. 16.
[46] Ibid.
[47] Ibid., p. 17.
[48] Ibid., p. 21.

Chapter IV: American Systems

Administrator. Governor Peterson had to wait until 1957 to fulfill his diplomatic ambitions, when he was successfully nominated and confirmed as Ambassador to Denmark.

Governor Peterson quickly established the fact that the shelter program was ended when he announced that he was not going to request Congress to appropriate large amounts of money for shelter development and construction. He announced that evacuation of the heavily populated urban areas was feasible and would be the alternative to expensive digging and construction projects.

His timing was as bad in civil defense matters as it was in diplomatic matters, for the thermonuclear bomb's effects differed radically from the fission bomb in one other aspect beside the infinitely greater magnitude of the fusion bomb—it generated massive fallout that threatened urban and rural areas alike. While it was true that the effects of the thermonuclear bomb were highly classified, and also true that Russia was not expected to develop the thermonuclear weapon for at least three or four more years, his new policy was quickly overtaken by events. The Soviet Union exploded a thermonuclear device on August 12, 1953. Evacuation as the major thrust of U.S. civil defense, however, lingered on until 1958, when the emphasis changed to the construction of fallout shelters.

The creation by the Federal Civil Defense Act of 1950 of the FCDA as a wartime mobilization agency with authority to designate civil defense tasks to other Federal departments and agencies, brought the FCDA into conflict with other mobilization agencies. As has been seen, the FCDA was a statutory agency created by the Congress under Public Law 920. Prior to the passing of that law, President Truman created other defense mobilization offices by Executive Order, placing them in the Executive Office of the President.[49] The non-statutory Office of Defense Mobilization was created on December 16, 1953, which transferred certain functions of the National Security Resources Board to the Director of ODM. On June 12, 1953, Reorganization Plan Number 3 was signed which abolished the statutory National Security Resources Board and transferred its remaining functions to ODM. The "cease fire" in Korea became effective on July 26, 1953.

Though the immediate emergency triggered by the Korean War was ended, the era of Cold War which ensued was regarded as a continuing emergency of highly dangerous international competition which could bring war at any moment. Under those conditions the prospect of mobilization of the country's resources for war-fighting or for recovery from an enemy attack was given an immediacy that had previously been lacking in peacetime. Though ODM had relatively meager financial resources appropriated to it, it was able to draw on far greater resources of other government agencies and departments by designating mobilization responsibilities they were obligated to perform.

Beginning in 1954, the FCDA began to exercise its statutory authority by delegating civil defense responsibilities to other Federal agencies and departments. Though some of those delegations required the commitment of relatively meager resources (such as the one to the Attorney General), others required the commitment or earmarking of considerable resources (emergency stockpiles of medicines by the Secretary of HEW, food stockpiles by the Department of Agriculture, etc.). Inevitably there was confusion and overlapping between the mobilization requirements of ODM and the FCDA. As FCDA's delegation program picked up, pressure built to combine all non-military defense activities under one Federal agency, an event which took place in 1958.

---

[49] Office of the White House, Executive Order 10193 (15 F.R. 9031).

In the aftermath of the explosion of the Soviet Union thermonuclear device there was a great deal of discussion in the United States about dispersing the Federal Government to make it less vulnerable to an enemy strike on Washington, D.C. in August 1954, the Federal Civil Defense Administration itself was moved to Battle Creek, Michigan. Although the intent might have been admirable, the net effect of moving the FCDA hundreds of miles from the center of the Federal Government was to further downgrade its prestige and effectiveness at a time when it required a major injection of Presidential authority and attention to successfully grapple with the numerous unresolved problems of civil defense in the atomic age.

C. History of Surface-to-Air Missiles

1. Background

The decision to develop a guided antiaircraft missile may be traced back at least to January 1944, when the AAA Board, in a recommendation to the AAA Command, called for a missile development program and specified the characteristics that such a missile ought to have. As was true in the case of early post war decisions to develop interceptor aircraft, there was little evidence of concern on the part of the AAA Board with a specific external threat. Rather, as indicated by the target characteristics included in the Board's recommendation, there was a perceived need for a missile capable of destroying B-29 or B-36 type aircraft; although, in 1944, the United States alone possessed the capability of producing such aircraft.

Had there been a visible external threat driving the surface-to-air missile program the program might have been much less instructive for the student of U.S. strategic decision making. The bureaucratic combat which characterized the program might at least have been subdued—if not crushed—in the face of an urgent need for a defensive missile. But the urgency which did attend the program was generated from within, and was the product of an intense rivalry between, first, the Army air and ground forces, and later, the Air Force and the Army. In fact, there is perhaps no better illustration of interservice rivalry during the first post war decade than the program to develop the surface-to-air missile.

2. The AAF-ASF Split

The program under consideration would eventually split into two separate programs—one to produce the Bomarc, and one to produce the Nike. But it all began as a single effort on January 31, 1945, when a letter from the Chief of Ordnance to Bell Telephone Laboratories (BTL) "authorized negotiations for a formal study of an antiaircraft guided missile."[50] Almost immediately thereafter, in February, the AAF and ASF jointly contracted with BTL for a missile feasibility study.[51]

The stage had already been set for the coming split between AAF and ASF, when the "McNarney Letter" allocated missile R&D responsibilities between the AAF and ASF, giving the former control over missiles lifted by *aerodynamic* forces, and the latter control over those depending upon *momentum*.[52] Competition between the AAF and ASF would for several years focus on the aerodynamic-momentum design issue.

BTL would not complete its antiaircraft missile feasibility study until July 1945,[53] but an interim oral report delivered on May 14 showed AAF which way the wind was blowing. In June, AAF withdrew its

---

[50] U.S. Army, Chief of Ordnance, "Letter," 31 January 1945.
[51] Byland, 24 April 1954.
[52] DA PAM 70-10, p. 6. Also see Chapter I, this report.
[53] BTL, Historical Summary of Nike.

support from the BTL study and immediately contracted with Boeing for a separate feasibility study to be completed in September 1945.

BTL (in July)[54] and Boeing (in September)[55] submitted final reports to their respective clients, in each case affirming the feasibility of developing a guided surface-to-air weapon suitably matched to the client's design interests. BTL's paper study of Project Nike, "AGM Report: Study of an Antiaircraft Guided Missile System," included the following recommendations to ASF:

(1) Extend radar and computer techniques, and explore supersonic flight;
(2) But start now, without waiting for the completion of related research;
(3) Employ known devices, techniques, and methods to the greatest extent possible.

Boeing's report on Project GAPA (Ground-to-Air Pilotless Aircraft) conveyed a similar sense of urgency to AAF, but such stimulation was unnecessary for a client already lagging its competitor—ASF—by several months.

3. Work Begins on Nike and GAPA

On September 13, 1945, ASF approved BTL's Nike development plan; and on September 21 the development contract was initiated under the direction of the Rocket Branch of the Chief of Ordnance. Western Electric (BTL) was made the prime contractor and was given responsibility for the radar, computer, and guidance systems.[56] Subcontracts were let as follows:

(1) Douglas: airframe, booster, and launcher
(2) Aerojet: sustainer and booster
(3) Picatinny: warhead
(4) DOFL: fuse
(5) JPL: consultant.

In December 1945, AAF responded to Boeing's GAPA report by asking Boeing for a contract proposal to design the missile deemed feasible in September; in February 1946 Boeing was awarded the design study contract.[57]

The intra- and interservice rivalry over surface-to-air missiles during the 1946–1955 period was primarily a jurisdictional dispute which impacted only obliquely on the technical progression of the Nike and Bomarc programs. However, the technical histories of the two systems are interesting in their own right and are summarized here apart from the later discussion of the bureaucratic combat which surrounded them for a decade.

4. The Race of the Engineers

Shortly after awarding Boeing the GAPA design study contract, AAF initiated two parallel defensive missile study contracts. In March 1946, General Electric was given the contract to carry out Project Thumper, a study of "interceptor weapons for ballistic missile defense." In April AAF asked the University

---

[54] Semmens, BDM, *Chronology*.
[55] Air Materiel Command, Development of Guided Missiles.
[56] Semmens, BDM, Chronology; BTL, Historical Summary of Nike.
[57] Air Materiel Command, Development of Guided Missiles.

of Michigan to study, under the project name Wizard, the feasibility of a supersonic missile capable of reaching 500,000 feet. Thumper was intended to collide with a target similar to the German V-2 rocket. Wizard, a much more sophisticated weapon, was intended for use against a 4,000 mph target at an altitude anywhere between 60,000 and 500,000 feet.[58] Both Thumper and Wizard, because of their importance to later developments in the ballistic missile defense program, are treated in greater detail in section D, this chapter.

Meanwhile, Project GAPA was well under way. By the spring of 1947, it was estimated that the GAPA's development would be completed by 1949, at a total cost of $16.4 million. Already, in March 1947, 31 GAPA missiles had been successfully test fired; and it was promised that the fully developed system would be effective against a 0.9 Mach target at 70,000 feet—a capability superior to that expected of the Nike.

Both the GAPA and Nike programs continued apace into 1948, when the GAPA program was mortally wounded in the budget area. Adjustments to the FY 1949 budget, which spanned the period during which GAPA RED was to be completed, reduced GAPA funding to such a degree that only 70 test vehicles, rather than the intended operational arsenal, were to be produced. (In fact, over 100 vehicles were produced before the program was terminated.)

The GAPA program waned and waxed in 1949. It was first marked for termination, then rescued by an infusion of previously appropriated but unspent funds. General Electric's Project Thumper was terminated, freeing additional resources to sustain GAPA. However, a JCS review of the overall U.S. guided missile program concluded that there were too many short-range missiles being developed; it was determined that GAPA would be phased out entirely by 1951. As Richard F. McMullen has suggested: "In 1949 . . . a reshuffle of missions in the air defense field eliminated GAPA as a factor in air defense. The Joint Chiefs of Staff decided that the short range air defense missiles would thereafter fall within the purview of the Army, thereby preparing the way for what eventually emerged as the Nike antiaircraft missile."[59]

While GAPA was in its death throes, Nike was, comparatively speaking, thriving. Like GAPA, Nike had been somewhat set back by the 1946 missile R&D budget cut which had reduced overall missile funding from $29 million to $13 million, effectively eliminating 11 of the 28 active missile programs. Nike R&D funding fell from $5.2 million in 1946 to $3.0 million in 1947. But unlike GAPA, Nike recovered, enjoying annual increases in its R&D budget through 1952, when it reached a yearly high of $19.7 million.

Engineering progress was relatively steady in the Nike program. Having been given a 1-A priority by Army Ordnance in September 1946, the program generated a successful, 16-launch flight test series in 1948. By October 1949, the fragmentation warhead design had been accepted and frozen in OCM 33057.[60] Two months later, the ground portion of the missile tracking system was successfully tested. By March 1950, the experimental Nike had proved itself worthy of conversion to an operational weapons system, and Army Ordnance initiated the development of the Nike-1.

By this time, GAPA and the USAF were far behind in the race against Army's Nike. In addition to being concerned over an apparent loss of jurisdiction in the missile field, USAF was also worried that the cancellation of GAPA would lead to the dissolution of the dedicated missile R&D team which had been assembled at Boeing. In January 1950, USAF directed Boeing and the University of Michigan to conduct

---

[58] Semmens, BDM, *Chronology*.
[59] McMullen, p. 90.
[60] OCM 33057.

Chapter IV: American Systems

talks aimed at marrying the GAPA and Wizard technologies. The offspring of this shotgun wedding between GAPA and Wizard would be dubbed Bomarc.[61]

By June 1950, planning for the new missile had been completed.[62] It would not be a short-range missile like those thought by JCS to be in too great supply. Instead, its range would be eight times that of the Nike (200 nm vs. 25 nm). Its altitude capability would exceed Nike's by 33 percent (80,000 ft. vs. 60,000 ft.), and its maximum speed would be 3.0 mach, compared to Nike's 0.9 mach. Flight testing of the Bomarc was scheduled to begin in July 1951 and end in October 1954; IOC was expected in 1956.

While Bomarc was generally considered to be solely an antiaircraft system, Air University was to claim later that: ". . . the Bomarc was developed specifically for interception and destruction of enemy aircraft *and missiles* (emphasis added) before they approach target areas."[63] A USAF ADC Historical Study, however, suggested that Bomarc was "impotent" against Soviet ICBMs and that by October 1962, the Bomarc 1M-99B had only about a 50 percent chance of target interception against even aircraft.[64] Some confusion among laymen about Bomarc capabilities against ICBMs may have resulted from its interception tests against GAM-77 and Regulus Missiles; at any rate, Bomarc was not tested against ICBM target nosecones.[65]

It was in July 1950 that Nike-1's characteristics (summarized above) were officially reported to the three services. The system was described in these words: "Based on known capabilities or determined by analytical and experimental work, these objectives defined a defense weapon that would be effective not only against presently known designs of bomber aircraft but also against those predicted for . . . the near future."[66]

January 1951 was an important milestone for both the Bomarc and the Nike-1. USAF designated Boeing the prime contractor for the development of the missile whose characteristics had been defined in June 1950—i.e., the Bomarc. Also in January, K. T. Keller, the SECDEF's Director of Guided Missiles, told the Secretary that "immediate acceleration of production processes for Nike-1 (was) necessary in order to get the missile system out of R&D into the tactical weapon stage at the earliest practicable data."[67] The stated intent of this acceleration was to produce 1,000 missiles by the end of 1952, develop by the same date a production capacity of 1,000 missiles per month, and develop by the end of 1953 a capacity to produce ground support equipment for three battalions per month.

This acceleration of the Nike-1 program was echoed later in 1951, when USAF accelerated the development schedule of the Bomarc. By year's end, 12 test missiles had been produced by the Bomarc industrial team[68]:

(1) Boeing: airframe
(2) Aerojet: booster
(3) Marquadt: ramjet
(4) Westinghouse: target seeker
(5) DOFL: fuse
(6) Picatinny: warhead.

---

[61] McVeigh, *Development*.
[62] Ibid.
[63] Fundamentals of Aerospace Weapons Systems, p. 399.
[64] McMullen, "History of Air Defense Weapons 1946–1962," p. 350 & 366.
[65] Ibid., p. 348 & 353.
[66] BTL, Historical Summary of Nike.
[67] Keller, "Letter."
[68] Semmens, BDM, *Chronology*.

However, the original goal of commencing flight tests in July 1951 was not met. The first such test was conducted on September 10, 1952; like most of the tests which would follow, this first one was a failure.

Blame for the failure was laid on Aerojet, which had been unable to produce a satisfactory booster. In the spring of 1953, Reaction Motors was added to the Bomarc team as a hedge against further Aerojet failures. But by November 1953, Bomarc had amassed a considerable number of failures, and USAF decided to extend experimental work on the system for an additional year. Before the end of 1953, it was also decided that the Sage system being developed by Lincoln Laboratories would be used to control the Bomarc.[69]

In early 1954, WADC established a new schedule for the Bomarc development program, at the same time simplifying the program's objectives. Flight testing was to resume in May 1954, nearly three years after the original target data. Flight tests were to terminate in January 1956, with an IOC expected in 1959.[70] If the Bomarc had ever been in serious competition with the Nike, the competition ended with this acknowledgement that the system would not even be fully tested, much less deployed, during the first post war decade.

In contrast to the GAPA-Bomarc programs, the Nike had come a long way by 1955. In February 1951, the first Nike-1 production contract was let, with Redstone Arsenal responsible for overseeing production. Nine months later, in November 1951, Nike was first fired against an aerial target.

By the following spring, the Nike-1 program was advancing rapidly on several fronts. On March 11, 1952, the Ordnance Department initiated feasibility study of an alternate, nuclear warhead for Nike-1.[71] In April, the Department of the Army approved the allocation of 32 Nike battalions to 14 geographic areas. On April 10, the conventional Nike-1 warhead was tested and successfully destroyed a B-17 drone. On April 24, a complete Nike-1 system destroyed its target.

By July 1952, the program had advanced to the point of testing production-line missiles. The first such test was conducted on July 22—successfully. Seven months later, work began on the first Nike variant, Nike-B. On February 1, 1953, the project was undertaken by Westinghouse, with the prediction that the new system could be experimentally demonstrated in about three years. By October 1953, Nike-1 had reached the point of being fired by tactical units; and by the end of the year the first Nike Ajax was on site at Ft. Meade, Maryland.

The year 1954 was occupied with development of the Nike-B and refinement of the Nike-1. In September 1954, development of a cluster warhead for Nike-B was initiated. On October 1, a study was undertaken to examine the capabilities of the Nike-1 against low-altitude targets. On November 8, the SECDEF was informed of the conclusions of a most important study: the Nike-1 system could be modified to control the Nike-B without affecting the ability of the system to fire unmodified Nike-1 missiles. This conclusion virtually guaranteed a future for the Nike-B, a missile which would have probably faced severe difficulties if it had been deemed incompatible with the Nike-1 system. The year ended with the publication in OCM 35654 of the following developmental priorities:

(1) Nike-1
(2) Nike-B
(3) Improvement Program
(4) Solid propellant Nike.

---

[69] McVeigh, *Development*.
[70] Ibid.
[71] BTL, Historical Summary of Nike.

Chapter IV: American Systems

5. The Bureaucratic Struggle Over Missile Programs[72]

The McNarney letter set the stage for an intense struggle between AAF and ASF (later USAF and AGF) over control of air defense missile programs. On February 13, 1946, the Deputy Chief of Staff, USA, requested that major Army commands review the McNarney letter and recommend modifications to facilitate efficient performance. Despite the fact that his command had fared well in McNarney's allocation of responsibilities, the commander of AGF responded with a recommendation that the issue be reopened and new directives be prepared. This is not to say that AGF was prepared to yield any ground. On the contrary, what AGF sought (among other things) was complete operational control over surface-to-air, surface-to-surface, and sea-coast-defense missiles.

It was in fact this matter of operational control which would become central to the bureaucratic struggle. The USAF, for a variety of reasons, would eventually concede on the issue of RED jurisdiction. But for the duration of the first post war decade the battle would rage over operational control of air defense weaponry, especially surface-to-air missiles.

The battle over operational control was joined on the issue of AAA forces. In May 1946, the AAF achieved a victory in the form of a War Department circular (WDC 138) which assigned AAF ADC responsibility for the air defense of the CONUS. AAF was designated to control and train those AAA units assigned to it, and it was left to AAF to recommend to the War Department just how many such units should be assigned.[73] At a June meeting of the Air Board, it was decided to propose complete integration of antiaircraft artillery into the AAF.

Later that same month, AGF proposed a somewhat self-serving compromise: AGF should be responsible for air defense within the area covered by ground weapons; AAF's mission should be the defense of those areas which AGF's weapons couldn't reach. This would, of course, mean AGF control over guided antiaircraft missiles as well as AAA.

AGF advanced this same argument in an August 26 letter to the Army Chief of Staff.[74] The letter noted that missile programs were sufficiently advanced to warrant a decision on operational control and that AGF was the logical recipient of that control.

On September 18, the War Department (WD) took a middle position in the debate. It agreed with AAF's argument that air defense must be unified, but claimed uncertainty on the future role of *missiles* in air defense, thereby encouraging a continuation of the AAF-AGF struggle over control of the most glamorous weapons in the air defense arsenal. WD did underwrite the integration of AAA units into AAF's ADC, but left AGF responsible for the technical training of these units.

AGF suffered a dramatic setback on October 7, 1946, when the Army Chief of Staff rescinded the McNarney letter and bestowed upon AAF responsibility for "R&D activities pertaining to GM (guided missiles) and associated items of equipment." Eight days later, AGF responded with a request for authority at least to establish the characteristics of those missiles which AGF would ultimately control. AGF further requested a determination on the issue of operational control of guided missiles.

---

[72] Discussions of the bureaucratic struggle as it occurred in the context of ABM decision making may be found in this chapter, section D. See also the related material in this chapter, section G.
[73] WD, *WDC 138*.
[74] Commanding General, Army Ground Forces, Letter to Chief of Staff.

Early in 1947, AGF conducted its own study on policies regarding control of ground-launched missiles. The study concluded that AGF should control all such missiles. But later in 1947, the National Security Act and the JCS extensions thereto affirmed that the USAF would be responsible for "defense of the CONUS against air attack." At this point in the struggle, the eventual outcome was already apparent: USAF would not gain control of all missile RED budgets, but would instead be the executive agency over all air defense operations. AGF would retain possession of systems such as the Nike, but their operation would be ultimately commanded by a USAF lieutenant general. When the National Security Act became law, it specifically stated that "missiles designed for employment in support of Army tactical operations" would be assigned to the Army, but that missiles designed for employment in "area air defense" would belong the USAF.

Though the outcome of the struggle had been predictable in 1947, the battle for control of the SAMs (as well as AAA) raged on into 1948. In preparation for the March 1948 Key West Conference, USAF directed its own Air Defense Policy Panel to develop an AF position on air defense doctrine. Predictably, the Panel recommended, among other things, that AAA be integrated into the Air Force.[75]

But USAF's grab for complete *ownership* of AAA assets was in vain. At the March 11–14 Key West Conference, the Secretary of Defense insisted that the Army "organize, train and equip AAA units and provide them 'as required' for air defense." (JCS was directed to work out the necessary joint doctrine and procedures—a task which JCS would prove incapable of meeting.) However, USAF's claim to *operational* control of all air defense forces was substantiated by an April 21 SECDEF order which assigned "primary responsibility for air defense of CONUS to USAF . . . Army to provide forces 'as required.'"[76]

On March 16, two days after the close of the Key West Conference, the Army renewed its fight for operational control of SAMs. In a letter to the Organization and Training Division of the U.S. Army Staff, AFF recommended that existing agreements "be reworded to indicate that USAF has a primary interest in . . . air-launched guided missiles and the Army in ground launched guided missiles."[77] The Committee on Guided Missiles of the Research and Development Board allied itself with AFF by recommending on June 9 that "surface-to-air missiles be the responsibility of Army Ordnance." AFF advanced the same argument again on March 24, 1949, and on May 16, the secretary of the Army recommended to the SECDEF that Army be given R&D responsibility for all land-launched missiles, Air Force to retain only air-launched systems. This, in effect, was a request that the 7 October 1945 WD Memorandum, which had granted the AAF responsibility for ground-launched systems, be overturned.

On November 17, 1949, JCS rendered its "decision" on the SAM control issue: "It is impracticable at this time to assign the several services, in accordance with their assigned functions, responsibility for the entire guided missile field. As a general rule, guided missiles will be employed by the services in the manner and to the extent required to accomplish their assigned functions."[78] However, some encouragement was given to the Army by the attendant JCS decision that guided missiles which supplanted AAA would, indeed, be assigned to the Army.

---

[75] Semmens, BDM, *Chronology*.
[76] Ibid.
[77] U.S. Army Field Forces, Commanding General, "Letter to Director, Organization and Training Division, U.S. Army Staff," 16 March 1948.
[78] Semmens, BDM, *Chronology*.

Chapter IV: American Systems

By the summer of 1950, accord was near in the struggle for control of AAA forces. On July 11 it was officially stated that ARAACOM would assume command of all AAA units allocated to air defense. On August 1, Generals Lawton and Vandenberg, Chiefs of Staff of the Army and Air Force, agreed upon a nested command structure which conceded AAA command to Army, but attached these AAA commanders to various echelons of the USAF command structure. In each case the appropriate USAF division commander would exercise operational control of AAA "insofar as engagement and disengagement of fire is concerned." This structure having been established, ARAACOM was given responsibility on December 1, 1950, for planning all AAA defenses within the CONUS.

In April 1952, this nested command structure was refined in ADC and ARAACOM's "Mutual Agreement for the Air Defense of the United States." As previously agreed, deployed AAA units would be operationally controlled by USAF commanders, with control being exercised through local Army AAA commanders. A further refinement in June did away with separate AAA staff sections in ADC and established a process of coordination between the counterpart staff elements of collocated headquarters.

Later that same month, on June 20, Undersecretary of the Army Karl Bendetsen reinvigorated the Army-Air Force squabble over control of guided missiles. Surveying the events of the previous few years, Bendetsen concluded that the Air Force was attempting to usurp "Army's responsibility in the guided missile field." He urged that Army take on all responsibility—research test, procurement, and operation—for ground-launched missiles, regardless of range.

By 1954, however, USAF's hold on U.S. air defense assets was firmly established. In January, the JCS agreed to establish a joint command for air defense of the CONUS. In August, Continental Air Defense Command (CONAD) was instituted as a joint command under the JCS. CONAD was charged with coordinating and integrating the air defense capabilities of the three services under the control of a single commander. USAF, of course, was designated the executive agency.

D. History of Antiballistic Missiles

1. The Technological Problems

The history of U.S. efforts directed toward ballistic missile defense in the 1945–1955 period can best be characterized as a series of ongoing studies and established requirements. Although these efforts were not necessarily lackluster, neither did they fall within the limelight of research or policy attention. This was primarily due to the more immediate and pressing problems of development such as the need for improved air breathing threat defense systems. And while the guiding idea of many studies during this period was an eventual solution for the "hitting a bullet with a bullet" problem, the actual solution must be dated much later: it was not until 3 June 1960 that one U.S. guided missile intercepted another (a Nike Hercules destroyed a Corporal)[79] and not until 14 December 1961 that a Nike Zeus intercepted a Nike Hercules.[80] Even these interceptions were rudimentary in concept; it took until 19 July 1962 before a Nike Zeus actually successfully intercepted an ICBM target nosecone, and then under test conditions which some considered to be unrealistic.[81]

---

[79] Semmens, BDM, *Chronology*.
[80] Ibid.
[81] Ibid. For date only.

Beyond the missile interception problem was the lack of solution during the 1945–1955 period to a series of infinitely more complex and related problems of then-unknown dimensions: the effects of decoys, penetration aids, multiple reentry vehicles, saturation, blackout, and "soft" system components on a viable ballistic missile defense (BMD) system. To varying degrees, these problems were to plague U.S. BMD efforts throughout the 1960's; the longevity of these difficulties suggests the overwhelming task which faced pioneer researchers in the field.

In tracing the significant BMD study efforts conducted and requirements established before 1956, it is therefore obvious that the full multidimensionality of the BMD problem was not clear at that time. Hence the history itself does not address all aspects of the defense problem as it was to develop. The trail of these early research activities is also fraught with dead ends which failed to pan out developmentally upon further examination. For example, the familiar Project HAWK was initiated in December 1950 under a Research and Development Board guidance objective stating (among other things) a requirement for a SAM with the capability to destroy incoming guided missiles of specified speed and altitude characteristics.[82] By 15 March 1951, however, the Army contract awarded to Fairchild Aircraft Corporation for the HAWK study had limited the desired missile to an antiaircraft capability, a specification which is better known to most students of air defense.[83] Other study efforts during those years show similar changes in emphasis; as a consequence the history detailed here does not attempt to enumerate all such marginally informative cases but rather addresses decisions and projects in the mainstream of activities.

2. World War II Experience

Navy, Air Force (then AAF), and Army activities in BMD can be traced to the World War II years and the establishment of service guided missile and missile defense programs. The German V-2 missile was a threat faced by our European Allies, and was to motivate U.S. antimissile study efforts; the Japanese Kamikaze threat led to creation of the Navy KAN-1 (Little Joe) guided surface to air missile.[84] Even more specific on antimissile efforts, from the Navy standpoint, was a July 1944 Navy Bureau of Ordnance directive requesting an analysis and evaluation of task force protection against guided missiles launched from enemy aircraft.[85] By December 1944, the Chief of Naval Operations had directed that such a development project be undertaken under the code name Bumblebee; it was conducted at the Johns Hopkins Applied Physics Laboratory.[86]

From the Bumblebee research grew a family of surface-to-air missiles—the May Bee (later Terrier), Must Bee (later TalosX), and the Tartar. Of these three missiles, the much larger Talos with its range in excess of 100 nautical miles and altitude of 80,000 feet was to emerge in 1959 as the Navy's ABM alternative to the Army Zeus.[87]

3. Post War Developments

The earliest major air force effort in the SAM field which was to lead into their ABM development efforts was the GAPA (ground-to-air pilotless aircraft) project, active from 1945 to 1949.[88] This effort was

---

[82] DA Pam. 70-10, p. 202.
[83] Ibid., p. 203.
[84] *Air Defense: An Historical Analysis*, Vol. III, p. 37.
[85] Ibid., p. 48.
[86] Ibid., p. 48 for date. Adams, p. 18 for location of research.
[87] Ibid., p. 49 on range of Talos. Adams, p. 18 for location of research.
[88] Ibid., p. 50.

Chapter IV: American Systems

pure research directed at developing a family of missiles much as the Navy Bumblebee research was to concurrently develop—but in the case of the air force, over 100 experimental missiles of different configurations were eventually fired.[89]

At about the same time that GAPA was being initiated, the Army ground force and air force efforts in these early years were prodded by the McNarney letter (discussed in greater detail in Chapter 1 and in this chapter, section C), issued as an Army directive 2 October 1944. In January 1947, however, this division of responsibilities changed significantly—the War Department allocated all research and development responsibilities for guided missiles to the Army Air Force.[90] As indicated in the GAPA discussion (section C, this chapter), this allocation of responsibilities was to be effected yet again in 1949.

The antimissile study efforts resulting from these assignments of responsibilities in the guided missile field were to be developed concurrently by the separate services in consonance with service desires for a continued role in the field; the assignment of roles and missions was part and parcel of the actual research efforts.

Of greater importance than the GAPA developments were the Thumper and Wizard projects initiated in March and April 1946, respectively.[91] Thumper was an Army Air Force Project awarded by contract to GE for the study of interceptor weapons for BMD, and was the first program of its kind.[92] Thumper was to develop the "... 'collision intercept' method for destroying a ballistic missile..." and was later functionally merged with the similar Wizard program.[93] Wizard, too, was an Army Air Force contracted study, awarded to the University of Michigan's Aeronautical Research Center to investigate the possibility of developing a supersonic missile capable of reaching 500,000 feet altitude.[94]

Specifically, the study was an engineering project to determine the design for a missile capable of intercepting and destroying a V-2 surface-to-surface missile, although advanced missile threats were also to be encompassed. Operating at speeds of 4,000 to 5,000 MPH, Wizard was to have a 50 percent kill probability against a V-2.[95]

The general missile which Army Air Force planners envisioned as developing from both the Thumper and Wizard studies was to be 60 feet long and 6 feet in diameter, with a range of 550 miles.[96] The desired long range of this missile placed it far in the future in terms of development. By the spring of 1947, it was estimated that it would be five to ten years "before the necessary long-range ground radar, long-range and highly accurate guidance systems and long-range radar seekers could be developed for the test support of any antimissile missile devised by General Electric or the University of Michigan."[97]

The slowly evolving and futuristic nature of these projects, combined with the previously mentioned funding crisis of 1947, relegated Wizard and Thumper to less attention—by the summer of 1947 they were individually reduced to a long-term study basis, with General Electric to receive $500,000 a year and the

---

[89] Ibid., p. 50. GAPA and related programs are discussed in section C of this chapter.
[90] Barnard, p. 25.
[91] Semmens, BDM, *Chronology*.
[92] Ibid.
[93] Adams, p. 18.
[94] Semmens, BDM, *Chronology*.
[95] Air Defense: An Historical Analysis, Vol. III, p. 50.
[96] McMullen, "History of Air Defense Weapons, 1946–1962," p. 48.
[97] McMullen, op. cit., p. 49.

University of Michigan $1,000,000 a year for this purpose.[98] This situation continued until 1949, when the Thumper contract was allowed to lapse on 30 June since it in many ways duplicated the Wizard efforts.[99]

Parenthetically, Wizard developmental work was to continue beyond 1955; by the 1958–1959 period, however, the Air Force had concluded that the proposed Wizard system, advocated as an alternative to Nike Zeus, was indeed not cost effective.[100]

The Navy Bumblebee and Air Force Wizard studies paralleled an Army program which was to serve as the actual mainstay of U.S. BMD efforts in the post-1955 years. This comment is retrospective because in the 1945–1955 period, there was not and could not, because of the rudimentary state of research, be any clear choice among nascent BMD system concepts. The fact that the Army Nike Zeus program, not the Navy Talos or Air Force Wizard programs, was to evolve into the Nike X, and then the Sentinel and Safeguard BMD systems adds weight to the predisposition to treat Zeus more thoroughly than these other programs. Zeus, and its associated Plato System, also serves to demonstrate the role which BMD studies played in these early years of considering possible air defense against missiles—it was not until February 1955 that the Army concluded that the state of missile technology had advanced enough to warrant initiation of an economic and technical feasibility study for an anti-ICBM missile.[101] But Nike Zeus had its study antecedents long before that time.

The efforts can be traced generally to guided missile development programs initiated during World War II. Project ORDCIT (Ordnance–California Institute of Technology) was initiated in May 1944 to conduct development work on long-range missiles, ramjets, and associated launch equipment.[102] Along with ORDCIT went an appreciation for the long-term, potential threat posed by the German V-1 and V-2 rockets; the Army project Hermes, contracted with General Electric in November 1944, investigated characteristics of the V-2.[103]

By 8 February 1945 project Nike had been initiated, but was not initially concerned with BMD—the Bell Telephone Laboratories were tasked in this program to investigate the possibilities of an antiaircraft defense with characteristics superior to contemporary conventional artillery.[104] In late March of that year, the Army Assistant Chief of Staff, G-3, assigned roles to the Ground and Air Forces for establishing military characteristics and employment doctrine for surface-to-air missiles.[105] The roles were split depending on whether the missile was to complement AAA or fighter interceptors. On 20 June the Army Ground Forces Equipment Review (Cook) Board submitted its report on equipment for the post war Army, and included the following task: "High velocity guided missiles . . . capable of . . . destroying missiles of the V-2 type, should be developed at the earliest practicable date."[106] While the Cook Board task was a restatement of a need realized earlier (and was itself to be restated that August by Subcommittee No. 4 of the Guided Missiles Committee)[107] it was followed rapidly by the initiation of related study efforts—in July the Signal Corps established two basic research radar

---

[98] McMullen, op. cit., p. 49.
[99] McMullen, op. cit., p. 90.
[100] The date selected depends on which event is emphasized: the 16 Jan. 1958 Sec. Def. McElroy allocation of ABM development responsibility to the Army (Adams, p. 27) or the early 1959 USAF position on Wizard cost-effectiveness (Adams, p. 33).
[101] DA Pam. 70-10, p. 181.
[102] Ibid., p. 4.
[103] Ibid., p. 7.
[104] Ibid., p. 8.
[105] Ibid., p. 8.
[106] Ibid., p. 10.
[107] Ibid., p. 10 (refers to date in parentheses).

Chapter IV: American Systems

projects suitable for use in an antimissile defense system.[108] By this time work had also begun on the White Sands Proving Grounds, where it was to be continued through the fall assembling captured V-2 components and (at nearby Fort Bliss) German scientists recruited in project Paper Clip.[109]

At about this period of time, research developments, role designations, and related events began at a rapid pace. Juxtaposing all of these happenings together leaves a cloudy picture of which information was, or was not, significant for later occurrences. It therefore becomes much easier to trace separate but related "tracks" of activities individually through to 1955 rather than to consider all together in a year-by-year progression. Three such tracks have been chosen and will be discussed sequentially:

(1) The assignment of guided missile responsibilities to Army Ground and Air Forces, and later to the Army and USAF
(2) Statements of antimissile missile requirements
(3) Studies and operational tests conducted on systems related to Nike-Zeus and Plato

Two caveats must be added before the first track can be addressed. First, the popular name "Zeus" was not actually assigned to Nike II until 15 November 1956, so the history of the pre-1956 years cannot trace Nike-Zeus per se—only those activities which were related to Nike II. The same general observation applies to Plato, which significantly evolved in 1952. Secondly, the historical discussion must of necessity limit itself to events closely related to the selected tracks. It is clear, for example, that the assignment of guided missile RED roles to the military services is only part of a much larger picture involving decisions about offensive versus defensive U.S. strategies, budgetary considerations, and overall service roles and missions. This larger picture is covered in other portions of the study.

The McNarney letter of 2 October 1944, which allocated R&D responsibilities in the guided missile field to the military services (see earlier detailed description), was to serve as the guiding document on such roles for a short period of time. Although there was discussion within the War Department in February 1946 regarding possible changes to the McNarney allocations, nothing concrete resulted.[110] By late March the Joint Chiefs of Staff had directed the Joint Committee on New Weapons and Equipment to submit recommendations on the allocation of these responsibilities.[111] During August there were some reports of friction between the Army Air Forces and the Army Ordnance Department regarding these responsibilities, and the Commanding General of Army Ground Forces recommended to the Chief of Staff that the responsibility for any ground launched missile should be held by AGF.[112] On 7 October 1946, however, the Army Chief of Staff rescinded the McNarney directive, giving the Commanding General of Army Air Forces R&D responsibility for guided missiles.[113] This was not the end of the argument—in mid-October, Army Ground Forces requested the Chief of Staff to be given authority to establish military characteristics for missiles they would use.[114] By mid-January 1947, an AGF study recommended that they be given responsibility for operational employment of all ground launched missiles.[115]

---

[108] Ibid., p. 10.
[109] Ibid., p. 11.
[110] Ibid., p. 12.
[111] Ibid., p. 13.
[112] Ibid., p. 15.
[113] Ibid., p. 15.
[114] Ibid., p. 15.
[115] Ibid., p. 16.

Similar recommendations and apparent differences of opinion were to occur both before and after the National Security Act of 1947 became law on 15 September 1947.[116] The Act commented on the assignment of surface to-air missiles to the newly established services: "Security missiles designed for employment in support of Army tactical operations will be assigned to the United States Army . . . Missiles designed for employment in area air defense will be assigned to the United States Air Force."[117] Although on 20 March 1948 R&D responsibilities for guided missiles to be used by Department of the Army were transferred to it by USAF, a larger question was looming on the horizon—the assignment of single or split service responsibility for *all* guided missile activities.[118]

Three milestones regarding this problem were to occur between then and the end of 1955. The first was on 17 November 1949 when, in JCS 1620/12, the Joint Chiefs unanimously reached the conclusion that: "it is impracticable at this time to assign to the several services, in accordance with their assigned functions, responsibility for the entire guided missile field. As a general rule, guided missiles will be employed by the services in the manner and to the extent required to accomplish their assigned functions."[119]

Between that date and the fall of 1953, this statement (and its additional comments about guided missile types "normally" to be employed by each of the services, effecting the earlier discussed GAPA), stood as the only basic paper on the problem on which agreement had been reached by the three service chiefs.[120] Four other related and split JCS papers in the interim were never acted upon.[121] The second milestone occurred in mid-November 1953 when the Secretary of Defense reaffirmed the existing division of guided missile responsibilities—the Secretaries of the service Departments were authorized to approve the missile programs of their respective departments, and such approval was recognized as sufficient authority for subsequent fund obligation and program implementation.[122] Although this authorization did not address the division of interservice responsibilities, it did reflect official realization from the highest level of an already operating reality. The third milestone was to significantly alter the missile responsibility assignments made in JCS 1620/12. It did so in JCS 1620/95 on 9 September 1954, when responsibilities were divided thus:

> The U.S. Army will develop, procure, and employ such surface-to-air guided missiles . . . designed for effectiveness against enemy aircraft and missiles out to a range of approximately 50 nautical miles. b. The U.S. Navy will develop, procure, and employ such surface-to-air guided missiles as are required by its assigned functions. c. The U.S. Air Force will develop, procure, and employ such surface-to-air guided missiles . . . [for] continental defense . . . of greater than 50 nautical miles horizontal range.[123]

Throughout the period, we thus see a slowly changing but eventually more distinct picture in the division of SAM responsibilities between the Services. However, JCS 1620/95 was not the end of controversy—the story continues in the post-1955 years where it will be discussed again.

The second major track to be elaborated upon encompasses the series of established requirements and statements of need for antimissile missiles. The first part of this story has already been mentioned in conjunction with World War II threats, and left the sequence of events during the fall of 1945. It continued

---

[116] Ibid., p. 17 for date only.
[117] Ibid., p. 17; this is not a direct quote from the Act, however.
[118] Ibid., p. 18; also see pp. 19–21.
[119] Ibid., p. 23.
[120] Ibid., p. 33.
[121] Ibid., p. 33.
[122] Ibid., p. 34.
[123] Ibid., p. 37.

Chapter IV: American Systems

in early January 1946 when the Commanding General, Army Ground Forces, both raised the problem of defense against the V-2 and established a requirement for a study program on the issue.[124] In early February, the Joint Committee on New Weapons and Equipment restated this antimissile need in its report on a Proposed National Program for Guided Missiles.[125] By 1 April Secretary of War Patterson had concurred on implementation of a national guided missile program; at the end of May the Stilwell Board established a requirement for a guided missile with a 100,000 yard range capable of intercepting missiles of the V-2 type.[126] Although the need for an antimissile missile was thus seen quite early in these years, it was not until January 1949 that the Army established a formal requirement for a SAM system to combat ballistic missiles.[127] It seems likely that the lack of practical results in the guided missile program contributed to the lack of a formal BMD requirement in earlier years; the program, in fact, was moving along quite slowly.[128]

Things were to continue in this same vein—in an 8 February 1950 memo to the Secretary of Defense: "The Secretary of the Army emphasized that as of that time there was no guided missile or other device in sight for protection against enemy supersonic guided missiles. That gap, he stated, existed because of the extreme technical difficulty in meeting or overtaking a missile traveling at supersonic speed."[129]

By mid-August of that year, a practical program looked even further away. At that time, Army Field Forces Board No. 4 commented on the absence of any Department of Army project to fulfill the antimissile missile requirement. The associated Signal Corps radar projects were considered not very active, and the board recommended that further antimissile missile studies be postponed until radar developments showed more promise.[130]

The seeds of Plato were sewn on 20 October 1952 when an Army G-4 conference designated the need for a theatre of operations antimissile system, which was the guiding idea of Plato.[131] Although studies were conducted on this idea and the overall need for a BMD system was restated by the Army Field Forces in late 1954, it was not until mid-1955 that this area of requirements was again viewed with deep criticality. This new found impetus was a direct result of an early 1955 Bell Telephone Laboratory Study, discussed as part of the third track.[132]

Overall through this time period, the desire for a ballistic missile defense system was thus stated and restated. The central reason for the lack of specificity in this perceived need was the rudimentary state of technology—the state of the art had not yet caught up to something which looked like a good idea.

The third track encompasses the studies actually conducted during these years on Army antimissile systems, and lacks clarity to the same degree that the second track does. The Nike program and Signal Corps radar projects have already been mentioned, and comprised the bulk of pre-1950 activities, along with general guided missile efforts. The Signal Corps projects were funded at $500,000 for FY's 1950, 1951, and 1952, but progress was slow because much basic research remained to be done.[133] On 18 December

---

[124] Ibid., p. 11.
[125] Ibid., p. 11.
[126] Ibid., p. 14.
[127] Ibid., p. 21.
[128] Ibid., p. 18 on the lack of practical results as reflected in Secretary of the Army Kenneth Royall's 17 April 1948 expression of concern for the same.
[129] Ibid., p. 23.
[130] Ibid., p. 25.
[131] Ibid., pp. 31, 37.
[132] Ibid., p. 37 on AFF requirement.
[133] Ibid., pp. 24–25.

1950 the JCS approved the Army's initiation of an antimissile project.[134] At the behest of the Secretary of the Army, Army Field Forces studied a preliminary report on Bomarc to assess its possible fulfillment of the recently established Army antimissile missile requirement.[135] On 18 October 1951, however, this study indicated that Bomarc would only partially fulfill the requirement.[136] By mid-September 1952 a contract had been awarded to Aerophysics Development Corporation for a feasibility study on ballistic missile defense. The content of their report, completed 15 May 1953, is instructive as to the level of development operant at the time: "The study defined the threats and critical problem areas and recommended research concentrated on the radar problem and the conduct of preliminary design efforts."[137]

Several similar studies aimed at determining feasibility were conducted during these years, and included (with starting dates): November 1952, Signal Corps—antimissile radar study; June 1953 Bendix Aircraft Corporation missile acquisition radar study (concluded in 1955 that the radar was feasible); September 1953 Sylvania Study (Plato) on antimissile missile feasibility; 25 May 1954 Cornell Aeronautical Laboratory study (Plato) on the previous Sylvania topic.[138]

Ongoing research conducted under these studies contributed to the Army decision in February 1955 to conduct an economic and technical feasibility study for a system to combat the ICBM.[139] The Bell Telephone Laboratories conducted this study beginning in March, with emphasis on the replacement of Nike I (Ajax) and Nike B (Hercules) in about 1965.[140] In May, a special Plato evaluation committee concluded that BMD was technically feasible; Plato study efforts were to continue through the end of the year with major efforts by Sylvania, Cornell Aeronautical Laboratories, and Pennsylvania State University.[141] By late fall 1955, the feasibility of the Plato theatre of operations system (using the Nike II—later Zeus—missile) and of the Nike II anti-ICBM concept were clear—at least to the Army.[142] In early December, based on this assessment, the Army requested $7.7 million in supplemental FY 1956 funds for the antimissile missile program.[143] It also called for a Department of Defense assignment of service responsibility for the area.[144]

The year thus ended on a positive note from the Army standpoint; that continued development was also favored by DOD would become clear in January 1956 when FY 1956 funds previously withheld were released for antimissile missile developmental work.[145]

E. History of Jet Interceptors

1. Background

The period from 1944 to mid-1948 constitutes a unity in respect to strategic planning and approaches to weapons development. However, owing to the considerable time lag between the appearance of new perceptions and approaches and their ultimate realization in concrete form, many consequences of devel-

---

[134] Ibid., p. 26.
[135] Ibid., p. 28.
[136] Ibid., p. 28.
[137] Ibid., p. 191.
[138] Ibid., pp. 191–192.
[139] Ibid., p. 181.
[140] Ibid., p. 181.
[141] Ibid., p. 192.
[142] Ibid., p. 42; see 5 December 1955 Director of R&D comments.
[143] Ibid., p. 42.
[144] Ibid., p. 42.
[145] Ibid., p. 182.

Chapter IV: American Systems

opments in 1944–1948 were still of major importance as late as 1953 or 1944; they will be traced in this section rather than in the rest, which treats the new developments of the period 1948–1955.

As the last year of World War II began, the military power of the United States had reached a tremendous level, both qualitatively and quantitatively; but military planners were already considering the implications of new technologies that promised to make the weapons and strategic concepts of the war obsolete. The first intercontinental bomber, the B-36, was under construction; both the Germans and the Americans had operational jet aircraft (the Me-262 and the P-80); German rockets were already in use as military weapons; and development of the atomic bomb, whose strategic implications transcended all foresight, was entering its final stages.

If the implications of these new developments were already partially apparent, the identification of a potential enemy whose military threat would require an urgent effort to build an extensive air defense had not yet been clearly made. It was mid-1945 before a new hostility and aggressiveness on the part of the Soviet Union began to manifest itself, and some years later that the military threat of this nation, with technological capabilities that were initially rated low by most Western observers, with an industry that had been severely damaged during the war and no wartime experience of strategic bombing, took shape as a long-range bomber fleet armed with atomic weapons. By the time the Soviet military threat attained these dimensions, the United States was in the process of developing an interceptor capability to confront it. An understanding of the nature of this development procedure, and a clarification of what forces, under immediate post war circumstances, drove or hindered it and to what extent the resultant weapons were commensurate with the Soviet threat, are of major importance to an understanding of the strategic arms race.

In 1944, the B-29 could well be considered to represent the most advanced bomber capability of the time. It was the fastest, longest-range bomber in the world, and its combat ceiling of more than 30,000 feet put it beyond the effective reach of almost any fighter plane in existence—a fact which made possible, for instance, the unescorted bombing of Japanese targets in 1944–1945. Beginning in 1944, the Army conducted tests in which the interception of B-29's flying at 30,000 feet was attempted with the new P-80 jet fighters. Although the service ceiling of the P-80 was well above that of the B-29, it had insufficient maneuverability at that altitude to make a successful interception. Although the tests established the fact that bomber capabilities were at the moment superior to fighter capabilities (a situation that had appeared and been reversed in the past), and undoubtedly gave some impetus to fighter development, the fact that the Soviets possessed no long-range bombers of their own manufacture in 1945 robbed the circumstance of much of its urgency.

A number of different propeller-driven aircraft types were assigned air defense roles in 1945–1946. Foremost among these was the P-47, a day-fighter with an excellent wartime record, which was phased out of active air defense service during 1947 but was used by the Air National Guard until early 1953. Another superb day-fighter, the P-51, was assigned to SAC for air defense. The twin-fuselage P-61, which had been used only sparingly during the war, was the primary night-fighter used for air defense until 1949, but with a combat ceiling of well under 30,000 feet it would have been of little use against a bomber such as the B-29. In January 1944, the development of the P-82, a double P-51, was begun, with an interceptor role envisioned. This aircraft, which became operational in 1949, proved unsatisfactory and was quickly phased out after limited procurement.

2. The Shift to Jet Interceptors

Although several jet aircraft were already being successfully flown (P-80) or were contracted for development (P-84, P-86) when the war came to an end, none of them was planned as an interceptor. The first decision to produce a jet interceptor came in late 1945 and resulted in the F-89. The process of making this decision seems to have been a complex one: the initial AAF design request, made in August 1945, was for a propeller-driven plane, but by November the idea of a jet design had been accepted. This jet aircraft was to be a successor to the P-61, but was to be effective in daylight as well as at night or in inclement weather. The day-fighter requirement was dropped in 1946 on the grounds that a heavy radar-equipped all-weather fighter would be no match for a small day-fighter.[146]

Because the F-89 was both the first and the only truly new interceptor design for which a prototype was contracted in the period 1944–1948, its origins merit consideration in some detail. The original August 1945 specifications for the propeller-driven plane call for a considerable increase in speed and rate of climb over the conventional planes than available or under development,[147] leading to the question why a jet aircraft was not originally specified. The cause was surely not a lack of appreciation of jet technology, and it is improbable that budgetary constraints were a major factor, in view of the relatively low cost of aircraft development: the initial development contract was for only $4 million, a very small amount compared with the $48 million spent on procurement of 48 production models of the F-89A in 1949.[148] In view of the large number of serious difficulties that beset the F-89 program between its inception and the end of 1952, it seems a reasonable supposition that planners felt the development of a propeller-driven model would offer a relatively quick and reliable development process, in which the problems encountered in developing all-weather electronics would not be compounded by the necessity of matching them to new and advanced airframe and engine designs with their own highly unpredictable problems.

When six manufacturers submitted design proposals in March 1946, most of the designs were for jet-powered planes, but a few were for conventional planes[149]; the fact suggests that the AAF had not changed to a hard-and-fast specification of a jet design, but had decided to admit that alternative as a result of initiatives from some of the manufacturers, since the characteristics originally specified would have been much easier to achieve with jet power.

Although the results of the interceptor tests with the B-29 were well known to Gen. LeMay, the Deputy Chief of Staff for Research and Development, who had planned the bombing missions over Japan in preparation for which they were conducted, the characteristics that were specified for the new plane at least partially under his authority were inferior to those of the P-80, which had been unsuccessful in the tests. It appears that a strong imperative to match the best U.S. offensive weapons with comparable defensive weapons was not yet felt in AAF aviation planning circles, although it was not long before the practice gained currency and urgency.

Flight tests on the XF-89 began in August 1948, and by October it had proved superior to other models being tested (the XF-87 and the Navy XF-30). Although the plane was viewed by some as the "best of a bad lot," the decision to procure it was made, and in May 1949 a contract for 48 F-89A's was signed.[150]

---

[146] Grant, p. 47; Semmens, BDM, *Chronology*, 28 August 1946.
[147] OSD, *Chronology*, p. 9.
[148] Ibid., pp. 31, 87.
[149] Ibid., p. 25.
[150] Ibid., p. 87.

Chapter IV: American Systems

The appearance in October 1947 of 48 Tu-4 bombers, copies of the B-29, during the celebration of the Russian Revolution,[151] was an event which served to focus and intensify U.S. perceptions of the Soviet air threat. The successful production of the Tu-4 meant that the Soviets now had a long-range bomber capability; in addition, it suggested that Soviet technological and industrial capabilities were greater than had been supposed, and that other unpleasant surprises might be in store. On the other hand, we know (with the benefit of hindsight) that the threat was a limited one. The Tu-4, like the B-29, was not an intercontinental bomber; with midair refueling it could possibly strike parts of the U.S. over the North Pole, but only on a one-way mission. Only a limited number of planes, however, was available at first and the usual malfunction problems, along with the necessity of using some of the planes for refueling, would reduce the number available for bombing considerably. Even more important, the Soviets did not yet have the atomic bomb. Clearly, the threat was not great; but reliable intelligence about Soviet capabilities was extremely scarce; the U.S. had no interceptor that was a match for the Tu-4; and it was not the job of U.S. military planners, especially those in SAC and ADC, to underestimate the threat of Soviet bomber capabilities.

The implications of this event in U.S. strategic thinking and weapons planning belong to the following section of this chapter, but the interim measures that were undertaken before new ideas and plans could be implemented belong to the present discussion. It was clear that more energetic pursuit of air defense was necessary, and one of the first steps that was taken was the transfer of jet F-84's, which had begun to be available in June 1947, to Air Defense Command. By 31 March 1948, ADC had 79 of them on hand, compared with 57 in the possession of the Tactical Air Command. The merger of ADC and TAC into the Continental Air Command (ConAC) in December 1948 made a total of 309 of the planes potentially available for air defense.[152]

The initial transfer of F-84's to ADC is especially striking in view of the fact that they were designed as fighter-bombers and would normally have been assigned chiefly to TAC. As interceptors, they were not very satisfactory: their speed and ceiling gave them only limited effectiveness against a B-29 or similar plane, and structural defects were a continuing problem.[153] Moreover, they were usable only as day-fighters; the night-fighter role was assigned to the conventional P-61, and briefly to the P-82, until new night and all-weather fighters became available beginning in late 1949.

The F-80 was somewhat more satisfactory as an interceptor, although it too was only a day-fighter, designed for a tactical role. Before the formation of ConAC, ADC had only 2 F-80's, but a total of 186 became available in ConAC, and 9 fighter-interceptor squadrons of F-80's had been assigned as of December 1948.[154] Notwithstanding the addition of the F-84 and the F-80 to the air defense force, the interceptor situation, particularly in bad weather, and against B-29 capabilities, was far from satisfactory. The Northwest maneuver in May 1948 produced the following results:

> The limitations of the defensive fighters in adverse weather conditions were emphasized during the maneuver. The P-61 fighter is of no practical value. Its speed and altitude limitations make it ineffective against today's bombers. . . . The P-80's were not equipped to penetrate an overcast. Replacement of instruments to relieve this limitation is in progress. The ground controller could not pick up, track and direct a P-80 with success. . . . The operation of the P-51's was hindered by adverse weather in the mountainous terrain.[155]

---

[151] Semmens, under date.
[152] *USAF Statistical Digest*, 1948, pp. 22, 29.
[153] See note 11.
[154] *USAF Statistical Digest*, 1948, pp. 26, 29; Grant, p. 50 (chart).
[155] Sturm, et al., p. 145.

Of the F-84, ConAC had the following opinion in November 1950: "The F-84D aircraft have little value as a fighter-interceptor . . . in view of the continued wing failures that have been encountered and the general inherent characteristics of the plane."[156]

In order to improve the capability of the interceptor force, yet another fighter originally intended for a fighter-bomber role was pressed into service. This was the F-86, originally designed for the Navy under the designation XFJ-1 as a carrier-based fighter and acquired by the AAF when the Navy decided not to procure it; the initial AAF development contract was signed in May 1945.[157] In speed, maneuverability, and combat ceiling the F-86 was far superior to any of the other Air Force jets, and it rapidly became the backbone of the interceptor force and the nearest approach to a truly satisfactory weapon among the interim models. Accepted for quantity procurement in the winter of 1948–1949, it achieved 10C at the end of May 1949; 12 squadrons were assigned to air defense by December 1950, when the phase-out of the F-80 was complete and that of the F-84 was under way. The day version of the F-86 was deployed on a large scale until 1954, when various all-weather aircraft took over virtually all interceptor duties.[158]

An all-weather jet interceptor capability was quite late being achieved. In view of the crippling delays in the development of the F-89, the Air Force was surely in need of an alternative. Work on the all-weather modification of the Sabre, the F-86D, began in 1949. The first F-86D was delivered in March 1951, and so urgent was the need to get this plane into service that it was targeted for production before the fire control and engine control systems had been proven. At that time, 341 were ordered; the number was raised to 979 2 months later. Unfortunately, in 1952 problems with the fire control and engine control systems delayed the program. Airframes piled up and could not be put into service; by January 1953, 2,500 planes were on order but fewer than 90 had been accepted.[159] Thereafter, the buildup in the number of planes in active service was rapid: more than 20 squadrons were in service by the end of 1953.[160]

In 1949, the year that work on the F-86D began, Lockheed proposed the rapid conversion of the T-33 trainer to a night-fighter. The T-33, based upon the F-80 design, was suitable for the purpose because it was a two-seat aircraft and thus afforded the space necessary for the radar equipment that was to be added. The modification program was completed rapidly, and deliveries of the interceptor, designated the F-94A, began in the second quarter of 1950.[161] By the end of the year six squadrons had been assigned, procurement orders having been greatly increased following the explosion of the first Soviet atomic bomb. In FY 1951, 176 F-9413's were delivered; another 180 were delivered in the first half of FY 1952.[162] The F-94C, an all-weather version, became operational in mid-1953, at about the same time as the all-weather F-86D, to which it was second in total numbers deployed.[163] These two fighters, together with a small number of F-89's, had the bulk of the interceptor duties until the F-101 and F-102 began to be operational in 1956.

When the F-86D began to arrive in air defense units, many pilots were dissatisfied with it because of the difficulty of using the intercept radar and piloting the plane at the same time.[164] Although pilots even-

---

[156] Sturm, et al., pp. 147–149.
[157] Semmens, under date.
[158] Grant, p. 52.
[159] Semmens, under dates.
[160] Grant, p. 50 (chart).
[161] *USAF Statistical Digest*, January 1949–June 1950, pp. 164–165.
[162] Semmens, June 1951, January 1952.
[163] Grant, p. 50 (chart).
[164] Sturm, et al., p. 156.

Chapter IV: American Systems

tually overcame this difficulty, it was clear that the limits of successful operation of a single-seat interceptor without the aid of some sort of ground control were being reached. The stage was set for an intensive effort to deal with this difficulty when a new generation of supersonic interceptors began to be developed in the early 1950's.

The later history of the F-89 involved many frustrations. Deliveries of the F-89 to operational units fell behind schedule from the beginning, and by June 1950 several deficiencies were apparent in the experimental models.[165] By late 1951, delivery was slowed considerably by defects in the aircraft, some of which made the interceptor ineffective above 30,000 feet. Since current plans called for the F-89 to constitute 25 percent of the ADC interceptor force, the aircraft had to be made combat-ready. But immediate improvement was not forthcoming, and during the first six months of 1952, the F-89 had seven accidents resulting in eight fatalities. Most of the defects were traceable to the attempt to increase output before the model had been adequately tested, in response to the extreme pressure to build up the interceptor force rapidly after the explosion of the Soviet atomic bomb.[166]

Although modifications were undertaken, at a cost of $17 million, the aircraft was grounded on 3 October 1952 until the major defects were corrected. The cost of the aircraft ultimately became triple that of an F-86D or F-94C; accordingly, when cuts in aircraft procurement were required, the F-89 program was a convenient place to begin. A further delaying factor was the lack of an adequate fire control system; armament development remained several years behind aircraft development throughout the post war years. Ultimately, production of the F-89 was accelerated during the second half of 1953, so that by the end of FY 1954 the Air Force had on hand a total of 349 F-89's of various models; of these, only 124 were assigned to ADC; the major air defense role had by then been assigned to the F-86D and F-94C. The F-89C almost reached obsolescence before it became operational in 1954; all versions of the F-89 left active service by the end of that year.[167]

3. Summary

The overall pattern of interceptor deployment over the period 1946–1954 is shown in Figure 1.[168]

On the whole, American interceptor development before the advent of the Century Series in the 1950's was not fully adequate to counter the Soviet threat that arose in the late 1940's. The constraints were primarily conceptual and technological rather than budgetary or organizational.

The emergence of the Tu-4 threat in 1947 and Soviet possession of the atomic bomb in 1949 were considerably in advance of expectations, and by the time these events occurred the U.S. was committed to a new development program that promised to be marginal at best in its capability for meeting the threat. The shifts in the earliest statements of performance specifications for the F-89, as well as the heterogeneous nature of the industry response in March 1946 indicate how unclear the conception of the exact nature of air defense needs was. The haste engendered by the successive escalations of the perceived threat resulted in a speed-up of the only long-range program in process (the F-89) to a level that produced serious defects in the product; a rush to fill the air defense gap with planes developed for other purposes first brought in

---

[165] Grant, p. 49.
[166] Ibid., pp. 49, 52.
[167] OSD, *Chronology*, p. 180.
[168] McMullen, *History*, p. 197.

Figure 1—Fighter-Interceptor Squadrons by A/C Type

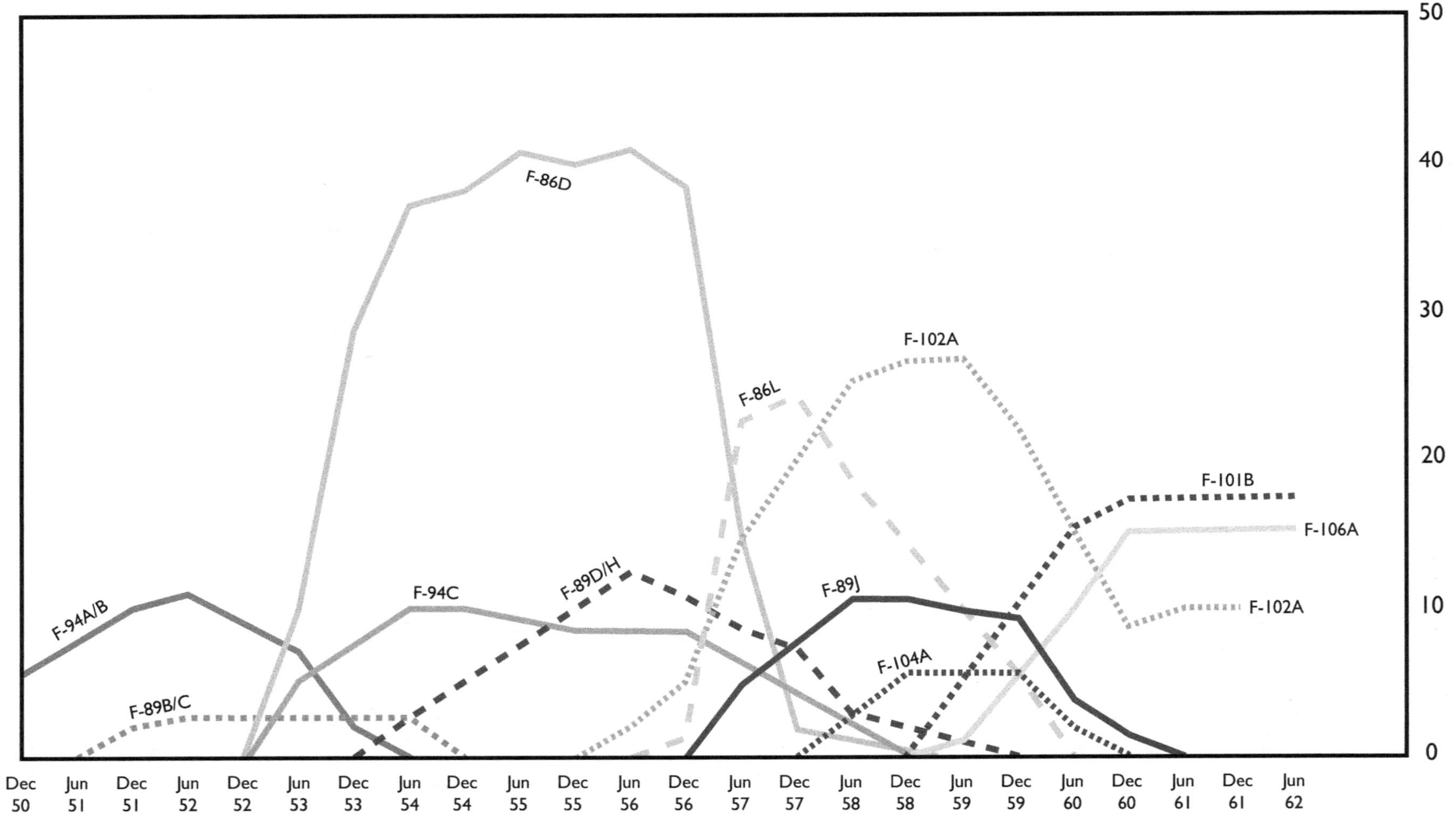

planes (the F-80 and F-84) that would have had only limited effectiveness against a B-29 type aircraft, but ultimately a strenuous effort at modification of other non-interceptor aircraft produced two interim interceptors, the F-94C and the F-86D, that did have a fair all-weather capability against the Tu-4. The overall picture is largely that a relatively unplanned effort to patch together an interceptor defense, which was conceptually remedied by decisions taken in late 1948 but could not be relieved in concrete terms until the middle of the next decade.

A second limiting factor was the unpredictability of technological advance during the period. Faced with the necessity of adopting and improving a bewildering variety of new technologies in the construction of aircraft with a more specialized mission than had been required before, the industry responded with strenuous efforts; but these efforts were not always successful, owing to the technological newness of so many components of an interceptor and to the prevailing relatively haphazard method of developing different elements such as airframe, engine, radar and fire control independently and then bringing them together as well as their characteristics would permit. (It should be noted, however, that difficulties similar to those encountered in the development of the F-89 and F-86D later slowed down the development of the F-102, which *was* planned as an integrated system.) Fortunately, the success of the industry in producing unexpectedly good aircraft for other purposes helped to redress the balance by making possible the modification of these aircraft (e.g., the P-80/T-33 and the F-86) for air defense uses.

Neither budgetary limitations nor service rivalries seem to have had a major retarding effect upon fighter development during the period. Budget cutbacks affected the total number of aircraft procured during the period, but the limiting factor in the jet interceptor force was quality, not quantity. RED costs were so small compared to procurement costs that R&D programs suffered comparatively little from the cutbacks, and even the costs of a major modification program such as that undertaken on the F-89 only led to reductions when it became clear that better and cheaper airplanes had become available.

The Air Force–Navy rivalry that continued through the period and culminated in the charges and countercharges of the B-36 hearings in 1949 focused almost totally upon the strategic offensive, leaving air defense largely unaffected. As the Army remained skeptical of the tactical value of jet aircraft until 1949 at the earliest,[169] there was little competition over jet development priorities from that quarter, and when a major shortage of procurement funds arose, it was frequently the tactical programs that were cut back. The two most important aircraft programs that were cut back in the period and the years immediately following were the F-93 (a fighter-bomber version of the F-86) and the F-88 (a penetration fighter, a type involved in a secondary mission of SAC).[170]

4. Decisions for Supersonic Interceptors, 1948–1955

Although the change of attitudes and methods in the area of strategic arms was a continuous process, the year 1948 has a good claim to be considered a watershed year in the history of interceptor development as well as in the larger strategic arena.

The increased clarity of strategic thinking which had been emerging for some time was signalized by the formulation by the Joint Chiefs of Staff of a definite conception of strategic operations against the Soviet

---

[169] *Aviation Week*, 25 July 1949, p. 16.
[170] Futrell, *Ideas, Concepts, Doctrine*, p. 225; Semmens, May 1951.

Union in early 1948.[171] Much thought had been devoted to the future development of this threat, and in 1948 both the report of the President's Air Policy Board and NSC 20/4 named the time at which the danger from Soviet power would likely become critical: 1 June 1953 in the former case and 1955 in the latter.[172]

In air defense, 1948 was the year in which plans were laid for an advanced interceptor to meet the anticipated Soviet capabilities of the middle 1950's. The successful realization of these plans, over a period of ten years, is the single instance in the entire post war period of a deliberately planned interceptor program that resulted in an operational aircraft fully equal to the role for which it was designed. The F-89 program that had gone before must be judged at least a partial failure; all other interceptors, before and after the 1954 Interceptor, were adaptations of aircraft originally designed for other roles. In a real sense, therefore, the interceptor program that was initiated in 1948 represents, in spite of the many difficulties that arose during its course, the high point of interceptor development efforts.

When, in October 1948, the decision was made to begin the development of a new all-weather jet interceptor, the pressure of the Tu-4 threat was still making itself felt in the decision, which opted for early availability of the aircraft rather than for a capability sufficient to deal with aircraft more advanced than the Tu-4—the anticipated Soviet B-47 type and B-52 type aircraft.[173] By January of 1949, however, a longer view was being taken, and the development of a capability beyond that of the expected future Soviet intercontinental jet bombers was being projected. The plane was dubbed the "1954 Interceptor," being expected to become operational in that year.[174]

In early 1949 the results of interceptor trials against the new B-36B bomber, which was then undergoing final testing, were made public. In the test, F-86A's, the best fighters then available, attempted interception of a B-36B at 43,000 feet. The fighters were able to reach this altitude, but maneuverability problems and lack of an adequate ground control severely limited their performance.[175] This test represented a continuance of the USAF policy, in the absence of reliable intelligence, of obtaining information on its requirements by matching its offensive and defensive weapons against each other. Its announcement, coupled with the announcement of coming requests for new design proposals (to lead to the first really new fighter prototypes since 1946), served to pave the way in Congress for acceptance of the new developmental proposals. It had the further consequence of further provoking the Navy, which was moving toward a showdown with the Air Force over the strategic mission, and which, viewing the Air Force announcement as a move to further increase its share of aircraft procurement funds, promptly offered to intercept a B-36 with its own McDonnell Banshees. The test never occurred, and since the conflict, insofar as it involved aviation, was really over the strategic offensive mission, had little effect on the AF interceptor development program.[176]

Discussions which ranged over the total air defense problem were held with industry representatives in May 1949. The development of a complete weapon system comprising airframe, power plant, armament, ground and airborne radar, communications, service facilities, and other aspects, was planned; the competition for the fire-control and electronic and control systems was held prior to the airframe competition, as

---

[171] At the Key West and Newport meetings in 1948.
[172] Futrell, op. cit., p. 209; Chapter I of this history.
[173] Semmens, 8 October 1948.
[174] Semmens, 13 January 1949.
[175] *Aviation Week*, 21 March 1949, p. 7, B-36.
[176] *Aviation Week*, 30 May 1949, p. 13; 6 June 1949, p. 11; B-36, Banshees.

Chapter IV: American Systems

the longest development period was expected in these areas.[177] By July 1951, three of six firms that had submitted airframe proposals, Convair, Lockheed, and Republic, were given contracts for "preliminary design and mock-up"; in this way small amounts were to be spent in acquiring initial information and the major production delayed.[178] But this sponsorship of closely competing programs was soon ended, and within two months the AF had made an initial commitment to Convair alone, placing the other design proposals on the back burner.[179]

The explosion of an atomic bomb by the Soviet Union in 1949 and the beginning of the Korean War in June 1950 greatly increased the pressure upon the AF to attain its advanced interceptor capability as soon as possible. But it soon became apparent that none of the original proposals would result in an operational aircraft by 1954. In particular, expected delays in delivery of the fire-control system and the engine put the projected availability of the Convair aircraft as late as 1956.[180] In view of this time lag, a reexamination of the interceptor program by the Board of Senior Officers revealed that a gap would exist between 1953 and 1955 during which the estimated speed of enemy bombers was Mach 0.8 to 0.85, a speed too great for the interim interceptors. Therefore, it appeared that, once again, an interim aircraft was needed.[181] Accordingly, in November 1951 the Air Force decided to expedite the development of the Convair plane with a different engine, under the designation F-102. Production of this "interim interceptor" was to be followed by completion of the "ultimate interceptor" as originally planned under the designation F-102B (later F-106).[182]

Production of the F-102 accordingly proceeded, encountering difficulties that entailed redesign of the fuselage into the "Coke bottle" shape and retooling to reduce the airframe weight; the resulting F-102A made its first successful flight on 19 December 1954 and became operational in mid-1956[183]; at this time the *complete* weapon system proved unsatisfactory, and modification and retrofitting extended the period before an acceptable level of overall effectiveness was attained to late 1958.[184]

The requirements for the F-102 had called for a rather short combat radius of 375 nautical miles, but after work had begun on it the U.S. radar defenses were considerably expanded northward, culminating in the 1954 decision to build the DEW Line within the Arctic Circle. As this expansion called for the coverage of a considerably larger area than that for which the F-102 had been planned, the Air Force on 19 February 1954 outlined requirements for a two-place long-range jet interceptor. In June 1954, the Air Research and Development Command recommended that the single-seat F-101, which originally was accepted in 1951 by the Air Force as a long-range escort fighter under the designation XF-88, but was cancelled in the same year for budgetary reasons, be adapted to serve as a long-range interceptor.[185]

The Air Defense Command was willing to accept the F-101, but the Air Force preferred to delay a decision until it could hold a design competition to get information on the possibility that an optimum long-range interceptor could be developed. Held in the summer of 1954, this design competition would stimulate interest that would eventually yield the design of the F-108, but it promised nothing that could

---

[177] Marschak, p. 99.
[178] Ibid., p. 101.
[179] Ibid., p. 102.
[180] Ibid., p. 102.
[181] Grant, p. 53.
[182] Marschak, p. 102.
[183] Ibid., pp. 102–109, gives a detailed account of the difficulties.
[184] Ibid., p. 109.
[185] Futrell, op. cit., pp. 484–485.

soon be available. The Air Defense Command apparently wanted more than industry could provide prior to 1960 or later, unless the Air Force would be willing to accept a four-engine fighter of virtually the same size as an airborne early warning aircraft. Facing these facts the Air Council on 16 February 1955 directed the procurement of two-place F-10113 Voodoo fighters to serve as interim long-range interceptors.[186]

When the Air Force issued its requirements description for the 1954 Interceptor electronics design competition on 18 August 1950, it noted that manual techniques of aircraft warning and control would impose "intolerable" delays under jet-age combat conditions, but did not attempt to describe the new ground environment that would be needed.[187] It was not until 1952 that a full-scale study of the needs and possibilities of a large-scale integrated ground control system was made; this study, conducted under the auspices of the Air Force–sponsored Project Lincoln, resulted in the construction of SAGE (Semi-Automatic Ground Environment), first on a trial basis in 1953, and then on an expanding scale throughout the continental U.S. over the rest of the decade. The 1954 Interceptor, ultimately the F-106, was designed to operate within this system.[188]

The adaptation of the F-104 as an interceptor belongs to the period after 1955, but the fact that it was substituted for the incomplete 1954 Interceptor justifies its mention here. The F-104 was developed by Lockheed by extensive modification of its unsuccessful entry in the interceptor competition of 1950–1951, which had been won by Convair.[189] Problems that had been encountered with the use of jet aircraft in the Korean War had strengthened the hand of tactical-fighter advocates in the Air Force and created an increased demand for a light tactical fighter. Lockheed won the contract in March 1953, and the first flight of a prototype took place in February 1954. In mid-1954 an impasse developed in the Air Force: heavy-fighter advocates, particularly in ADC, wanted a heavyweight fighter as best suited for all-weather use; light-fighter advocates, mostly from TAC, pointed to the events in Indochina as indications that the United States might soon be involved in another limited war, which would require advanced tactical fighters. The conflict was resolved at the instance of a third group, who suggested adding more equipment to the F-104 and switching to a more powerful engine. In the fall of 1954, the Air Force signed a contract for 17 F-104A airframes at a cost of $39 million; the first F-104A had its initial flight in February 1954.[190]

Since the F-104 had not been designed as a fighter-interceptor and possessed electronic equipment that was not compatible with the semiautomatic ground environment that the Air Defense Command was installing, ADC was reluctant to take the day fighter; but it recognized that it could get the F-104 without great delay, and in April 1955 it asked for six squadrons of the plane. While the F-104 was a flashy performer, it never met air defense requirements. In August 1957 the Air Force eventually limited F-104 programming to only two wings of aircraft and cancelled further production of the plane. At this time the Air Defense Command was rescheduled to receive only four squadrons of F-104's.[191]

5. Summary: 1950–1955

By 1955 the Air Defense Command possessed a good system to meet the threat of the Tu-4 offensive, and there was optimism that the air defense system could continue to outdistance the Soviets.

---

[186] Futrell, op. cit., p. 485.
[187] Futrell, op. cit., p. 484.
[188] Futrell, op. cit., pp. 486–487; Grant, pp. 73–74.
[189] Marschak, p. 110–111.
[190] Marschak, pp. 111–112, 114–115.
[191] Futrell, op. cit., p. 486.

Unfortunately, the Soviets achieved "qualitative surprise" and demonstrated on 1 May 1955 that their offensive capabilities had risen to a new plateau much sooner than had been anticipated. "We now have a good system to fight the Tu-4," observed General Partridge, who became Commander-in-Chief, Continental Air Defense Command on 20 July 1955. "Unfortunately, the Russians came along a little more rapidly than we anticipated in their technical developments, and they introduced the jet bombers and the Bear more rapidly than was forecast." Partridge also warned that "the defenses which we are . . . planning . . . take care of the Soviet threat up through the manned bomber, but the Soviets are said to be building an intercontinental ballistic missile, and we must somehow devise a defense against this type of attack."[192] The immediate air defense problem in 1955–1956 concerned the development of capabilities to counter the Soviet Bison and Bear, both of which would likely possess a standoff missile capability equivalent to the Hound Dog. With one aerial refueling, the Soviet Bear, moreover, would be able to fly a circuitous route that would evade existing early warning lines in the Arctic. Since it was a turboprop aircraft, the Bear would not only have a very long range, but it would also be able to operate effectively at low altitudes.[193] The stage was set for another round of air defense planning.

F. History of Early Warning Systems, 1945–1955

1. Introduction

This portion of the larger study traces five distinctive tracks related to air defense early warning systems throughout this ten-year period. Track I covers the chronological developments and technical characteristics of the Distant Early Warning (DEW) line. Track II covers the history, technical characteristics, and effectiveness of the Lashup system; Track III traces the evolution of the Supremacy plan into the "Permanent" early warning system; Tracks IV and V describe the mid-Canada and Pinetree lines, respectively. Although admittedly these systems evolved during the same general time period, the decision was made to trace each separately so as not to confuse the reader with a plethora of information about all systems during short time periods. This procedure has the additional merit of being an innovative approach to the construction of an early warning system history; many studies on the same subject tend to lump all developmental decisions together, and in these cases it is difficult for the reader to discern any clear pattern of evolution for single systems.

2. The DEW Line

Planning for the creation of a DEW line began in 1946, when the Army Air Force first advanced a definitive[194] proposal for such a system. This plan was discarded shortly thereafter because of Congressionally inspired post war economies, which were to similarly restrict other air defense planning goals. By 1948, with the release of the USAF plan for a Supremacy air defense system of vast proportions (see detailed description in Track 111), it looked as though plans for a DEW line were dead. The USAF Air Defense Command (ADC) disagreed with Supremacy, for no provision was made in it for the Alaska to Greenland net with flanks guarded by aircraft and picket ships which ADC felt was necessary for 3 to 6 hours of

---

[192] 84th Congress, 2d Session, *Study of Air Power*, pp. 252–253.
[193] Futrell, op. cit., p. 488.
[194] Ray, p. 1.

warning time.[195] Supremacy was rejected in favor of a more limited eventual system because of post war budgetary priorities, and nothing was to develop on DEW for some time.

In September 1949, the Soviet Union exploded its first nuclear device. This calamitous event was followed in October 1949 by the establishment of Project Charles at MIT, a USAF-sponsored study of air defense.[196] The Project Charles report, completed in August 1951, showed the vulnerability of the U.S. to air attack and the real need for a DEW facility to provide the requisite early warning of impending attack.[197] By August 1952, the Project Charles recommendation had been seconded by the report of the Summer Study Group at MIT's Lincoln Laboratory. This report urged that a DEW line be built along the 70th parallel with water extensions to Hawaii and Scotland. Cost of such a line was estimated at a third of a billion dollars with an operational target date of late 1954 if the project took on a high priority designation.[198]

But the Summer Study Group report on DEW ran into stiff opposition in November 1952 when USAF and RAND concurred that DEW was an idea ahead of its time—their joint judgment was that insufficient funds and rudimentary technology combined to eliminate DEW from short-term consideration.[199] USAF was still seriously interested in studying the early warning problem, however, and in December, therefore, contracted with Western Electric for two test installations in light of the earlier RAND report.[200]

DEW had become an issue of some public concern by the spring of 1953; previous reports favoring the system combined with the ongoing Korean War and the new look it had engendered toward U.S. defense efforts brought the attentive public into the picture. The Alsop brothers and other journalists surfaced the DEW issue at that time, which was propitious for DEW since President Eisenhower had just taken office and the new administration brought with it new policy ideas.[201] In July the Secretary of Defense, in conjunction with other Eisenhower initiatives toward a restudy of American military needs, appointed a special group headed by Major General Harold Bull. The Bull report not only confirmed the views of the Summer Study Group, but also recommended the expenditure of $18 billion to $25 billion in the next five years to automate air defense systems and establish a DEW line.

New impetus was given to a rethinking of American defense efforts by the August 1953 Russian test of a hydrogen bomb; by October, the National Security Council had approved the Summer Study report, including the DEW line.[202] Within the context of other Eisenhower initiatives on increasing air defense which had been sent to Congress in January 1954, the NSC report of the previous fall was in turn approved by the President in February.[203] With this approval the DEW project was given to USAF; Western Electric was the contractor for what was labeled as Project Counterchange (later renamed Project Corrode) and for Project 572 to test communications in the early warning field.[204]

By June of that year, the Canadian–U.S. Military Study Group had recommended approval of the DEW line; the concept of the line was well on its way with the increased attention being directed at it.[205]

---

[195] Ray, p. 1.
[196] Ibid., p. 6.
[197] Ibid., p. 6.
[198] Ibid., p. 7.
[199] Ibid., p. 9.
[200] Ibid., p. 11.
[201] Ibid., p. 11.
[202] Ibid., p. 11.
[203] Ibid., p. 12.
[204] Ibid., p. 12.
[205] Ibid., p. 16.

Chapter IV: American Systems

In August, a USAF-RCAF committee was set up to develop mutually agreeable criteria for the tentative line. They endorsed a route from Herschel Island to Padloping Island, and integration of DEW with the "Alaska Ring" radar net. According to their report, the area from Kodiak Island to Hawaii would be covered via aircraft and picket ships; the Eastern extension on the opposite side was to go to Cape Farewell, Greenland, and then to the Azores.[206] Disagreement arose over placement of the line. USAF believed (along with the Navy) that the line should go to Iceland and Scotland on the Eastern side; ADC nonconcurred with this belief, objecting to it on the grounds that the route would be subject to "spoofing" raids by the U.S.S.R.[207] The Navy additionally wanted to change the Pacific route to a Midway-Adak line.[208]

By November, the Locations Study Group had combined these varying requests and had settled on a route from Cape Lisburne, Alaska, to Cape Dyer, Baffin Island. The tempo of events picked up rapidly from that time on. In December 1954 Western Electric was named the prime contractor for the system; in January 1955, the JCS approved the route previously suggested by the Locations Study Group. In May, formal agreement was reached with Canada to establish the DEW line in Canadian territory; by June, actual land construction of the line had begun.

Even in this flurry of activity, however, IOC for the line was somewhat in the future—in July, a contract was signed committing the contractor to complete DEW installation by mid-1957. Once this date had been established, personnel requirements could be dealt with—in August, authority was granted by the Secretary of the Air Force to staff the line with contract civilians. Carrying the story through the end of 1955, in December the JCS reconsidered placement of the line and accepted the Navy's earlier recommendation—they authorized the Midway-Adak route, plus some gap-filler radars for the Aleutian Islands.[209]

---

[206] Ibid., p. 16.
[207] Ibid., p. 16.
[208] Ibid., p. 16.
[209] Ibid., p. 19. Included below is technical information about the DEW radars. All information is from Ray *except* the information on picket ship and aircraft systems. This data is from Wohlstetter, Appendices D, E, F, and N.

DEW Radar Systems

A. Technical
The central part of this line was built using specially designed equipment to withstand the existing environmental conditions.
  1. Search Radar—AN/FPS-19
  (1)   L bank 1220–1350 MHz
  (2)   Two back-to-back antennas, each 36' wide x 11' high. One for low beam, one for high, each with its own radar. Rotation rate 1.25 rpm. Detection range about 160 nautical miles from altitudes of 5000 to 7000 feet.
  2. Fluttar Radar—AN/PFS-23
CW Doppler system. Receivers and transmitters spaced alternately along line. 475–525 MHz, 1 Kw power. Antennas were 6' wide, 20' high and elevated from 100–400' above ground. These were for low-level detection, and were designed to work down to 200' elevation over land and 50' over water.

B. Technical
  1. Radars—For the Alaska to Labrador Section
  (1)   Search radars
AN/FPS-19 L band search, two antennas per radome with one for high beam and one for low beam, 180° apart. Range 160 nautical miles for detection altitudes of 5000 to 7000 feet
  (2)   Doppler
AN/FPS-23 Fluttar systems
475 – 525 MHz, 1 Kw power, detection down to 200' over land, 50' over water
  (3)   Picket ships
Combination of DER (Destroyer Escort/Radar) and YAGR (Converted Liberty Ship) with AN/SPS-6C surveillance radar and AN/SPS-8 height finder. Range about 40 miles at 500' elevation due to earth's curvature
  (4)   Aircraft
Navy WV-2 or USAF RC-121 (converted Lockheed Constellation) using AN/APS-20 surveillance and AN/APS-45 height finder.

The most interesting portion of the DEW story thus clearly occurs after 1955, for the line was not operational until 1957. It was only then that full costs could be assessed for the system; it was only then that bugs could be worked out of the radars, one radar of which initially was to generate false alarm rates as high as four per minute from such sources as clouds and icebergs. The full details of these problems and costs will be covered in the second portion of this history.

3. Track II—Lashup

The story of the Lashup radar system is a short one of small proportions compared to later early warning nets. In October 1948, the Commanding General of the USAF Air Defense Command, General Stratemeyer, received $561,000 to start Lashup I by expanding the five-station radar net then in existence.[210] Lashup was tied to a renewed emphasis on defense given increased cold war hostilities at that time—earlier that same year, Czechoslovakia had fallen to communist control, and the Soviet blockade of Berlin had begun.

By early 1949, siting had been completed and some stations were in operation.[211] USAF also issued plans at that time for Lashup II to cover the Northeast, Northwest, and Sandia-Los Alamos areas.[212] It was also envisioned that as personnel and equipment became available the San Francisco, Los Angeles area would be covered.[213] On 1 June 1950, the completed Lashup net went into operation. In all, 44 stations were included and used World War II equipment—the system was a stopgap measure which had to suffice until the new "permanent" or "P" system installations had been completed.[214] By 1952, Lashup stations were gradually being phased out as the "P" system stations came into operation.[215]

But although Lashup was a short-lived system, its deployment proved beneficial in working out problems for later, more sophisticated nets. ADC admitted that Lashup was only good for training since outdated equipment in poor repair was used, and not enough personnel were available for 24-hour operations of even that equipment.[216] ADC's opinion of Lashup was that it was of prime benefit in showing what needed to be done to improve the system rather than as an effective early warning net.[217] They also believed that Lashup helped to promote greater harmony among air defense protagonists when they saw how bad the operation of Lashup actually was.[218]

The problems of the Northwest Lashup provide an example of the problems of the entire system. That portion of Lashup ran only 8–12 hours a day during its life span. Stations were undermanned by unskilled personnel; replacement parts were difficult to get; and there was a general lack of height finders among the stations.[219] Throughout Lashup, the AN/CPS-5 proved to be the system "workhorse" among the radars, although the AN/CPS-1 was considered to be the best unit.[220] The worst operational radar units were the AN/TPS-1B and the AN/TPS-10A.[221]

---

[210] "Organization and Responsibility for Air Defense."
[211] Ibid.
[212] "The Air Defense of Atomic Energy Installations."
[213] Ibid.
[214] "Chronology of Blue Air Defense Systems."
[215] "Organization and Responsibility for Air Defense."
[216] Ray.
[217] "The Air Defense of the United States."
[218] Ibid.
[219] "The Air Defense of Atomic Energy Installations."
[220] "The Air Defense of the United States."
[221] Ibid.

Chapter IV: American Systems

But these problems of Lashup had to be expected because of the nature of the system—it was a crude attempt to answer a much larger question.

4. Track III—Supremacy and the "Permanent" System

After the end of World War II, the early warning radar net then in existence was decommissioned as part of the general return of men to civilian life. This left CONUS with no early warning facility, so the USAF attempted to plug the defensive gap by formulating the Supremacy plan. This plan called for a complex net of 223 CONUS radars and 37 Alaskan radars[222] and was approved for construction by the USAF Chief of Staff in November 1947.[223] When these plans were released in early 1948, ADC complained bitterly because there was no provision for land-based radars along upper North America. ADC wanted to include a system from Alaska to Greenland with the sea flanks guarded by picket ships and airborne radar placed to furnish three- to six-hour warning times. With the nation's general relaxation from the war effort, however, ADC's case was not stated vividly enough for either the USAF or the public to be impressed. General opinion was that the idea of a SAC deterrent force was sufficiently powerful to preclude attack on the United States, thus making an aircraft early-warning network unnecessary.

Budgetary restrictions continued to plague the military in this early postwar period, and in late 1948 the Supremacy plan was withdrawn for a more modest one called the Interim Program.[224] This was essentially Phase I of Supremacy and proposed to use radars either on hand or already on order, thus requesting funding only for facilities construction. The FY 1949 request was $45 million for this purpose. A "First Augmentation" was also requested at the same time. This augmentation was essentially Phase 11 of Supremacy and included funds for more radars, height finders, and their installation.[225]

In March 1949, Congress approved a permanent post war radar net for CONUS and Alaska. The bill signed by the President authorized the USAF to build a 75 station "permanent" aircraft control and warning net which was essentially the proposed Interim Program and its First Augmentation.[226]

After approval of the program and while waiting for an appropriation to clear Congress, the USAF diverted $50 million from aircraft procurement funds to get the program started. The USAF deemed coverage of the northern approaches to the continent to be of prime importance, so only $18.8 million of the diverted funds were earmarked for continental stations, with the bulk going to support the Alaska priority stations.[227]

A Congressional appropriation of $85.5 million was finally received in October of 1949 for construction of the "permanent" radar net.[228] Planning progressed for the priority Alaskan stations, and construction was ordered for 24 of these in December 1949. This first building phase was started in March of 1950 as soon as weather conditions became more favorable.[229]

Construction of the original "permanent" or "P" radar net was to in June of 1952.[230] Even before the net was finished, extensions into Canada to increase warning time for critical areas of the United States were being planned.

---

[222] "Organization and Responsibility for Air Defense."
[223] "Chronology of Blue Air Defense Systems."
[224] Ibid.
[225] "Organization and Responsibility for Air Defense."
[226] "Chronology of Blue Air Defense Systems."
[227] "The Air Defense of the United States."
[228] "Chronology of Blue Air Defense Systems."
[229] Ibid.
[230] Wohlstetter, Appendix N. Included below is technical information about the "Permanent" system radars.

5. Track IV—The Mid-Canada Line

In October of 1952, Canada started plans for its own early-warning radar line crossing the middle of the country at about the 55th parallel.[231] These plans appear to be an effort on Canada's part to gain its own entry into the early warning system at not too much expense and gain an additional hour's warning time for most of its population centers. The United States was glad to cooperate with these plans and in October of 1953 the plans were approved by the Joint Canadian–U.S. Military Study Group.[232]

Shortly after the plans were approved, construction agreements were reached (the United States paid a share of the cost) and 1957 was set as the target year for operations to begin.[233]

The line was built approximately on the 55th parallel from Dawson Creek, B.C., to Hopedale, Lab. It was composed of 90 detection and 8 section control stations. All detection stations were unmanned and telemetered their data to the section control stations for analysis. The radars used were CW Doppler sets, either the U.S. AN/FPS-503 or the Canadian MK II Fluttar set.[234]

6. Track V—The Pinetree Line

While the U.S. "permanent" system was being built, planners were at work to extend its coverage northward. The first extension of the P system into Canada is sometimes called the Pinetree line, the "radar extension program," or the "Canadian extensions." In August of 1951 an exchange of notes between the United States and Canada constituted formal agreement to build the line.[235] A total of 33 sites were planned, mostly in the southeastern part of Canada. When costs were discussed, Canada bridled until the United States offered to pay two-thirds of the total. Construction was essentially complete by June of 1954, when all but one of the sites became operational.[236]

Figures 2 through 5 are graphic displays of the systems discussed in this section.

G. History of Command and Control, 1945–1955

1. Introduction

This segment of the larger history limits itself to some fairly well-defined subfields in the area of command and control. *Omitted* from detailed description are air defense weapons, the specific threat to CONUS, air defense outside of CONUS (including early warning systems), and the military hardware of command and control systems. Command and control roles and missions as they apply to surface-to-air weapons are discussed in detail in this chapter in section C.4. *Included* in the central focus of this segment are the roles, missions, and interservice relations in the formative periods of the Air Defense Command (ADC), Continental Air Command (CONAC), Army Antiaircraft Command (ARAACOM), and Continental Air Defense Command (CONAD) during the 1945–1955 period.

The difficulties involved in structuring the scope of the study in this manner have already been well put by a similar study:

---

[231] Ray.
[232] Ibid.
[233] "Chronology of Blue Air Defense Systems."
[234] "Operation of the Mid-Canada Line."
[235] "Chronology of Blue Air Defense Systems."
[236] Ibid.

Figure 2—Early-Warning Systems

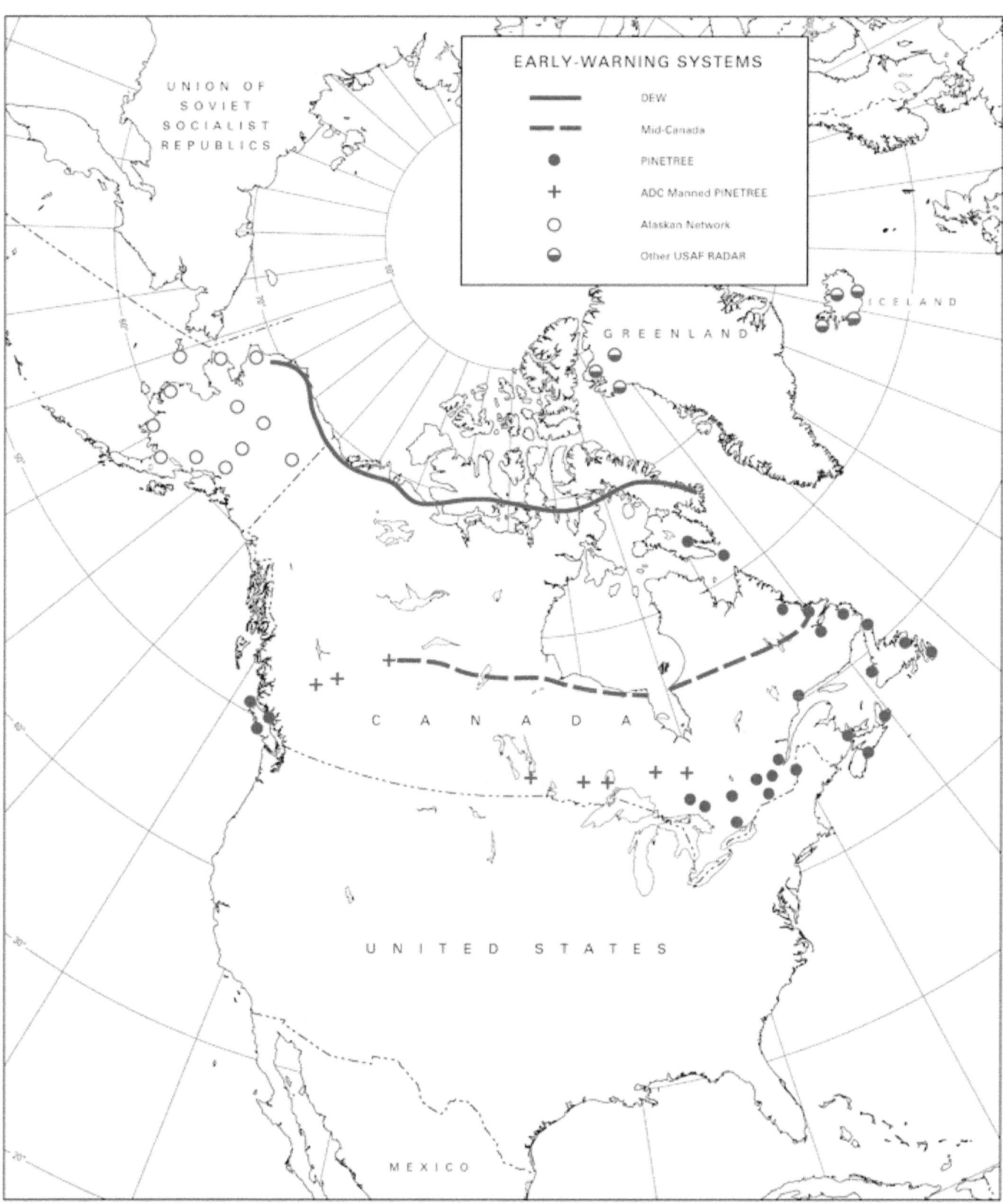

Figure 3—Lashup, Completed by April 1950

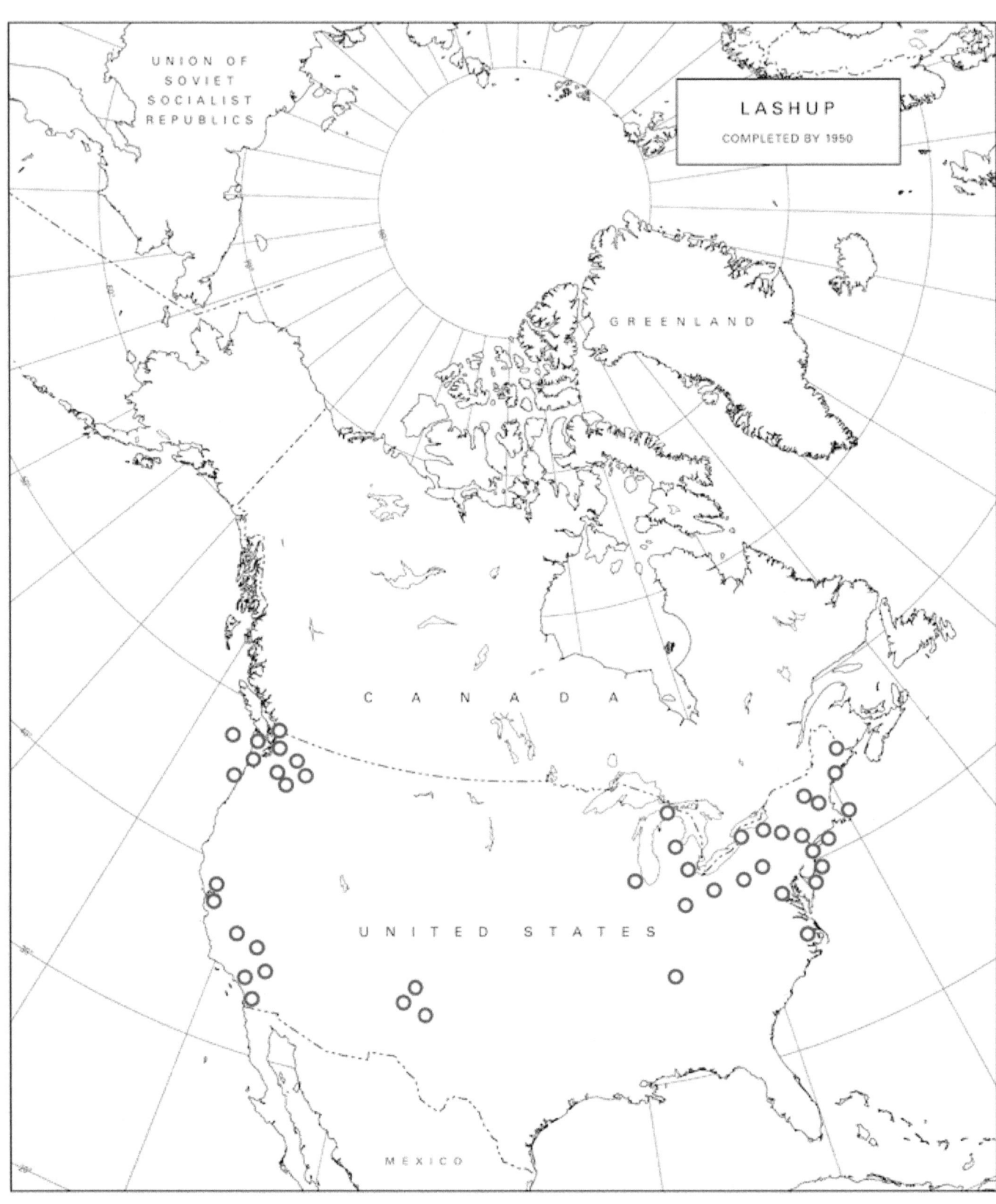

Figure 4—Permanent System

Figure 5—Planned Deployment of Contiguous System (as of June 1955)

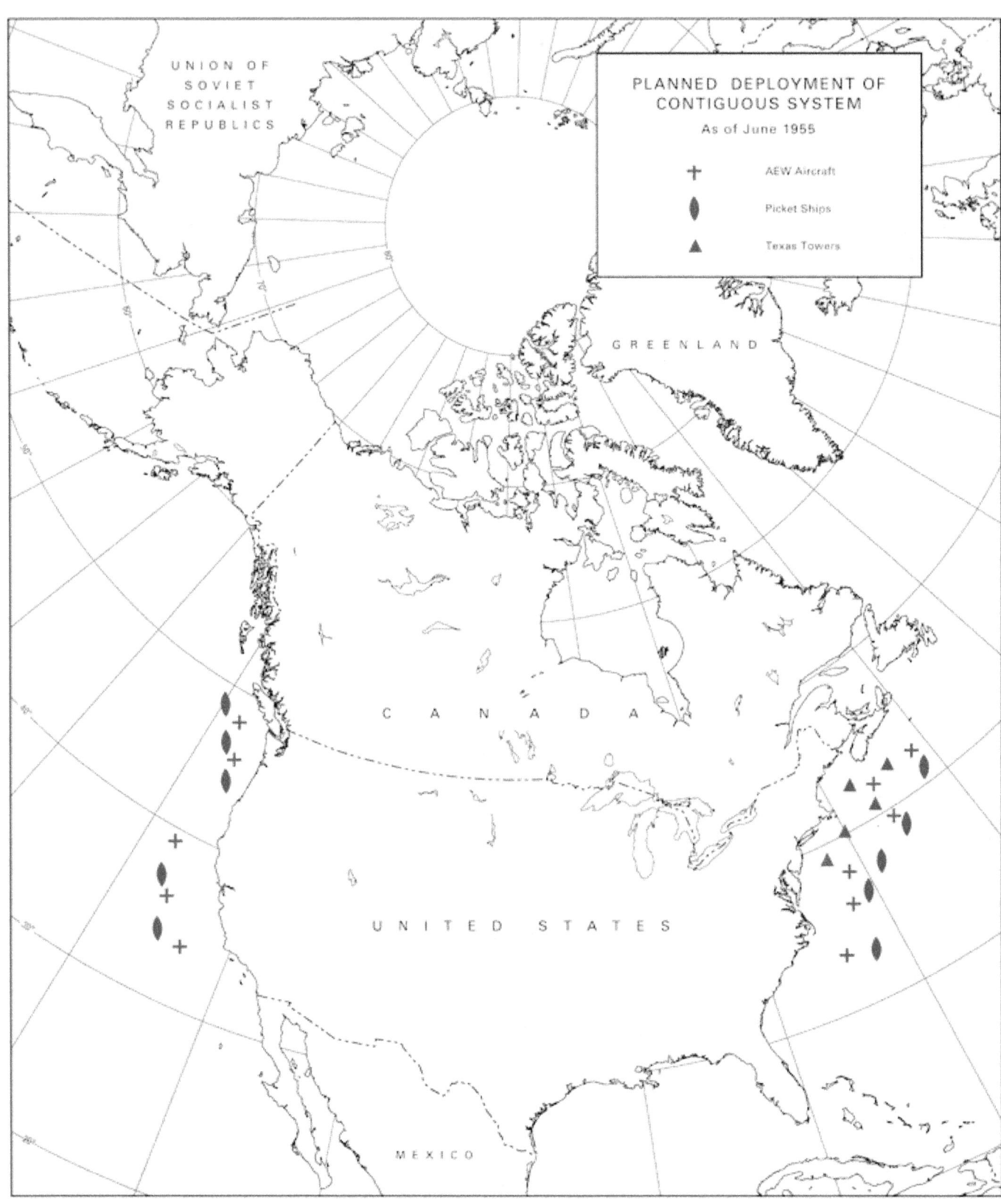

Chapter IV: American Systems

Isolating the organizational story from the history of the growth of the radar, fighter and antiaircraft forces was the most difficult problem. . . . To have ignored the influence on organization of the various expedients applied to the build-up of forces would have been to treat the evolution of the organization in a vacuum. On the other hand, to have made more than the merest reference to the force developments would have led to an obscuring of the central theme.[237]

In addition to the problem of scope is the fact that several comprehensive histories have already been written which trace the evolution of these organizations through the same period of time. While it is obviously more stimulating to "break new ground" in such an endeavor, this is not possible in this field. Primary source documentation has already been used by these other studies (especially in the classified literature) in an attempt to accurately portray the course of events and extent of service competition in the formation of air defense organizations. This effort can therefore not be pretentious; the best it can hope to do is to elaborate an accurate perspective on salient events during the time period.

2. Pre-1945 Decisions

The choice of 1945 as the first year of this history does not dovetail neatly with the formation of the first active air defense organization in the post war period. The Air Defense Command (ADC) is the first of the previously mentioned organizations to be discussed; there were actually three ADC's: one from 26 February 1940 to 2 July 1941; the second from March 1946 to July 1950; and the third from January 1951 through and beyond the end of our time period, 1955.[238] Therefore, discussion of the ADC initiated in 1946 must include information from the earlier period to reflect the state of affairs from 1945 on.

The earliest ADC grew out of a suggestion in November 1939 by then Chief of the Air Corps Major General Henry H. Arnold to the War Department that a unit be established to study the problem of CONUS air defense, an effort then absent.[239] The result of this suggestion was the establishment of an ADC on 26 February 1940, a planning body tasked to study the problem of attacking planes over the United States.[240] The study efforts of this first ADC fed into a War Department assignment of the mission of organizing, training for, and operating the air defenses of the United States to the Commanding General, GHQ Air Force in March 1941.[241] However, this responsibility was primarily for mobilization—under wartime conditions four newly created CONUS air defense commands were actually to be responsible for defense operations.[242] Thus CG GHQ air defense prerogatives were to be released to defense commanders once hostilities began. This problem of responsibilities was not particularly crucial, however: ". . . in spite of the increased emphasis on defense planning, the entire question of air defense was still generally considered to be an academic one in 1941, as it was to be later, in 1946–47."[243]

After Pearl Harbor, the concern for air defense took on a new seriousness. As an operationally dependable air defense system grew during the war, the question of doctrinal responsibilities for air defense roles and missions continued to evolve. Precursors of post war problems in the assignment of responsibilities are seen in two major documents developed during these years. The first is found in Field Manual 1-15, issued by the War Department in April 1942. Entitled "Tactics and Techniques of Air Fighting," this document

---

[237] Sturm, "Foreword."
[238] "The Air Defense of the United States," p. 11.
[239] Ibid., p. 10.
[240] Ibid., p. 11.
[241] Ibid., p. 13.
[242] Ibid., p. 14.
[243] Ibid., p. 17.

stated a position of much future controversy between the Army Air and Ground Forces: "The interceptor command must have operational control over all antiaircraft artillery, searchlights and barrage balloons in the defense area."[244] This control problem will be picked up again in the post war years.

Also significant was the historic Field Manual 100-20, *Command and Employment of Air Power*, issued in July 1943 by the War Department with initiation from AAF. As a precursor to the formation of the second ADC in 1946, the manual specified organizationally that: ". . . the normal composition of an air force includes a strategic air force, a tactical air force, an air defense command and an air service command."[245] Leading directly to post war interservice competition for roles and missions was the statement that: "Land Power and Air Power are co-equal and interdependent forces . . ." and that ". . . neither is auxiliary of the other."[246] Even more pertinent to the later controversy was a statement about air defense responsibilities of the air forces under a unified command structure such as existed in combat theaters: "When antiaircraft artillery searchlights, and barrage balloons operate in the air defense of the same area with aviation, the efficient exploitation of the special capabilities of each . . . demand that all be placed under the command of the air commander responsible for the area. This must be done."[247]

Within CONUS during the war, some disagreement continued over the assignment of operational control over antiaircraft artillery to either Army Air or Ground Forces. Little had been settled by the war's end, however, and it has been suggested that during this time the air defense mission was kept ". . . in a state of suspension between AAF and AGF."[248]

3. Immediate Post War Decisions

With the War Department reorganization of forces in the spring of 1946 to meet post war needs came air force organization along functional lines—but the establishment of priorities and the division of functional missions still remained moot points. An Air Defense Command was created in March 1946 (along with the Strategic and Tactical Air Commands and the Air Materiel Command) and was tasked with the interim mission to ". . . organize and administer the integrated air defense system of the continental United States . . . exercise direct control of all active measures and coordinate all passive means of air defense."[249] While this major mission statement appeared specific on the extent of control ADC was to have, the War Department by directive on 8 April 1946 also gave Army Ground Forces (AGF) a defensive mission:

> Under the general plans of the War Department, and in conjunction with designated air and Naval commanders, prepare for, and on order, or in imminent emergency, execute planned operations for the defense of the United States.
> Coordination. Coordinate ground plans, including coastal defense and antiaircraft projects, with designated air and naval commanders.[250]

Although it appeared that a broad charter had been granted to ADC, AGF also thus had a piece of the action—and the situation demanded clarification. By May the War Department sought to eliminate the existing confusion over air defense responsibilities with issuance of Circular 138. This circular had the

---
[244] Ibid., p. 26.
[245] Ibid., p. 26.
[246] Ibid., p. 26.
[247] Ibid., p. 27.
[248] Ibid., p. 29.
[249] McMullen, "History of Air Defense Weapons 1946–1962," p. 16.
[250] Barnard, p. 17.

Chapter IV: American Systems

net effect of satisfying neither the ADC nor the AGF. The assignment to ADC of control over CONUS air defense in 138 was not specifically defined to their satisfaction nor was AGF pleased since ADC was to control antiaircraft units.[251] The existence of this displeasure continued. The War Department was requested to clarify its position after issuance of Circular 138, but it only did so by "refusing to modify the definition of air defense enunciated in WD Circular 138, and, in effect, by sustaining the AAF contention that AA should not revert to exclusive Ground Forces control. At most, however, this hedged upon the broader issue involved, and retained the dual assignment of antiaircraft artillery to AAF and AGF previously announced by the War Department."[252]

This lack of mission and control clarity may well have been caused by the unstated view of the War Department and the Army Air Force (parent to the ADC) that air defense should be viewed as a mobilization effort rather than as something performed by an ongoing, active military organization with organic defense hardware.[253] At any rate the lack of clarity was to restrict ADC activities through 1947, along with constraints imposed by shortages of personnel, forces, and the weapons to perform its assigned mission.[254] ADC took third priority after SAC and TAC, a position which was to limit ADC to a small role including supervision of the air reserves and planning an air defense system for CONUS.[255]

But while ADC remained at dead center regarding its mission and equipment, the Army Air Force gained a distinct advantage over AGF in September 1946. The War Department resolved the antiaircraft gun control issue by deciding that: "AAF would control AA units with air defense missions."[256] Therefore although ADC was relegated to a relatively powerless role, AAF was on its way to a more powerful position which was to be reinforced by the creation of a separate U.S. Air Force in 1947.

The tempo of events picked up rapidly in 1947. Three plans formulated by ADC for the air defense of CONUS went unapproved by AAF through the spring and summer, for the services were anticipating resolution of the more important issue of separating the Army from the Air Force.[257] The National Security Act had been sent to Congress on 27 February; by July the Act was passed, and the USAF came into being in September.[258] In July the Commanding Generals of Army Ground and Air Forces, respectively Generals Devers and Spaatz, had agreed that the ADC had responsibility for AGF units participating in air defense within the zone of the interior (CONUS).[259] But the exact meaning of this declaration remained unclear, overshadowed by the larger event of service reorganization. Creation of an independent Air Force in September did little to help ADC; on 17 December USAF directed ADC to base future force planning on the premise that the "Air National Guard [would] constitute [ADC's] major source of Air Defense Units."[260] Ironically, this reinforcement of ADC's lack of organic hardware was followed two days later with a formal mission directive for which the command had been waiting for months. Air Force Regulation 20-13 was issued on 19 December, and specified that air defense was to be the command's "chief mission."[261]

---

[251] Barnard, p. 17.
[252] "The Air Defense of the United States," p. 46.
[253] Futrell, "Ideas, Concept, Doctrine . . . ", p. 187.
[254] Sturm, p. 5.
[255] McMullen, op. cit., p. 22 on "Third Priority." Sturm, p. 5, on other information.
[256] Barnard, p. 20.
[257] McMullen, op. cit., p. 22.
[258] McMullen, op. cit., p. 22.
[259] Barnard, p. 22.
[260] McMullen, op. cit., p. 23.
[261] Sturm, p. 6.

Although these decisions clarified ADC's mission and status vis-à-vis the USAF, interservice roles remained to be agreed upon. In pursuance of such agreement Secretary of Defense Forrestal held a series of conferences at Key West, Florida, 11–14 March 1948, which resulted in service approval of the Air Force's air defense responsibilities. The Key West Agreements specified that:

> The Air Force was formally assigned the responsibility for defense of the United States against air attack, while the Army received the task of providing antiaircraft artillery units. Thus the Key West Agreements concluded the discussions and agreements which had been going on since early 1946. Although the Air Force accepted responsibility for air defense, and hence operational control of AA, they did not achieve the integration of AA into the Air Force. The details of implementing these agreements were left to the two services.[262]

During this same period of time in 1948, the cold war began to intensify but did not lead to an immediate strengthening in the U.S. air defense establishment. Among other things, in February communist control was attained over Czechoslovakia; in June the Russians began the Berlin blockade. While these occurrences contributed to the hardening of Soviet and U.S. policy positions, a domestic recession had greater impact on air defense efforts than overseas events. A budget surplus predicted in 1948 for FY 1949 quickly turned into a deficit of almost $2 billion.[263] With advice from the Bureau of the Budget in the summer of 1948, President Truman established an arbitrary defense budget ceiling of $14.4 billion for FY 1950.[264] The handwriting of fiscal austerity was on the wall for the Joint Chiefs; although FY 1950 was roughly a calendar year away at the time, the necessity for cutting back on desired programs seemed a certainty. It was within this context that any likelihood of new-found impetus for ADC was to drag on: ". . . although the urgency of clearing ADC's mission-laden decks was recognized in many official statements, little was done until the formation of the Continental Air Command (CONAC) in December 1948."[265]

In conjunction with the budgetary situation President Truman ordered the Air Force to reorganize for more economical use of available (especially civilian) assets on 15 October 1948.[266] As part of the subsequent reorganization, the administrative and logistical functions of ADC were doled out to the territorial air forces and the command itself became an operational headquarters under CONAC as of 1 December 1948.[267]

But while ADC was dissolved as a major command with the creation of CONAC, the pooling of available hardware that resulted brought about something ADC had long requested: an increase in operational forces. "On 30 November 1948, ADC had seven manned and equipped fighter squadrons earmarked for air defense purposes. The following day 16 manned and equipped fighter squadrons were available for air defense use."[268]

Developments internal to CONAC were to continue slowly during calendar year 1949 despite its auspicious beginnings in late 1948. Congressional action on Defense planning activities slowed during that year due to the Navy super-carrier–USAF B-36 controversy, and by the end of 1949 CONAC found itself with a small force increase over the strength of a year earlier—a total of ". . . 20 manned and equipped interceptor squadrons dedicated to air defense."[269]

---

[262] Barnard, pp. 23–25.
[263] Futrell, op. cit., p. 222.
[264] Futrell, op. cit., p. 222.
[265] "The Air Defense of the United States," p. 53.
[266] Barnard, p. 29.
[267] "The Air Defense of the United States," p. 201.
[268] McMullen, op. cit., p. 30.
[269] McMullen, op. cit., p. 55.

Chapter IV: American Systems

Interservice agreement on the role which CONAC should play still remained to be worked out although the Air Force had temporarily solved its internal air defense organizational problem with the establishment of CONAC. The mission directive issued to CONAC 11 January 1949 indicated that its purpose was "to conduct the active air defense of the United States, cooperate with land and amphibious forces, supervise the Air Force reserve programs, and ready all forces under its jurisdiction."[270]

Joint Army and Air Force discussions continued during the winter of 1948–1949 over the exact meaning of these CONAC responsibilities. The problem was not a particularly crucial one for the Army, because although there was disagreement over which service should control AA fire (the then-prime contribution of the Army to air defense) there was only one regular army AA battalion in existence during early 1949—and it was stationed at the Army Antiaircraft Artillery School at Ft. Bliss.[271] By decision of General Omar Bradley, Army Chief of Staff, on 18 February 1949, "Army units . . . [were placed] under operational control of the Air Defense Command (ADC); with command exercised by AA Sections belonging to the ADC staff."[272] Disagreement within the Army below the level of the Chief of Staff over the meaning of the term "operational control" was to continue through 1949, and the situation remained unresolved until 1950.[273]

In the meantime ADC was further degraded within the CONAC structure. The transfer of organizational and operational responsibilities within CONAC under a general reorganization during 1949 eliminated the need for a command level between the CONAC commander and field commanders with area air defense responsibilities.[274]

> Consequently, in September [1949], the Headquarters Air Defense Command was reduced to record status.
>
> It remained in this state of limbo until 1 July 1950 when, in consonance with the sweeping reorganization of the command which took place at that time, it was completely dissolved.[275]

The on-paper reorganization of USAF's air defense efforts in September 1949 had led to the activation of two regional commands—the Eastern and Western Air Defense Forces. Predating this activation was the Soviet explosion of an atomic device in August 1949, which had given impetus to a more effective air defense organization; the newly created area commands were partially a result and were placed on the same command level as the numbered air forces, a situation which looked more workable than the continuation of an understaffed ADC HQ.[276]

Operational control arrangements between the two services for air defense hardware still remained to be worked out, however. The 1949 USAF position that AAA units should be placed under operational control of ADC, coupled with differences of opinion on the DA staff over the Bradley decision on air defense responsibilities, serve as examples of the continuing problems in determining appropriate service roles.[277]

---

[270] Sturm, pp. 22–23.
[271] Barnard, p. 37.
[272] Ibid., p. 37.
[273] Ibid., pp. 37–39.
[274] Sturm, pp. 27–31.
[275] Ibid., p. 30.
[276] McMullen, op. cit., pp. 55–56 and Sturm, p. 43 on Russian A-bomb threat and the ADC.
[277] Futrell, op. cit., p. 284 on 1949 USAF position; Barnard, p. 43 on DA staff disagreement.

4. The Korean War Period

An increase (albeit a slow one) in the number of manned and equipped AAA units available led the Army to reconsider the AAA operational control problem in a conference 4–6 January 1950.[278] The issue at hand, from the Army standpoint, was the establishment of measures to prevent over control in air defense by the Air Force.[279] From this conference grew the recommendation that in the short run, an Army AA staff section should be established at CONAC; the Air Force concurred with this idea on 9 March of that year.[280] As a long-range plan for solution of the same problem, the conference recommended formation of an Army Air Defense Command, something which would in fact be established on 1 July 1950 as the Army element of CONAC under a slightly different name: the Army Antiaircraft Command (ARAACOM).[281] A series of USAF-Army agreements during the spring and summer of 1950 worked out joint target defense efforts, the most significant agreement of which occurred on 1 August 1950: "In a memorandum of agreement . . . Generals Vandenberg [USAF] and Collins [USA] decided between themselves that targets to be defended would be decided upon jointly by the Departments of Army and Air Force . . . and that Air Force air defense commanders would exercise operational control over antiaircraft artillery insofar as engagement and disengagement of fire is concerned."[282]

With this statement of agreement, the Army's operational control of AAA was definitely weakened; or as stated more strongly by an Army historian, the agreement ". . . significantly damaged AA's effectiveness."[283] The balance of air defense hardware control was clearly shifting in favor of the Air Force.

Providing a stimulus for a further review of air defense efforts during this time was the North Korean invasion of South Korea on 25 June 1950. The associated Congressional and service attention to CONUS defense, coupled with resultant manpower and materiel allocation increases for the services, fed in to the reestablishment of the USAF Air Defense Command as a major operational command on 1 January 1951.[284] On that date, an important reassignment of forces from CONAC to ADC occurred; ADC acquired: "The two Air Defense Forces, the air divisions, the fighter wings, groups, and squadrons, the AC&W groups and the radar squadrons, plus all of the other organizations whose primary duty under CONAC had been air defense. . . ."[285]

ADC had therefore become a command in its own right. The hardware strength of ADC was to move both up and down from the January baseline during 1951; while the size of the USAF weapons force doubled in the early months of that year, the need for overseas fighter units constrained any rapid increase in ADC-committed forces.[286]

Although ARAACOM HQ was collocated for closer liaison with the reinstituted ADC at Ent AFB, Colorado, on 15 January 1951, continuing problems remained to be worked out between the two organizations and between their parent services in the air defense field. ARAACOM, as ADC, had drastically increased its size in a short period of time; regarding ARAACOM, "From 11 July 1950 to 10 April 1951,

---

[278] Barnard, p. 43.
[279] Ibid., p. 46.
[280] Ibid., pp. 46, 53.
[281] Ibid., pp. 47, 55.
[282] Futrell, op. cit., p. 284.
[283] Barnard, p. 73.
[284] Ibid., p. 66.
[285] Sturm, p. 45.
[286] McMullen, op. cit., pp. 97–98.

Chapter IV: American Systems

[the] command increased from twelve men . . . to sixty-one units of assorted types and sizes."[287] Thus while earlier differences of opinion had existed between the services over roles and missions, the flavor of post-1950 discussions was modified by the fact that both of these service air defense organizations now had considerable physical strength. It took some time before new accommodations were to be reached between the two; the newly strengthened organizations individually found too many internal organizational problems to be dealt with in the short term to come to serious grips with any revision of the existing Collins-Vandenberg agreement. ARAACOM expanded from 23 battalions in mid-April 1951 to 45 battalions by the end of that year; internal headquarters reorganizations and the establishment of operational defenses for selected areas occupied most of the available time through that period.[288] ADC was similarly involved at this same time with CONUS sector divisions and manpower staffing assignments.

The next major interservice agreement occurred in the Chidlaw (CG, ADC)-Lewis (CG, ARAACOM) memorandum of July 1952. From this agreement ARAACOM gained the following:

a. Definition of the term Gun Defended Area (GDA). [Note: GDA was essentially a AAA free-fire zone]
b. Commitment by ADC to exercise operational control through AA defense commanders
c. ADC's pledge to designate GDA's as soon as possible
d. ADC's guarantee to provide space for AA staff sections
e. Assurance that ARAACOM would continue to prepare plans for AA defenses
f. The right to participate in ADC exercises
g. That ADC would relay intelligence data to ARAACOM
h. That cross service agreements could be used to support AA units defending Air Force Bases.[289]

Although ARAACOM had clearly gained by these points in the area of operational control compared to the earlier agreement since ADC would exercise its control through AA commanders, it was still obvious that ADC had the upper hand in the overall picture. ARAACOM was bargaining with ADC, not vice-versa.

Actions by ARAACOM and ADC from the Chidlaw-Lewis agreement through the end of 1953 are set within the context of organizational introspection. During this period, the Department of the Army demobilized National Guard units which had been mobilized to serve in Korea, and regular army units were activated to replace them. ARAACOM participated in this changeover, along with deploying a new gun weapons system (the 75-mm. Skysweeper) and modifying the responsibilities of its various headquarters for greater efficiency.[290] ARAACOM was also extremely busy with the conversion of gun battalions to Nike Ajax battalions. Although the first Nike Ajax unit was not on site until December 1953, prior activities to meet that deployment date required the development of individual and unit training plans, logistical studies, site selection, and unit reorganization schemes as major areas of concern.[291]

During this same period of time, ADC was striving to realize a previous planning goal for the projected 1953 ADC of 57 squadrons.[292] Although the ADC "pie in the sky" goal of late 1952 was for an eventual "ultimate" air defense force of 151 interceptor aircraft squadrons plus 30 Bomarc squadrons, by mid-1953

---

[287] Barnard, p. 75.
[288] Ibid., p. 92.
[289] Ibid., p. 117.
[290] Ibid., pp. 123, 133.
[291] Semmens, BDM, *Chronology*.
[292] McMullen, op. cit., p. 98.

they actually controlled 46 manned and equipped squadrons compared to 39 at the end of 1952.[293] ADC continued to strive for the goal of 57 squadrons through the end of 1953; this figure was eventually realized at the end of 1954 (although 2 of those so-designated had not yet been manned or equipped).[294]

Overlapping these events were the activities of the Joint Air Defense Board (JADB), established by the Air Force Chief of Staff in early 1952 to coordinate procedures and doctrines between the services. The "joint" nature of the board is in some doubt because of the source of establishment of the board; Lieutenant General Lewis (former ARAACOM CG) later described JADB as ". . . entirely useless and a waste of personnel."[295] Interservice work of the board was complicated by the extent of control the Air Force had already assured itself in the air defense field. ADC reflected their own view of this control in some basic tenets of air defense organization they set forth in early 1953, the most pertinent of which is the following: "Air Division Commanders should have control of all air defense tools in his (sic) area which are necessary for the active air defense."[296] An Army historian stated this tenet as an accomplished fact when he said that: "Since the Collins-Vandenberg agreement, the United States Air Force had operational control of AA units."[297] At any rate, the Joint Air Defense Board came to be viewed as an unacceptable solution to the problem of coordination in light of this Air Force control.

Somewhat predating serious reconsideration of the JADB but impacting on it was President Truman's acceptance of a set of recommendations about air defense from the National Security Resources Board. By acceptance of the recommendations, Truman ". . . thereby ruled that a continental defense system capable of withstanding any eventuality should be ready for service by the end of 1955."[298] Although this was a requirement established by a President who was to be out of office within a month, it contributed in a general way to the revision of the JADB by its statement—new attention was being directed at air defense.

5. Post–Korean War Developments

Other events were also to impact on the JADB issue and the larger issue of joint command. President Eisenhower took office in January 1953, and during the same month (July) that the Korean armistice was signed ordered the JCS to take a fresh look at U.S. military capabilities.[299] Chairman of the JCS Radford and Air Force Chief of Staff Twining began considering better solutions to interservice air defense coordination than the JADB in August of that year as part of their response to the President's request, and determined that a CONUS air defense command should be placed directly under the JCS rather than the then-current arrangement.[300] On 20 August 1953, the Soviet Union successfully tested a hydrogen bomb; this development plus the emerging need seen at the highest decision-making levels for a new look at U.S. defense capabilities served as a backdrop for the emerging reorganizational activities. Although ADC and ARAACOM continued to develop internally, the overall organization for air defense was now a question to be resolved by higher authority within the context of a new overall strategy. In October, the Chairman of the JCS requested that the NSC issue fundamental guidance on U.S. strategy; the response was NSC-162,

---

[293] McMullen, op. cit., pp. 98–100.
[294] McMullen, op. cit., pp. 100–101.
[295] Barnard, p. 159.
[296] Sturm, p. 69.
[297] Barnard, p. 159.
[298] Futrell, p. 304.
[299] Futrell, op. cit., p. 380.
[300] Barnard, p. 159.

Chapter I: American and Soviet Strategy: A Comparison

which recommended increased spending of about $1 billion per year on air defense. President Eisenhower approved this recommendation and sent it to Congress on 7 January 1954.[301]

Continued consideration was given to modifying the existing air defense organizational structure during January. The JCS tasked the Joint Strategic Plans Committee to prepare the Terms of Reference for a joint command to replace the JADB; its report, completed in March, suggested that Army, Navy, and ADC views be obtained on such a command.[302]

As might have been anticipated, ADC and ARAACOM disagreed over the composition and organization of a new joint command. LTG John Lewis, CG, ARAACOM, basically recommended a command similar to that which then existed, with "the Air Force component, as the executive agent of the JCS, preparing and submitting plans, requirements, doctrine and procedure. When AA units deployed to tactical positions ADC would exercise operational control."[303]

But General Lewis' position received little support. Instead, the recommendations of General Benjamin Chidlaw, CG, ADC, held sway; without repeating his argument, the ideas are reflected in the CONAD decision:

> On 2 August 1954, the services resolved their differences, and JCS established Continental Air Defense Command (CONAD) on 1 September 1954. The United States Air Force was the victor in the settlement of the dispute. ADC assumed the dual role of a joint command. Its echelons picked up added designations as joint headquarters.... Although representatives from the Army and Navy were on the joint staffs; [sic] commanders and key staff officers were Air Force officers. In a sole concession to General Lewis, component forces retained the status of operational control upon deployment, as opposed to the attached status advocated by General Chidlaw....[304]

The handwriting was on the wall; the Air Force had won the roles and missions argument. USAF was designated the executive agency for CONAD by JCS; General Chidlaw became the first CINCONAD, with the Army and Navy CONAD component force commanders as his "advisors" on antiaircraft and Naval force employment matters, respectively.[305] The extent of service control over CONAD is thus clear. A look at the organization's charter illuminates the CONAD mission. The "terms of reference" established for CONAD with its creation (serving until revision in September 1956), set out the extent of CONAD's control through the end of the time period covered here. Briefly, "CONAD's operational control... [consisted of] ... the authority to direct the tactical air battle, including engagement and disengagement of weapons and control of fighters; specify the conditions of alert; station the early warning elements; and locate and deploy the combat elements of the command in accordance with JCS-approved plans."[306]

CONAD, through USAF, was therefore in the driver's seat of CONUS air defense efforts.

Although by the end of 1955 ARAACOM's 79 weapons battalions outnumbered the interceptor squadrons of ADC (which continued to work toward attainment of the USAF-projected ADC strength of 69 squadrons for mid-1957, a net desired increase of 12 over those authorized by the end of 1954), it was clear that ARAACOM's numerical unit strength would not offset the predominant Air Force role which had been established with the creation of CONAD.[307]

---

[301] Futrell, op. cit., p. 381.
[302] Sturm, pp. 85–86.
[303] Barnard, p. 160.
[304] Barnard, p. 162.
[305] Sturm, pp. 89–90.
[306] Air Defense: An Historical Analysis, Vol. III, p. 110.
[307] McMullen, op. cit., pp. 100–101.

6. Summary

Throughout the 1945–1955 period, organization for air defense was stimulated by a number of factors including response to threats and events external to the United States. Significant external stimuli included: Soviet and other communist actions in Eastern and Western Europe during the late 1940's; Soviet atomic capabilities as evidenced in their nuclear weapons tests; and, the impetus the Korean War gave to a build-up of U.S. military forces. However, the exact extent to which these events brought about modifications in the size of, and organization for, air defense is difficult to determine.

Air defense organization was also affected by AAF/AGF, and later USA/USAF competition for roles, missions, and operational control of air defense hardware. Within this context, ARAACOM was the product of Army disagreement with the extent of the USAF ADC's role in air defense. CONAD resulted from an ADC desire for complete control over air defense roles and missions.

Command and control organizations were first constrained, and later assisted, by budgetary considerations. CONAC grew out of a budgetary austerity program under President Truman; ADC, ARAACOM, and later CONAD became flush with larger monetary allocations. The impact of the defense budget level on air defense efforts should not be underestimated, for it proved to be a more potent factor than external threats in determining the size of these efforts during the 1948–1950 period.

Finally, although it is guesswork to assess the efficiency of these air defense organizations in actually countering the then-existing threats, it does appear ironic that shortly after CONAD came into existence the first significant reference was made to the obsolescence of air defense because of the increasing sophistication of long-range missiles.[308]

The following chart (Figure 6) depicts major changes in U.S. organization for air defense in the 1945–1955 period.

---

[308] Murdock, pp. 34–35 on the November 1954 statement by Secretary of the Air Force Harold Talbott.

Figure 6—Major Changes in Air Defense Organization, 1945–1955

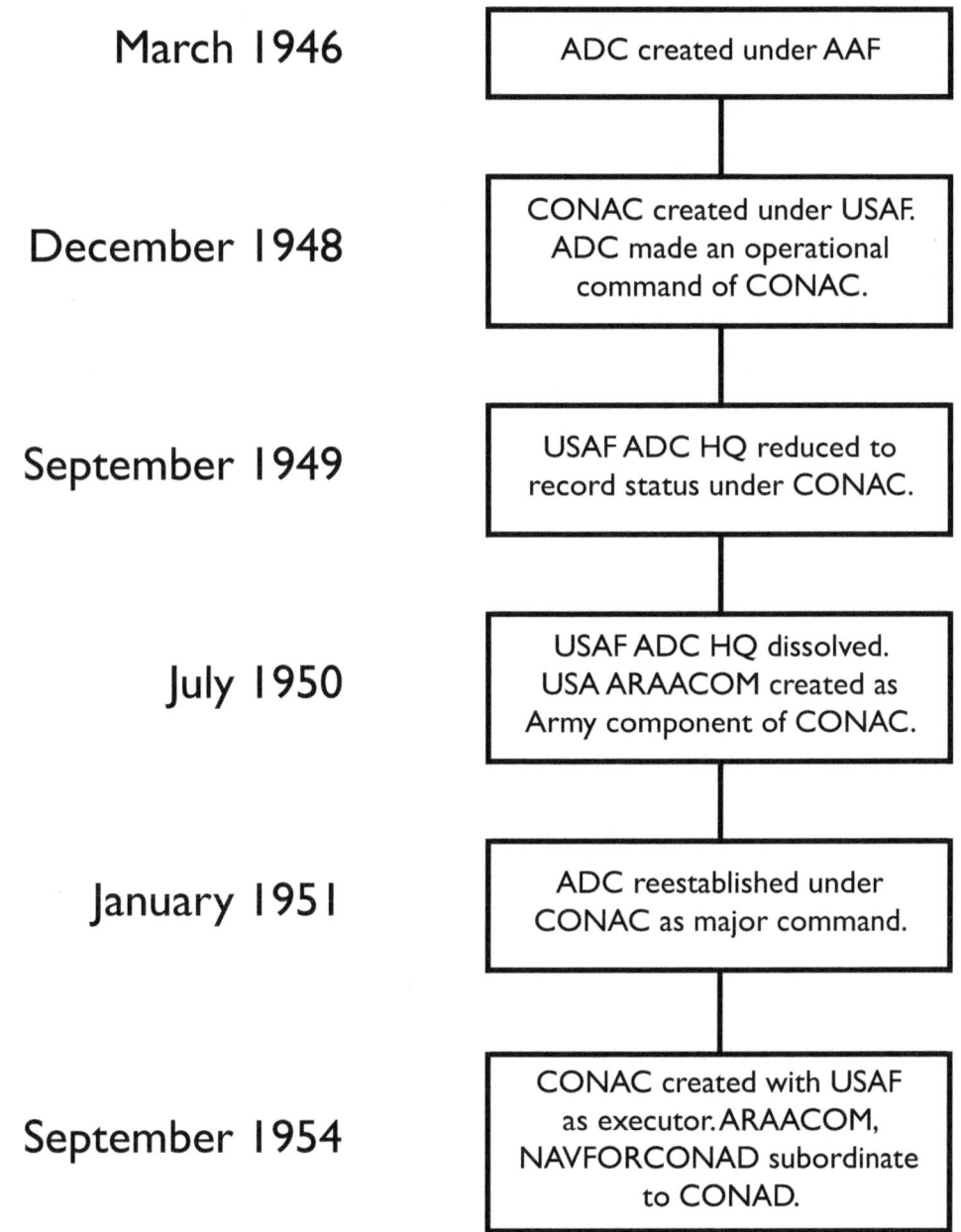

Chapter V

Soviet Systems

A. Introduction

From the Soviet perspective, "The development of antiaircraft defense after the Second World War may be divided into two periods: the first, from 1946–53, and the second, from 1954 to the present."[1] The break between the two periods is delimited by the formation of PVO (Strany) as a co-equal with other services of the Soviet armed forces in May of 1954. Coincidently, the 1953 date conforms to more general Soviet military histories, which acknowledge 1953 as the year of Stalin's death and the year in which the Soviet Union demonstrated its first thermonuclear weapon. A third stage seems also to be doctrinally accepted which acknowledges "the revolution in military affairs." This last phase is marked by the formation of the Rocket Forces as another service in 1960 and the adjustment of military doctrine to nuclear and missile weapons. Within these divisions, Soviet writers usually characterize the first period as one in which Soviet air forces were equipped with modern jet aircraft. The second period is generally characterized by the deployment of missiles for both ground and aviation air defense components. The third period might be characterized by attempts at ABM defense. In keeping with the Soviet view of the earliest period, this history will focus on the decisions involved in the process of aircraft modernization and the development of jet technology. Subsequent volumes will focus on surface-to-air missiles and Soviet ABM programs in turn.

Not only does the focus on jet aircraft accord with the Soviet view of early post war history, it also takes advantage of unique insights into the Soviet process of decision making. Aircraft designers and test-pilots occupy a special status among Soviet heroes. They write and they talk more freely about their activities than other segments of the society and they appear somewhat open about their activities with members of the aviation press—that is if a decent period (about 20 years) has passed to preclude possible disclosure of military secrets. In addition to the remembrances of key figures in the Soviet development community, there are also a number of defectors who round out the picture of Soviet aviation, particularly in the areas of applied research and aircraft production. Thus, in retrospect, a fair picture emerges as to how decisions were made with regard to aviation in the late Stalinist period; it is a picture which is substantially corroborated by intelligence of the period and by more recent Soviet official documents.

From the standpoint of historiography, the focus on aircraft developers and development decisions may be dangerous. It may distort conclusions drawn with the benefit of a wider focus. This potential bias is acknowledged, but discounted, for several reasons:

(1) The personal role of Stalin in military decisions, particularly aviation matters
(2) The purge and politicization of air force leadership in 1946

---

[1] Dzhordzhadze, "The Role of Historical Experience," p. 41.

(3) The subordination of the air forces to ground forces requirements and leadership

(4) The continuing pattern of political domination of the military establishment and military force structure decisions which persisted after the death of Stalin

(5) The exclusion of members of the military and political leadership from weapons decisions made among Stalin and his principal advisors.

These factors lend credence to the picture of Soviet decision makers portrayed in the following materials. A further, and compelling, reason is that few data exist to develop alternate foci. Therefore, the following materials approach aviation decisions through the designers and include additional data which broaden the perspective.

Rather than detail what strategic defense forces developed, or how, the intent is to ask "why?" It is the contention here that design activities provided a menu of weapons from which a number were chosen for production and deployment. It is in this context, that one gains a grasp of "why?"

By extension, understandings gained from a study of aviation decisions can be applied to developments in the realm of antiaircraft artillery, surface-to-air missiles, and radar systems. In two major respects, however, decisions related to complementary defensive systems differ. First, it seems they did not involve Stalin as frequently. Second, they took place in a framework where domestic institutions were less well developed and where reliance on foreign technology was higher. This chapter thus discusses the observable developments within these other categories of systems. It closes with a discussion of civil defense developments to complete an overall appreciation of the strategic defense effort.

B. History of Fighter Aircraft of PVO

1. Pre-War Experience

Patterns of organization, institutional behavior, and decision making in Soviet aviation derive from the pre-WWII formation of the Peoples Commissariat for Aviation Industry and from the emergence during the late 1930's of a group of young and competent designers who since have been sustained in their independent development activities. The industry was *highly competitive* in the process of designing alternative prototype aircraft, *political* in the allocation of resources and *centralized* in the exchange of information.[2] It became an establishment in which the designers played a key role protected by a ministerial-level institution along with key producer industries. Within this establishment, the user organization, the air forces, did not necessarily have the predominant voice.

The character of the Soviet aviation industry was much influenced by the purges of scientists and engineers during 1927–1929. In effect, these purges, which culminated in the Industrial Party (Promparty) Trial of 1930, virtually wiped out the entire technician class of that generation.[3] The principal designers of the thirties—Nikolai Polikarpov, in fighters, and Andrei Tupolev, in bombers—fell into disfavor in 1929 and Polikarpov was imprisoned for industrial sabotage or "wrecking."[4] During this period, the Central Design Bureau was organized under the State Political Administration (GPU or Secret Police). Among its facilities was the "Seventh Hangar" organized under the "internal prison" (Vnutrennaya Turma), where Polikarpov

---

[2] See Institute for Research in Social Science, and Alexander R&D for detailed description.
[3] Solzhenitsyn, pp. 377–399. Of approximately 30–40,000 engineers in the U.S.S.R., Solzhenitsyn estimates that 5,000 were arrested (p. 387).
[4] "Prolific Pioneer," Flying Review International, July 1968, p. 405.

Chapter V: Soviet Systems

and other aviation notables lived and worked under heavy guard.[5] During that period, Alexander Yakovlev, Sergie Iluyshin, and probably Artem Mikoyan received their training in this same Central Design Bureau Complex. In 1933, after the successful flight of his I-5 prototype, Polikarpov was released. By 1934, it was Tupolev's turn. He received a ten-year sentence for sale of military secrets to Germany, but worked his way out after two years with the design of the gargantuan eight-engine "Maxim Gorky" propaganda and passenger craft.[6] He was returned to prison on two later occasions in 1937 and in 1940.[7] In 1937, another name in Soviet aviation gained prominence—that of Semyon Lavochkin. The design of the LAGG-I and the team of Lavochkin, Gorbunov, and Gudkov emerged, again from prison.[8]

a. Structure of the Aviation Industry

Four basic functions were organized under the Commissariat and the Ministry of Aviation which succeeded it. They were and (in 1975) still remain:

(1) Basic Research
(2) Prototype Design
(3) Testing and
(4) Production.

Basic research is conducted within the Central Aerohydrodynamics Institute (TsAGI) for airframe problems and within the Central Institute of Aviation Motor Building (TsIAM), the All Union Institute of Aviation Materials (VIAM), and the Scientific Institute for Aviation Equipment for related subjects. Design activities are the province of the Central Design Bureau (TsKB) and of semi-autonomous Experimental Design Bureaus (OKBs) which operate under it in the fields of airframes, engines, and armament. Testing is conducted by centralized testing establishments, most notably the Flight Test Institute (LII) and the Scientific Testing Institute of the air forces (NIIVVS). Production is organized among individual factories responsible to the Ministry.[9]

b. Elites

Within Soviet air forces, there are two parallel series of ranks; one for the operational side and another for the technical. The operational ranks range up to Chief Marshal, but the engineering ranks stop at the next-lower Colonel-General rank. Notably, only Army officers are eligible for the highest rank, Marshal of the Soviet Union. This, however, does not indicate that officers of the Aviation Engineering Services carry less weight; quite to the contrary:

> It is more difficult to obtain an engineering rank than an executive one, as the prefix "engineer" is only given to those who have received the highest technical air education, and is usually reserved for those who have passed through the Zhukovski Military Engineering Academy. Exceptions are occasionally made for distinguished inventors. In the schools and experimental stations of the Soviet Air Forces, the technical side outranks the non-technical. For example, an Engineer-Major may even hold a post which would normally be filled by a non-technical Major-General.[10]

---

[5] Ibid. and Yakovlev, *Target*, p. 84.
[6] "Chief U.S.S.R. Aircraft Designer," *Air Intelligence Digest*, Jan. 1950, p. 16 CONF.
[7] "Soviet Big Five Aircraft Designers," *Air Intelligence Digest*, Feb. 1954, p. 32 CONF.
[8] "Lavochkin" *Air Intelligence Digest*, Mar. 1950, p. 36.
[9] Institute for Research in Social Science, and Alexander, *R&D*.
[10] Tokaev, *Soviet Imperialism*, p. 42.

The Zhukovski Academy is a centralized post-graduate institution devoted to aviation studies (and Marxist-Leninism of course). Its students and graduates are distinguished by special pay, privileges, social access, uniforms, and bearing. Its senior staff members frequently enjoy direct access to the Politbureau and some relief from political imperatives which are imposed on the remainder of the Soviet population. Alumni of the academy share a "scientific" ethic and generally recognize each other on the basis of individual competence. ". . . We are therefore school-mates. A strong comradely friendship binds us. We frequently consult with each other and help each other solve complicated problems."[11] Among names frequently mentioned in this study, Yakovlev, Mikoyan, Iluyshin, Lavochkin, and Tokaev were Zhukovski graduates. Tupolev, Polikarpov, Klimov, and Yakovlev were at one time staff members. Those who do not fare as well, Sukhoi, for example, appear to be graduates of other technical institutes.

The ethic which binds the technical elite extends, in part, to their subordinates. The open literature contains several examples of direct appeals as high as Stalin[12] for review of sentences on behalf of technical staff and of confrontations with political officers to allow individuals to continue with competent work with less interference.[13] This "backing up" of personnel may explain the strength and loyalty of design teams.[14]

c. Design Competition

The tradition of design competition evolved during the 1930's as a number of designers began working independently of the major institutes. In 1936, a requirement was issued for a light multipurpose fighter. Four designers responded with development programs. Later that same year, the specification was revised to favor the light bomber role and a Sukhoi prototype (the Su-2), developed independently of his mentor Tupolev, was accepted.[15]

The epitome of design competition was that held in late 1939. Over 20 designers were given assignments to provide prototypes against two or three basic requirements. A fairly detailed account of that competition is resorted to because it is prologue to the decision patterns and criteria that prevailed until Stalin's death in 1953.

The competition derived from a conference in the Oval Hall of the Kremlin. Among those present were "all who had proved themselves to be aviation designers or inventors and who had in recent years made some contribution to aviation."[16] The meeting was presided over by Stalin, V. M. Molotov (Premier), and K. Y. Voroshilov (Minister of Defense), with Molotov moderating. What ensued was a general review of the status of Soviet aviation and a debate over the utility of four-engined bombers. Subsequently 20–25 engine and airframe designers were again called to the Kremlin for personal interviews before a panel of Stalin, M. M. Kaganovich (Commissar for Aviation), Molotov, Voroshilov, F. A. Agal'Tsov (Assistant Director of the Air Force), and another member of the Politburo.[17]

Among Yakovlev's recollection of his interview is the following dialogue:

---

[11] Yakovlev, *Target*, p. 416.
[12] Ibid. p. 420.
[13] Takaev, *Comrade X*, pp. 112–115.
[14] "Tupolev," *Air Intelligence Digest*, Jan. 1950, p. 15.
[15] Nemecek, Feb. 1966, p. 373.
[16] Yakovlev, *Target*, p. 163.
[17] Ibid.

Chapter V: Soviet Systems

[Stalin] ". . . Are you aware that we have ordered this kind of fighter from several other designers, and the winner will be the one who not only gives the best fighter in terms of flight and combat qualities but also delivers first, so that we can get it into series production sooner?"

[Yakovlev] "I understand, Comrade Stalin."

[Stalin] "It's not important if you understand. You've got to produce it sooner."

[Yakovlev] "What time limit?" [the key question!]

[Stalin] "The sooner the better. By New Year's?"

[Stalin] "We ourselves are very much aware that we don't need that many planes. But, the good Lord willing, out of all these we'll get five or six that can be put into series production. And that many new aircraft won't confuse us."[18]

Yakovlev states that he left the meeting "inspired with the spirit of creative competition and with unwavering intentions of beating our rivals."[19] Eleven other designers were competing against the same requirement, but Yakovlev produced before his counterparts—by the New Year's deadline. The first three available prototypes (YAK-1, MiG-3, LAGG-3) were committed to production before testing was completed. On January 9, 1940, Yakovlev was appointed by Stalin to be Assistant Commissar for Aviation Industry at age 35.[20]

Several points are illustrated by this vignette which characterize subsequent aviation decisions during the Stalinist era. The points are underscored because they represent a pattern repeated in post war decisions:

(1) The dominant role and personal involvement of Stalin
(2) The weight of *political* and *technical* representation in the process as opposed to the one representative of the air forces general staff
(3) The importance of the design community in the process
(4) The official encouragement of the competition concept
(5) Compressed lead times and the importance of arbitrary and seldomly explicit dates
(6) The rewards, both in terms of production commitment and of other honors, which attend the design of the first prototypes fielded (reinforced by the negative rewards of Hanger Seven)
(7) The continuity of the key figures in the decision pattern. Yakovlev remained Assistant Commissioner until 1948, and the competing bureaus are, for the most part, still active.

d. Information Flows

Among Yakovlev's innovations in 1940 were the design handbooks and reorientation of the TsAGI. The design handbooks amounted to a standardization program for the aviation development community. The multiplication of independent design activities necessitated a common code of procedures. An initial version was produced in 1940. The second edition which appeared after the Soviets entered WWII consisted of 11 parts:

(1) Aerodynamics
(2) Hydromechanics
(3) Strength of materials
(4) Flight tests of aircraft and equipment
(5) Engines
(6) Aircraft equipment

---

[18] Ibid., p. 165.
[19] Ibid., p. 166.
[20] Ibid., p. 169.

(7) Aircraft armament
(8) Landing gear and mechanisms
(9) Standard systems
(10) Materials
(11) Semiproducts[21]

Among contributors to the handbooks were the foremost Soviet authorities on aviation science and design with a leavening of test pilots. The second edition was intended to incorporate construction and combat experience gained from the immediate pre-war generation of fighters. The design handbooks became a virtual encyclopedia of Soviet aviation and the principal means of communicating research results to the practical engineering level. They also provided a medium for reconciling conflicting perspectives of the military, scientists, engineers, production specialists, and maintenance people. The handbooks are a feature of Soviet aviation today and are thought to be a principal source of continuity and conservation in Soviet aviation technology.[22]

e. Use of Foreign Technology

In its early years, the Soviet aviation establishment relied heavily on foreign technology, but with the express aim of freeing itself from dependence on such assistance as soon as possible. Before 1925, Italy, France, England, and the Netherlands had supplied the Soviet Union with most of her planes and as late as that year a German-directed Junkers Company produced 500 aircraft in Russia.[23] Independent Soviet airframe designs began to emerge during the mid-1930's with independent engine designs emerging somewhat later. Purchases of foreign aircraft were not completely stopped and a concentrated effort to obtain U.S. technology followed the resumption of U.S.S.R./U.S. relations in 1933. As late as 1936, U.S. aircraft were purchased under license.[24]

During the pre-war period, a diversified program to exploit foreign technology accompanied the reorganization of design activities. Emphasis was placed on legitimate procurement of equipment and information, along with official visits and student exchanges. Generally, material was open for sale one year after it began production.[25]

During the war, the United States and Britain sent about 18,000 aircraft to Russia. These are compared by the Soviets to approximately 126,000 Soviet-produced craft to demonstrate that "the Soviet Union fought with its own strength."[26] It is the opinion of Robert Kilmarx that of these thousands of these lend-lease craft were held back to conserve them for use during the later period of transition to jet aircraft.[27] According to General John R. Dean, head of a U.S. military mission to the U.S.S.R., "we never lost an opportunity to give the Russians equipment, weapons, or information which we thought might help our combined war effort."[28]

The overt Soviet effort was supplemented by covert and grey activities. Toward the end of the war, the Soviet Purchasing Commission in Washington numbered over 1,000 people and high priority was given to

---

[21] Yakovlev, *50 Years*, p. 40.
[22] Alexander, *R&D*, pp. 15–16. Declining influence of the handbooks is discussed in Alexander, 1973 Trip Report, p. 9.
[23] Institute for Research in Social Science, pp. 58–59.
[24] Ibid.
[25] Kilmarx, pp. 165–166.
[26] Yakovlev, *50 Years*, p. 97.
[27] Kilmarx, p. 208.
[28] Ibid.

collection of information on jet aircraft. An effort to obtain information on America's first jet (the P-59) and on General Electric and Westinghouse jet engine developments is well documented.[29] Andrei Schevchenko, a legal representative to Bell Aircraft and later of Amtorg who engaged in espionage, reportedly mentioned a Lenin prize of 500,000 rubles for a jet aircraft design by the end of 1945.[30] Another report of the 1945 deadline is attributed to a Russian in this country.[31]

2. Performance of Soviet Aviation During WWII

In its simplest, the story of Soviet Air Forces during WWII is one of initial debacle and remarkable recovery aided by the overextension of German power. Despite the massive destruction of Soviet aircraft in June of 1941, a credible local defense began to be marshaled around Moscow in that same autumn. The winter-enforced lull in the air war, coupled with increasing numbers of new Soviet fighters, changed the momentum of the air battle. Stalingrad appears to have been the turning point where German aviation operated with impunity during the early stages of the siege, but suffered increasing losses as the campaign wore on. German losses exceeded resupply, while the Soviets were rapidly increasing their air forces based on industrial capacity, recovering from relocation to the east of the Urals.

In January of 1943 USAAF daylight raids combined with RAF night attacks on Germany to force the build-up of Luftwaffe homeland defenses at the expense of forces supporting the Eastern Front. As this homeland air front began to absorb over half of Germany's air resources, the balance shifted overwhelmingly in favor of the Soviets. By late 1943, a Soviet force of from 12,000 to 15,000 thoroughly modern aircraft faced a German Eastern Front air strength of from 2,000 to 3,000. During the Kuban and the Kursk-Orel campaigns in the summer of 1943, Germany did mass to contest the air, but at heavy cost in aircraft and crews. The Soviets could absorb losses; the Germans could not. Thereafter, local Luftwaffe commanders came to regard unfavorable odds of 12:1 as routine.[32]

a. Lessons Learned—Fighter Aviation

Despite Western historians who credit Soviet successes to improved airbase attack, the following emerged in 1949 as doctrine distilled from WWII experience. It relates to the relevance of fighter combat as opposed to other techniques of air defense or air superiority[33]:

(1) The experience of the past war showed that fighter aviation is the decisive factor in the struggle for air superiority. It also showed that the outcome depends mainly on air combat, which is the most effective way of destroying enemy aircraft.

(2) The experience of the war undermined the theory of German-fascist military circles about destroying an enemy air force by lightning war consisting mainly of strikes against enemy air bases.

(3) It also undermined the theories of Anglo-American military circles about gaining air superiority through air strikes at the military economy of the enemy, especially against his aircraft industry, his fuel reserves and his air training establishments. (Concentrated actions against the centers of the enemy's aircraft industry are certainly useful in gaining air superiority and they can hasten the

---

[29] Hearings, Un-American Activities, Jet Propulsion, p. 121.
[30] Ibid., p. 120.
[31] Ibid., p. 121.
[32] Lee, 1959, p. 70.
[33] Volkov, Col. A., "Fighter Aviation in Contemporary War," Voennaya, Mysl', Feb. 1949, pp. 55–69. From extracts. Note that a separate doctrine of "Air Defense Operations" was emerging among PVO troops during this period. See above Chapter V.

defeat of the enemy air force, but this can be only a supplementary means of winning air superiority. The main method must be destruction of enemy aircraft in the air and on air bases.)

(4) The struggle for air superiority and with it the main efforts of fighter aviation should be centered primarily about the ground effort. The reason for this is that only by means of ground action can the strategic aims of the war be attained. No independent air action can achieve results equal in importance to those air actions carried out in the interest of the success of the overall effort. In this context, air combat becomes as a rule extremely savage and calls for the greatest pressure and energy. Both belligerents can expect to suffer heavy losses as new air reserves are brought into action in the effort to secure freedom of action for the ground forces.[34]

From the contemporary U.S. perspective of "strategic," these lessons appear to relate to "theater" applications. However, from the Soviet experience, the Wehrmacht was Germany's strategic instrument. From the Soviet view:

> ... Soviet military science considers that the outcome of war under contemporary conditions is decided on the field of battle by means of the annihilation of the armed forces of the enemy and that one of the most important tasks of aviation is active assistance to the ground and naval forces in all forms of their combat activity. This definition of the fundamental mission of aviation is not contradicted by the need to employ part of its forces to strike the deep rear of the enemy, or his military-industrial targets, but our military science does not consider such blows an end in themselves, but only a helpful means of creating favorable conditions for the success of the combat operations of the ground and naval forces. The structure of our military air forces is established on the basis of the scientific definition of the role and significance of aviation in contemporary war.[35]

In the context of early post war decisions these doctrinal statements are interesting in that they obscure the difference between frontal and defense aviation. The perception of an integrated air superiority mission epitomized by fighter-versus-fighter battles simplified potentially conflicting priorities by way of establishing a single set of interceptor requirements. Such a perception was not without foundation until 1957 when SAC released its fighter wings to the Tactical Air Command; U.S. B-36 doctrine called for fighter escort.[36]

b. Lessons Learned—Institutional

Beside the sanctification of fighters as the primary instrument of air power, the WWII experience confirmed the "correctness" of institutional arrangements in Soviet aviation. During the war years the Soviets produced 126,000 to 157,000 aircraft[37] of a quality comparable to those operational anywhere in the world—the German jets excepted. The Soviet perception was that "Our aircraft surpassed the enemy's in both quality and quantities."[38] While this perception of Yakovlev was self-serving since he was then Deputy Commissar for Aviation Industry, it is nevertheless important because he continued in that position through the period of significant postwar decisions. Moreover, it soon became a test of loyalty among the Soviet population at large to put down everything that was foreign and to proclaim the superiority of Soviet technology.[39]

---

[34] Nikitin, Col. Gen. of Avn. A., "Soviet Aviation," Voennaya Mysl', Feb. 1949, p. 62. Quoted in Garthoff, p. 173–174. An early post war attempt to define a strategic doctrine more in line with Douhet's theories was unsuccessful. (Ibid., p. 172.) This does not deny that an extremely high priority was given to long range developments which would lead to an intercontinental "strategic" weapon. See Tokaev, Stalin Means War, pp. 91–121.

[35] 85th Cong. 1st Sess. DoD Appropriation for 1958, HR, Hearings, pp. 917–918. Quoted in Futrell, Ideas, Concepts Doctrine, p. 465.

[36] From Soviet figures, Yakovlev, 50 Years, p. 97. These figures are slightly conservative when compared with U.S. intelligence estimates circa 1949. The range is accounted for by the addition of Jan.–June 1941 (pre-war) production to the lower figure.

[37] Yakovlev, Target, p. 286.

[38] Tokaev, Stalin Means War, pp. 107–108.

[39] Lee, 1959, pp. 143–144.

Chapter V: Soviet Systems

The perception of design and industrial success on the part of the Soviets was appropriate in many regards. From the design standpoint, Asher Lee summarizes a widely held respect for the machines that were produced after 1943:

> ... Their own YAK, MiG and LAGG fighters were more than equal in performance to the British Hurricanes and American Aerocobras and Kittyhawks—even the improved versions which they were getting in hundreds every month under Lend-lease. Indeed, the technical gap between the German and Soviet single-engined fighters had virtually closed by the end of 1943. French pilots who have flown the YAK, the Spitfire and the Messerschmitt 109 declare that the Soviet plane was the equal of its German and British counterparts....[40]

From the production standpoint, the Soviet perception of success also is justifiable when compared with the production of its enemy. By 1944, Soviet monthly aircraft production was running ahead of the German industry. Despite the fact that over half of the Soviet aviation industry was relocated in 1941, production recovered within the year. In 1944, the last full year of the war, Soviet production reached 40,300 and German production was 40,953.[41] (No less remarkable than the Soviet recovery, however, was the German success at maintaining such a production rate in spite of allied air attack by dispersed use of underground facilities and other expedients.) The Soviet 1944 monthly production rate of 3,300 compares with a peak wartime U.S. rate of 7,100 although such comparisons ignore the large proportion of bombers in U.S. production which would reflect on an alternate measure of airframe weight. Despite qualifications, the perspective of institutional success appears justified. The Soviet aviation establishment had fielded a force roughly equivalent to that of its primary enemy; on the other hand, that enemy had other battles to fight. On the Eastern Front the Soviets had a rough 6 to 1 numerical superiority toward the end of the war.[42]

c. Lessons Learned—Design

A primary effect of the war was to emphasize the producibility of Soviet designs and modifications:

> The designer cannot forget for an instant that any improvement, no matter how necessary for increasing the quality of a piece of armament, must be introduced only with the consideration that it be reflected minimally in fulfillment of quotas. Therefore, the designers were in closest contact with the series production plants. Prior to introducing any innovation into an existing piece of armament, they had to anticipate in their own minds in minute detail what difficulties this improvement might entail in the mechanical processes. The designers had to effect their changes in such a way that they might be put into series with only a minimal loss in the daily output quota of aircraft sent to the front. This was an extremely difficult task, especially difficult when a new type of aircraft entered into series production. Under war-time conditions, the designer must also consider this fact in developing a new aircraft and his new product must make maximum use of existing technology in a given series factory.[43]

Another basic lesson was that of a relation between simplicity and utility in combat. Simplicity affected predictability but it also affected how fast weapons were available at the front. To train for the use of simple weapons was easy.[44]

The over-riding lesson was the necessity for technical capability. "To the designer, war is a difficult school. However, the lessons he learns stay with him throughout his life and serve as the motto: 'Be ahead!'"[45]

---

[40] Kilmarx, p. 318.
[41] Leë, 1959, pp. 69–74, passim.
[42] Yakovlev, *Target*, p. 337.
[43] Ibid., p. 357.
[44] Ibid., p. 358.
[45] Ibid., p. 357.

d. The Commitment to Jet Interceptors

The Soviet aviation establishment was left in an uncomfortable position during later stages of the war. Work on advanced designs was discouraged in order not to divert resources from the production effort.[46] However, as Soviet forces penetrated Eastern Europe, the aviation community became aware of the array of weapons its enemy had in prototype and on the drawing boards. In late 1944, Soviet forces captured a quantity of Junkers JuMO-004 and BMW-003A jet engines and a number of these were provided to Soviet designers for experimentation.[47] Later when the German plants were occupied, they were returned to production as Soviet plants tooled up to produce the engines also. About the same time, a program was initiated to copy U.S. B-29 bombers, four of which began to fly into Soviet hands in August of 1944.[48] In November of 1944 with these precedents, a special committee under the Council of People Commissars, headed by Malenkov, was created to oversee the exploitation of the German economy.[49] This appears to have coincided with the focusing of intelligence collection efforts on U.S. jet designs.[50]

It was not until 1945 that a jet aircraft design effort was given official sanction by Stalin. The date may have been either in February[51] or in May when, with the German surrender, aircraft production was sharply curtailed.[52] In June, a party of about ten senior officers was dispatched to Berlin to organize the exploitation of German aeronautical science. By August 15, a Soviet program was initiated for flight testing the German Me262 jet. Meanwhile, during the autumn of 1945, the Aviation Commissariat had developed a detailed review of the "dangerous situation" in advanced technology and design.[53]

Among proposals surfaced in conjunction with the Commissariat review was one to commit the Me262 to production. During the presentation of the Commissariat's proposals to Stalin, however, Me262 production was opposed by Yakovlev on the basis that the aircraft was unstable and unsafe, that such production would divert resources from native designs and that more advanced prototype would soon be forthcoming from both his own and the Mikoyan-Gurevich design teams.[54] The proposal was rejected and a tentative deadline, the August 46 Tushino air show, was set for the new prototypes. Detailed project designs were approved for Lavochkin, Mikoyan, Sukhoi, and Yakovlev at about the same time. Concurrently, the Commissariat was reorganized as the Ministry of Aviation Industry and M.S. Krunichev was appointed as Minister replacing Kuznetsov. The name and the appointment accompanied a general realignment of Defense Ministries. Nonetheless, it would be Krunishev's responsibility to give concrete form to the Party commitments.

In all, four designer teams were involved in building fighter prototypes around the captured Junkers and BMW jet engines. Those which received the more powerful Junkers engines of 2,000 lbs. thrust, Yakovlev and Lavochkin, focused on a single engine design. Those which received the 1,800 pounds of thrust BMW engines, Sukhoi and the Mikoyan/Gurevich team, would focus on a two-engine design. Within both the single- and double-engine approaches, divergence emerged as to the conservatism of

---
[46] Lee, 1959, pp. 231–232.
[47] Green, "Billion Dollar Bomber," July 1971, p. 105.
[48] Kilmarx, p. 213.
[49] Hearings, Jet Propulsion, p. 121.
[50] Air International, "First of Many," p. 233.
[51] Yakovlev, *Target*, p. 362.
[52] Ibid., p. 363.
[53] Yakovlev, *50 Years*, p. 102, and *Target*, pp. 363–364.
[54] Air International, "First of Many," p. 233.

design. On the single-engine side, Yakovlev took the more conservative approach of fitting the new engine to an established airframe—that of the YAK-3 fighter. Meanwhile, the Lavochkin team committed itself to a new design. Among the two-engine competitors a like phenomenon was observed. The Sukhoi design focused on a refinement of the general concepts of the Me262 while the Mikoyan-Gurevich collective attempted a new design. Meanwhile, the aircraft engine establishment attempted to bring both the engine types into series production—the Jumo as the RD10 and the BMW as the RD20. Although the intention does not appear to have been documented, the program decisions for a successful jet were well hedged. Should either engine prove unworkable, an alternative was available. Should either the MiG or the Lavochkin designs fail, a more conservative back-up design was in progress using either engine. Should either domestic engine program fail, East German factories were kept in operation. A matrix of this hedging effect appears in Figure 7. Predictably, Yakovlev's re-engined version of the established conventional aircraft was the first of the four ready for testing in October of 1945. Not predictably, all four prototypes were basically successful.

Figure 7—Hedging Effect of Initial Jet Prototype Design Decisions

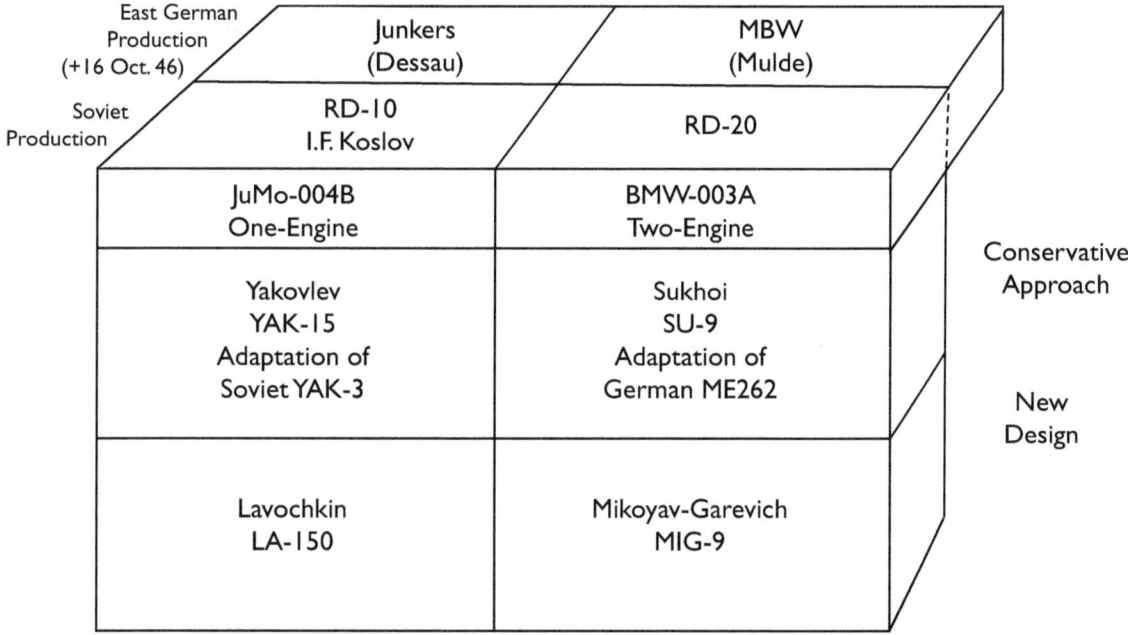

The claims about which Soviet jet aircraft was first to fly are[55] in dispute. Supposedly it was settled by the toss of a coin. Full flight of Yakovlev's aircraft had been delayed pending wind tunnel tests during the winter of 1945, while airfield conditions delayed both Yakovlev and Mikoyan until April 24, 1946.[56] With the coin toss, Mikoyan's air craft flew first and Yakovlev's followed. Both aircraft were supposedly demonstrated at the Tushino show on August 19, although only the MiG-9 was reported by USAF intelligence. The Su-9 flew in August and the La150 in September.

---

[55] Yakovlev, *Target*, p. 365.
[56] Ibid., p. 371.

3. Post–World War II Developments

a. The Ministry of Aviation Production Plan

In December of 1945 the status of Soviet aviation had come under debate in the Party Central Committee. The Aviation Commissariat proposals debated at that time culminated in a comprehensive program to eliminate any lag in the field of aircraft design or research. In March of 1946 a party of senior aviation personalities, Yakovlev among them, visited Germany to assess first-hand what could be obtained there. By April 2, a long-range plan for the development of jet fighters was laid before Stalin.[57]

The strategy for post war development of jet fighters was based on the rapid achievement of superior jet engine capability. Although the Soviets had some background in jet turbine design dating back to 1937, the work of its most experienced jet technician, Arkhip Lyulka, had been interrupted during the war. After working on an unheralded rocket aircraft project, Lyulka returned in 1942 to jet turbine work. By the end of the war he was bench testing an experimental engine of 1,543 pounds thrust and had initiated work on a 2,866 pounds thrust engine intended for flight testing.[58] It was apparent, however, that these engines were behind the world standard and would require extensive development while German engines were already available. The Commissariat plan would allow attention to be given to advanced engine design while native designed aircraft would be based on engines of foreign derivation. Key to the strategy was the purchase of British Rolls Royce centrifugal compressor engines—the Nene and the Derwent. In reacting to this strategy, Stalin is said to have remarked, "Just what kind of fool would sell his own secrets!"[59] Nevertheless, the Russians had had considerable experience with the British unclassified lists during the war and were aware that licenses for production of these engines were being sold in a number of countries. The successful attempt to purchase these engines would proceed.

The 1946 Plan addressed three stages of engine development with associated design activities[60]:

(1) Transitional aircraft based on 1,800–2,000 pounds thrust German engines. This stage was nearing fruition as the YAK-15 and MiG-9 were already in preliminary testing.

(2) Combat capability based on British Nene and Derwent engines of 3,500–4,850 pounds thrust. A requirement for such aircraft would emerge concurrently with the plan.[61] All four fighter design teams would submit prototypes which evolved to the MiG-15, the YAK-23, Su-II, and the La-15.

(3) Advanced aircraft based on engines by Klimov, Mikhulin, and Lyulka in the range of 6,600–17,600 pounds thrust. It was planned that these would be available in 5 to 6 years. Eventually, the Klimov VK-1 would power the MiG-15 bis, and the MiG-17; the Mikhulin AM-5 would drive the MiG-19 and YAK-25; the Lyulka AL-7 eventually powered the Su-9 and Su-11 of the late fifties.

The 1946 plan coupled with the December 1945 commitment of resources by the Central Committee would allow the Soviets to achieve superiority in jet engine technology in the early 1950's.[62] It facilitated early emphasis on advanced technology by leap-frogging intermediate stages of development with adapta-

---

[57] Air Enthusiast, "Lyulka," pp. 297–298.
[58] Yakovlev, *Target*, p. 372.
[59] Ibid., and Yakovlev, *50 Years*, p. 103.
[60] Flying Review International, "Mikoyan Quarter Century," Nov. 1965, p. 159.
[61] A regression analysis of Soviet and U.S. jet engine characteristics, conducted by RAND, concludes that Soviet jet engine technology led U.S. technology until roughly 1950–1953 depending on whether U.S. or Soviet forecasting equations were used. See Alexander and Perry, 1972, pp. 30–32.
[62] U.S. evolution from British technology is described Ibid., pp. 11–19.

Chapter V: Soviet Systems

tions of foreign designs. In effect, the Soviets would be mastering British jet technology almost concurrently with the United States.[63] In the meantime, native airframe designs would continue on a par with those of other countries. One consequence of the resulting engine allocations, however, was that available power may have prejudiced the success of early prototypes in the program. It appears that early success may have prejudiced later success.

b. The Debate Over Use of German Technicians

Among issues addressed in conjunction with the April plan was the question of how to use German personnel:

> During the meeting the question arose relative to the possibility of using German specialists who were working in East Germany in aircraft factories. Khrunichev and I expressed doubts of the wisdom of such steps. We felt it unwise to expose our newest research institute secrets. However, with a wide-spread research experimentation at the base of our Soviet institutes, the activities of the German specialist would be fruitless. They would be able to create nothing.
>
> However, this consideration was paid no heed. I was looked upon not so much as Assistant Minister as a designer and it was obviously assumed that in fearing competition from German scientists and designers, I might not be sufficiently objective on this question.
>
> As is well known, German specialists arrived in the Soviet Union, but attempt to use them were unsuccessful, although costing a great deal.[64]

During the summer of 1946, Germans who had been working with the Soviets were transported to the U.S.S.R. in a well-coordinated surprise movement. On October 21, 1946, dozens of trains in one night moved some 40,000 Germans under a five-year "contract" to various Soviet locations. Some 3,000 of these were aviation specialists.[65] The program was not without difficulties, however, as a conversation five months later between Col. G. A. Tokoev and Stalin discloses:

> " . . . we certainly need more German specialists. There are a great many who are being wasted at present, through being given completely unsuitable jobs."
>
> "But why should that be. Why can't you rope in all the Germans you need?"
>
> "Principally because the Germans fear to enter our service more than anything, Comrade Stalin," I answered. "Since German specialists were removed wholesale to the U.S.S.R. in 1946, whether they wanted to go or not, the whole population are afraid of us. And some of our own officials, for their part, are prejudiced against employing Germans. For instance, Doctor Kurt Tank, who was chief designer during the war for the firm of Focke Wulf, offered of his own free will to join us. He was turned down by General Kutsevalov, and General Lukin, on the grounds that he had been a member of the Nazi party."
>
> "And what are your own feelings on that point?"
>
> "I don't agree with the Comrades concerned."
>
> "Where is Tank now?"[66]

What ensued was a comic-opera effort to kidnap Tank, involving the Dictator's son Vassily Stalin, and the then Deputy Chief of the KGB Ivan Serov. Added to this duo, the main task of which was to pursue the exploitation of remaining German aviation talent, was the same General Lukin who had a notorious reputation among Germans for the pillaging and deportation of their aviation industry and technicians in the

---

[63] Yakovlev, *Target*, p. 371.
[64] Stockwell, pp. 42–45, from German press accounts.
[65] Tokaev, *Stalin Means War*, p. 116.
[66] Tokaev, *Comrade X*, p. 316.

previous year.⁶⁷ Notably, serious efforts to improve voluntary cooperation were lacking. Tokaev, the senior Soviet technical advisor on aviation matters in Berlin, by his admission, discouraged a member of potential collaborators by his honest portrayal of the reality of their service.⁶⁸ The upshot of the story is that Tokaev defected and Kurt Tank eventually designed jet aircraft for the Peron government in Argentina.

The same General Lukin (by Tokaev's account)⁶⁹ and Vasily Stalin (by Solzenitzn's account)⁷⁰ were the source of denunciations which eliminated the top echelon of the post war Soviet air forces. In March 1946 the Commander-in-Chief of Soviet air forces Chief Marshal of Aviation Alexander Novikov was arrested and imprisoned along with his Deputy, Colonel-General Repin, the senior officer of the Aviation Engineering Services.⁷¹ Although reasons for the arrests vary, the purge accompanied a reorganization and a tightening of political controls within the armed services. Marshals Vershinin and Sudets took their places in the high command. So it was that Sudets had a role in the formalization of the requirements for the MiG-15⁷² and the date of the Air Forces requirement is placed at the time of the April plan. More importantly, the Air Forces leadership was in a state of upheaval while the future of its capabilities was being decided by the Ministry of Aviation Industry.

c. Success of First Prototypes (YAK-15 and MiG-9)

Although the political and strategic implications of the April date of the first jet flights are unclear, the implications on fighter characteristics were. A month after its first flight, the initial prototype nosed into the ground killing its pilot. Another prototype was made available in July to continue the test program. Mark Gallai, the test pilot, relates that during his baptism with the second machine, the trim controls were reversed, the engines would not throttle back fully, and the nose-wheel collapsed.⁷³ Nevertheless, both the YAK and MiG aircraft were ready for the Tushino show on 19 August 1946. Stalin demonstrated his jets in the first post war Aviation Day flying display. If haste was evident in the construction of the prototypes, what followed demonstrated even more vividly the priority attached to the program.

The day following Tushino, Mikoyan and Yakovlev were summoned to the Kremlin. There Stalin directed that 10–15 aircraft of each type be prepared for the October Revolution Parade 80 days thereafter. Both designers were dispatched to production plants with an Assistant Minister of Aviation to act as expediter. Despite the obvious enormity of the task, 15 MiGs and 15 YAKs were ready by 7 November. In spite of all the effort, the November parade was weathered in—the scheduled fly-by was grounded.⁷⁴

Curiously enough, U.S. intelligence only observed the MiG-9 at the August show.⁷⁵ However, 50 YAK aircraft were observed during the following May Day celebration while only 40 MiGs were seen. The MiG being the more difficult of the two aircraft to build suggests the MiG and YAK were concurrent programs. Nonetheless, the above landmarks are standard features of more recent Soviet aviation history.⁷⁶

---

⁶⁷ Ibid., pp. 347–361, passim.
⁶⁸ Ibid., p. 317.
⁶⁹ Solzhenitsyn, p. 447.
⁷⁰ Tokaev, *Soviet Imperialism*, p. 43.
⁷¹ Gurevich, p. 17.
⁷² "First of Many," Flying Review International, p. 237. Also in Gallai.
⁷³ Ibid.
⁷⁴ "Soviet Air Shows," Air Intelligence Digest, Oct. 1949, p. 4. passim. thru 1955. CONF.
⁷⁵ Izmaylov (Ed.), p. 630.
⁷⁶ Flying Review International, "First of Many," p. 237.

Chapter V: Soviet Systems

The MiG was the more successful of the two aircraft owing mainly to the greater power available from the two-engine configuration and to its all-metal construction. Its 560-knot speed compared favorably with its contemporaries, the U.S. Shooting Star and the British Vampire. Gallai recounted recently:

> In the air the MiG-9 turned out to be unexpectedly simple to fly—its characteristics were modest and unassuming. One might even go so far as to term them agreeable. I say 'unexpectedly' advisedly, as before the service introduction of jet aircraft, there was a certain fear among [Soviet] fighter pilots that these novelties would be difficult to handle in the air; it was widely believed that jets could be flown only by 'extra special' pilots and then only after protracted training. In the event, reality proved very different—the MiG-9 could be flown by the average fighter pilot. Indeed, it was easier to fly than its contemporary, the YAK-15.[77]

Sometime afterward, Yakovlev was to explain that the YAK-17, a refinement of the YAK-15, intentionally designed as a transition aircraft with the specific purpose of allaying fears of the new technology. "We made up our minds to create an aircraft in which only the engine would be new and everything else possible would remain the same as in a piston aircraft. The flier . . . would find himself in a familiar setting and not feel the difference between jet and piston aircraft."[78]

Despite its lack of performance, the YAK was a notable step forward. It made lesser demands of the airframe industry used to working in mixed wood and metal designs and the single-engine arrangement caused less demand on engine production. As later modified, it would provide training aircraft and early combat aircraft for the Soviets, the Chinese, and the East Europeans.

d. The Unsuccessful Prototypes

A similarity between Sukhoi's SU-9 and the Messerschmidt 262 was to serve him poorly. A number of modifications were incorporated into the German concept, including the retrograde return to tapered as opposed to slightly swept wings, but the SU-9 was doomed by two characteristics. First, it was later than the YAK and MiG; it first flew on 18 August, only two days before its predecessors were committed to production by Stalin. Secondly, by following the basic architecture of the ME262, it appeared to contradict Stalin's December decision. Following Yakovlev's argument, the political mind was probably loath to support a Soviet design which appeared to copy that of the former enemy.

Nevertheless, the basic design was sound. Due to a higher surface (wetted) area, the craft was inherently somewhat slower than the similarly engined MiG and it had a slightly lower ceiling. Nevertheless it had a comparable climb rate and was notably superior to the MiG-9 in endurance and ammunition capacity.[79] Indeed Yakovlev, himself, would resort to similar underwing-pod engine mountings four years later.

The Lavochkin aircraft suffered as did Yakovlev's from lack of power from the single Jumo engine. First flying in September of 1946, it was late for the production decision. Although more advanced in concept than Yakovlev's plane, it was too complex a design for the performance it promised. Various alternate prototypes (the LA-152, 154, and 156) were attempted which compromised somewhat with the YAK concept. Anticipating the more powerful British engines, the LA-152 was rebuilt with 35° swept wings in 1947.[80]

---

[77] Yakovlev, *Target*, p. 365.
[78] Nemecek, "Turbojets and Tribulations," pp. 489–490.
[79] Green, "Last of Lavochkins," p. 220.
[80] Gurevich, pp. 19–42. The design achieved a ceiling of 40,000+ feet.

Although the design (LA-160) was little more than an experimental adaptation, its early testing served to assuage the reluctance with which the Soviets (among other nations) approached swept-wing designs.

e. The MiG-15

The YAK-15 and MiG-9 were obsolete before they flew. In March or April 1946, before the first jet flights, an air force requirement was probably incorporated in the Aviation Ministry Plan brought before Stalin on April 2, 1946. According to an account attributed to Gurevich, the specifications envisioned "aircraft to climb rapidly to a height of ten kilometers [38,000 ft.] and to maneuver quickly at that altitude at a good speed and with a heavy cannon . . . . We were to provide for only one pilot and to stay aloft for one hour. Otherwise we were not restricted in our design besides the usual strength requirements and the need for close attention to metal working."[81]

The requirement was based on a 4,400 pound thrust engine that was to be available within a year.[82] In fact the British granted permission to export ten of the 4,800 pound Nene engines to the Soviets in September of 1946. In all, 55 Nene and Derwent engines were shipped to the U.S.S.R. in 1947.[83] At the time the design started, however, all that was available was the RD-21, a slightly improved version of the BMW-003 rated at about 2,200 lbs. In effect, reliance on British engines facilitated a design based on twice the power then available from native engines.

It has been common to erroneously attribute the MiG-15 to a design by Kurt Tank, who had been chief designer for Focke-Wulf during WWII. Although the fuselage arrangement bears a superficial similarity to Tank's later Pulqui II aircraft, the wing planform is decidedly different. Further, Tank himself went through a straight-wing configuration in 1947 before producing his Argentine swept-wing prototype in 1950.[84] In fact, the Soviets may have understood theoretical aspects of transonic flight some three years before the West.[85] An effort began in 1942 to develop a unified general theory of supersonic wings. Results of the coordinated inquiry were published in 1946 and 1947. Among the contributions was an exploration of the application of conical flow theory to delta wings; it was written by Mikhail J. Gurevich. Therefore, it seems appropriate that one consider the theoretician Gurevich and the production expert Mikoyan perfectly capable of developing an impressive machine. The apparent similarity between the U.S. F-86 Sabre, the MiG-15, and Tank's designs derives from a common reliance on the 1940's technology and from the principles of aerodynamics as given practical meaning by extensive German wind tunnel testing available to all competing post war nations.

The MiG-15 had several faults, most notably its dangerous spin. It was found necessary to send air force test pilots to units converting to the aircraft in order to demonstrate proper spin recovery measures. For a period spinning was banned, pending the investigation of a number of accidents; even afterward, special clearances were required for the maneuver.[86] Early attention was given to a trainer version and use of YAK-17 trainers, but numerous pilots graduated directly to the MiG from conventional aircraft.

---

[81] Ibid., p. 19.
[82] Nemecek, "Turbojets and Tribulations," p. 492.
[83] *Janes All the World's Aircraft 1956–57*, pp. 39–40.
[84] "Soviet Aerodynamics Research," *Air Intelligence Digest*, Nov. 1955, pp. 9–11. CONF.
[85] "From Cambodia to Cuba," *Air Enthusiast*, p. 303. Per memoirs of the test pilot Pyotr Stefanovsky.
[86] Opinion of Kilmarx, p. 239. Summaries of pilot opinion appear in Stockwell, pp. 50–54. See chart on comparative characteristics, Section III.

Chapter V: Soviet Systems

Beside the spin problem, the aircraft was poorly armed. It mounted two 23-mm. and one 37-mm. cannon. The 23-mm. lacked punch and the 37-mm. lacked firing rate. All three lacked sophisticated ranging devices.

That the MiG-15 was a brilliant accomplishment became apparent in Korea. It had put Soviet aviation ahead of European rivals and nearly equal with the United States. It out-climbed, out-maneuvered, out-accelerated, and flew higher than its principal opponent, the North American Sabre. It maintained a speed advantage until the F model of the Sabre appeared late in the Korean war. Its record was marred by poor guns and bad pilots.[87]

The MiG-15 first flew on December 30, 1947, barely three months after the American F-86.[88] The Gurevich account talks of an initial prototype, however, which flew on July 2 and was to have been ready for the Tushino show—a plausible objective.[89] This otherwise undocumented prototype purportedly crashed soon after its first flight. (This portion of the account may be intentionally confused with the first MiG-9 prototype.) Nevertheless, the MiG-15 as we know it flew only some 20 months after the first Soviet jets and confirmation of the requirement. The design was thought to be so successful that a production commitment was made in March 1948—before aircraft tests were half through. This rather drastic step is a measure of the importance attached to the MiG-15 program.

f. MiG-15 Competitors

The same type of hedging pattern observed in the program for the first jet prototype can also be seen, to a lesser degree, in the program which resulted in the MiG-15. Yakovlev continued to upgrade the YAK-15 straight-wing configuration with the Derwent engine as opposed to the Nene engine used in the MiG-15. Lavochkin was also allocated the less-powerful and wider Derwent but would work both swept and straight wings. Eventually, he too would proceed to a Nene-based prototype.[90] Meanwhile Sukhoi re-engined his two-pod SU-9 to produce a multipurpose fighter capability, the SU-11, with Derwent engines.

1) The YAK-23

Yakovlev had improved the basic YAK-15 with a tricycle landing gear, a slightly improved version of the Jumo engine (the RD 10A), and more metal components. The result was the production version of the YAK-17 which appeared in mid-1947. Before the YAK-17 entered production, however, another aerodynamic and all-metal improvement, the YAK-19, appeared. Although the YAK-19 was not produced, a second prototype proved useful as a flying test platform for the Derwent engines and as an experimental predecessor for the YAK-23.

The YAK-23 was the Derwent-powered MiG-15 competitor or, possibly, back-up. The first prototype flew in June of 1947 and conformed to a possible pre-Tushino deadline. Notably, the successful flight nearly coincides with the ill-fated MiG prototype referred to in the Guervich account. Yakovlev's incremental approach again assured that he would be first to fly, but even though a production decision was favorable,

---
[87] First F-86 prototype first flew October 1, 1947. First production model flew May 20, 1948. Janes All the World's Aircraft 1956–57.
[88] Gurevich, p. 42.
[89] "How Russian Stormed Sonic Barrier," *Aviation Week*, Sept. 12, 1965, p. 22. From the Soviet Journal Ogonyok, and Green, "Last of the Lavochkins," April 1968, pp. 221–222.
[90] "Yakovlev's Lightweight—the Yak-23," *Air Enthusiast*, May 1973, p. 230.

the bolder design of the MiG-15 drew more attention, offered more promise, and was produced in greater number. The YAK-23 was ordered into production with minor modifications in March of 1948 after a complete and successful test program.[91] The MiG was ordered to production about the same time without complete tests.

A common contention is that the YAK was an intentionally tapered wing back-up to the more risky MiG design. It is equally likely that both were in response to the same air force's requirement, with Yakovlev adopting the more conservative approach to ensure meeting an implied, if not specific, Tushino deadline. This strategy had worked successfully in 1939 and 1946. It did not work in 1947. The divergence in designs probably became apparent when a preliminary MiG concept known as the "pre-project" was submitted for Ministry of Aviation and Air Force approval. If this logic holds, it explains when and why a YAK-25 swept-wing design was abandoned and why that number was also assigned to a later and more important aircraft.[92]

In its own right, the YAK-23 was a successful machine in a league with the British Gnat. It was used widely as a transition lightweight fighter for many of the Warsaw Pact forces. Even ten years later, in 1957, it would set world climb-to-altitude records for 3,000 and 6,000 meters.[93]

2) The La-15

While Yakovlev had taken an incremental approach, and MiG a bold one, Lavochkin's efforts scattered. Despite his experience with the swept-wing La-160, his treatment of airframes for the British engines was hedged by an additional retrograde straight wing, but thin-wing, design. Given the more powerful Nene engine, he then committed himself to the swept-wing which he himself had popularized. His timing and the engine allocation were against him. It appears he spent too much time with the advanced swept-wing mated with the German technology engine. The La-160 flew only three months before the MiG-15. By the time his Derwent-powered prototype came out, the MiG had been committed to production. Nevertheless, the resulting La-15 was produced in limited numbers after state acceptance in June of 1948. Because of a lower ceiling than the MiG (incurred as a result of the Derwent-type engine) the aircraft was used as a ground-support, rather than interceptor, aircraft. Subsequently, Lavochkin did receive a Nene engine and the prototype which carried it was credited with being the first Soviet aircraft to break the sound barrier in a dive.[94] While this event of 26 December 1948 is marked in Soviet aviation history, interceptor development was by then focused on the MiG-15 and its successors.

3) The SU-11

In the meantime, Sukhoi had become involved in a multitude of programs which diverted him from the mainstream of interceptor development. Among these were a conventionally powered two-engine reconnaissance plane, and a four-engine light bomber. Both designs were powered by Derwents.[95] As in the MiG-15 case, the bomber with the more powerful Nene engine was produced, in this instance the IL-28. Nonetheless, the Sukhoi Bureau did participate in interceptor development with the British engine, again

---

[91] Ibid., p. 231.
[92] Ibid., p. 229.
[93] Green, op. cit., May 1968, p. 291.
[94] Nemecek, "Turbojets and Tribulations," pp. 491–492.
[95] "From Cambodia to Cuba," *Air Enthusiast*, p. 203.

Chapter V: Soviet Systems

the Derwent. Apparently he had not learned from the SU-9 experience and again reverted to the unpopular "German" twin-pod configuration. Although the prototype SU-11 flew before the MiG-15, it lacked the speed and maneuverability of all its rivals.

g. Soviet Engines

The 1946 plan for native designed engines met with fruition at the turn of the decade. In 1950, Vladimir Ya Klimov produced a much improved centrifugal flow engine. Although it was based on his early experience with the Nene, the RD-45 copy and some of its minor improvements, the VKl was generally larger but also lighter. The result, with water injection, was thrust improved from 5,952 pounds to 6,750. With a 200-pound weight reduction it contributed significantly to the performance of the MiG-15.[96]

Meanwhile, Arkhip Lyulka was testing a design for the AL-5 in the realm of 10,000 pounds of thrust. This engine continued to be associated with unsuccessful prototypes until much later it reached production status with Tu-110. By that time it had been upgraded to 12,000 pounds thrust.[97]

Most of the Soviet jet engine designs concentrated on centrifugal compressors focused on mass of the airflow. This resulted in engines with large frontal areas which were difficult to incorporate into efficient fighter designs. It seemed this basic technology would not support supersonic flight.[98]

For the Soviets, the breakthrough came about 1950 with Mikhulin designs based on axial compressors. The first of these was a low-pressure, single-rotor configuration believed to have powered the prototypes of the Mya-4 and Tu-16 bombers which appeared in 1954. While the engine was large compared with Western standards, the technology promised improvements with multiple rotors, higher pressures, and higher heats. The effect would be higher thrust-to-weight ratios, improved fuel consumption, and, especially important in fighter designs, smaller sizes and weights with a much improved thrust-to-frontal area ratio. Pending the development of such engines the design of suitable all-weather area interceptors was frustrated as the 1948 attempts demonstrate.

h. 1948 Attempts at an All-Weather Capability

Among Sukhoi's ill-fated activities was a 1948 attempt at an all-weather interceptor, the SU-15. It featured a curious staggered fuselage arrangement of the production version of the Nene engine, the RD-45. The SU-15 would have been a heavy machine with a radome to house an Air Intercept scanner mounted over a common opening which served both engines. The aircraft would have featured a good 750-mile radius and transonic speed, but unfortunately it disintegrated in one of its first flights.[99]

Lavochkin in 1948 also attempted to create an all-weather fighter. As with the Sukhoi aircraft, it featured two engines, probably RD-45's, mounted in the fuselage. A radome would have been housed inside a large circular intake which served both engines.[100]

Likewise, Mikoyan and Gurevich participated in the all-weather interceptor design activity. The MiG prototype, the I-320, had similar features and performance as the other two aircraft. Of three aircraft the MiG

---

[96] "Lyulka," *Air Enthusiast*, p. 299.
[97] Inferred by USAF Intelligence, *Air Intelligence Digest*, "Mikhulin," Nov. 1954, p. 21. (CONF.)
[98] Nemecek, op. cit., p. 499.
[99] Green, "Last of Lavochkins," June 1968, pp. 349–350.
[100] "Plane Facts," *Air Enthusiast*, March 1973, p. 140.

was the first to successfully fly. The SU-15 crashed in 1949, the MiG performed successfully in the winter and the Lavochkin flew in February. But the Mikoyan designers also resorted to another approach.[101]

It is likely that none of the three models were passed after it was found that the rather primitive Izumrud radar could be fitted to the MiG-15. The fuselage mounting of two large centrifugal engines in the fuselage was an ungainly, inefficient and expensive arrangement without compensating advantages in range. Further, the short acquisition range of the Izumrud may have made greater demands on maneuverability than either aircraft seemed to offer, especially when compared with the MiG-15. Nevertheless, the SU-15, the La-200, and the I-320 do indicate the order of Soviet priorities. Attention was first focused on the achievement of a world standard day interceptor. Then, and only then, did the focus shift to an all-weather capability. The requirement appears to have been dropped when it was found to be technologically inconvenient; a simpler expedient was adopted instead.

The failures of the SU-15 with the post war purges did cast a long shadow through Soviet aviation history. Sukhoi's post war record, to those who did not appreciate a number of his technical innovations, appeared to be a series of disasters. Judged by a more objective standard, he was the only major designer who had failed to create a jet prototype suitable for series production.

During the post war period when it seems that every sector of the Soviet society required a ritual "cleansing"[102] Sukhoi's was the obvious target among the design bureaus. Although Sukhoi does not appear to have been imprisoned, his design bureau was disbanded in 1949.[103] The long shadow is this. On the Sukhoi drawing boards was a design, the SU-17, which might have been the first totally supersonic Soviet aircraft.[104]

Such was the success of Sukhoi's 1956-version SU-9 and SU-11 that he is sometimes credited for breaking the sound barrier with the earlier design that never flew. Advanced aircraft concepts such as were seen in 1956 might have been available to the Soviets three or four years earlier had it not been for the purge of the Sukhoi bureau.[105]

i. Improvement of the MiG-15

Such was the perceived success of the MiG-15 that alternative fighter designs stagnated at the turn of the decade. Although the Soviets were aware of its failings quite early—the spin proclivity, for example—it was a thoroughly capable aircraft in well-trained hands. Early attention was given to a two-seat trainer version to ease the earlier mentioned difficulties of conversion training. Moreover, the basic configuration accommodated an improved engine and a rudimentary air intercept radar. During 1950, these modifications appeared in two separate adaptations of the basic aircraft: the MiG-15 bis clear weather fighter which featured the improved native-designed VK-1 engine accompanied by a general trimming of weight and the MiG-15P which added the Izumrud radar to the improved single seat model.[106]

The MiG-15, however, remained a poor transonic airframe aerodynamically.

---

[101] Alternate translation to "purge."
[102] Nemecek, op. cit.
[103] Green, "Sukhoi," p. 353.
[104] Assuming availability of Mikhulin engines—an assumption which would have required a somewhat earlier emphasis on smaller axial-flow configurations.
[105] "From Cambodia to Cuba," *Air Enthusiast*, pp. 304–306.
[106] Ibid., pp. 307–311.

Chapter V: Soviet Systems

j. The MiG-17

In parallel with the above programs, a general reworking of the design was undertaken to extract full advantage of the improved power plant in speed regions near Mach 1. The result was the MiG-17. While changes in the fuselage were minimal—a lengthening by 41 inches—the MiG-17 featured an entirely new wing and modified tailplane. The new wing was larger, thinner, and more swept with parallel but rounded tips, while the tailplane was also more swept. The result was a transonic design which retained the maneuverability of the MiG-15 for subsonic combat.

The MiG-17 evolved to a limited all-weather variant as did its immediate predecessor. The Izumrud radar was fitted along with two beam-riding missiles.[107] The nose was extended somewhat to accommodate the radar equipment. This MiG-17P was available in 1953, but production was limited. By that time, more effective all-weather aircraft were in development.

k. Stagnation of Development

The period from 1950 until 1955 is marked by a dearth of significant interceptor prototypes except for the 1953 appearance of the MiG-17. Several reasons for this may be apparent:

(1) Production of the MiG-15 which continued until 1954 occupied a great deal of Soviet production capacity. This consumption of capacity had been sparked by the Korean War. The transfer of this capacity to the similarly constructed MiG-17 represented a least disruptive means of modernizing the force.

(2) The attention of the aviation industry may have turned to bomber aircraft which were nearing production.

(3) Two technological constraints seemed to prohibit major advances. The first was the lack of an efficient axial flow engine and the second was the size of Soviet second generation air intercept radars. The extent to which these factors constrained an effective all-weather design was apparent in the 1948 prototypes.

(4) On a more speculative point, it had become apparent that other elements of the air defense system, particularly the control and warning system, required attention before better interceptors could be effectively utilized. Likewise, the Korean War had emphasized the necessity of adequate pilot training. This coincides with the evolution of PVO Strany between 1948 and 1954.[108]

(5) The political leadership was satisfied with the Mikoyan-Gurevich product. As in WWII, production focused on great quantities of a standard design once it was proven. The Korean war and the necessity of equipping the newly formed Warsaw Pact forces emphasized the production commitment. It is also apparent that minor changes in the MiG-15 were adopted in favor of the more disruptive change to the MiG-17. The 20-month development cycle observed in the generation between MiG-9 and MiG-15 indicates that such a rework of a basic design as the MiG-17 could have been available in 1950 or 1951 had it been wanted. Instead, development proceeded at a more leisurely pace.

(6) Of ultimate importance, Stalin did not want new designs; he had become committed to Mikoyan.

l. The Decision to Develop the YAK-25

The first all-weather area interceptor of the Soviets, the YAK-25, did not appear until 1955. Its designer explains the stagnation of the design process and claims credit for the innovation. Since his story is fairly

---
[107] See Chapter IV above.
[108] Barrage aircraft—one which patrols in the air, defending objectives from air attack (Trans). Roughly translated "area interceptor."

complete, concise and essentially correct in its fit with observable facts, it is quoted in its entirety. Possible controverting evidence from other participants—Stalin, Beria, Mikoyan, and Mikhulin—is not available:

> In 1951 the MiG-15 fighter was in series production and used as armament in the Air Force. It was our Army's basic swept-wing jet fighter, and a fine machine.
>
> At that time we were developing several types of new swept-wing fighters, but all our proposals met with Stalin's objection: "We have the fine MiG-15, and I have no intention of creating new fighters in the immediate future. It would be better to continue improving the MiG...."
>
> I was highly upset by the situation, which was arising in our Design Bureau. Behind me there were several hundred people who might lose faith in me as a design team leader. I also understood that if all our experimental works were limited to modernizing existing series aircraft and not creating new more advanced models, this would inevitably lead to a lag in the shortest possible time. And so, day and night I was tormented with the questions of what stand to take.
>
> I felt that we had to create something new in quality. At that period I got close to the engine designer Alexander Alexandrovich Mikulin. I felt then and I feel to this day that he was our foremost and most perspicacious aircraft engine designer. His AM-3 and AM-5 jet engines were for a long while the power source basic to Soviet aircraft.
>
> In 1950 and 51, he and I had the idea of creating an economical light jet engine. Mikulin had formulated the idea that a jet engine with small dimensions would be more effective from the viewpoint of economy, reliability and other aspects. I supported him in this.
>
> Mikulin began work on a light-weight small-size jet engine with a thrust of 2000 kg. I decided to develop an aircraft for this engine which in addition to good, simple flight qualities would have great endurance and flight range—qualities enjoyed by no other jet fighters of that period, either in the Soviet Union or abroad. It was then felt that jet engines were very uneconomical in terms of fuel consumption and therefore although we might talk of fairly long endurance and range for heavy aircraft such as bombers with large fuel reserves, for jet fighters an increase in range and endurance seemed an insurmountable obstacle. With two of Mikulin's engines subsequently designated the AM-5, we succeeded in designing an aircraft which had double the MiG's flight range and endurance. It would require a crew of two, and would carry heavy armament—two 37-mm. cannons with large supplies of ammunition.
>
> For its time, this was an innovative aircraft in the fullest sense of the word. With my idea for this aircraft, I decided to skip the usual steps of going through the Ministry and Air Force, and wrote directly to Stalin. I had no other recourse: I was afraid that my proposal might get bogged down in going through normal channels.
>
> Three or four days after I sent my letter, Aviation Industry Minister M. V. Khrunichev called me. Mikhail Vasik'yevich well understood the difficult, complicated situation and attempted to ease my position, but could not do much.
>
> I went to him at his office. He was alone. He stood up from behind his desk with a kind smile.
>
> "Stalin just called. He got your letter and has read it. He said that your proposal is quite interesting. He is surprised that you can promise a fighter with such range and endurance. He also asked whether it would be possible to use your aircraft as an all-weather barrage[109] interceptor and supports your proposal. He said that you should keep working on your idea, and he'll contact you in a few days."
>
> And in two days Stalin did call in Khrunichev, Artem Mikoyan and me.
>
> In Stalin's office we found Bulganin, Beria and Malenkov. Stalin took my letter from the table and read it aloud.
>
> "Well?" he asked. "Does this mean we can make a fighter with this jet engine that will have great flight range and duration? That's very important. At what expense will you achieve it?"
>
> I explained that the idea might be achieved only if we were able to work together with Mikulin, whose engine would, in combination with several structural features of the aircraft, be a success. Stalin was completely in favor of the idea in principle, but said that we would have to be able to put out such an aircraft in a barrage fighter-interceptor version.

---

[109] Sukhoi was a nonperson at the time of the conversation. This is a possible explanation of omission of Su-15.

Chapter V: Soviet Systems

"We need this kind of interceptor, which could stay in the air a long while and search out the enemy not only during the day, but at night as well, and in bad weather. We ordered Mikoyan and Lavochkin to develop such a fighter, but something didn't work out, and their flight endurance is less than you propose."

Not long before this, heavy fighter-interceptors had in fact been developed and tested under the designation La-200 and I-320.[110] I do not know precisely or, more accurately, I don't remember the reasons why both these fighters failed their test flights. However, it's not a questions of what the reasons were—what was important was that the country was lacking a much-needed all-weather night fighter-interceptor.

I replied that Mikhail Vasil'yevich had already given me authorization and that we were working in this direction and would probably encounter no difficulties. It should especially be remembered that the engines in my aircraft were located under the wings and in this way the nose of the fuselage allowed a great deal of area for installing a powerful radar unit which had previously been created by our designers working in radar.

At this point Stalin raised the point of whether this aircraft would be capable of use as a high-speed observation aircraft. I found no objection to this.

Satisfied in principle with these questions, in conclusions Stalin said that he had received an offer from Artem Mikoyan as well, who wanted to use Mikulin's same engines in creating a long-range fighter model based on the MiG-17 series aircraft.

"Well, we'll have both an interceptor and a high-speed observation plan. Yakovlev will make this one, and Mikoyan will give us our long-range fighter," concluded Stalin.[111]

As is the procedure in the Soviet Aviation R&D, Yakovlev returned for formal approval of the "pre-project,"[112] a more or less formal proposal submitted for technical evaluation of the design concept. The pre-project is used to establish the priority for a project and for assigning its place in the overall Soviet system of industrial planning; it differentiates required designs from the ongoing development work of the Design Bureau. It is at this stage that the politics of Yakovlev's design activities were laid bare:

On July 30th [1951] and in the same company we again gathered with Stalin to examine and evaluate placing Mikulin's AM-5 engine in both the YAK-25 two-seat all-weather barrage jet night interceptor with its YAK-25R modification serving as an observation aircraft as well as the fighter which was serving as the basis for the well-known MiG-25 [*sic* MiG-19].

The project was sent to Stalin in short time. He was already familiar with it and, with almost no notes, he indicated that he had no objection.

At this point Beria opened his briefcase and withdrew some sort of document.

"Comrade Stalin," he said, "here is another proposal by the designer Lavochkin."

"What proposal?" asked Stalin irritatedly. "I don't know anything about any proposal by Lavochkin."

To this Beria replied in an intentionally indifferent tone, attempting to emphasize his objectivity:

"He sent it in a long time ago . . . Some sort of unusual interceptor. And it's equipped for night and blind flying. Everything's here on three pages . . . ." And he started to read: "Radar, radio, radio compass, instrument landing system, etc., etc . . . ." The whole list. "He proposes building it on the basis of the La-200."

All the instruments which Beria had listed are basic requirements on any interceptor, including the one I had proposed. But Beria had to play out this entire scene and give Stalin the impression of a long list of equipment only to destroy my proposal and reverse the decision which had been taken—in a word, to stab me.

Stalin blazed up.

"Why didn't you report this to me?" he asked Khrunichev.

Khrunichev at first started to lose his temper, but then he replied that the La-200 had already been rejected once as a complete failure and therefore there could be no basis for using it as the source of a new aircraft. Besides, the entire list of equipment was also on the YAK-25.

---
[110] Yakovlev, *Target*, pp. 394–396.
[111] Alexander, *R&D*, pp. 17–18.
[112] Yakovlev, op. cit., pp. 396–399.

Stalin wanted to hear none of this, but simply repeated, becoming more heated:

"Why didn't you report it? Why didn't you report it?"

Finally, Mikhail Vasil'yevich succeeded in clarifying that Lavochkin's proposal had been examined in the Ministry and that it had received no approval basically because Lavochkin had planned on using his own unsuccessful fighter, which had already been rejected. Subsequently Lavochkin succeeded in gaining permission to pursue this work, but his aircraft never did materialize.

I was terribly frightened both for my own concern and for Mikhail Vasil'yevich. In those days nothing was worse than being looked upon as a fraud in Stalin's eyes. Meanwhile he, without quieting down, continued demanding of Khrunichev:

"Why didn't you report it?"

It would seem that Khrunichev had purposely concealed Lavochkin's proposal. Finally Stalin understood what the situation was and said:

"We will not go back on the decision we've already made, but we'll look at Lavochkin's proposal separately."

The proposal was accepted, but in signing it Stalin suddenly turned to me:

"And why is this written here at the end: 'Upon construction of the aircraft, to allow you overtime and piece-work pay and set aside money as a prize?' Why should you have such an advantage? You know what they're saying behind your back? They tell me your self-seeking."

"They have misinformed you," I replied.

"What do you mean, misinformed?" Stalin again flew into a rage.

"Well, prize money and overtime and piece-work money are at the disposal of all the designers: Tupolev, Ilyushin, Lavochkin and Mikoyan. This is no exception to the rule. On the contrary, the exception to the rule is that our design team has for the last two years not had this privilege, while all the others have had it and continue to."

"And how is this so?" Stalin asked, surprised.

Khrunichev verified that this was in fact so. Then Stalin, still irritated, came back to me:

"I want you to know what they're saying behind your back."

"Thank you for telling me. What complaints have there been against me?"

"They tell me that you have been using your position as Assistant Minister to build yourself the largest factory."

"That's slander. I have the smallest factory."

Stalin turned to Khrunichev:

"Is this so?"

Khrunichev pulled from his pocket a notebook which he always kept on him and in which was written all necessary information concerning the production areas of the different factories, the amount of equipment, the number of workers, etc., and said:

"That's true Comrade Stalin, Yakovlev has the smallest factory."

"They say that you've grabbed a lot of machine-tools."

"That's also untrue. I have fewer machine-tools than any other designer," I replied.

Again Khrunichev verified that I was telling the truth. Mikhail Vasil'yevich quoted the number of machine-tools in our Design Bureau and, for comparison gave the number in Tupolev, Mikoyan, Ilyushin and others' experimental Design Bureaus.

"They say you've gotten hold of laboratory equipment like no one else has."

"That, too, is untrue. I have nothing the others don't have."

And again Khrunichev proved the veracity of my words.

"How can this be so?" said Stalin, gradually calming down. "I had completely opposite information. Strange. . . . "

"It's unobjective and made-up information to weaken faith in me. Incidentally, I anticipated the possibility of such accusations and so doing my eight years of work, first at the Narkomat, then in the Ministry, I have done nothing which might subsequently justify even one of the reproaches which you have been throwing at me."

"And you haven't received any prizes in recent years?"

"That's precisely right, I haven't."

"I don't understand a thing," Stalin voiced his amazement and, to the amazement of those present, turned to Khrunichev and Bulgarin and said:

"Well, if this is so, we have to create conditions for him no worse than for the others. He's done a great deal for our aviation and will do more."[113]

From the 1955 May Day fly-by, U.S. observers reported two new types of fighters. One appeared to be a twin-jet clear-weather fighter capable of supersonic speeds—the MiG-19. The other was identified as a Yakovlev designed all-weather interceptor. Both were displayed in sufficient numbers to indicate they had been committed to serial production.

The YAK-25 featured two engines carried in underwing pods in a configuration similar to that of Sukhoi's early SU-9 and 11 and of the Me-262 which Yakovlev himself had much maligned. Further, the wing bore a striking resemblance to that which appeared on the 1950 Pulqui II design by Kurt Tank. The fuselage featured a large radome which housed a radar much improved over the Izumrud. The remainder of the fuselage allowed sufficient fuel for a much extended range.

Lavochkin did produce the prototype mentioned in the Yakovlev account. The La-200B features a nose radome of similar dimensions to that on the YAK-25. However, he retained the VK-1 centrifugal-flow engines which were fed by intakes on both sides of the radome for the forward engine and a larger lower scoop for the rear engine. Somehow the nosewheel was housed among the lower ducting. Range was extended by two large underwing fuel tanks and two crew members sat abreast. Not surprisingly, the YAK-25 was chosen with the more efficient engine, serviceable installations and stable wheel positioning, not to mention greater speed, range, and altitude. If for no other reason, the La-200B deserved to die from sheer ugliness.

The YAK-25 was committed to series production and eventually some 580 were produced.[114] Meanwhile, Pavel Sukhoi had been reestablished following the death of Stalin in 1953. Already in progress was an aircraft which would fill out the PVO all-weather force.

4. Observations Based on the Evolution of Interceptor Designs

a. Introduction

The foregoing material provides a basis for some generalizations about the nature of Soviet force-posture decisions particularly as they relate to the aviation element of early post war air defenses. Although the generalizations are inherent within the foregoing material, supplemental evidence will be drawn upon to round them out.

---

[113] See production data, Section III.
[114] Izmaylov (Ed.), p. 631.

b. Perception of Strategic Defense

From the outset, it is essential to disregard the contemporary U.S.-conceived dichotomy between strategic and theater defense. It seems clear that the Soviet aviation establishment in the early post war period conceived of fighters and bombers. Fighters were further broken down into interceptors and ground attack. Among interceptors there was a separate category of "barrage" or area defense aircraft. Otherwise, an interceptor was an interceptor whether it was assigned to PVO Strany or to the forward area. As is conveyed in the strategy chapter, PVO Strany and the integrating concept of air defense operations evolved some 15 years and a world war after the patterns of weapons creation were established. A dichotomy between frontal and defense aircraft evolved as PVO Strany evolved, but that was well after the program of post war aviation modernization was well under way.

c. The Role of Planning

It is clear that there was a plan, such as Yakovlev documents, which governed the development of jet aircraft. Such a plan would have coincided with the decision cycle of the Fourth Five-Year Plan. Despite what may seem to Westerners to be virtual obeisance to "the Communist Party's and Soviet Government's concern and attention for aviation,"[115] a high priority was set for aviation development and a political consensus supported it. Throughout the period of the Fourth Five-Year Plan (1946–1950), either three or four programs were instituted to compete against each interceptor requirement. In addition, a multitude of prototypes continued to be developed in the course of ongoing design bureau activities—these aside from the formalized requirements cycle. It is no coincidence that Stalin's attitude changed to "no intention of creating new fighters in the immediate future" at the same time as the Fifth Five-Year Plan.

It is clear also that this type of long-range plan evolved in the industrial and design establishment. Military participation was negligible except within the Central Committee. Military participation came in the formal requirements cycle which gave priority to certain specific types of aircraft already being developed. In the case of the MiG-19, La-200B, and YAK-25, it is evident that the requirements were formalized between Stalin and the designers, with pernicious participation by Beria and separate perfunctory staffing by the air force.

d. The Role of Institutions

The perception of two categories of aircraft, bombers and fighters, was reinforced by the structure of the Ministry of Aviation. Of ten bureaus, three design-oriented bureaus were devoted to fighters, bombers, and engines. Thus, categories of aviation were conceived in this manner. This division parallels the 1930's institutionalization of bomber design activities in the Zhukovski Academy under Tupolev and of fighter design activities in TsAGI under Polikarpov. Major Designers schooled under either of these two men basically remained working in either one category or the other. Sukhoi was the exception of a Tupolev protégé who worked in fighters. But the exception supports the rule somewhat. His aircraft tended to be heavy fighters more appropriate to ground attack and he mixed fighter and light bomber design activities with a lack of success. Only in the late 1950's did his heavy aircraft come into vogue.

e. The Flow of Information

Although the pre-war centralization of basic research in the TsAGI infers a common downward flow of basic aerodynamic findings, it is clear that the sharing of information did not work very well. Somehow,

---

[115] Tokaev indicates that it was the Mikoyans' influence that saved him from expulsion from the party in 1937. *Comrade X*, p. 72.

Chapter V: Soviet Systems

during the development of the MiG-15, Mikoyan and Gurevich knew much more about swept wings than did Lavochkin. One suspects that the MiG bureau had better access to wind tunnels and to German test results. (Alternately, the MiG team might have acquired its own test facilities.) Likewise, Lavochkin appears to have been ill-informed about the capabilities of the Derwent engines he was to work with. Although a partial explanation of the MiG-15 success can be attributed to the theoretical talents of Gurevich, better information also seemed to support the MiG collective's single-minded pursuit of a bold design. The system includes competition for information.

f. Allocation of Engines

One is struck by the manner in which engine allocations prejudiced the success of a particular prototype. The double JuMO configuration had an obvious power advantage over a single-engine BMW-powered design. Likewise the Nene engine's greater thrust and smaller frontal area offered advantages of a similar magnitude over the Derwent engine. Both allocations favored Mikoyan and Gurevich.

g. Intelligence, Risk, and Luck

A great deal was at stake for the Soviets to base their long-range planning for aviation on the assumption that British engines could be obtained. To be sure, back-up programs were under way, but the weight of development effort appears to have been committed to third-generation engines while lengthy negotiations were ongoing. This is risky policy behavior, but the payoff was enormous. In light of the outcome, it was quite a reasonable risk based on good intelligence about British commercial procedures and about British Labor Government politics.

h. Rewards and Incentives

As the Yakovlev account reveals, there was a competition among design bureaus for personnel, equipment, and facilities. There was also a system of materialistic rewards in the form of overtime pay, bonuses, and state prizes which operated in the aviation industry. All of these things flowed from "successful" designs. Successful designs were those which were committed to serial production. There was also a system of negative rewards. It can be represented by Hangar Seven of the internal prison which operated during the 1930's. In the post war years it was represented by the fate of the Sukhoi bureau.

i. Conflict of Objectives

Between the Stalinist criteria which prevailed until 1950 ("the winner will be the one who gives us the best fighter . . . and also deliver first") is a very real conflict. One with a mathematical bent will point out that either delivery time or performance can be optimized. Yakovlev made his reputation by delivering first; Mikoyan made his by delivering best. In the post war period, Mikoyan and Gurevich played the better mixed strategy between these two objectives. Lavochkin also played a mixed strategy, but his timing appears to have been out of cycle.

j. Personal Politics

Soviet wartime and post war fighter aviation was dominated by two men: Alexander Yakovlev and Artem Mikoyan. These two represented the foremost among a very small group of heroes, the Design Bureau Chiefs, after whom aircraft were named. These men were literally "Heroes of Socialist Labor." Among this group was a collegial relationship supported by a similar education, the same mentors, common work experience, and intramural competition. These men shared a common ethic with the Aviation Engineering Service of the air forces.

One of these men—Yakovlev then Mikoyan—was Stalin's personal advisor on aviation. Their influence extended beyond fighter aviation matters. Yakovlev held a favored position because of his two-hat assignment as Deputy Commissar (later Minister) of Aviation. Mikoyan held a favored position because he was the brother of Anastas Mikoyan, an even closer associate of Stalin generally in charge of the consumer goods area in the post war period. An active area of Anastas' interest was foreign trade; he had been charged with responsibility for foreign aid during the war, and he was later to be foreign policy advisor to Khrushchev.

The Mikoyan relationship worked in at least two ways during post war aviation development. First it clarified the opportunities inherent in British technology to both the design and trade portions of the government. Second it allowed Artem Mikoyan a separate channel to the Politbureau—one that he used for political relief on behalf of others in the aviation establishment as early as 1937.[116] Stalin's preference among designers changed in 1946 after the success of the MiG-9, when Yakovlev resigned his position as Deputy Minister. Thus Mikoyan was in a favored position in the competition for information and resources from the time of the first jet prototypes on. In addition, he used his favored position well. His were the best of the post war designs. Thus, securing himself in this favored position, his design objectives, which emphasized speed and altitude, predominated over alternate design approaches which might have favored range or improved supporting systems. Personal politics helps explain why the MiG-15 was a success and how Stalin came to be committed to improvement of the MiG as the route of aviation development.

k. Design Objectives Versus Requirements

A recent Soviet text for industrial engineers in the aviation industry states the following: "The basic task of the technical preparation of production is the creation of designs . . . whose quality is *not worse than the best world models*, and the period of their development and introduction into series production is minimum" (emphasis added).[117] Yakovlev's personal motto was "Be Ahead."[118] Mikoyan's Bureau slogan is said to be, "Speed and Altitude."[119] Stalin, at the 1947 Tushino Show enjoined the aviation industry to create aircraft which would "fly higher, faster, and farther" than any in the world.[120] This slogan harks back to a speech to the Eighteenth Party Congress (1939) which stated: "We will henceforth fight to increase quantity, improve quality and decrease the cost of our aircraft so that our pilots can fly higher, farther, and faster than anyone in the world."[121] An even earlier precedent is a July 1929 Party Central Committee Decree which includes: "We consider the greatest challenge in building the Red Air Force to be the improvement of its quality as fast as possible to the level of the foremost bourgeois countries . . . "[122] While the list of these slogans can be extended, it is evident that throughout postwar interceptor decisions they represent a set of lenses through which the Soviet aviation industry sees the world and which "color" their perceptions. It is the contention that these perceptions profoundly influenced the menu of weapons from which Soviet plan-

---

[116] Tikhomirov and Paramonov, p. 152.
[117] Yakovlev, *Target*, p. 357.
[118] Green, "Mikoyan Quarter-century," p. 156.
[119] "Soviet Air Shows," *Air Intelligence Digest*, Oct. 1949, p. 5.
[120] Yakovlev, *Target*, p. 153.
[121] Ibid., p. 147.
[122] AID, "Soviet Bloc AAA: An Interim Solution," April 1957, p. 34.

ners built their post war strategic defensive force. Such a contention goes a long way toward explaining that Soviet interceptor aircraft were *not* designed against the early U.S. bomber threat. Instead, they were designed in technological competition with foreign interceptors.

On the other hand, the 1948 attempt at an all-weather prototype confirms that there was a perceived need among the air forces for an all-weather interceptor and that it had matured to the point of a "requirement." That the requirement resulted in a less-than-satisfactory weapon is evident. An interim solution was arranged, the MiG-15P, and the design process continued without regard to the night and all-weather threat. A more appropriate weapon awaited an engine design breakthrough and Yakovlev's initiative. The 1948 requirement also coincides with the emergence of PVO Strany as an independent force. It is inferred that this type of two-engine, long-range aircraft is what the PVO wanted. Instead, it got the short-range MiG-15P. Either aircraft would have been equipped with a short-range radar. Thus, planning attention in aviation was directed to the engine and the airframe; other element of a weapons system were added on—if it was technically convenient.

C. Antiaircraft Artillery and Surface-to-Air Missiles

1. World War II Experience

During World War II, antiaircraft artillery was the basic element of the static air defense of the important centers of the country. Other related ground-operated systems included antiaircraft machine guns, barrage balloons, and antiaircraft searchlights. The primary systems used by the Soviets were the 25-mm., 37-mm., 76-mm., and 85-mm. antiaircraft guns. These guns were further supplemented by 90-mm. and a few 120-mm. U.S. guns which were supplied under Lend Lease and by captured German 85-mm., 105-mm., and 128-mm. guns.[123] According to Marshal Batitskiy, the medium caliber guns were completely replaced with 85-mm. guns during the war.[124]

In the tactics of antiaircraft artillery general principles were worked out for the construction of a powerful, deep-echelon antiaircraft defense for large objectives with the use of systems of weapons of various calibers, and on the basis of the control of rather large groupings of antiaircraft forces. So that antiaircraft defense would be flexible, and equipped to respond quickly to any changes in the nature of the air enemy's actions, mobile groups were established which included small units of antiaircraft artillery, antiaircraft machine guns, and searchlights. These groups were used for battle with aircraft on their flight routes (operating from ambush), for temporary cover of small individually important objectives, and for strengthening the defense on the exposed operational axes of enemy aircraft. Extensive use was made of armored antiaircraft trains which were assigned the missions of protecting railway communications and objectives primarily in the pre-frontal sector.[125]

The scale of Soviet use of antiaircraft artillery grew steadily throughout the war. For example, the Soviets in 1941 had some 1000 antiaircraft guns defending Moscow. By 1945 the number had risen to over 2,000.[126]

Lessons learned from World War II included the need to increase the range and effectiveness of the guns, to improve the lethality of the antiaircraft shells, and to provide better fire control. In addition, it was

---

[123] Batitskiy, *Voyennaya Mysl'*, p. 35.
[124] Ibid., p. 36.
[125] Batitskiy, *Voyska Protivovozdushnoy Oborony Strany*, pp. 101–102.
[126] Ibid., p. 327.

also necessary to improve their tactical employment, mainly through the achievement of better concentration of fire.[127]

2. Post War Development (1945–1955)

During the period from 1947 to 1954, the Soviets introduced three new antiaircraft artillery guns of larger caliber (57-, 100-, and 130-mm.). Gun-laying radars were included in the composition of antiaircraft artillery batteries.[128] In order to improve the concentration of fire, the batteries were equipped with eight guns rather than four as before, and the individual guns were positioned more closely together. In order to increase the defensive depth, antiaircraft batteries were deployed along concentric perimeters around the areas being defended.[129]

Thus, throughout the first decade after the war, the Soviets continued to improve the technical characteristics and tactical concepts of their antiaircraft artillery. At the same time, the Soviets were also working on a new weapons system, the surface-to-air missile, which would take over and greatly expand on most of the role of antiaircraft artillery.

By the end of the war, the Soviets had captured a considerable number of German missile scientists. One group which had been working on surface-to-air missiles was put to work at Scientific Research Institute 88. Under projects R-113, these scientists were directed to design a surface-to-air missile utilizing the design principles of the German World War II Wasserfall missile as a point of departure. The missile was to be effective from 16,000 to 98,000 feet and was to carry a 500 Kilogram warhead. The German scientists worked by themselves in isolation from any Soviet counterparts. They apparently were being tasked to develop specific missile system components, although the project encompassed the total missile system. The work was conducted from 1947 to 1951. Four units were delivered for testing; the first in 1948, the last in 1950. In 1951, the group was disbanded.[130]

In 1951, construction was begun on a network of surface-to-air missile launch sites and associated radar installations surrounding Moscow. This was the SA-1, a missile with an effective maximum altitude of 60,000 feet and an effective minimum altitude of 3,500 feet. The first sites became operational in 1954 with deployment continuing into the next period (post 1955).

Deployment of the SA-1 was limited to the area around Moscow. It apparently was designed to counter the perceived threat of mass bomber formations flying at what was then considered to be a high altitude (i.e., up to about 50,000 feet). The SA-1 lacked mobility, a 360 degree radar capability for each site, and autonomous control for each site. These factors probably led to the decision not to deploy the SA-1 more extensively and to begin the development of the SA-2, a mobile system, probably in the 1950–1952 period.

3. An Evaluation

Antiaircraft artillery, as the Soviets deployed it and continued to modernize it, was a large and costly system. Still, the decision was made to expend the resources on a system which would soon be largely

---

[127] Batitskiy, *Voyennaya Mysl'*, p. 37.
[128] Yakimanskiy, p. 70.
[129] CIA/SI 17-56, 1 December 1956, "Contribution of German Scientists at Branch 1 of Scientific Research Institute (NII) 88 to the Soviet Guided Missile Program," pp. 5–6, (S).
[130] Research and Development Associates, "Comparison of U.S. and U.S.S.R. Land-Based Battlefield Air Defense Systems."

Chapter V: Soviet Systems

replaced. The 130-mm. antiaircraft gun actually began deployment after the first SA-1's had become operational. Concern for defense was such that even new guns were about to become obsolescent within about three years after their deployment. The rationality of the final antiaircraft artillery deployments was even more questionable in light of the problem of defending a target area against the mass destruction capabilities of nuclear bombs.

As the first decade ended, the SA-1 was setting the pattern for the future in which surface-to-air missiles would largely replace antiaircraft artillery and would also assume ascendancy over fighter aviation as the premier arm of the national air defense system.

The story of Soviet air defense missiles and also of antiballistic missiles belongs essentially to the period after 1955. The early developments will therefore be retraced as the post-1955 period is analyzed.

D. History of Early Warning Systems

1. Pre-1945 Developments

The Soviet early warning systems prior to and during World War II were heavily dependent on visual and sonic methods. Radar, although somewhat developed, was not deployed and was used only to a very limited extent. In 1941, the Soviets had, in its completed state, their first known radar. The development for this radar took place at the University of Kharkov and later relocated to the Red Army Signal Labs at Hytischi. At this time, another Soviet group, the Leningrad Development Group, was working on a C-W Doppler operating at about 50 MHz.

The later years of World War II found the Soviets in the position to receive samples and/or significant information concerning nearly all of the major operational radars in the United States and United Kingdom. The sets of primary significance were the U.S. SCR-584 fire control radar, which in turn became the Soviet Son-2; the British searchlight control radar "Elsie"; and the U.S. types SCR-545, 527/627, 582/682, 602.[131] The control or knowledge of these radars proved to be the means for the late wartime and post war Soviet radars.

2. Assessment of Post War Requirements

The Soviets, as a result of World War II, were well aware of the limitations of their offensive and defensive systems. This, combined with the known offensive potential of the West, dictated that the Soviets attach a high priority to air defense. The Soviets decided that their wartime approach to early warning was clearly inadequate.[132] Indeed, it was necessary to greatly expand the use of radar equipment of various kinds. A particular concern, during World War II, was how to combat massed enemy flights at night under the conditions of the use of radio and radar interference.

In their post war analysis, the Soviets noted that the need for early warning was a lesson which should have been learned from observing the German offenses against Poland, Norway, and France. But it was a lesson which they did not heed sufficiently. This was evidenced by the German surprise air attack on June 22, 1941, in which the Soviets lost some 1,200 aircraft while simultaneously sustaining many losses to all other border air defense forces. In relation to the defense of so vast an area (U.S.S.R.), the efforts of

---

[131] Ibid.
[132] Batitskiy, *Voyska*..., p. 333.

interceptors must obviously be closely coordinated with a highly efficient early warning system. Russia saw this flaw in her defenses and made strenuous efforts to improve the situation. From the evidence which has so far come to light, it is apparent that Soviet planners sought to cover the whole of the U.S.S.R. by a comprehensive air warning organization.

3. Developments After 1945

Throughout the 1945–1955 period, the early warning systems of sonic and visual sighting remained extremely important. This system continued to maintain an active role in the detection, tracking, and primarily the identification of aircraft due to the system's invulnerability to electronic jamming and direct air attack. The short-range limitations of this system were not important enough to phase it out; therefore it continued to serve not only as a secondary means of warning and a supplement to radar systems but also as a gap filler.

Organizationally, in order to establish control, the country was subdivided into regions with each region administratively subordinate to the PVO Headquarters in Moscow. Direct communication links were established between each region and Moscow headquarters.

The responsibility for air defense of each region was placed on the Military Commander of each area.[133] The Military Commander had at his disposal tactical air forces, aircraft artillery, and an air warning system. (Satellite countries are set up on a similar basis even though it appears cruder and less effective.) From 1950 to 1952, there appears to have been considerable expansion and reorganization of the air warning system in both the PVO and the Field Armies. One important change was the increasing use of radar. In conjunction with this, Air Defense Centers were set up at Air Army, Air Corps, and Air Division levels and these ensured a much greater degree of coordination of existing facilities.

Technologically, progress after 1945 was deeply dependent on Western knowledge, acquired by three means: first by lend-lease; second by capture; and third through post war German scientific assistance. One of the most significant events, as far as U.S. knowledge is concerned, was the publication of the MIT Radiation Laboratory series of books, which in effect became the Soviet developmental "Bible" for some time to come. Western knowledge provided the core of Soviet Air Defense prior to 1951.

With respect to lend-lease, the growth of mutual distrust between the U.S. and U.S.S.R. prompted the end of the Lend-Lease Policy to the Soviet Union and others in 1945. However, by this time, the Soviets had enough knowledge to manufacture copies of Western radars, through the assistance of German scientists and engineers. Certain foreign radars were adapted to Soviet requirements and placed into production.

During 1945–1946 and later, we find that Germans were apparently being forcibly evacuated and taken from East Germany. As far as this forced work on radar systems was concerned, these Germans were primarily put to[134] work in the Scientific Research Institute 160, about 22 miles from Moscow. This was primed for the exploitation of German scientists who were prominent in the electron-tube field. Before 1950, the German group had completed the development of X-band and S-band tubes for radar jamming purposes. The department was evidently still engaged in development of jamming the KU-band, which is the region in which practically all U.S. airborne and U.S. ground radar operated. This and other works indicates that the Soviets knew what they needed for effective electronic countermeasures.

---

[133] SRI, "An Analysis of the U.S.-Soviet Strategic Interaction Process."
[134] "Soviet Electronic Countermeasures," *Air Intelligence Digest*.

Chapter V: Soviet Systems

By 1950, the extension and development of air warning network had been most marked. By then they afforded continuous coverage in fair depth and density for the entire country with the exception of the least vulnerable portions of the national frontier. However, it was obvious that these systems were not confined to the Soviet Union. The zone extended to Eastern Europe, to Poland and likewise to other satellite countries.

The air warning networks had the following characteristics:

(1) Their performance was still unimpressive by Western standards
(2) Restricted range necessitated their use in great numbers to give continuous coverage
(3) Russia's great size permitted radar positioning far in advance of the area to be defended
(4) The system was simply built and easily maintained
(5) Most of the equipment was mobile and extremely easy to conceal (no high concrete towers; thus recognition was difficult from the ground and almost impossible from the air).

There were three primary sets in use by 1950: RUS-2, Pegmatit, and Dumbo. RUS-2 was a highly mobile ground radar developed early in the World War II period. The complete equipment consisted of two trucks or one truck and a trailer. One vehicle contained the radar equipment and its operators, the other housed the generators. In addition to its high degree of mobility and aptness for concealment, the RUS-2 was a very simple form of radar and already obsolete by Anglo-American standards during the 1945–1950 period. The primary disadvantages of the RUS-2 were its inaccuracy in measurement of range and bearing, its lack of height-finding capability, and its poor range against low-flying aircraft.

The Pegmatit was the first relatively static radar installation; although a trained team should be able to dismantle and reerect it on another site in a matter of days.[135] The radar was generally placed inside of a building or house with an aerial array protruding through the roof or nearby ground.

Dumbo was the third major radar system at this time. The Dumbo radar was first reported in 1946 and represented an improvement over the RUS-2 (1943) in range and accuracy. Although not mobile the set was easily transportable. This set was also easily concealable and was often erected in wooded areas with only aerials clear of the tree tops. Dumbo proved to be the primary post–World War II early warning radar. However, this system was quickly followed by a family of radars characterized by metric frequency, the use of Yagi antenna, goniometric techniques and nearly identical transmitters.

By late 1951 Token, the next radar system to develop, stood out as the beginning of a generation of Soviet-built radars. This generation consisted of two subgroups, V-beam radars, and multisearch radars. By mid 1952, at least 50 V-beam radars, were spread across the U.S.S.R. and surrounding satellites from East Germany to Vladivostok.[136] This radar was obviously inspired by the U.S. AN/CPS-6 V-beam set. Although not provided for or available under the lend-lease program, it was contained in the MIT series. This set was constructed with IAGC and FIC circuitry: basic ECCM features which produced a limited capability against long pulse jamming and jamming with low modulation frequencies.

During the post-1950 period, Scan Odd was developed with German technical assistance. This was the first Soviet AI radar with limited all-weather capability. This set became field operational and was deployed in 1954.[137]

---

[135] "The Use of Radar in Soviet Antiaircraft Defense," Air Ministry Secret Intel. Summary.
[136] Background Intelligence Data for Posture Statement on Strategic Initiatives.
[137] Ibid.

Knife Rest A and GAGE, a Soviet designed EW and surveillance radar mounted on a bunkered building, made their appearance in 1952. The oldest radar in the Soviet inventory with the strict purpose of early warning, Knife Rest A had limited accuracy and detection capabilities, but was inexpensive and easily maintained. Knife Rest A has been found to operate in the 70–80 MHz frequency range. Gage proved to be the first really permanent radar of any significance that was employed by the Soviets as a search finder.

In 1953, a height finder was produced by the Soviets. This radar (Patty Cake) did not follow the usual Soviet development pattern—because it was uniquely Soviet in design—not a copy of Western technology. This, as stated, was contrary to the pattern followed in the V-beam early warning radar (Token) and fire-control radar (Whiff) which were directly derived from Western radar technology. Patty Cake remained the sole Soviet operational height finder from 1953 to 1956. Although the Soviet Union and the Soviet satellites were still using U.S.-made and British-made radars, in addition to the Soviet-made copies of U.S. and British radars.

In 1954, the number of Token radars increased markedly. Soviet technicians were clearly more successful at maintaining them at an operational level than the U.S. had initially anticipated. The difficulties that the United States had expected the Soviets to encounter were based on U.S. experiences with the AN/CPS-6, a similar radar. It was found, however, that the basic design of the Token radar was considerably simpler.

Observations during the 1954 time period showed that the Soviets were developing a radar system that made concurrent use of two sets as a single unit. The most commonly used sets were GAGE (search finder) and Patty Cake (height finder). The advantages of this system, in relation to Token, proved to be:

(1) Less complicated installation
(2) Simpler maintenance and operation
(3) Increased range and height finding capabilities.

The Soviets took this one step further by building radar installations with four radars. These radars were situated in pairs with Gage and Patty Cake comprising each pair. This appeared to represent a movement away from the mobile V-beam, Token, to a static system of radar defense.

By 1955, the Scan Can radar system was developed for use on missile armament. It is believed that this system was developed from Scan Odd. The nodding height finder was also introduced in 1955, apparently to provide reasonably accurate altitude readings on modern manned aircraft.

4. Summary

At the end of World War II, the Soviets found themselves in an outdated position regarding offensive and defensive war systems. They chose to place high priority on development of their defensive system. Development of radar systems was obtained through lend-lease, capture of wartime radars, German scientific assistance, and Soviet developments.

Throughout the 1945–1955 period, the Soviets primarily worked to reduce surprise, increase coordination, and increase the capabilities of their early warning system. The introduction of jet aircraft and tactical bombers increased the necessity for early warning and low altitude capabilities. By the end of 1955, radar systems were deployed and in the development stage to counter these problems.

Chapter V: Soviet Systems

Although advance raid warning was now primarily dependent on radar, visual reporting was still highly organized in 1955 with 750 visual reporting posts in active operation.[138]

E. History of Civil Defense in the Soviet Union, 1945–1955

1. Introduction

Civil defense in the Soviet Union played a key role in defense measures after the 1920's, but the destruction suffered during World War II and the advent of weapons of mass destruction prompted a new emphasis on Civil Defense shortly after the war.

Reconstruction and other problems surrounding immediate postwar recovery took priority until 1948; thereafter, and especially after the outbreak of hostilities in Korea, new civil defense programs and policies emerged.

Since the Bolshevik Revolution ended in 1917, the Soviets have nurtured the expectation of an impending attack by capitalist powers. During the 1920's, cities and other targets were prepared for protection against chemical and conventional attack. In 1927, OSOAVIAKHIM, a paramilitary training organization, was established with Civil Defense training as one of its prime functions.[139] During the 1930's, as concern over air power and the German threat began to grow, the first nationwide civil defense program was begun. However, it was not until World War II, when old civil defense programs proved inadequate, that shelter construction and compulsory training programs, designed mainly for civil defense workers, actually began.

2. Post-War Developments: General

Immediately after the war, interest in civil defense declined, primarily because of the precedence given to reconstructing the nation's social, economic, and military complex. However, around 1948, reports were filtered to the West from returning German POWs of a shelter construction program in all new buildings.[140] In 1949, basic radio communications designed to improve defense command and control was ordered. A call, in 1950, for "tens of thousands" of instructors preceded the formation of DOSAAF in 1951.[141] This organization, a paramilitary group cooperating with the Army, Navy, and Air Force, replaced OSOAVIAKHIM and became the principal civil defense training group. In the next two years, as DOSAAF took on more responsibilities, mandatory study circles began, followed by a 20-hour compulsory civil defense training program for all members, then numbering approximately 16 to 20 million.[142] The XIXth Party Congress, meeting in 1952, called for "all out" defense measures, to include civil defense. In 1953, an antiaircraft general, Nikolay F. Gritchin, was made DOSAAF chairman, indicating the growing importance of this group in relation to the military, and air defense in particular.[143]

Although the Soviets were aware of the existence of nuclear weapons at the end of World War II, little or no mention was made of these in public literature until 1954, nine years after Hiroshima and five years

---

[138] "Air Warning System of the Soviet Union," RCAF Intel. Summary.
[139] "Civil Defense of the U.S.S.R.," *Intelligence Review*, p. 15.
[140] Goure, *The Soviet Civil Defense Program*.
[141] CIA, "Civil Defense in the U.S.S.R."
[142] Goure, *The Soviet Civil Defense Program*.
[143] CIA, "Civil Defense in the U.S.S.R."

after the U.S.S.R. exploded its first atomic bomb. The turning point in civil defense thinking occurred at this time when civil defense literature publicly announced a growing concerning with nuclear and bacteriological weapons. This awareness precipitated changes in policy and eventual debate in the late 1950's over the effectiveness of civil defense programs, shelters, evacuation and dispersal procedures, and various other aspects of the existing system. More immediate results involved, in 1955, the assignment of Colonel General of Aviation O. Tolstikov, a First Deputy Minister for Internal Affairs, as head of Civil Defense and the onset of a 10-hour compulsory training program for the adult population.[144]

3. Organization

Civil defense, until 1961, was an integral part of the Soviet Antiair Defense (PVO) and was supervised by the Main Directorate of Local Antiair Defense, or GU MPVO. This controlling body operated under the Ministry of Internal Affairs (MVD) and was responsible for planning and assisting the Council of Ministers in developing civil defense policy and cooperating with the Defense Ministry's Main Directorate of Antiair Defense of the Country. Also, under the jurisdiction of the Council of Ministers was the principal civil defense training organization, DOSAAF.

Subordinate to the GU MPVO were Republic, Region (Oblast), District (Rayon), and City MPVO organizations. Within these areas, the civil defense structure paralleled that of the civil administration and employed administrative and managerial personnel from government and industry in its own commands and staffs.[145] For example, the Council of Workers Deputies of the City maintained responsibility for civil defense in their area. The chairman of their Executive Committee was the Chief of the MPVO in the city, and he directed the program through the MPVO staff. His duties included staff and personnel training, planning, financial and materiel coordination, and organizing civil defense training programs for the population. In addition, the MPVO controlled the services of fire fighting crews, emergency engineers, medical personnel, the sanitary processing and decontamination groups, the security groups, those involved in warning and communications, transportation personnel, shelter and cover service, and various other facilities that could assist in any facet of civil defense.[146]

Several aspects of the city or point concept indicate that the Soviet Union had not yet modified its civil defense structure to accommodate a nuclear threat. The existing system was geared towards a World War II or conventional bomber mode of attack. It was not until the early 1960's that the need for a state-wide, rather than city-wide, system of civil defense was evolved.[147] In addition, there was not, as yet, significant cooperation with the military, indicating that the actual integration with the air defense contingent of the U.S.S.R. had not been fulfilled.

4. Training

Comments on the organizational concept of civil defense between 1945 and 1955 would be incomplete without some attention to the birth and rise of DOSAAF, the paramilitary organization with responsibility for Civil Defense training of the entire population.

---

[144] Goure, *The Soviet Civil Defense Program.*
[145] "Civil Defense of the U.S.S.R.," *Intelligence Review*, p. 16.
[146] Ibid., p. 17.
[147] CIA, "Soviet Civil Defense: Policies and Priorities," p. 13.

Chapter V: Soviet Systems

Paramilitary organizations have always handled Civil Defense training, beginning in 1927 with OSOAVIAKHIM. In September 1951, DOSAAF succeeded OSOAVIAKHIM as the "Volunteer Society for Cooperation with the Army, Air Force, and Navy" with Colonel General Vasiliy I. Kuznetsov as its head.[148]

Kuznetsov's leadership of DOSAAF was uneventful and he was replaced in 1953 by Lt. Gen. Nikolay F. Gritchin, a former World War II antiaircraft artillery officer. This appointment caused various analysts to note that there may have been increasing emphasis on the cooperation of civil and air defense at this time because of Gritchin's background. In any event, Gritchin initiated a successful campaign to urge new KOMSOMOL recruits into DOSAAF and to integrate DOSAAF with the trade unions and their various enterprises. In July 1954, a plenary session of the Central Committee of DOSAAF was held, emphasizing its roles and calling for a sports competition which would measure such abilities as marksmanship, grenade throwing, and PVKho (antiair and antichemical defense) to be held the next month.[149]

The PVKho section of DOSAAF retained the main responsibility for supervision of civil defense training, beginning with the study circles which originated prior to the formation of DOSAAF. Members of these circles who passed various civil defense examinations were awarded the badge of "Ready for Antiair and Antichemical Defense." In 1948, the stated goal of the mass training program was the preparation of 4 to 5 million persons a year to qualify for the badge. The Soviet press placed considerable emphasis on this program, evidenced in a *Pravda* item noting that in 1951, 21,434 persons from Tadzhik SSR were trained and received the badge and that the number of such trainees was growing "yearly by the hundreds of thousands."[150]

These various reports made civil defense and DOSAAF progress look effective, at least on paper. The three civil defense manuals of 1952, in particular the "Handbook for Exercises," reaped praises of civil defense excellence on "heroic people contributing to Civil Defense during the Great Patriotic War" and to DOSAAF and its work.[151] The contents of the manual included sections on means of attack against the rear and antiaircraft defense, protection against bombs and their consequences, protection against gases, and rules of conduct for the population in antiaircraft defense. However, the outlined procedures did not demonstrate that the Soviets had achieved any profundity in civil defense that could not be achieved in any other country subject to aerial attack. Surprisingly enough, they lacked any significant reference to atomic or thermonuclear warfare and its consequences, a matter which seemingly should have been assuming more importance as the Cold War was taking shape. One of the few references to atomic weapons appeared in the Soviet press in 1947, before OSOAVIAKHIM was disbanded: "The present program of civil defense includes the training and protection of the population against atomic air raids. OSOAVIAKHIM aims only at the discipline of the people; the preparation of such defenses as 'insulation layers' is being left to the scientists. At present, sham maneuvers are held for those people in strategic areas who would have to be moved away rapidly, and personnel are being trained in the detection of radioactivity. The training is similar to that for chemical warfare."[152]

---

[148] "Military Notes: U.S.S.R.," *Intelligence Review*, p. 16.
[149] CIA, "Civil Defense in the U.S.S.R."
[150] "DOSAAF Trains Soviet Civil Defense," *Air Intelligence Digest*, p. 14.
[151] Ibid., p. 14.
[152] Ibid., p. 13.

Whether this statement indicated that the press was merely naive or was printing what it was authorized to print is unknown. As a propaganda move, it could have been intended to reassure the population regarding any knowledge they might possess of nuclear threat. The mention of "scientists" handling problems related to civil defense indicates that the Soviets may have been awaiting technological developments in shelter capabilities before either publicizing a problem they could not yet counter or making any massive changes in the existing system.

Guards Colonel General P. A. Belov became the new commander of DOSAAF in 1955 and perhaps initiated the first drive for better cooperation between the military and the civil defense organs when he stressed the need to use demobilized reserve officers and soldiers for leadership and instruction in areas of civil defense.[153] Eventually, not reserve but high-ranking active duty officers became a part of the directorate. Various sources have mentioned that, after 1955, civil defense was endorsed by the Soviet leadership.[154]

5. Shelters, Evacuation, and Dispersal

Although some sources refer to basement shelters constructed in new apartment buildings as early as 1946,[155] the general consensus puts the year around 1948 when German POWs reported sighting shelter buildings being inspected and supervised in recent construction. It was believed that civil defense officials had authority to conduct these inspections to insure that construction was meeting certain regulations. However, it was also noted that priority was given to shelter protection for industrial, administrative, and economic facilities and to major cities, thus disregarding a greater part of the population,[156] particularly the agrarian community. The most prevalent shelters, those of World War II vintage, were not capable of protecting more than 10 to 15 percent of the population against fallout,[157] and new shelters were designed merely to withstand the collapse of the building. This did not account for the thermal and blast effects of nuclear explosion. The advantage of existing underground structures was demonstrated in 1954 when shelter construction was begun in subways.

The preceding data were partly responsible for spurring the civil defense debates of the late 1950's over the cost-benefits of updating present shelters to withstand nuclear attack.[158] It was not until then that a massive evacuation program was promoted to compensate for both the shortage and inadequacy of the existing shelters. Very little emphasis was accorded to a formal evacuation program prior to 1958.[159] Although one source said there was "fairly reliable evidence" that industrial evacuation plans were updated in 1950, an interview in 1953 with Moscow citizen did not yield any evidence of a city-wide air raid drill during the two-year period the interviewer had been a resident there.

A summary of rules the population was to follow during a "critical situation" involved learning the location of the nearest air raid shelters, and *when none exist* to "prepare trenches, dugouts, and similar facilities,"[160] indicating the inefficiencies of the shelter program. Also, implied is the Soviets' reliance on early warning of attack. Civil defense elements maintained close communications with the "local elements

---

[153] CIA, "Civil Defense in the U.S.S.R."
[154] "Civil Defense of the U.S.S.R.," *Intelligence Review*, p. 20.
[155] SRI, Soviet Strategy, Objectives, and Force Postures in Response to U.S. BMD, 1968–1980.
[156] Goure, *The Soviet Civil Defense Program*.
[157] CIA, "Soviet Civil Defense: Policies and Priorities," p. 7.
[158] Ibid.
[159] CIA, "Changing Soviet Civil Defense Concepts."
[160] "Civil Defense of the U.S.S.R.," *Intelligence Review*, p. 20.

of the air defense command . . . especially VNOS," the ground observation early warning service.[161] This approach may have been appropriate when bomber attack was the primary threat, but dependence on such a primitive early warning system (which later improved with more advanced radar technology) in order to prepare the population, was hardly an efficient and secure plan.

According to observations during a 1961 trip, which could easily apply to this early period, Leon Goure theorized that the population was indifferent to civil defense, possibly because of the effects of World War II destruction. He noted that the general fear of war and feeling of helplessness against the weapons of war left the people with little confidence in shelter programs. "Mere physical survival was not reassuring when they knew the great damage brought by war: and were still recovering from World War II."[162] If this is true and if the leadership of the Soviet Union considered the civil defense programs as a propaganda tool in boosting the morale and nationalistic altitudes of the population, then they were unsuccessful in attaining this goal.

Uncertainty exists concerning the relationship of industrial dispersal in the Soviet Union and civil defense activities. However, it seems that the reasons for relocation of industry to the Ural regions during the 1930's and from 1941–1945 were attributed primarily to both protection from conventional military invasion and the discovery of new locations of resources,[163] from which air and civil defense would only indirectly benefit. Budgetary considerations alone would make such a transfer impractical except in extreme cases. Although one source assigns to the MPVO the peacetime functions of "town planning" (and thus the ability to *ensure* proper dispersal of plants and provisions for air raid facilities in new building construction),[164] it is doubtful that it was able to do more than recommend guidelines for such purposes.

6. Summary

It would seem that, as the Soviets were recovering from World War II damage and beginning their strenuous drive to gain technological and military parity with the West, they also found time to reassess and begin improvements on other internal programs. Civil defense acquired renewed attention by 1948 and paralleled the growth of air defense in the Soviet Union.

Beginning with lessons learned from World War II, including the effects of German air attack on their homeland and the accounts by returning Soviet military of U.S. bomber damage in Germany, Soviet leaders realized the need for a stronger, more organized civil defense program. Not only did they realize that the ability to protect their military/economic/social complex would be a more difficult mission with the development of new weapons technology, but perception of immediate threats such as the proliferation of the United States' Strategic Air Command, the establishment of NATO in 1949, and the Korean conflict of 1950–1953 (when it was possible to actually witness and assess the new aircraft technology developed since the war) reinforced the Soviet's early views concerning adequate defense. The following changes within the Soviet Union after 1950 had a profound effect on defense posture:

(1) Development of strategic weapons of mass destruction;
(2) Increasing vulnerability due to urbanization and industrialization;
(3) Polarization of the global struggle into an East/West power bloc;

---

[161] Ibid., p. 20.
[162] Goure, *The Soviet-Civil Defense Program: A Trip Report*.
[163] Cole and German, A Geography of the U.S.S.R., The Background to Planned Economy, p. 75.
[164] "Civil Defense of the U.S.S.R.," *Intelligence Review*, p. 20.

(4) Cold War intensification;
(5) The feeling that civil defense can contribute to the overall military posture of the Soviet Union.[165]

Thus, it could be claimed that the Soviet civil defense program was a result of mere common sense, of the recognition of the need to protect not only the military-industrial segment of the society but also to maintain the morale of the population, now considered a prime factor in effective recovery from mass attack.

Of course, the success of such a vast institution relies heavily on popular support. As stated earlier, considerable apathy has been reported, and one sources mentioned that "pressure is being applied by the Communist party and other groups" to promote membership and participation.[166] The advent of a compulsory training program in 1955 probably came as a result of little success with "voluntarism." Therefore, again it must be that the program at least looked "good on paper," but to the extent it was successful is not known. By 1955, with the acknowledgement of nuclear weapons, civil defense appeared to be more heavily endorsed by "those who can make a difference"; also, the impressive leadership status of such organizations as DOSAAF, and Tolstikov's appointment as Chief of Civil Defense in 1955 implied a trend toward greater integration with the military and air defense components.

A quote from a 1953 article states: "Today, the Soviet Union is reasonably well prepared in civil defense matters to cope with air attack."[167] The key words here seem to be "air attack," because Soviet civil defense preparations were certainly keyed to a World War II–type of aerial threat through 1958. Even the publicized awareness in 1954 of a nuclear threat did not immediately change civil defense thinking, although it precipitated greater military/political concern with civil defense and the eventual transition of the system from a civilian-administrated/city-oriented program to a military-directed/nationwide institution.

---

[165] Goure, *Civil Defense in the Soviet Union*.
[166] "Civil Defense of the U.S.S.R.," *Intelligence Review*, p. 20.
[167] Ibid., p. 15.

Appendix A

Concepts of Air Defense Before 1945

A. The U.S. Heritage of the Interwar Period

1. Early Premises

U.S. concepts for air defense during the 1920's were strongly influenced by various developments in U.S. national policies, the perception of the threat and technological advances. These were supported by "lessons" drawn from World War I operational experience and subsequent developments.

U.S. national defense policies rested on the premise that attack by a potential enemy was unlikely. Indeed, during the decade of the 1920's, Army and Navy planners found it difficult to determine *any* enemy or enemies who might be *capable* of threatening the United States. After the 1922 Washington Disarmament Treaty and the termination of the Anglo-Japanese alliance, the United States seemed to have little to fear either from hostile air attack launched from carriers (because of tonnage limitations in the Washington Treaty of 1922) or from land-based aircraft (because of their inherent range limitations). As a consequence, the conclusion was general that the United States was in no danger from air attack. This conclusion was not reinforced by prevailing service doctrine but still became the conventional wisdom.

2. Origins of Air Force Doctrine: Early Air Defense Concepts

Air officers in the Army were convinced from the end of World War I that the best defense was a good offense. Many who held this view felt that the Army General Staff was primarily interested in the "defensive use" of aircraft and had neglected the "fighting side." General Mitchell carried on an extraordinary effort for a separate aviation department while arguing the need for a defined role for an expanded Air Service in the Army. Mitchell's paper entitled "Tactical Application of Military Aeronautics," proposed in January 1920, defined the principal mission and secondary employment of aeronautics. "The principal mission of Aeronautics is to destroy the aeronautical force of the enemy and after this, to attack his formations, both tactical and strategical, on the ground or on the water. The secondary employment of Aeronautics pertains to their use as an auxiliary to troops on the ground for enhancing their effect against hostile troops."[1]

Based upon a visit to France, Italy, Germany, Holland, and England in the winter of 1921–1922, Mitchell advocated unity of "air command." The air commander, he wrote "should control not only the observation aviation but also all antiaircraft weapons, searchlights and barrage balloons."[2]

Two years later, General M.M. Patrick, who had headed the Air Service with the AEF in France, proposed a reorganization and expansion of the Air Service within the War Department to give the Air Service

---

[1] Futrell, *Ideas, Concepts, Doctrine: USAF*, pp. 32–33.
[2] Ibid., p. 37.

a status analogous to that held by the Marine Corps within the Navy Department. He wrote on 19 December 1924, "I am convinced that the ultimate solution of the air defense problem of this country is a united air force.... Future emergencies will require at the very outset... the maximum use of air power on strategic missions...."[3] Such views were disputed by some critics.

In early autumn of 1925, the Secretaries of War and Navy jointly requested President Coolidge to support a board to study the best means of developing and supplying aircraft in U.S. national defenses. The President appointed a board, The Aircraft Board, headed by Dwight W. Morrow. After extensive hearings, this board published a report on 25 November 1925 stating: "We do not consider that air power, as in some of the national defense, has yet demonstrated its value—certainly not in a country situated as ours—for independent operations of such a character as to justify the organization of a separate department."[4]

The board concluded that the United States was in no danger from air attack and stated that the "belief that new and deadlier weapons will shorten future wars and prevent vast expenditures of lives and resources is a dangerous one, which, if accepted, might well lead to a more ready acceptance of war as the solution of international difficulties."[5]

Over the next decade, advances in aircraft range, speed, and altitude persuaded the Air Corps to urge upon the War Department the development of interceptor aircraft with at least 20 percent greater speed than proposed bombardment planes. In addition, the Air Corps recommended steps to provide a ground observer corps and aircraft warning and reporting unit in the United States and its overseas possessions.

While the Air Corps was seeking a better interceptor capability, it was also urging an improvement in early warning systems.

Detection research had progressed deliberately after World War I. By the 1930's, increased concern for defense (i.e., a growing U.S. desire for effective warning of a hostile approach either by sea or air) caused existing programs of visual and sonic research to broaden and include other radio-optical research for detection. That area showed promise and progress. Both the Army and the Navy reported success in detecting and tracking aircraft by reflected infrared rays. The Army, in 1926, had detected an aircraft, and, in 1932, the Navy had tracked a blimp using reflected IR means. The Army's Signal Corps experimented in tracking ocean liners in the early 1930's using a thermo locator. From a location at Fort Hancock, the Mauretania was tracked to a distance of 23,000 yards in 1934. A year later, the Normandie was tracked to 30,000 yards and, a few months later, the Aquitania to a distance of 18,000 yards through a fog.[6] Radio location soon took over, however, from heat locating and ranging.

May 1937 is often cited as a principal turning point in Army technical history, based upon the successful demonstration of a short-range AA radio locator, the SCR-268, developed for searchlight control.[7] Designed to locate aircraft at night in range, elevation, and azimuth accurately enough so that searchlights would instantly illuminate them when they were turned on, the SCR-268 was a mobile item of equipment. Designed for AA use, it did not provide continuous tracking and could not be brought to bear against low-flying aircraft. With relatively limited range, the SCR-268 provided only about five minutes' warning.

---

[3] Ibid., p. 43.
[4] Ibid., pp. 48–49.
[5] Ibid., p. 49.
[6] Terrett, *The Signal Corps: The Emergency*, pp. 38–39.
[7] Ibid., p. 46.

Appendix A: Concepts of Air Defense Before 1945

Although it was obviously not immediately useful for interceptors, the new locator was impressive enough to prompt the Army Air Corps to seek development of an early warning radio locator to provide warning at ranges up to 120 miles. Following further development and testing during 1938, the SCR-268 mobile radar for AA was standardized and put into production in the winter of 1939. Concurrently, development of early warning radars for the Air Corps progressed until the SCR-270 was established as basic equipment for the purpose. With these developments, the United States, as well as the British and the Germans, had radar for air defense when World War II began.[8]

In addition to these developments in the doctrine and technology of early warning and interception, the Army fostered improvements in antiaircraft artillery.

3. U.S. Army AAA Developments

AAA developments during the 1930's in the U.S. Army advanced to the degree that appropriations permitted. In 1938, the 90-mm. gun development project was completed and by 1940 was standardized as a replacement for the 3-inch AA gun M-3 which had been adopted in 1928. The 3-inch gun began to phase out as the 90-mm. AAA gun was adopted as standard in February of 1940. By the fall of 1940, the 90-mm. requirement called for more than 1,000 guns; yet during 1941 only 171 complete units were produced. The 37-mm. AA gun was adopted as standard in 1939 but this automatic weapon was just getting into production in 1940, when 170 were produced. By January 1941 this weapon was being produced at a rate of 40 per month. In the following month the 40-mm. Bofors AA gun was approved for standardization, although it took more than a year to get production rolling on the Americanized version of the 40-mm. AA gun.[9] The caliber .50 AA machine gun remained a low-altitude defense weapons from its adoption as standard during the early 1920's.

The U.S. Army AAA regimental organizations at the time were of two basic types: mobile and semi-mobile. Mobile regiments consisted of two battalions; the first battalion (guns) contained three gun batteries, each having four 3-inch guns and one searchlight battery of 15 searchlights. The second battalion was made up of automatic weapons, with those batteries of 37-mm. automatic weapons each having eight 37-mm. guns with one .50 caliber machine gun battery or, as was the case earlier, four .50 caliber machine gun batteries. The semi-mobile regiment consisted of three battalions; the first two battalions were gun battalions, each with the armament of the mobile battalion; the third was an automatic weapons battalion of four batteries.

At the outbreak of World War II in September 1939, the U.S. Army included seven skeletonized active AA Regiments, plus a number of National Guard and Organized Reserve AA Regiments, in the inactive forces.

4. Expansion Program

Keeping pace with increased performance of military aircraft, AAA developments influenced U.S. Defense planning. In addition to greater interest in AAA, in June 1939, the Army began an "Aviation Expansion Program" which authorized a three-fold increase in the combat strength of the Air Corps. That branch planned to attain within two years an overall strength of 24 groups—including seven pursuit

---
[8] Ibid., p. 127.
[9] Green, et al., *The Ordnance Department: Planning Munitions for War.*

interceptor groups. As the war in Europe developed, the U.S. Army Air Corps looked more closely at air combat operations in that theater for their implications concerning air power theories which stemmed from Douhet's thesis that airpower and command of the air would enable the destruction of an enemy nation. Increasingly the Army Air Corps argued that the air defense of the United States was best served by having strong offensive air capabilities. The best defense was a strong offense.

U.S. air officers generally agreed in the fall of 1939 that the Luftwaffe had substantiated American theory in its essentials because, although German air operations in Poland were mainly in support of ground fighting, the Luftwaffe had established control of the air by destroying the Polish Air Force on the ground on its air fields. German victories over British and French forces in the west further underscored the theory and increased pressure for meeting U.S. bomber requirements. Recommendations for increases in U.S. long-range bomber forces were pressed with the view that, rather than investing heavily in interceptors for defense, strong U.S. bomber forces could carry destruction to an enemy homeland or destroy his air power.

Development and success of the B-17 and B-18 gave rise to the Air Corps Tactical School 1938 teaching: "The possibility for the application of military forces against the vital structure of a nation directly and immediately upon the outbreak of hostilities in the most important and far reaching development of modern times."[10]

5. U.S. Air Defense Planning and Organization for CONUS

Thus, as early as 1938 U.S. planning had to include the possibility of attack on the continental United States. Because of the prospect that this possibility would involve air attack, air officers became more deeply involved in U.S. defense planning. "Indeed, they tended to feel that the problem was exclusively theirs and to attach slight importance to collaboration with ground troops. . . ."[11]

An Air Defense Command was organized on 26 February 1940, with headquarters at Mitchell Field, Long Island, New York, under GHQ, Air Force. It was a planning body with authority to organize combined air-ground operations but it had no territorial responsibility over either aircraft or antiaircraft artillery. Directly subordinate to the GHQ Air Commander, the Air Defense Command's organization and operations were greatly influenced by lessons from the Battle of Britain and the growing autonomy of the Army Air Corps. The Air Corps, for example, established an intermediate echelon between its wings and the GHQ Air Force in 1940 by dividing the United States into four air districts. Ostensibly organized for training and administration, these districts were later proposed to have, within each of them, a bombing command and an air defense command, the former to conduct offensive operations, the latter defensive operations, "within the theater of the Air District."[12] In other parts of the Army, it was held that the air districts should not be identified as theaters of operations.

In March 1941, the War Department ordered the establishment of four defense commands in the United States—Northeastern, Central, Southern, and Western. Each defense commander would be responsible for planning all measures against invasion of the area of his command. The commanding general of each of four armies was designated as the commanding general of the defense command within which his head-

---

[10] Futrell, op. cit., p. 84.
[11] Greenfield, et al., *Army Ground Forces: The Organization of Ground Combat Troops*, p. 116.
[12] Ibid., p. 117.

quarters was located and the Army staffs were used as the staffs of the defense command. This same War Department order replaced the previously announced four air districts with four numbered air forces. Each air force included a mobile echelon comprising a bomber command and an interceptor command, the name chosen to replace the "air defense" command. The four air forces remained directly under GHQ Air Force and were not subordinate to the defense commands.[13] The directed organization appeared somewhat similar to the basic British structure which had been set up for UK air defense under the RAF.

By June 1941, the Army Air Forces became an autonomous element in the War Department and direct responsibility for Army aviation matters was given to the Chief, Army Air Forces. Within his staff, the Air War Plans Division was charged with preparing "overall plans for the control of the activities of the Army Air Forces."[14] In effect, the AAF would make aviation plans for the numbered air forces in the defense commands. But the War Department order of 17 March 1941 establishing the defense commands stated explicitly: "When the War Department, to meet an actual or threatened invasion activates a Theater of Operations (or similar command) in the United States . . . the commander of the theater (or similar commander) will be responsible for all air defense measures in the theater."[15]

This same order provided that antiaircraft artillery, searchlights, and barrage balloons be attached to interceptor commands during operations.[16]

How these ground elements would be controlled, however, was not clear. Experience in the Battle of Britain had shown that tactical coordination was needed and that rapid, reliable communications and intelligence were essential, among other reasons, to clarify responsibilities and to avoid possible harm to friendly aviation. In the summer of 1941, the AAF proposed that the fire of all AAA be controlled by regional officers of the interceptor command. This was deliberated through the spring-summer of 1941, first, by an Air Defense Board made up of the Chief of Coast Artillery, Chief Signal Officer and the Commanding General of the GHQ Air Force which concluded that an exception should be made for combat zones. This view was personally contested by General McNair (first commander of Army Ground Forces) who pointed out that coordination of air defenses was just as necessary in the combat zone as elsewhere. He urged unity of command for all air defense forces and suggested that all antiaircraft units should be assigned or attached to interceptor commands.[17]

6. Early Air Defense Doctrine

During the following months, the AAF prepared a draft Field Manual, entitled "Air Defense," which included doctrinal concepts which integrated pursuit/interceptors, AAA, barrage balloon units, and Signal air warning units into a coordinated air defense establishment. This draft manual which drew heavily on British air defense experience in the Battle of Britain, distinguished for the first time between the term "air defense," which was a direct defense against enemy air operations and "counter air force operations," which were said to be not properly within the scope of air defense. While not officially approved and published,[18]

---
[13] Ibid., p. 119.
[14] Futrell, op. cit., p. 100.
[15] Greenfield, op. cit., p. 123.
[16] Ibid.
[17] Ibid.
[18] FM 1-25, *Air Defense*, was finally published by the War Department on 24 December 1942, but it was substantially revised from this draft.

this draft manual strongly influenced U.S. air defense training and organization. Much of its substance was incorporated into War Department Training Circular No. 70, 16 December 1941, which implicitly reflected some of the lessons drawn from the attack on Pearl Harbor and the need for unified command as it stated: "All antiaircraft artillery and pursuit aviation operating within the same area must be subject to the control of a single commander designated for the purpose." Two days later, War Department Training Circular No. 71, 18 December 1941, set forth the concept of "antiaircraft commands" to operate under the "command" of interceptor commanders.[19]

In addition to these concerns with the proper organization for air defense, the Army Air Forces newly established Fighter Command School in the summer of 1942 also contributed to the evolution of air defense doctrine. The Air Defense Directorate of that school set about to develop air force doctrines, tactics and techniques of air defense, to test air defense equipment and operational procedures and to recommend measures for the organization of air defense for the Unites States and overseas theaters.

7. Organizing AAA Combat Units

The concept of an arm of one of the Army's branches to be configured for operational employment as part of a larger integrated fighting force was new and pointed up the growth of specialization and new techniques and interdependence of U.S. combat forces. Within the Army Ground Forces the Coast Artillery Corps, which was traditionally responsible for ground-based air defense, confronted a number of problems in meeting demands of a great and rapid expansion. Gradually a new antiaircraft branch emerged within the Coast Artillery Corps and the new element exceeded the importance of the coast defense functions.

The requirement for operational air defense units grew amazingly, and the antiaircraft operational function became increasingly technical. As an indication of growth, during the three years after the fall of 1940, when the President declared a national emergency and U.S. defense efforts accelerated, Infantry increased by 600 percent; Field Artillery by 500 percent; but Antiaircraft Artillery jumped by 1750 percent.[20] Only a small part of this expansion resulted from the call to active service of Antiaircraft Artillery units from the National Guard and original reserves. Thus, there was an immediate and difficult job of organizing, training, and equipping substantial numbers of AAA units.

To build required, new AAA units became an important, pressing task. No other ground areas had to ship units—organized, trained, and equipped for combat—as rapidly as antiaircraft. In the early phases of the defense buildup and initial period of the war the demand for AAA was exceptionally heavy both in overseas theaters and bases and in the defense commands in the United States. Units had to be put together and deployed quickly. The effort was built on the base of available active units which, by 30 June 1941, included 43 mobile AAA Regiments, 6 semi-mobile Regiments, 13 separate AAA Battalions, and 1 Barrage Balloon Battalion.[21]

As an early step to facilitate rapid organization and training, the AAA regimental structure was replaced by designating the battalion as the fundamental unit, making it self-contained tactically and administratively. In addition, the number of different kinds of units was reduced. As the Army moved to eliminate the

---

[19] Greenfield, op. cit., p. 126.
[20] Ibid., p. 418.
[21] Cibula, *History of the Antiaircraft Command*.

Appendix A: Concepts of Air Defense Before 1945

AA regiments, a new tactical organization, the group, was set up to provide a means of having a flexible composition of AA battalions. As groups would have a number of battalions, varying with the situation, so would brigades constitute a varied number of groups with attached battalions. At the same time, the Coast Artillery designation of AAA units also was dropped.

As part of a major reorganization of the Army in March 1942, the Antiaircraft Command was set up within the Army Ground Forces and made responsible for readying any required AA forces needed for operations. Many handicaps attended the organization and training of new units by the Antiaircraft Command. Combat experiences were not available to pre-test or guide the effort. There was no proven doctrine and much to learn from on-going operations. To regularize training policies was difficult in the face of heavy demands for more complete training.[22]

8. Lessons from the Battle of Britain and American Combat Experience

The Battle of Britain clearly influenced U.S. thinking about coordinated air defense. The British experience impressed itself in various ways on U.S. organization and operations. First, that experience seemed to discredit the U.S. concept that a hostile air force could be destroyed on the ground. The RAF not only showed that a well-dispersed air force was a difficult bombing target, but also argued that it was effective and efficient to destroy hostile aircraft in the air by fighter attack. Second, fighter tactics used by the RAF were proved effective because of electronic early warning and fighter control established on the recommendations of a special committee for the scientific survey of Air Defense under the chairmanship of Sir Henry Tizard, Rector of the Imperial College of Science and Technology.

U.S. Army Air Corps observers attributed severe losses taken by the Luftwaffe in the Battle of Britain to the firepower volume of British fighters, poor rear defenses of the German bombers, vulnerability of dive-bombing tactics, large formations, and poor air discipline. Yet the growing significance of radar was implicit in the basic report of the RAF victory submitted by General Spaatz on 29 February 1941 when he said: "A numerically inferior air force has been phenomenally successful in stopping the unbroken chain of victories of the world's strongest air power." That same month, General Arnold, while commenting on U.S. air defense deficiencies, wrote: "During daylight in good weather, when pursuit aviation is present in strength in an area, it can pretty near bar the air to the bomber."[23] (Within a few years, senior U.S. air officers would claim that bombers could overwhelm any defense.)

The British experience soon stimulated conceptual planning for a U.S. continental warning system. From the spring of 1941, GHQ Air Force had responsibility for organizing and training for air operations and defense against air attack in the continental United States. Many other War Department agencies were actively engaged in different aspects of the development of U.S. air defense capabilities. Under the AF GHQ, the Army Air Force organized interceptor commands to carry out air defense operations. It was anticipated that these commands would exercise operational control of AAA units of the Coast Artillery Corps and air warning units of the Signal Corps.

---

[22] During 1942, the SCR 268 was the only gun-laying radar available for AA units although it had not been designed for that purpose. Since these radars were also needed overseas, very few were available for units in AA training center in the United States. Target practice against airborne targets was difficult because of limitations on availability of Air Force aircraft for tow target missions. AA Command pioneered expedients such as the rocket target and other training devices.
[23] Futrell, op. cit., p. 97.

"When war came [radar warning] sites had been picked for thirteen radar stations along the East Coast and eight of the stations were approaching completion."[24] On the West Coast at the outbreak of war 10 radar sites were scheduled to be set up to provide coverage of the 1200 miles between Seattle and San Diego.[25] Each radar chain was to be complemented with ground observers; the East Coast was to have 4,000 ground observer stations and 2,400 were supposed to be active along the Pacific coast.

But, while progress had been made, the air defense system of the United States was still in a formative stage when the war broke. There was no GCI (Ground Controlled Intercept) capability and it was "not until late 1943 that the continental defenses were generally equipped with VHF radio and a workable system for controlling interceptions at night."[26] While radar siting activity was "feverish" during 1942 and 1943, by the fall of 1943, the danger of air attack had decreased to the point that the numbered Air Forces which had been assigned to the defense mission were then reassigned to the control of the Army Air Force.

Early in 1942, the Army was reorganized into three principal elements: Army Ground Forces, Army Air Forces, and Army Service Forces. None was directly responsible for air defense combat operations. Under the Army Ground Forces, the Antiaircraft Command was given the mission of organizing, training and equipping AAA units for assignment to operational commands. In addition, AA Command was responsible for developing AA materiel and equipment. Major General Joseph A. Green, then Chief of Coast Artillery, headed the AA Command and his headquarters were staffed by personnel from the Office of the Chief of Coast Artillery. From April 1942 to September 1945 the AA Command trained and sent overseas 451 separate AAA units; the balance of a total of 613 AAA combat units were trained for use within the continental U.S. Under the Army Air Forces, four numbered air forces based in the U.S. not only organized and trained air units but shared air defense activity at home. The Army's Chief of Ordnance and Chief Signal Officer had significant roles in the procurement, delivery, and maintenance of air defense equipment under the Service Forces.

Since operational activity in continental air defense never actually involved active combat, the growing overseas experience of U.S. units increasingly affected organizational and training activity in the zone of interior and also influenced equipment developments for air defense. From the Philippines, Panama, the Antilles, Alaska, and the Central and South Pacific reports of operations during 1942 began to build a varied body of operational experience which was looked upon as a validation and extension of existing U.S. doctrine, organization, and equipment for air defense.

Because it was the first major air-ground offensive in World War II, operations in North Africa beginning in November 1942—with new theories being expounded and tested there and greater emphasis given to armored warfare—soon gave rise to demands for more effective close air support and air defense tailored to the needs of mobile, widely dispersed combat formations. These demands also led to concepts of increased centralization of air power.

General Montgomery wrote in January 1942 that the greatest asset of air power was its flexibility and maintained that this flexibility could be realized only when air power was centrally controlled by an air officer who maintained close association with the ground commander. The following month General Spaatz

---

[24] *History I Fighter Command, 1941–1944*, p. 104ff, cited by Sturm, et al., *The Air Defense of the United States*, p. 21.
[25] Ibid.
[26] Ibid., p. 22. GCI involved U.S. commitments to air defense improvements for many years after the war. Considerable effort and money have gone into improving the potentials of GCI, including adding to the speed and altitude of interceptors, and to the lethality of their armament. Much effort has been given to improving the coverage and sophistication of ground based radar nets. Yet the war time role of GCI was never really clarified with respect to possible theaters.

Appendix A: Concepts of Air Defense Before 1945

organized the Northwest Africa Allied Air Force and gave it command over a Strategic Air Force, a Coastal Air Force and a Tactical Air Force. Writing to General Arnold the next month, General Spaatz said: "the air battle must be won first . . . Air units must be centralized and cannot be divided . . . among several armies or corps. . . . When the battle situation requires it, all units, including medium and heavy bombardment must support ground operations."[27] Within a few months, the Army Air Forces published Field Manual 100-20, "Command and Employment of Air Power," which said:

> The inherent flexibility of air power is its greatest asset. This flexibility makes it possible to employ the whole weight of the available air power against selected areas in turn; such concentrated use of the air striking force is a battle-winning factor of the first importance. Control of available air power must be centralized and command must be exercised through the Air Force commander. . . . Therefore, the command of air and ground forces in a theater of operations will be vested in the superior commander charged with the actual conduct of operations in the theater, who will exercise command of air forces through the air force commander and command of ground forces through the ground force commander.[28]

Published by the War Department, but without the concurrence of the Army Ground Forces, FM 100-20 was greeted with mixed reactions. In the Army Ground Forces, it was viewed with "dismay" and described as the "Army Air Forces' Declaration of Independence." Among U.S. air officers, too, there was some reserve; for example General Orvil Anderson considered the division of air power, as represented by a tactical air force, to be wrong and it was suggested that the Air Force had "swallowed the RAF solution to a local situation in Africa hook, line and sinker without stopping to analyze it. . . ."[29]

In effect, relatively new and essentially untried principles were being applied on the battlefield to the needs of the war. Trial and error experience in the field did not offer American schools adequate time for thoughtful development of doctrine. Nevertheless "trained" units had to be deployed with the latest "doctrine." With incidental changes, the previously developed draft on air defense, which had originated in the Army Air Forces in October 1941, became War Department Field Manual 1-25 on 24 December 1942. But little actual operational experience could validate the manual.

In North Africa, the Luftwaffe remained active and contested with the several allied air forces for local air superiority. The demands for air defense capabilities, therefore, intensified and the rate of growth for antiaircraft units continued high throughout 1943. This continually expanding requirement for AAA combat units not only consumed programmed manpower, but increasingly sophisticated and varied technical demands developed as a result of combat experience and the growing capabilities of improved weapons, ammunition, and material.

Within the Army Ground Forces, AAA was viewed primarily as a "defensive" capability, required and useful only so long as U.S. air power could not provide air superiority. Air defense requirements for resources were of less concern to the AGF which felt that the AAA represented priority and specialized requirements for support in men, equipment and facilities. AAA was useful and worthwhile if it supported ground combat forces but otherwise air defense artillery was of lesser interest.

Command arrangements in overseas areas governing air defense frequently were deficient for coordination of operations; long periods of inaction limited operational proficiency because of lack of arrangements and facilities for continued training. AAA units needed target practice and this entailed Air Force support, to

---

[27] Futrell, op. cit., pp. 121–122.
[28] Ibid., pp. 122–123.
[29] Ibid.

fly the tow-target missions. Such conditions fostered a proposal for the transfer of the AA Command to the Army Air Forces. The issue first came to a head in February 1943. Originated within the War Department General Staff, by the G3, General Edwards, who was an Air Corps officer, the proposal was supported by General Arnold, Commanding General, Army Air Forces.[30] The main reason for the proposal, according to the memorandum setting it out, was that AAA and fighter aviation should be trained together because they should operate as a team in combat.

General McNair, the AGF commander, agreed with the need for training of AAA units with Air Force units but he also believed there was a need to train AAA units with mobile ground units, despite the fact that few ground troops had, up until that time, engaged in mobile operations.[31] He could not see how branch or unit training of AAA, a necessary preliminary to combined training of any kind, would be improved by a transfer of the Antiaircraft Command to the Army Air Forces.[32] The Operations Division of the War Department General Staff agreed, and the proposal for AAA to be shifted to the AAF was dropped.

By the summer of 1943, however, the issue surfaced again.[33] Reflecting the growing significance of AAA as part of active air defense operations overseas, a substantial body of antiaircraft officers were assigned to duty at various Air Force headquarters throughout the world. Their assignments ranged from instructing at the School of Applied Tactics at Orlando, Florida, to flak analysis for operational Air Forces overseas. Many AAA units were actively committed to air field defense. AAA officers on duty with the Air Force had a kind of functional headquarters in the office of the Special Assistant for Antiaircraft to General Arnold, headed at the time by Major General Homer R. Oldfield, who was named to the post after having served for several years as the Commanding General, Panama Coast Artillery Command. In that assignment, General Oldfield had commanded the antiaircraft defense of the Panama Canal with more than 600 operational positions manned in an extensive deployment throughout Panama for defense of the canal.

In September 1943, General Oldfield was named to head a War Department Board to survey the antiaircraft problem, following the shooting down of U.S. aircraft by friendly antiaircraft in the Sicilian Campaign. That board submitted a number of findings, including the following:

(1) Air commanders, in the defense of fixed installations in the theaters of operations, should exercise command over their supporting antiaircraft units,
(2) Air commanders should control the allocation of all antiaircraft units,
(3) Army Ground Forces regarded AAA as a defensive weapon,
(4) Combined training of AAA had been bad, and
(5) The dissemination of technical knowledge and training doctrine in the theaters had been inadequate.

---

[30] War Department Memo, 9 February 1943, subj.: "Integration of AAA with AAF," cited by Greenfield, op. cit., p. 420.
[31] In the North African campaign, the utility of self-propelled AAA had been demonstrated effectively and spurred the requirement for this special type of automatic weapons battalion. One AAA unit in the initial landings had been equipped as a self-propelled battalion for test of the concept. Organized with a headquarters and, each consisting of two platoons, one an automatic weapons platoon, the other a machine gun platoon, AAA SP battalions were standardized in 1943 to provide the AW platoon with nine M-15 gun carriages, consisting of one manually operated 37-mm. gun coaxially mounted with two air-cooled .50 caliber AA machine guns. The M-15 was a lightly armored, half-track carrier. The machine gun platoon was equipped with eight M-16 carriages; each consisting of four air-cooled .50 caliber AA machine guns on a power-operated revolving turret mounted on a lightly armored half-track carrier. Subsequently, each platoon was organized to have an equal number of M-15 and M-16 mounts.
[32] Memo, General McNair for G3, WD, 19 February 1943, subj.: as above, cited by Greenfield, p. 421.
[33] OPD Memo for G3, WD, 23 February 1943, same subject, cited by Greenfield, Ibid.

Appendix A: Concepts of Air Defense Before 1945

As a remedy, the Oldfield Board recommended the transfer of antiaircraft training to the Army Air Forces.[34] The War Department disregarded the Board's recommendation.[35]

9. Contribution of the SCR-584

By the summer of 1943, improved gun-laying radars, the SCR-584 and SCR-545, were being reproduced in quantity to equip AAA gun units. The SCR-584, a microwave development, proved to be an outstanding piece of equipment and came into great demand because the SCR-268 was increasingly vulnerable to German jamming. Everyone wanted the SCR-584. The Air Force commanders in North Africa complained that their 268's were being jammed and could not satisfactorily direct either searchlights or night fighter operations.

U.S. AA searchlight units had been trained in cooperative tactics with fighter aircraft; one searchlight in each platoon was designated as an orbit beacon and the U.S. standard 60-inch searchlight, with a beam of 800 million candle power, capable of illuminating targets to 19 miles under normal atmospheric conditions, had been adapted to spread the focus of the beam. While decreasing the intensity of the beam and lessening effective range by this focus change, the wider beam made it ideal for use against high speed targets at close range as well as being useful against night-time parachute attack and raids and providing artificial "moonlight" for friendly night operations or surveillance.

With the advent of the SCR-584, however, field commanders increasingly called for AAA which could defend effectively against hostile air attack by day or night. Air Force commanders and principal staff officers saw the improved AAA capability as lessening demands for night fighters and for airborne intercept radars. Such factors helped to sustain continuing requirements for more AAA units.

10. Strategic Factors and Related Influences on AAA Developments in World War II

Despite the popularity of AAA units for defense, strategic factors soon brought a decline in their training and overseas deployment. Toward the end of 1942, estimates of the limits of U.S. capacity to produce materiel and ceilings on the manpower available to the Army had come sharply into view. Limitations on shipping capacity were also felt as the submarine menace continued. These, combined with the evolution of changed Allied strategic concepts, constrained the fuller development of the ground army.

From 1 April 1942 to 2 September 1945, 451 separate AA units were trained and shipped overseas by the AA Command. Included among them were: 80 AAA Gun Battalions, 176 AW Battalions, 18 Searchlight Battalions, 6 Airborne AAA Battalions, and 83 additional separate AA units, such as airborne AA MG batteries, AW batteries and operational detachments. Such units were largely organized, trained and equipped during the period that manpower and logistical limitations in the Army were becoming of great concern. Indicative of this, the proposed organizational structures (TO&Es) for these kinds of units were critically reviewed by the War Department in late 1942 to justify the personnel and equipment needed to carry out the AAA mission. As a result of this review, the organization of AAA units, as proposed by the AA Command, was cut from 10 to 15 percent in personnel and equipment. Still, the War Department requirement for AAA

---

[34] Memo, Major General Oldfield and others for G3, WD, 27 Sept. 1943, subj.: AAA, cited by Greenfield, Ibid.
[35] WD Memo, WDCSA 351.17 (13 Oct. 1943), Gen. McNarney for Gen. McNair, 13 Oct. 1943, same subject., cited by Greenfield, Ibid.

units in 1943 continued to rise. At the end of 1942, AAA troop strength in the Army approximately 7 percent; the following year, the same percentage held true.

By the end of 1942, however, the basic outline of U.S. strategy seemed pointed to an even greater development of air power for offensive purposes, substituting for defensive AAA resources. The strategic factors included the following:

a. Allied Strength

By late 1942, it appeared that the Soviet had passed from a strategic defense to the offense. Massive ground forces (400 divisions by 1945) engaged the bulk of German ground forces and helped to neutralized Japanese forces along the Manchurian Border.

b. Allied Naval Strength

Naval successes by this time enabled the employment of U.S. forces at advantageous times and places.

c. Increasing Allied Air Power

Reduced effectiveness of the Luftwaffe and increasing effectiveness of Allied air would permit employment of ground forces under conditions of favorable, local air superiority. In this light, and because of shipping constraints, U.S. strategy began to allocate a larger proportion of U.S. resources to naval and air power and to support of U.S. allies. AA equipment furnished the U.S.S.R., for example, included more than 250 90-mm. guns, 5,500 40-mm. guns, 2,200 multiple mount AW, including 100 self-propelled M-15 sets, and many different radars, and, of particular importance, 49 SCR-584 sets.[36] The War Department therefore revised its 1943 mobilization troop basis to emphasize a basic preferences for light, easily transported units having offensive combat capabilities. This emphasis promoted a lighter, flexible, more interdependent ground army with its main strength in infantry, backed by significant fire support and with armored divisions designed to exploit breakthroughs. Such an emphasis on the ground offensive meant that the proportions of armored and AAA units in the ground army would gradually be reduced. While more than 800 AAA battalions had been planned, in October 1943 the War Department reduced the planned figure to 575 and checked what had been a continuing AA expansion.[37] By the spring of 1945, AAA constituted less than 4 percent of the strength of the Army. At the same time, it was 11.5 percent of the strength of the Army's ground combat forces.[38]

Other undulations also affected the organization, training, and equipment of AAA units during World War II. For example, by the end of 1943, every item of primary armament and equipment—guns, radars, automatic weapons, and searchlights—then being issued to AAA units either did not exist at the time of Pearl Harbor or had been considerably modified and improved. (A comparable situation existed among Army Air Forces units.) To realize these improvements and modifications, however, required a great variety of tests and a considerable analysis of suggestions, devices, and prototype equipment. While a number of advanced developments were contemplated, the basic strategic approach formalized by the War Department in late 1942 may have tended to slow or impede development of AA guided missiles during World War II.

---

[36] Jones, *The Roads to Russia*.
[37] Greenfield, op. cit., p. 423.
[38] Ibid., pp. 203, 395.

Appendix A: Concepts of Air Defense Before 1945

The 120-mm. AA gun (Ml) was standardized by 1944 as a result of development begun in 1939 for a gun with greater range than the 90-mm. gun. A need for guided missiles to reach very high flying aircraft or high rockets, such as the rumored German "V" weapons, however, was stated by Headquarters AA Command in 1943. The 120-mm. gun was a high-velocity weapon with a muzzle velocity of 3100 fps, able to fire a 50-pound projectile to 56,000 feet using semi-fixed ammunition and employing a power-operated ammunition tray and rammer. Excessive barrel wear was anticipated and this fact, together with technological progress, prompted a stated need for an AA missile.

11. Guided Missile Development

In January 1944 the Antiaircraft Artillery Board outlined the military characteristics for a controlled antiaircraft rocket projectile and recommended that AA Command initiate a development program using those characteristics. The Commanding General, Army Ground Forces quickly forwarded these recommendations to the Commanding General, Army Service Forces, and on 9 February 1944 requested that a project for the development of an antiaircraft rocket weapon with associated control mechanism and directing radar be initiated immediately and be given the highest priority.

The development of the missile itself would be an Ordinance responsibility; but the guidance package would be electronic and therefore a concern of the Signal Corps. The latter took the stand that until Ordnance determined the kind of missile and its flight characteristics, work on a control system would not be pursued, "due to limitations of personnel."[39] Thus, in April 1944, the Signal Corps saw the project "to be desirable for LONG range investigation but one which the Signal Corps should not attempt at the present time. . . ."[40] When the German V-1 and V-2 weapons began to hit the UK in the summer of 1944, U.S. research in rockets and guided missiles quickly accelerated.

In the meantime the Army also began other projects to meet future requirements. In May 1944, Army Service Forces awarded the California Institute of Technology a contract involving an estimated $3,900,000 for research and development work on long-range rocket missiles, ranjets, and launching equipment. The resulting "ORDCIT" Project was to focus on propellants, control mechanisms, and materials involved in missile design, as well as aerodynamics. The overall aim of the program was to gather research information on which to base the design of future missiles.

Later in 1944, the Ballistic Laboratory at the Aberdeen Proving Ground, which was assigned responsibility for all external ballistic missile work in connection with guided missile development, successfully performed the necessary tracking and computation of trajectories for testing the first missile developed by the California Institute of Technology.

While these development activities got under way, a struggle grew within the Army concerning control over the development of missile weapons.

In an attempt to clarify areas of responsibility, on 2 October 1944, Joseph T. McNarney, the Deputy Chief of Staff, issued a policy directive to the Commanding Generals, Army Ground Forces, Army Air Forces and Army Service Forces. That directive established responsibility for research and development in the field of guided missiles as follows:

---

[39] Thompson and Harris, *The Signal Corps: The Outcome*, p. 464.
[40] Ibid.

(1) Army Air Forces would have research and development responsibility, including designation of military characteristics, for all guided or homing missiles dropped or launched from aircraft.

(2) Army Air Forces also would have research and development responsibility for all guided or homing missiles launched from the ground which depended for sustenance primarily on the lift of aerodynamic forces. The Army Air Forces and Army Ground Forces would designate military characteristics when and as these affected their interests.

(3) Army Services Forces had research and development responsibility for guided or homing missiles launched from the ground which depended for sustenance primarily on missile momentum. The Army Air Forces and Army Ground Forces would designate military characteristics when and as these affected their interests.[41]

12. Continued Utility of AAA

A revolution in AA gunnery, stemming from the introduction of radar, helped to make very substantial contributions to the toll of enemy aircraft attacking areas defended by AA guns. In addition, by their volume of fire, AA guns forced aircraft to take evasive action which reduced the effectiveness of air attack. Concentrations of guns forced bombers to seek altitudes above effective zones of AA fire, and bombers flying above 20,000 feet lost considerable bombing accuracy.

U.S. AAA proved particularly effective against the German "long-range" bombardment weapon, the V-1. This relatively small, automatically controlled, jet propelled monoplane carried a ton of high explosives at a speed between 300 and 400 mph at altitudes from 600 to 10,000 feet for 250 miles.[42] The V-1 missile attacks against the United Kingdom began during the night of 13 June 1944 and ended 29 March 1945.[43]

V-1 activity against the United Kingdom occurred in three periods. The first from 13 June to 5 September; the second, when the V-1 was air-launched, from early September to mid-January 1945; and the third, from 3 March to the end of the month. A combined U.S.-British air defense, including fighters and AAA, was setup against this new weapon.

At the start AA guns were formed in an inland belt between the Channel and London, the prime target of attacks. AAA was restricted from firing whenever RAF aircraft were over the area. Their success was limited. Soon the defense shifted, based on a desire to destroy V-1's over the ocean. To lessen the danger to personnel and property from falling V-1's and to eliminate mutual interference between AAA and fighters, the defense was realigned after a month. AAA was moved to the coast and set up in a 5,000-yard belt along the Channel coast which permitted guns to fire 10,000 yards out to sea. The fighters were to intercept further out in the channel and beyond the belt of guns. Over the gun belt fighters were restricted; they had to fly over 8,000 feet in that area and AAA guns could fire up to 6,000 feet. Following this, and with the proximity fuze available and authorized for use, AAA quickly reached a high order of effectiveness against the V-1.

On the continent, the capture of Antwerp and the opening of port facilities there saw the rapid growth in importance of that city as an Allied supply base. Germany made a determined, large-scale effort to neutralize Antwerp and its port facilities beginning on 24 October 1944 and maintained nearly continuous V-1 attacks against the area until 30 March 1945. Of nearly 5000 V-1 missiles launched by the Germans against Antwerp only 211 (4.3 percent) fell within the area which was designated to be vital. AAA provided the principal defense against the V-1 attacks on Antwerp. About 12,000 personnel participated in the AA defenses.

---

[41] Letter, C/S USA, to CG AGF, et al., subj.: "Guided Missiles," 2 October 1944.
[42] General Board, ETO, *Tactical Employment of AA Units, Including Defense Against Pilotless Aircraft (V-1)*, Report No. 38.
[43] Welborn, *V-1 and V-2 Attacks Against the UK*, Tech. Memo ORO-T-42, p. 1.

Appendix A: Concepts of Air Defense Before 1945

In the early days of the Antwerp defense, the effectiveness of the defense was degraded considerably by restrictions placed on AA fire in order to protect friendly flight activity. A number of airfields in the vicinity of the city complicated control and protection of friendly aircraft from AA fire. Because of adverse weather in the fall season, visual recognition was difficult and to eliminate the mutual interference problem, a "Inner Artillery Zone" (IAZ) was established. Friendly aircraft continually violated the IAZ; during the period 26 November–11 November 1944 available records reportedly indicate 375 friendly aircraft in 129 flights violated the prescribed zone.[44] Nevertheless, while large amounts of AA equipment, ammunition, and personnel were required, the AA defense of Antwerp essentially made the V-1 obsolete as a tactical weapon.

In the various theaters of operations, AA units provided defense against air attack on friendly forces and installations both in the combat zone and in the rear areas. Allocation of AAA for the defense of specific units or vital areas was established on the basis of priorities directed by the U.S. forces or area commander. No AAA units were assigned as organic or integral elements to other combat organizations; generally AAA units provided air defense protection and, on occasion, especially during later stages of the war, ground fire support to U.S. ground combat forces. But no organic AAA was provided U.S. divisions.

13. Anomalies in Command and Control Air Defense Resources

In the European theater the requirements for U.S. AAA units were derived from British organizational allocations of antiaircraft artillery. This situation stemmed from a combination of factors that included U.S. deference to British sovereignty and experience, U.S. adherence to the British pattern of action, and the functional air defense planning and operational responsibility among U.S. forces being vested with U.S. Army Air Forces. In turn, this raised a question concerning the control of organically assigned AAA units. If AAA units were not specifically assigned to a parent unit or organization, functional command of a "coordinated" air defense might require an Air Force command of these units.

Several anomalies were apparent in the general situation, reflected by the allocation of U.S. AAA units in the ETO in October 1944. At the time, AAA units either were assigned or attached as follows:

	Armies			6th Army Group	12th Army Group	IX ADC
	First	Third	Ninth			
Gun Battalions	5½	5	7	1	1	7
Automatic Weapons	17	13	11	2	2	20
Searchlight	—	—	—	—	—	3
Self-Propelled AW	6	6	3	1	2	—

Noteworthy is the fact that the Army group and Army elements had: 19½ gun battalions versus 7 for IX Air Defense Command; 45 AW Battalions versus 20; and all 18 self-propelled AW battalions were with the operational combat forces. Yet none of these AAA units was organic to any of these field forces.

---

[44] *The Flying Bomb: The Defense of Antwerp and Brussels*, par. 33–40; U.S. Army Hq Antwerp X, "Infringement of IAZ, 26 November–11 December 1944" (Air University Archives, 539.667B, Folder 33) cited in Chapter 4, *Air Defense Historical Analysis*, U.S. Army Air Defense School, p. 148.

As the flow of Allied operations moved east, these field forces were increasingly dependent upon AAA for effective local defense yet could neither effect nor cause the reassignment of any AAA units under the IX Air Defense Command to help provide air defense protection. In contrast, Air Force units under IX Air Defense Command could be reassigned, and be relieved from responsibility for any active air defense role. This actually happened. With a reduced threat, fighters were withdrawn from IX AD Command and only AAA was actively committed to the air defense mission. Accordingly, it was questioned whether IX AD command, the principal theater element for air defense had either been tested for or demonstrated then current air defense "doctrine."

The Air Force Commander in the ETO, with responsibility for the U.S. air defense mission (CG, Ninth Air Force), could deputize a subordinate Air Force command (IX Air Defense Command) to discharge the air defense responsibility and either authorize or direct that command to disengage Air Force units which were assigned air defense missions. Theoretically, at least, the situation could have developed that an Air Force commander could carry out air defense missions with only AAA units, thus exclusively using ground based air defense systems to provide the protection of rear areas. This appeared to violate the "doctrine" of coordinated, integrated air defense and rankled further because AAA units believed the air warning service in the IX Air Defense Command inadequately performed its air defense mission, being used more to control tactical air operations. At the same time, the Air Force component commander could also limit the use of AAA assigned to Army field forces by asking for augmented or more intensive ground-based air defense efforts for the defense of airfields located forward of army group rear boundaries.

Essentially, the Air Force element could dictate the scale of the AAA allotment needed for rear areas, citing the factors of British experience and the need for an Air Force command over any AAA resources committed in order to coordinate the several means being employed for air defense. With the authority that attended that responsibility, the Air Force commander could also scale down the commitment of air resources given to the task while limiting the transfer of ground AA units critically needed by ground force commanders in the field.

In Europe, all Air Force capabilities were considered to be available for support of the surface campaign. "Although the Ninth Air Force stood ready to maintain friendly air superiority, it was routinely committed to interdiction and close support operations."[45] Thus, Allied air resources, without being obliged to extended, static commitments for air defense because of the general decline of the Luftwaffe and the availability of AAA for protection, were free to pursue offensive operations against the enemy, including counter-air operations against airfields.

Nonetheless, it remained evident that air defense from AAA units was still valuable and significant in protecting forward areas against air attack. Anzio, Remagen, and Bastogne all provided apt illustrations of that fact. Between 18 and 23 December 1944 at Bastogne, for example, the U.S. 406th Fighter-Bomber Group was responsible for close air support to the 101st Airborne Division. The group flew 529 close air support sorties into the area; out of 60 operational P-47's at the beginning of the period, the group lost 17 shot down and had more than 40 damaged by German AA in the area.[46]

In a two-week period in March 1945, the Remagen Beachhead became the most heavily defended vulnerable area since Normandy. Normally, on a single day, 67 jet aircraft attacks were made on the bridge

---

[45] Futrell, op. cit., p. 162.
[46] Ibid.

Appendix A: Concepts of Air Defense Before 1945

which was defended by U.S. AAA. A total of 142 German aircraft were destroyed by AAA fire and 59 probably destroyed there from 8 March to 21 March 1945.

14. Interest in New, Improved Air Defense Weapons

As the war drew near its close, interest in the potential of new defensive weapons grew and greater expectations of effectiveness took hold with the prospects of maneuverable defensive missiles or projectiles. Gun developments had proved capable of handling high-speed targets and, with improved fire control, the defense could contemplate the prospect of jet aircraft without undue concern. The Army had begun work in 1944 on an improved fire control system, the M-33, to link a computer with guns, a tracking radar, plotting boards and communications equipment. (As developed, the M-33 system could compute, for the 90-mm. and 120-mm. guns, firing data for targets with speeds up to 1,000 mph.)

In February 1945, Bell Telephone Laboratories was given a contract, co-sponsored by the Office, Chief of Ordnance and the Army Air Forces, to explore the possibilities of a new antiaircraft defense system to combat future bombers invading friendly territory at such speed and altitude that conventional artillery would be unable to defend against them effectively. Bell completed a research plan to develop a practical weapon system of this type six months later. The plan promised such a system within a few years. To have a system available by the time an enemy could have high-speed, high altitude bombers in operation, it was recommended that the equipment be derived insofar as possible from devices, methods, and techniques already known and understood. By this time, however, the AAF had pulled out of the joint effort. The proposed project was named Nike and marked the beginning of the development of a series of missiles bearing that name and which eventually led to the antiballistic missile system known as Safeguard.

At about the same time the Army Ground Forces Equipment Review Board submitted a report on postwar equipment for the Army. Among its findings the Board concluded that high velocity guided missiles, preferably of the supersonic type capable of intercepting and destroying aircraft flying at speeds up to 1,000 miles per hour at altitudes up to 60,000 feet or of destroying missiles of the V-2 type, should be developed at the earliest practicable date.

Air defense remained a subject of high level attention for a variety of reasons. Prominent among them was the violent and growing use of Japanese suicide air attacks in the closing campaigns in the Pacific. Beginning as a reaction to U.S. landings in Luzon, the Japanese attacks, later known as Kamikaze attacks, grew in frequency and intensified. In effect, they proved very costly, decimating Japanese air strength but posing serious problems for U.S. leaders. While causing only relatively minor damage to U.S. ships at Luzon, the Kamikaze attacks on Okinawa in April 1945 helped the Japanese to sink 20 U.S. ships and to damage 157 others. Most of the sinkings (14) and damages (90) resulted from the suicide attacks. During May and June, these attacks continued. In all, Kamikaze attacks accounted for 26 of 28 U.S. ships sunk and 164 of the 225 ships damaged at Okinawa.[47] Destroyers, cruisers, battleships and carriers were all hit; some of the large ships suffered great damage and loss of life.

The Japanese objective sought to disable the U.S. fleet offshore to disrupt supply. In addition, Japanese air attacks were directed against U.S. airfields. During the operation Japan launched nearly 900 air raids. Nearly 4,000 Japanese aircraft were destroyed in combat including 1,900 Kamikaze planes. The intensity

---

[47] Appleman, *Okinawa: The Last Battle*, pp. 362–364.

and serious threat of Kamikaze attacks helped to promote a crash program for a shipborne air defense guided missile.

15. The Termination of World War II

Barely three years after denouncing the Japanese air attack on Pearl Harbor, President Roosevelt in early 1945 contemplated an "intensive bombing" campaign against the Japanese homeland to destroy Japan and its army. Admiral William Leahy, the President's wartime chief-of-staff, recorded in his diary in February 1945: "The President [Roosevelt] said that with the fall of Manila the war in the Pacific was entering a new phase and that we hoped to establish bases on the Bonins and to make plans for additional bombing of Japan . . . he hoped by intensive bombing to destroy Japan and its army and thus save American lives."[48]

The following month, the most destructive bombing raid in history took place when U.S. B-29's raided Japan and, according to the U.S. Strategic Bombing Survey, killed at least 83,000 people, injured 102,000 others and left 1,000,000 homeless.[49] Within six months, General LeMay's 20th Air Force could deliver 8,000 tons of bombs per raid.[50] During July 1945, LeMay's B-29's dropped 40,000 tons of bombs on Japan.[51] Navy carrier aircraft strikes against the home islands added substantially to that total. And, as part of the deliberate preparation to the planned invasion that was scheduled later that year, U.S. military power being redeployed from Europe to the Pacific would include the B-17's and B-24's that had been pounding Europe with mass bombing attacks. The U.S. capacity to bomb Japan was growing on a vast scale. Despite the fact that many primary targets in Japan were so badly burned they no longer represented useful targets, the U.S. program of putting 1,051,000 tons of bombs on Japan during 1945 moved ahead on schedule.[52]

Nonetheless, a unique "rain of destruction from the air, the like of which had never been seen on the earth" and "utter destruction" of Japan was spoken of by the United States in the summer of 1945 unless the Japanese surrendered immediately.[53] Propaganda leaflets dropped on Japan said: "You should take steps now to cease military resistance. Otherwise we shall resolutely employ this [atomic] bomb and all our other superior weapons to promptly and force fully end the war."[54] U.S. leaders clearly wished to avoid an invasion of Japan.

President Truman wrote in his memoirs that "General Marshall told me that it might cost half a million lives to force the enemy's surrender on his home ground."[55] Secretary of War Henry L. Stimson, soon after the war, recalled: "As we understood in July, there was a very strong possibility that the Japanese government might determine upon resistance to the end, in all areas under its control. In such an event the allies would be faced with the enormous task of destroying an armed force of five million men and five thousand suicide aircraft, belonging to a race which had already amply demonstrated its ability to fight literally to the death."[56]

---

[48] Leahy, *The Leahy Papers*, "Diary of William Leahy, 8 November 1947."
[49] Craven and Cate, *Matterhorn to Nagasaki: June 44 to August 45*, p. 617.
[50] Miller, *Men of the Contrail Country*, p. 39.
[51] Knebel and Bailey, *No High Ground*, p. 2.
[52] Arnold, *Global Mission*, p. 595.
[53] Truman, *Memoirs: Year of Decisions*, p. 422.
[54] Knebel and Bailey, op. cit., p. 170.
[55] Truman, op. cit., p. 416.
[56] Stimpson, "The Decision to Use the Atomic Bomb," *Harpers*, Feb. 47, p. 102.

Appendix A: Concepts of Air Defense Before 1945

Vannevar Bush had no doubt about the desirability of using the atomic bomb; he reportedly "knew it would end the war."[57] And, while a number of scientists opposed the use of the bomb only a relative minority of U.S. government officials opposed its use.[58]

Thus, the terrible retribution of Hiroshima and Nagasaki in early August 1945 when U.S. strategic aircraft delivered atomic weapons there, appeared as a capstone to the war which began for the United States as a result of a Japanese air attack. In effect, there seemed to have been demonstrated the overwhelming potential of strategic forces wielding nuclear weapons. The image portrayed was colored and given added dimension by other events and technical milestones of World War II. Taken together, there was projected a new security environment which would profoundly challenge conventional wisdom and "operational experience." This challenge elicited little recognition or response as the United States sought a transition from war to peace and failed to arouse notable interest even as the country's leaders began an exhaustive inquiry into the questions of Pearl Harbor where surprise air attack had brought America into the war.

The Pearl Harbor investigation saw lessons in that bitter experience centering on the need for better coordination among U.S. armed forces and improved intelligence. But the question of measures to defend against surprise attack by air were essentially ignored. Nonetheless, air and missile defense were a central security issue for the next twenty-five years. In the face of technological changes and advances in offensive capabilities operational procedures, tactics, techniques, and command and control procedures for air defense had to be adapted and fitted to the bounding development of new weapons and their projected potentials. Changes in the established pattern and structure of air defense concepts was inherent in the situation at the end of World War II.

B. Growth of Soviet Air Defense

1. The Interwar Years (1918–1941)

The origins of Soviet air defense can be traced to the first years of the regime when the Soviets had to defend against air attacks by the forces of foreign intervention and internal counterrevolution. During this period (1918–1920) small numbers of antiaircraft batteries and fighter aircraft were assigned to the defense of important centers such as Petrograd and Moscow. Because of the limited means which were available, the air defense had an "objective" or "point" character. The tactical approach of the time had the combat units of antiaircraft artillery spread out around the objective in such a fashion as to improve the mutual cover of a firing zones of adjacent batteries. Machine guns were placed on the roofs of buildings in order to do battle with low-flying enemy planes. Fighter aircraft assigned to defend an objective, as a rule, were based at the edge of the city and carried out combat operations up to the zone of antiaircraft artillery fire.[59]

The detection of enemy aircraft was the responsibility of a special air observation service which included nets of visual observation posts spread around the defended points to distances of 100–200 kilometers. Observers at these posts, upon visually or by sound detecting enemy aircraft, reported the information immediately to the air defense headquarters and the nearest airfield. The command of the air defense forces was concentrated in the heads of the chief of the air defense point. But because of inadequate

---

[57] Giovannitti and Freed, *The Decision to Drop the Bomb*, p. 324.
[58] Feis, *The Atomic Bomb and the End of World War II*, pp. 190–191.
[59] Batitskiy, *Voyennaya Mysl'*, p. 28.

communications the air defense commander could provide only initial direction. After which each unit commander acted independently in accordance with his own situation. Some centralized control did exist during battle, particularly in the linking of individual antiaircraft batteries in groups with each battery having its own sector of defense.[60]

Such were the origins of the Soviet national air defense system. The system is frequently identified as Soviet PVO. The term "PVO" is an abbreviation for two Russian words, "Protivovozdushnaya Oborona," which literally mean "Antiair Defense." Another term which is frequently encountered in transliteration from Russia is "PVO Strany," meaning "Air Defense of the Country," or, more conveniently, "National Air Defense."

In 1930, the Soviet air defense system began to come into much sharper focus. On 15 April 1930, a directive of the Revolutionary Military Council of the U.S.S.R. called for the Headquarters of the Red Army to prepare a national air defense plan and to present it to the Council of Labor and Defense for approval.[61] Specifically the plan was to encompass the following:

(1) identification of the most important state regions and points and specification of the means for their defense;
(2) presentation of measures which would secure the uninterrupted operation of industry during wartime;
(3) determination of measures of passive (local) air defense.

The commanders of military districts were then called upon to develop district air defense plans within the framework of the general air defense plan. The directive from the Revolutionary Military Council indicated that direct control of the air defense service in the districts was the responsibility of the chief of air defense of a district who was also designated an assistant chief of staff of the district.[62]

Within the Headquarters of the Red Army there was a Sixth Section which had been formed in 1927 and which handled matters of national air defense. This section was then upgraded in 1930 to the level of a directorate. It developed the General Plan for National Air Defense for 1930–1933.[63] Another document which was produced was the "Regulations on the Air Defense of the U.S.S.R." Under these regulations population centers and state installations of strategic, economic, or political importance which had to be defended against possible enemy air attack were designated air defense points or objectives. An air defense point encompassed all objectives located within its territory. The points were further distinguished according to whether they were to support the operations of the active army or were in the interior of the country.[64]

In accordance with the new regulations the air defense service of a point was organized and conducted on the basis of the involvement of all local military and civilian organs and also of public organizations. All resources were responsive to the chief of air defense of the point.[65]

During the period 1930–1932, the Headquarters of the Red Army organized and conducted several exercises in order to work on problems of the tactics of the air defense of the major centers and rear area objectives of the country. In the military districts special exercises were conducted with respect to the air

---

[60] Ibid., p. 29.
[61] Batitskiy, *Voyska Protivovozdushnoy Oborony Strany*, p. 43.
[62] Ibid.
[63] Ibid.
[64] Ibid.
[65] Ibid., p. 44.

Appendix A: Concepts of Air Defense Before 1945

defense at major points, the protection of rail movement against air attack, and the employment of barrage balloons. This latter step coincided with the formation of the first barrage balloon regiments.[66]

The gradual improvement of Soviet air defense continued apace until 1937 when the Soviet Government, noting the increasing danger of hostilities in Europe, implemented a new series of measures to strengthen air defense. Air defense corps were organized for the defense of the largest centers of the country, including Moscow, Leningrad, and Baku. These corps contained antiaircraft artillery divisions (the first such divisions had been formed only a few years earlier), antiaircraft search light regiments, observation, warning, and communication regiments, barrage balloon regiments, and machine gun regiments. Air defense divisions of similar but scaled-down composition were formed for the defense of certain other centers such as Kiev. The results of these and similar unit creations was to bring all air defense forces except fighter aviation together in combined arms formations. The fighter aviation which was assigned to the defense of the major centers of the country was subordinated to the air force commanders of the military districts. The basing of fighter aviation was accomplished under general air defense plans within a radius of 20–100 kilometers from the defended objectives. Fighter aviation participated in all general air defense exercises. In case of war, the fighter aviation was to come under the operational control of the air defense corps and division commanders for the performance of joint operations.[67]

As World War II drew nearer and then erupted in the West, additional changes were made. Practical experience was gained in the war against Finland and this was reinforced by observation of the pattern of operations in the West. The territory of the Soviet Union was divided into air defense zones (which coincided geographically with the military districts). In turn the zones were divided into air defense districts, and air defense points were identified within the districts. The zones were headed by air defense commanders who at the same time were deputies to the military district commanders.[68] At the national level, air defense was further upgraded with the establishment of the Main Directorate of Air Defense of the Red Army in accordance with a Defense Commissariat directive of 27 December 1940. The head of the main directorate was directly subordinate to the People's Commissar of Defense of the U.S.S.R.[69]

On the doctrinal side Soviet air defense concepts were put into a structured and balanced framework which contained the following basic points[70]:

(1) The massed employment of all air defense forces and means in order to combat enemy air action through the close coordination of all arms of air defense, avoiding the one-sided development of any single arm of air defense at the expense of the others;

(2) The grouping and concentration of air defense forces in those areas which were in the greatest danger of enemy air attack;

(3) The consistent implementation of the principle of the massed employment of air defense forces for the defense of the strategically most important points and objectives of the country;

(4) The maneuvering of air defense forces during the course of combat operations in accordance with the specific situation in order to reinforce the most threatened approaches and objectives;

(5) The close cooperation of National Air Defense Forces with the ground forces in accomplishing air defense in the frontal area.

---
[66] Ibid.
[67] Ibid., pp. 46–47.
[68] Ibid., p. 47.
[69] Ibid., p. 48.
[70] Ibid., p. 52.

2. Experience During World War II[71]

The Soviet Union's air defense forces began deployment and the taking of combat positions in a situation where the German had already initiated an invasion and where enemy air attacks were being mounted against major objectives in the border air defense zones. While the antiaircraft artillery units located along the western border were fully deployed and had taken their firing positions by the morning of 22 June 1941, many units located in the heartland were in camp and began moving out to defense objectives at a considerably later date. The Moscow alert batteries were combat-ready by about noon on 22 June. By that evening 102 out of 137 available batteries had taken their firing positions. The entire Moscow system was ready to repulse enemy air attacks by the morning of 23 June.

Full deployment of the air defense system to a combat-ready status took a considerably longer time. For example, the 18th separate Antiaircraft Artillery Battalion, which had the mission of defending the railroad bridge across the Dniester River near the city of Rybnitsa, did not reach its deployment position from camp until the sixth day after the war began. The aircraft warning service battalions stationed at the border continued their deployment during the first 2 days of the war with arriving reserve personnel. The second-line aircraft warning service battalions were not fully deployed until 25 June. As a whole, the antiaircraft defense of objectives located in zone up to 500–600 kilometers from the border, as well as Moscow and Baku air defense, was essentially deployed and ready to repulse an attack from the air by the evening of the second day of the war.

During the initial phase of the war the most important task of Soviet air defense forces was defense of major population and industrial centers; this involved utilization of the bulk of available fighter aircraft and medium and small-caliber antiaircraft artillery. Defense of lines of communication on the front occupied a secondary position during the initial phase. In addition to performing their immediate missions of repulsing mass enemy air strikes against airfields, personnel, cities, and lines of communication, air defense troops were compelled to take part in action against enemy tank and mechanized units. The brunt of the effort was handled by antiaircraft artillery, since fighter aviation was weakened by losses sustained during the initial days of the war.

The Germans were making a desperate effort to disrupt rail operations in the vicinity of the front. During the course of 1941 the Germans conducted approximately 6,000 air strikes against rail objectives. In spite of this effort only 1,504 raids (or 25 percent) succeeded in disrupting rail traffic as long as 6 hours.

At the end of 1941 major changes were made in the air defense system. By decision of the State Defense Committee a commander of National Air Defense Forces designated, and corresponding control entities were established: an Air Defense Fighter Aviation Directorate and Headquarters, and office of the Chief of Antiaircraft Artillery, etc. The air defense forces were removed from the jurisdiction of the military districts (fronts) and placed under the Commander of National Air Defense Forces and his command elements, with the exception of the forces defending Leningrad, which were left under the command of the Commander of Troops of the Leningrad Front. At the same time the previously existing air defense zones were replaced by the Moscow and Leningrad corps and a number of air defense divisional regions.

---

[71] The following account is based on an article by Soviet authors Dzhordzhodze and Shesterin, who summarize a much more detailed account by Marshal P. F. Batitskiy, op. cit.

Appendix A: Concepts of Air Defense Before 1945

The fighter aviation corps and divisions detached for air defense missions were operationally subordinate to the Commander of National Air Defense Forces, and locally to the corps and division air defense region commanders. Soon thereafter, at the beginning of 1942, aviation regiments and divisions engaged in air defense were placed entirely under the Commander of Territorial Air Defense Forces. In accordance with an order issued by the People's Commissar of Defense of the U.S.S.R., 56 airfield service battalions were assigned during this period to support air defense fighter aviation. These battalions were placed under the commanders of the corresponding fighter aviation corps, divisions, and detached regiments. This signified that one of the basic air defense arms—National Air Defense Forces Aviation—was organizationally constituted, but also that conditions had been created for organizing unified control of all air defense forces and securing more effective coordination of these forces.

The heaviest fighting involving air defense forces in the summer–fall campaign of 1941 was in the defense of Moscow and Leningrad. Actions in the defense of these cities essentially constituted air defense operations, as a result of which enemy air power sustained heavy losses. The following figures indicate the scale of these operations. From July through December 1941 a total of 18,000 German sorties were recorded in the coverage areas of the air defense forces defending Moscow and Leningrad. The troops of two air defense zones (Northern and Moscow) took part in action against enemy aircraft; these operations included the participation of more than 1,800 medium and small-caliber antiaircraft guns and 600–700 fighters. In the course of these actions air defense forces destroyed more than 1,700 enemy aircraft.

An important place in improving national air defense was occupied by matters pertaining to change in the organizational forms of the air defense troops, since these forms exerted a direct influence on combat activity, and on the efficiency of utilization of available manpower and hardware. This was linked in large measure with the over strategic situation, with the nature of enemy air and ground actions, as well as the nation's economic potential for the establishment and equipping of new air defense units. At the beginning of 1942 the Moscow Front and the Leningrad Air Defense Army were established on the basis of the former Moscow and Leningrad air defense corps. Development of an enemy air threat against the Baku oil fields led to the establishment of the Baku PVO Army.

Further development of air defenses and the art of employment of air defense forces came with changes in the character of the war. The Soviet Army, after the Battle of Stalingrad, retook two-thirds of the enemy-occupied territory. This fact had a definite influence on the character of air defense. It was reflected first and foremost in the maneuvering of units in the wake of the advancing forces, in organization of closer coordination with front and army air defense as well as change in the structure of national air defense control.

In June 1943, another reorganization took place in the air defense forces. This reorganization consisted essentially in the following. Two air defense front directorates were established—Western and Eastern. The Office of the Command of National Air Defense Forces was abolished, and supervision of the activities of the air defense fronts and zones, weapons planning and supply was transferred to the Red Army Commander of Artillery. The following elements were established under that commander: Air Defense Forces Central Headquarters, Air Defense Fighter Aviation Central Headquarters; Air Defense Main Inspectorate; Air Defense Forces Combat Training Directorate; Aircraft Warning Service Center. The fighter aviation defending Moscow was unified into the First Air Defense Fight Army.

As the gap increased, however, between the units of the advancing Western Air Defense Front, which were moving ahead in the wake of advancing forces, and the units of the Eastern Front, which had remained in place, the drawbacks of this reorganization became more and more obvious. While the Western Front, which was operating along the front lines, was heavily engaged against enemy aircraft, the troops of the Eastern Air Defense Front were rather idle, in view of a lack of regular enemy air operations.

Another reorganization took place in the spring of 1944: the Western Air Defense Front was changed into the Northern Front, while the Eastern Front was changed to the Southern Air Defense Front; this eliminated the above-mentioned drawbacks of the previous organization. At the same time a Transcaucasian Air Defense Front was established, based on the Transcaucasian Air Defense Zone.

After the Battle of Kursk the Germans lost their control of the air, which resulted in a change in the basic utilization of their air power. The Germans almost totally stopped bombing objectives deep in the rear areas, shifting their main efforts to action along the line of the front. In some cases the German command was able, by maneuvering units, to concentrate heavy air power to carry out major missions. For example, the Germans were successful in maintaining a fairly high level of air activity in the Ukraine and Belorussia in 1944, as well as on the approaches to Berlin in the winter of 1944–1945. An indicator of German air activity during this period is the fact that in February 1945 alone the Germans flew 18,000 sorties to prevent the crossing of the Oder River by the forces of the First Belorussian Front and to provide support for counterattacks by German ground troops.

In addition to maneuvering its available air power, the German command began employing other air attack weapons to destroy objectives in the front area: radio controlled bombs and aircraft, heavily loaded with explosives. The explosive force of such an aircraft exceeded that of a simultaneous strike by 10 to 12 bombers. For this reason they were employed chiefly against major crossing points, railroad junctions and other important objectives in the area of the front.

Protection of lines of communication along the front became particularly important in the third phase of the war; the Germans considered disruption of these lines of communication to be one of the principal missions of their air power. Large-scale strikes were employed. For example, in the winter of 1944, 1,200–1,450 combat aircraft were concentrated in the zone of action of the Ukrainian fronts; this comprised 53–56 percent of total German aircraft on the Soviet-German Front.

The Soviet command had concentrated more than 2,000 antiaircraft guns, 1,650 antiaircraft machine guns, approximately 450 fighters, and 300 antiaircraft searchlights for the purpose of protecting rail objectives in the south. The Soviet command countered massed utilization of enemy air power with massed utilization of air defense forces. As a result, in 1944 German aircraft succeeded in flying only 1,161 raids on rail objectives, while in 1943 the figure had been approximately 7,000. There were also considerably fewer cases of rail traffic disruption. There were 1,039 disruptions in 1943, while in 1944 there occurred only a few brief stoppages in a few rail traffic areas.

In addition to protecting lines of communication and immediate rear area objectives, the air defense forces were called upon to carry out other missions in close coordination with other armed forces branches. They took part in encirclement operations, provided protection for friendly troops in attack position and protected crossing areas, airfields, and supply trans-shipment facilities. Air defense forces were continuously redeployed behind the advancing forces in connection with occupation of new areas and entire countries. This was a distinctive feature in air defense forces utilization in the third phase of the war. For example, in order to strengthen the defense of rail centers and other important objectives in the area of the First and Second Ukrainian Fronts, two fighter divisions and more than 40 antiaircraft artillery regiments were rede-

Appendix A: Concepts of Air Defense Before 1945

ployed in May–June 1944 from the rear areas of the Southern Air Defense Front to the front. In the summer and fall of 1944 five air defense corps were moved from the heartland beyond the Soviet borders to protect objectives in the vicinity of the front. The continuous redeployment of air defense capabilities did not cease until the war came to an end.

The changes in the grouping of National Air Defense Forces manpower and equipment, the continued Soviet Army advance westward, and the movement of new air defense units behind the advancing troops caused certain control difficulties. The Southern and Northern air defense fronts proved unable to maintain efficient control over their units, which were dispersed over a large, deep area. In connection with this, in December 1944 the Northern and Southern Air Defense fronts were transformed into the Western and Southwestern air defense fronts respectively, while a new, Central Air Defense Front, with headquarters in Moscow, was established to control the units protecting objectives in the deep rear areas.

Development of the air defense system took place on a foundation of steady technological advances and the equipping of the Armed Forces with increasingly sophisticated weaponry. Important qualitative changes occurred, for example, in air defense fighter aviation. By 1944, there were mostly new types of aircraft (LA-5fn, LA-7, YAK-3, YAK-9). Radar came into extensive use for intercept vectoring. The equipment and weapons of the other arms of National Air Defense Forces also underwent improvement and modernization during the course of the war.

With these organizational changes, the basic principle of employment of air defense forces as a whole did not undergo major changes during the war. Antiaircraft defense remained essentially point defense, which was dictated by the technical level of available resources. At the same time improvement in the quality of air defense weapons and combat equipment particularly fighters, improvement in utilization techniques, the adoption of radio communications for control purposes, and improved communications reliability made it possible gradually to transition to new principles of PVO organization, from the defense of individual objectives to defense of entire areas and zones.

The development of the concept of zone defense can be illustrated with the example of the Moscow air defense during the first year of the war. In particular, the fighters defending Moscow were at the same time defending a number of cities and objectives in the Moscow industrial region. Deployment of radar facilities on the distant approaches to Moscow (the Rzhev, Sychevka, Vyaz'ma line) and the redeployment to that area of a number of air regiments greatly enlarged the Moscow air defense boundaries and made it possible to intercept any aircraft at some distance from Moscow. Fighters based in the immediate vicinity of Moscow were used to repulse major air attacks on objectives in the Moscow industrial region. In addition, the deployment of aircraft warning observer posts a considerable distance from Moscow and the establishment of a solid-coverage aircraft spotting zone, and organization of reliable control and warning communications which cover the entire area were testimony to the fact that the air defense system of such a major center as Moscow had developed beyond the framework of defense of a separate, although very important objective.

This air defense principle did not become the basic principle of the overall national air defense system. Examples of this type of defense, however, did occur even after the Battle of Moscow. Fighter units based within a radius of up to 200 kilometers from Kursk were used to repulse mass German air attacks on Kursk (June 1943), in spite of the fact that they had the mission of defending other objectives. In 1944, fighter regiments protecting the cities of Kiev and Zhitomir were used to repulse night air attacks on the Korosten'

Rail Center. During the defense of lines of communication along the front in 1943–1944, fighter units were assigned to protect not only major rail centers, bridges, and river crossing areas, but also entire main rail lines.

This experience demonstrated the feasibility of employing fighter aviation for the purpose of simultaneous protection of many objectives located within fighter effective radius of action. This principle made it possible to utilize the maneuver capabilities of fighter aircraft vigorously and fully, when necessary concentrating large numbers of fighters in a threatened area to repulse enemy air attacks. This utilization of fighter aviation became possible because of qualitative improvements and the extensive adoption within the air defense system of radio and radar equipment for fighter control and guidance.

Appendix B

A Chronology of American Air and Ballistic Missile Defense Systems

1944

2 October	Army issues directive to AGF, AFF, and ASF (the McNarney letter) allocating responsibility for R&D.

AAF has responsibility for all guided or homing missiles dropped or launched from aircraft.

AAF also has responsibility for all GM and homing missiles launched from ground that depend on the lift of aerodynamic forces. AGF and AAF will designate characteristics when and as they affect their interests.

ASF has R&D responsibility for all GM and homing missiles launched from ground which depend for sustenance primarily on missile momentum. AGF and AFF designate characteristics of interest.

1945

31 January — A letter from Office, Chief of Ordnance to BTL authorizes negotiations for a formal study of an antiaircraft guided missile.

8 February — Project Nike-I is initiated.

May — AAF signs its initial development contract for P-86, formerly Navy XFJ-1.

20 June — Army Ground Forces Equipment Review Board (Cook Board) submits its report on equipment for the postwar Army. "High velocity guided missiles, preferably capable of intercepting and destroying aircraft flying at speeds up to 1,000 miles per hour at altitudes up to 60,000 feet or destroying missiles of the V-2 type, should be developed at earliest practicable date."

July — BTL furnishes written report AAGM Report (Study of an Antiaircraft Guided Missile System). Signal Corps formally establishes Air Defense Fire Distribution System (ADFDS) Project 414A which will lead to development of AN/FSG-1 (Missile Master).

August — With the ending of World War II, early warning radar stations still operational in CONUS are inactivated.

14 August — Subcommittee Number 4 of the Guided Missile Committee recommends the services include in their R&D programs studies covering:

(a) A system for control of SAM missiles against simultaneous attacks from all directions.

(b) An effective short range SAM to replace the 40-mm.

(c) A guided missile for defense against other supersonic GM and aircraft.

	(d) An experimental program to determine the optimum warhead characteristics of surface-to-air missiles.
28 August	AAF makes initial design request for a propeller driven interceptor to replace the P-61; the request ultimately results in development of the jet-powered F-89.
13 September	Ordnance Technical Committee initiates a project for development of SAM based on military characteristics outlined by Antiaircraft Artillery Board in March 1945.
18 October	Patch Board submits its recommendations for an AAA organization which will effectively counter a future air threat incorporating rockets and guided missiles as major weapons.
November	The idea of a jet-powered interceptor as a replacement for the P-61 is accepted by AAF; military characteristics for the plane approved.

1946

4 January	CG, AGF in letter to CG, ASF requests a high priority study on defense against the V-2 and similar GM.
February	Boeing begins design studies for GAPA Project, a ram-jet vehicle capable of reaching an altitude of 60,000 feet at a range of 35 miles at supersonic speed. This will lead to development of Bomarc.
13 February	Army Deputy Chief of Staff requests major commands to review McNarney instructions of 2 October 1944 and recommend modifications to obtain most efficient performance.
27 February	CG, AGF in response to Army DCS 13 February letter recommends:
	(a) The GM Committee of JCS Joint Committee on New Weapons be disbanded.
	(b) A joint Army-Navy GM Board empowered to coordinate and guide or control GM development for Armed Forces be organized without delay.
	(c) A revised directive on the development of GM within the Army be published.
	(d) A directive be published establishing the division of responsibility between AAF and AGF for operational employment of GM. This would give seacoast defense, surface-to-air, and surface-to-surface to AGF.
March	AAF awards contract to GE for the study of interceptor weapons for ballistic missile defense. The first program of its kind and is designated the Thumper Project. It will parallel the University of Michigan Wizard Project initiated the following month.
	Six manufacturers submit designs in interceptor competition, most are for jets, a few are for conventional planes. One of four Northrop designs is accepted (ultimately the F-89).
27 March	HQ ADC activated at Mitchel Field, New York.
April	AAF awards University of Michigan a contract to study possibility of developing supersonic missile capable of reaching 500,000 feet (Project Wizard).
17 April	AGF submits to the GM Committee a summary of its program which includes requirements for both an antiaircraft GM with a range of at least 50,000 yards and an interceptor GM with a range of at least 100,000 yards, for engaging very high altitude supersonic missiles of the V-2 type.
14 May	WD Circular 138 stipulates the AAF, ADC will provide for the air defense of CONUS and will control and train such AAA units as may be assigned to it. AGF and AAF to cooperate in developing AAA tactics, deciding on types of weapons required, and

Appendix B: A Chronology of American Air and Ballistic Missile Defense Systems

	drawing up manning and equipment documents for AAA units. AAF will recommend to WD the means, including AAA, required for defense.
25 May	ASF, in connection with the Proposed National Program for guided missiles, outlines existing ordnance projects: ORCIT, HERMES, Nike-I.
29 May	The WD Equipment Board (Stilwell Board) establishes the following requirements:
	(a) An antiaircraft missile capable of destroying aircraft traveling 1,000 miles per hour at altitudes up to 60,000 feet at a horizontal range of 50,000 yards.
	(b) An interceptor guided missile with a range of 100,000 yards, capable of intercepting aircraft and guided missiles of the V-2 type traveling at speeds greatly in excess of the sonic.
4–6 June	At an Air Board Meeting, the decision is taken to propose integration of antiaircraft artillery into the Army Air Forces.
14 June	CG, AGF sends CG, AAF an AGF study of the air defense problem proposing:
	(a) Division of the air defense mission.
	(1) Local air defense to AGF.
	(2) AAF defenses beyond reach of ground weapons.
20 June	P-86 letter contract of May 1945 superseded by definitive R&D contract; three prototypes to be built.
26 August	CG, AGF informs Army CoS that a point has been reached in the development of certain missiles at which assignment of operational responsibility is possible. AGF position is that any missile launched from the ground is the responsibility of the Ground Forces as a part of their logical mission.
September	AMC dissatisfied with XP-89 mockup; many changes suggested.
18 September	In a summary sheet this date, WD expresses its agreement with AAF that air defense mission should be unitary but withholds decision as to the future role of guided missiles in air defense. It announces the AAF ADC will be integrated, incorporating AAA elements. ADC will ensure that assigned AAA units are trained in the ground combat role, and AGF will continue to provide technical training.
26 September	Army Ordnance, In OCM 31055, establishes the priority of the Nike-I System as 1-A.
7 October	Army CoS rescinds the McNarney Directive of 2 October 1944 and directs CG, AAF assume responsibility for R&D activities pertaining to GM and associated items of equipment.
15 October	AGF requests authority to establish military characteristics of those missiles of which it is the ultimate user and recommends an early decision on operational responsibility for guided missiles.
20 December	With P-86 prototypes still under construction, the first production order for 33 planes is issued.

1947

13 January	As a result of WD decisions in the field of R&D of GM, AGF undertakes a study to determine policy, particularly with respect to operational employment and concludes that AGF should be assigned responsibility for operational employment of all ground-launched missiles.
February	Fifteen YP-84A's delivered to AAF.

21 May	First postwar AC&W organization, the 505th AC&W Group, is activated at McChord AFB, Washington.
20 June	Army Ordnance Department establishes, as part of the HERMES Project, development of a two-stage missile with the code name Bumper.
July	AGF and AAF agree on air defense procedures prior to designation of overall theater commander.
25 July	Congress passes the National Security Act of 1947 creating three separate services, making permanent the JCS organization and creating the National Military Establishment.
19 August	CG, AAF and CG, AGF disagree over GM development priorities.
September	In extension of National Security Act of 1947, the JCS formulate a functions paper which defines Army and Air Force roles and missions.
15 September	The National Security Act of 1947 becomes law. Paragraph 3, Section IV, includes the following matters agreed between AGF and AAF with respect to SAM GM: (a) Security missiles designed for employment in support of Army tactical operations will be assigned to the United States Army. (b) Missiles designed for employment in area air defense will be assigned to the USAF.
18 September	The USAF is established.
23 October	A flight of 48 Soviet TU-4 (Bull) bombers is observed in the U.S.S.R., establishing a presumptive capability to bomb the continental United States by flying one-way missions.
21 November	USAF CoS approves Plan Supremacy for construction of an elaborate postwar radar network. The plan is withdrawn in 1948 in favor of a more modest initial program.
17 December	USAF grants ADC authority to use fighter and radar forces of SAC, TAC, and ANG in an emergency. The ANG would constitute a major source of air defense units.

1948

	Testing of the pilot model 75-mm. AA gun, Skysweeper, is begun.
February	An Air Defense Policy Panel recommends that AAA be integrated into the Air Force.
11–14 March	Secretary of Defense rejects demand for integration of AAA into USAF at Key West Meeting with JCS. The Army will organize, train, and equip AAA units and provide them "as required" for air defense.
16 March	CG, AFF recommends that existing agreements concerning employment of GM be reworded to indicate that USAF has primary interest in the command and employment of air-launched GM and the Army in ground-launched GM.
21 April	Secretary of Defense order assigns primary responsibility for air defense of CONUS to USAF.
13 May	The Bumper missile is fired successfully for the first time.
9 June	The Committee on GM of the Research and Development Board recommends that SAM be the responsibility of Army Ordnance if designed to be launched from the ground.
8 October	GOR for new all-weather jet interceptor issued. Early availability given precedence over capability against aircraft more advanced than Tu-4.

Appendix B: A Chronology of American Air and Ballistic Missile Defense Systems

25 October	The first air defense division organization, the 25th Air Division, is established at Silver Lake (Everett) Washington.
16 November	The 26th Air Division, the first division on the East Coast is activated at Mitchell Field.
1 December	The Continental Air Command (ConAC) is established with Headquarters at Mitchell AFB. ADC and TAC made into subordinate "operational" headquarters.

1949

	Army and Air Force Authorization Act of 1949 authorizes the Secretary of the Army "to procure materials and facilities, including guided missiles, necessary for the maintenance and support of the Army."
January	Army establishes a formal requirement for a SAM system to combat ballistic missiles.
13 January	ADO for "1954 Interceptor," to have a capability superior to that anticipated for Soviet intercontinental jet bombers, is issued. Coordinated development of the plane as an integrated system is planned.
February	A Panel on Air Defense recommends to General of the Army, Omar Bradley, Chairman, JCS, that an AAA staff section be added to HQ ADC and that ADC be given operational control of AAA units allocated to air defense by JCS.
19 February	Chief, AFF, establishes a requirement for a long range, surface-to-air GM capable of intercepting and destroying missiles of the V-2 type.
1 March	The six numbered air forces of CONAC are relieved of air defense responsibilities which are assigned to Eastern and Western Air Defense Liaison Groups.
21 March	Congress approves a permanent postwar radar net for CONUS and Alaska. The President signs a bill authorizing the Secretary of Air Force to construct a "permanent" aircraft control and warning system for CONUS and Alaska.
24 March	AFF states its position on GM responsibility as follows:
	(a) The Air Force has paramount interest in the command and employment of air-launched guided missiles and units.
	(b) The Army has paramount interest in the command and employment of ground-launched GM and units.
1 April	The 25th and 26th Air Divisions are transferred to ADC.
May	$48 million contract issued for modification of F-89 and 48 production models of F-89A.
	Procurement of F-86D recommended.
16 May	Secretary of Army recommends to Secretary of Defense that operational responsibility for all land-launched guided missiles be assigned to DA and that a National Military Establishment research and development program for GM be jointly undertaken and supported with each service being assigned primary cognizance for RED as follows:
	(a) Army Land-launched SAM and SSM.
	(b) Navy Ship-launched SAM and SSM.
	(c) Air Force AAM and ASM.
31 May	F-86 enters service.

8 August	The Joint Strategic Plans Group, in a "split" paper, advises JCS on the assignment of responsibility for major categories of GM. View "A," which the Group recommends for approval, assigns all land-launched missiles to Army, ship-launched to Navy, and air-launched to Air Force. View "B" advises postponing a decision on the basis that the missile art has not yet advanced sufficiently to make determination possible.
26–29 August	USAF detects a nuclear detonation "somewhere on the Asiatic mainland."
19 September	27 more F-89A's ordered.
23 September	President Truman announces an atomic explosion has taken place in the U.S.S.R.
October	Procurement order for F-94 raised to 288 following Soviet atomic explosion; later raised again to 368.
7 October	Initial procurement order for F-86D issued: 2 prototypes and 122 production models.
29 October	Congress appropriates $85.5 million for construction on a "permanent" aircraft control and warning system for CONUS and Alaska.
17 November	In JCS 1620/12 the JCS conclude that "it is impracticable at this time to assign the several services, in accordance with their assigned functions, responsibility for the entire guided missile field. As a general rule, GM will be employed by the Services in the manner and to the extent required to accomplish their assigned functions. Development in certain categories has progressed to the point where the fields of their normal employment may be recognized." GM supplanting antiaircraft artillery are assigned to the Army as are surface-launched GM which supplant or extend the capabilities of artillery.
December	Construction is ordered on 24 priority radar stations of the "permanent" aircraft control and warning system of CONUS and Alaska.
December	The missile tracking portion of the Nike ground system is successfully tested at White Sands Proving Ground.
December	F-86D chosen as backbone of interceptor force.
8 December	The 32nd and 28th Air Divisions are activated at Stewart and Hamilton AFB.
16 December	30th Air Division activated at Selfridge AFB.
22 December	F-86D makes first flight. During late 1949, the F-86A has been replacing the P-80 and P-84.
27 December	Eastern Air Defense Force publishes rules of engagement for Fourth Army.

1950

January	Joint Defense Planning Committee informs CONUS armies that joint agreements with air forces will be drawn up on the basis provided by the rules established 27 December 1949 by Eastern Air Defense Force. However, ConAC disapproves, especially the EADF/Army position that aircraft should be fired upon unless identified as friendly. ConAC assumes that no AC&W system, current or future, can undertake to warn AAA when friendly aircraft enter its area. The ConAC position, never abandoned, is that AAA must be in constant "hold fire" status until released by the air commander to fire at a particular aircraft. This controversy will be ended by the Collins-Vandenberg agreement of 1 August 1950.
January	ConAC Operations Plan 1-50, "Air Defense of the United States" is issued to Eastern and Western Air Defense Forces. It contains a listing of targets to be defended by AAA.

Appendix B: A Chronology of American Air and Ballistic Missile Defense Systems

	HQ USAF, authorizes around-the-clock air defense operations over the Atomic Energy Commission works at Hanford, Washington. HQ USAF, assigns units of the Air Defense Forces equal personnel priority with SAC and overseas units.
March	Construction of the "permanent" aircraft control and warning system begins.
March	Battery C, 518th AAA Battalion (120-mm. gun) becomes operational at Hanford, Washington. The remainder of the BN arrives on site 1 May.
	An ad-hoc interservice committee recommends sixty critical locations to be defended by AAA. The Army and Air Force finally agree on twenty-three which are to be defended by a federalized Army National Guard Force.
	Army Ordnance initiates development of a tactical Nike system (Nike-I).
	ADA study of AAA C^2 problems concludes that a AAA command is essential. This study is under review when South Korea is invaded.
May	Provisional HQ, Albuquerque Air Defense Sector, is established by USAF, ADC, at Kirtland AFB, New Mexico, to exercise operational control over the radar and fighter forces defending the Los Alamos and Sandia areas.
May	F-94 enters service.
15 May	AFF directs its Board Number 4 to study and formulate military characteristics for countermeasures against air-to-surface and surface-to surface missiles.
1 June	The Lashup radar network of 44 radar stations is completed. This network is to operate with World War II radar equipment until the "permanent" AC&W system is completed.
	The first Canadian-U.S. Emergency Air Defense Plan is approved.
	ConAC is formally authorized to establish a Ground Observer Corps.
25 June	North Korea invades South Korea.
27 June	Around-the-clock operations begin in United States air defenses.
July	Air Force puts electronics and control system for "1954 Interceptor" under development contract.
1 July	Army Antiaircraft Command (ARAACOM) is established with HQ in Washington, D.C. per DA, CO 20, 29 June 1950.
	CAA establishes Air Defense Identification Zones (ADIZ) in vital areas of the United States.
11 July	MG Willard W. Irvine is directed to assume command of ARAACOM and "to support the CG, ConAC, on basis of joint agreements between DA and DAF pertaining to policies and procedures for joint air defense of CONUS." When so directed by the JCS or in case of air attack on the United States, CG, ARAACOM, is to assume command of AAA units allocated to air defense.
15 July	ConAC recommends that 20 squadrons of the Air National Guard be called to federal service to buttress the air defense system.
19 July	The three armed services issue regulations establishing Air Defense Identification Zones.
August	F-94B begins to reach operational units.
1 August	A Memorandum of Agreement signed by General J. Lawton Collins, CoS, Army and General Hoyt S. Vandenberg, CoS, USAF, provides for joint decision at departmental

	level on targets to be defended by AAA, mutual Army/USAF agreement on locations of defenses (except that tactical dispositions are to be determined by AAA commanders), Army staff representation at each echelon of USAF command structure charged with air defense, and operational control of AAA by USAF division commanders "insofar as engagement and disengagement of fire is concerned."
7 August	A provisional Southern California Air Defense Sector is established with headquarters at Fort MacArthur, California, and given operational control of radar and fighter forces in the area.
14 August	AFF Board Number 4 informs Chief, AFF that DA has no projects to fulfill the requirement for an AMM and recommends that it be directed to prepare military requirements for search and tracking radar. Also, that certain Signal Corps projects in radar search and tracking research be provided funds and be pursued to completion.
18 August	Description of "pure interceptor" for 1954 issued for design competition.
24 August	President Truman authorizes interception and engagement of unidentified aircraft anywhere in the United States.
September	Public Law 778 gives the Civil Aeronautics Authority (CAA) power to regulate civil air traffic in peacetime.
	In reply to a proposal by LT General Whitehead, CG, ConAC, to establish a third Air Defense Force, LTG Norstad, Acting VCoS, USAF, suggests deferring change until current consideration by the JCS concerning a unified command for air defense reaches a conclusion.
1 September	Eastern and Western Army Antiaircraft Commands are established with HQ at Stewart AFB, New York, and Hamilton AFB, California. USARAACOM GO3, 28 August 1950.
20 September	27th Air Division is activated at Norton AFB, California, to replace provisional Southern California AD Sector.
28 September	First production model of F-89 delivered.
8 October	31st Air Division activated at Fort Snelling, Minnesota. The seventh division of ConAC is without area responsibility in EADF and will be reassigned to Central ADF on 20 May 1951.
November	A revision of DA Ops Plan for 1950 (DA-OP-US-1-50) includes a list of 23 targets, listed in alphabetical order, to be defined "to the extent appropriate units are available." The list has been jointly prepared and is the first approved list of vital objectives.
1 November	HQ ARAACOM, is moved from Washington, D.C. to Mitchel AFB, New York where it initially serves as the AAA element of ConAC staff.
December	By Executive Order, the CAA is empowered to require filing of flight plans by civilian aircraft operating within coastal, domestic, or international boundary ADIZ's. This gives the air defense system its first real control over peacetime air traffic.
December	The Committee on Guided Missiles of the Research and Development Board recommends that fiscal support for air defense be increased to permit initiation of new projects to fill serious gaps. A homing-all-the-way missile is specifically recommended. The HAWK Project is initially to be limited to development of a short-range, SAM to be effective against aircraft and guided missiles attacking at speeds up to 600 knots and from altitudes of 30,000 feet to 1,000 feet at 10 miles range and 500 feet at 6 miles range.

Appendix B: A Chronology of American Air and Ballistic Missile Defense Systems

1 December	CG ARAACOM, assumes responsibility for planning all AAA defenses within CONUS.
6 December	CG ConAC requests authority to call up 15 Air National Guard squadrons to federal service and to place 23 other squadrons on call.

1951

January	Airframe proposals for "1954 Interceptor" submitted.
1 January	ADC is reestablished as a major command of USAF with HQ Ent AFB, Colorado. Eastern and Western ADF, air divisions and other organizations with primary missions related to air defense are reassigned from ConAC.
5 January	34th Air Division activated at Kirtland AFB replacing the provisional Albuquerque Sector.
8 January	LT General Ennis C. Whitehead is appointed CG of the reestablished Air Defense Command.
10 January	General Collins, Army CoS, directs G-3 to prepare a study of "Preferential Treatment of Selected National Guard (AAA) Units" with a view to future employment of state-commanded AAA units.
10 January	Director of Guided Missiles for the Secretary of Defense, Mr. K. T. Keller, informs Secretary of Defense that immediate acceleration of production processes for Nike-I is necessary in order to get the missile system out of R&D into the tactical weapon stage at the earliest practicable date. The objectives of this effort are:
	(a) Production of 1,000 missiles by 31 December 1952.
	(b) Production facilities capable of producing 1,000 missiles per month by 31 December 1952.
	(c) Production by 31 December 1953 of sufficient ground support equipment for twenty tactical battalions.
	(d) Production facilities by 31 December 1953 capable of producing ground support equipment for three tactical battalions per month.
15 January	HQ, ARAACOM is moved to Colorado Springs, Colorado. The office of the CG is at Ent AFB, the remainder of the staff is located initially in the Antlers Hotel.
23 January	ConAC receives authority to call 15 National Guard Squadrons into federal service and to place other squadrons on call as requested 6 December 1950.
1 February	15 ANG fighter squadrons are federalized and assigned ADC.
19 February	The first production contract is initiated for Nike-I. A letter order is issued to the Western Electric Company effective until such time as a definitive contract is written.
March	341 F-86D's on order; number increased to 979 two months later. First F-86D delivered and tested. Plane targeted for production before fire control and engine systems proven.
1 March	Central Air Defense Force is activated at Kansas City.
	29th Air Division is activated at Great Falls, Montana.
2 March	Another six ANG fighter squadrons are federalized.
15 March	MG Maxwell D. Taylor, Army G-3, requests that Chief, National Guard Bureau, assure prior G-3 approval of further allocations of nondivisional Army National Guard AAA

	gun battalions, in order to preclude their federal recognition in locations far removed from planned vital objectives of air defense.
19 March	33rd Air Division activated at Tinker AFB, Oklahoma.
29 March	Committee on Guided Missiles approves Hawk as a SAM project for Army and requests that the Technical Evaluation Group study and make recommendations on optimum conduct of the program.
4 April	ARAACOM forwards the first master deployment plan: "Operations Plan for Antiaircraft Defense of the United States (AA-OP-US-1-51)."
10 April	CG, ARAACOM, assumes command of all AAA units allocated to CONUS air defense—six AW, nine 90-mm. and eight 120-mm. battalions plus four Bde and seven Gp HQ, eight AAA Ops Det and 15 Signal radar detachments.
24 April	Central ARAACOM established with HQ at Kansas City, Missouri. Organized 1 May 1951.
May	DA approves conversion of ARAACOM's AW battalions to Skysweeper by end of 1953.
	McDonnell XF-88 wins long-range escort fighter competition over six rivals; procurement delayed.
June	F-89 delivered to operational units.
	176 F-94B's accepted in FY 1951.
	Ten federalized Army National Guard gun battalions are assigned to ARAACOM—the first accession of such units during the Korean action.
14 June	AFF forwards to DA the Army military characteristics for a low-altitude, short-range, SAM guided missile.
20 June	Secretary of Army requests AFF to study a report published by Boeing and University of Michigan entitled "Preliminary Study of a Missile Defense System" and comment on the extent to which Bomarc fulfills the Army's requirement for an antimissile missile.
22–24 June	The first nationwide joint air defense exercise is conducted.
July	Convair gets prototype development contract for "1954 Interceptor." Republic and North America also receive contracts for their designs; soon afterward, Republic program terminates, North American design (F-103) kept only as "experimental aircraft."
1 July	35th Air Division is activated at Kansas City, Missouri. This is the eleventh division in ADC.
18 July	Secretary of Defense notified Chairman, R&D Board of his desire for Army to proceed with the Hawk Project and that funding is approved.
1 August	An exchange of notes constitutes formal United States–Canada agreement for building the Pinetree radar net extension in Canadian territory.
25 August	LT General Benjamin W. Chidlaw succeeds LT General Whitehead as ADC commander.
28 August	ARAACOM conducts its first unilateral exercise; 75 percent of its batteries occupy tactical positions for seven weeks until 18 October. *The exercise, planned to last only 30 days, is extended because of intelligence indications.*

Appendix B: A Chronology of American Air and Ballistic Missile Defense Systems

September	When it becomes clear that the "1954 Interceptor" with the specified characteristics will not be ready by 1954, the construction of an interim version (F-102) by Convair is automated.
September	HQ, 35th Air Division is moved to Dobbins AFB, Georgia.
5 September	Secretary of Defense notified Secretary of Army that Army is authorized to proceed with implementation of Hawk Program.
October	ARAACOM 25 percent Rotation Program initiated. All AAA battalions within six hours' travel of tactical sites are required to maintain one battery on-site at all times. Major Commanders are authorized to order deployment of other batteries under specified emergency conditions.
18 October	AFF, after reviewing Boeing–University of Michigan study of Bomarc missile, concludes that the missile will only partially fulfill Army antimissile requirements. AFF withdraws a Board 4 recommendation that Army give no consideration to support of Bomarc project, but agrees that the missile would only partially meet the need for a defense missile and would not affect the Army's responsibility in air defense in the foreseeable future.
30 November	ARAACOM submits to DA its first deployment plan for SAM.
	ARAACOM submits to DA its plan for the exploitation of ARNG antiaircraft potential.
	Designation of McDonnell Voodoo changed from F-88 to F-101.
December	The President orders procedures established for the control of electromagnetic radiations in an emergency.
31 December	ARAACOM includes 6 Bde HQ, 13 Gp HQ, 13 AAA Ops Det, 6 AW battalions, 24 90-mm. battalions, 15 120-mm. battalions, and 23 signal radar maintenance units.

1952

	F-86D program delayed because of difficulties in fire-control and engine system.
	F-89 has seven accidents, resulting in eight fatalities, in first six months of 1952.
January	180 F-94B's were accepted in first seven months of FY 1952.
	Convair's original letter contract for "1954 Interceptor" expanded to include start of production engineering and tooling program. Convair later authorized to proceed with building of two YF-102 prototypes and seven production aircraft for 1954.
15 January	McDonnell accepts F-101A contract.
18 January	ADC proposes a requirement for small, unmanned radars (gap fillers).
1 February	HQ 25th Air Division is moved from Silver Lake to McChord AFB, Washington.
15 February	HQ 32nd Air Division is moved from Stewart AFB to Hancock Field, New York.
	ARAACOM resubmits its 30 November 1951 plan for SAM deployments.
26 February	DA authorizes ARAACOM to coordinate planning for utilization of ARNG units.
	USAF withdraws delegated responsibility for development of ground-based electronic countermeasures against missiles from Army. Tendered by USAF on 18 February 1948 and accepted by Army on 3 April 1948.

10 March	The first Multiple Corridor System for identification of traffic arriving from overseas is placed in operation outside San Francisco.
31 March	Chief of Ordnance directs Picatinny Arsenal to study the feasibility of an atomic warhead for the Nike-I missile.
April	DA approves an ARAACOM recommendation concerning allocation of 32 Nike-I battalions to 14 defended areas within the United States.
	DA approves ARAACOM's basic concept for the integration of ARNG units into the Air Defense System.
	Phase-out of ARAACOM's 47 assigned ARNG AAA gun battalions is begun. By end 1952, 27 battalions, three brigades, seven groups, and eight operations detachments will be phased out and Active Army units activated in their stead.
1 April	The Multiple Corridor Identification System is made an integral part of the 28th Air Divisions' Identification System.
10 April	In early tests of warheads, a Nike-I destroys a maneuvering B-17 drone at a range of 17 nautical miles and an altitude of 10,000 feet.
10 April	ADC and ARAACOM draw up a "Mutual Agreement for the Air Defense of the United States." AAA units are to pass to the *operational control of appropriate USAF commanders* when deployed to tactical positions, but such control is to be exercised through local AAA Commanders. Defended areas are to be determined by mutual agreement between DA and USAF. ARAACOM's responsibilities include ascertaining ADC's AAA requirements and attempting to fulfill them, preparing detailed plans, providing AAA advisors, and prescribing conditions of readiness. ADC is responsible for all identification, prescribing alerts, establishing gun-defended areas—to be "prescribed as soon as practicable" and, establishing in coordination with ARAACOM, the basic rules of engagement.
17 April	On the basis of reported unknowns ADC declares an actual command-wide condition of Air Defense Readiness. This is a first.
24 April	Complete system test of Nike-I is concluded with round 92 whose live warhead instantly destroys a large bomber.
28 April	Major General John T. Lewis succeeds Major General Irvine as CG ARAACOM.
9 May	Office, Chief of Ordnance requests BTL to make a study of the feasibility of an antiaircraft guided missile carrying an atomic warhead using the Nike-I ground guidance system.
27 May	The original construction program for the "permanent" aircraft control and warning net is completed.
Summer	F-89F program cancelled.
	In view of the possibility of future wars resembling the Korean War, the development of a cheap mass-produced lightweight tactical fighter is suggested within the Air Force.
2 June	Separate AAA staff sections within HQ ADC and its major subordinate command headquarters are abolished in favor of coordination between counterpart staff elements of collocated HQ at appropriate echelons.
19 June	Assistant, Chief of Ordnance informs Assistant, Chief of Staff, G-4, that the following studies are being conducted:

Appendix B: A Chronology of American Air and Ballistic Missile Defense Systems

	(a) A study of the relative effectiveness of atomic warheads against bomber formations.
	(b) A preliminary study of an antiaircraft GM carrying an atomic warhead using the production Nike-I ground equipment.
	(c) A preliminary study of the feasibility of adapting the Corporal missile to a surface-to-air missile with an atomic warhead.
20 June	Undersecretary of the Army, Mr. Karl R. Bendetsen, in a memorandum states that USAF is undertaking an overall campaign to usurp the Army's responsibility in the entire GM field and takes the position that the Army should undertake to secure assignment of responsibility for all ground-launched guided missiles regardless of range, provided they do not require manned aircraft to launch, guide, or home. The Army G-3's position does not go as far with respect to the ICBM but considers that in the SAM field the Army must be responsible for research, test, procurement, and operations of those systems required to protect Army ground installations in a theater of operations. To avoid duplication of effort, the Army would also provide such weapons for the zone of interior.
1 July	The Federal Civil Defense Agency (FCDA) takes over operation of Civil Air Raid Warning net.
14 July	AFF Arms Board recommends that 15.61 percent of the Army's M-Day combat troop strength be allocated to nondivisional AAA.
15 July	Plan for Security Control of Air Traffic is signed by the Secretaries of Defense and Commerce.
22 July	The first production-line Nike-I makes a successful flight.
10 September	The first Bomarc test launching takes place at Cape Canaveral.
3 October	All F-89's grounded pending correction of major structural defects.
17 October	In a letter to Lincoln Laboratory, the Assistant Chief of Ordnance describes the lack of defense against ballistic missiles carrying atomic warheads and requests the laboratory to investigate and evaluate possible methods of defense utilizing and extending Projects Wizard and Thumper, considering defense against large missiles of the 50–400 mile range and ICBM.
20 October	At a conference sponsored by DA, G-4, it is decided that the antimissile system for the Army should be pointed toward the development of a system for use in a theater of operations. AFF is tasked to supply the following information:
	(a) The relative priority of competing characteristics appearing in currently approved military characteristics for the Army's antimissile requirement.
	(b) The minimum acceptable altitude coverage necessary for an interim antimissile surveillance radar.
	(c) A description of the types of missiles with flight paths that could be encountered in a theater of operations before 1960.
1 November	The first hydrogen bomb is exploded at the AEC Eniwetok Proving Ground.
31 December	President Truman approves a National Security Council policy statement calling for a strengthening of continental defense.

1953

January	2,500 F-86D's on order, of which fewer than 90 have been accepted.

1 February	The 29th and 34th Air Divisions are reassigned from Western to Central Air Defense Force. The 29th Air Division area is expanded to include North and South Dakota and Nebraska.
	Work on the development program for Nike-I-B is initiated by Western Electric who estimates that the system can be experimentally demonstrated in approximately three years.
16 February	ARAACOM region boundaries are changed to conform with ADC boundary changes of 1 February.
18 February	ADC promulgates instructions to all commanders to employ simultaneous engagement as necessary to effect maximum destruction of the attacking force. This follows testing in Western ADF which demonstrates the feasibility especially with the M-33.
March	The AW battalion at Castle AFB, California is converted to Skysweeper. The other three battalions in ARAACOM will be converted in October 1953.
3 March	Military characteristics of Nike-I-B (Hercules) are established.
9 April	Ordnance Technical Committee formally establishes a Hawk RED Project.
10 April	USAF adopts the Lincoln Transition System later to be renamed the Semi-Automatic Ground Environment (SAGE) System instead of the rival Air Defense Integrated System (ADIS) sponsored by the University of Michigan.
30 June	USAF reports only 66 active F-89's out of 164 first-line aircraft.
6 July	DA publishes criteria for designating ARNG AAA units as Special Security Force units.
22 July	The Continental Defense (Bull) Committee appointed by the National Security Council reports that continental defense programs, current and future, are inadequate.
27 July	An armistice is signed in Korea.
12 August	A thermonuclear explosion takes place in Russia.
21 August	USAF approves, in principle, as an interim measure, establishment of Inner Defense Areas (IDAs) around those targets in the United States which have effective AAA defenses. This has long been ADC and ARAACOM's recommendation, except that both considered IDAs to be necessary over the long as well as short term. IDAs differed from Gun Defended Areas in that all weapons would be used for defense.
25 September	The President approves a statement calling for increased emphasis on continental defense.
July	F-89 procurement accelerated in second half of year.
October	First YF-102A delivered.
	Last AW battalion phased out of CONUS Air Defense.
1 October	Secretary of Defense issues a revision of "Functions of the Armed Forces and the Joint Chiefs of Staff" commonly known as the "Key West Agreements."
	The first airborne early warning squadron is activated at McClellan AFB, California.
8 October	The Canada–United States Military Study Group recommends establishment of a Mid-Canada Line of early warning radar along the 55th parallel.
28 October	A Nike-I missile is fired for the first time by a tactical unit, Battery A, Package Number 2, 1st Guided Missile Group, at Red Canyon, New Mexico.
3 November	Canada agrees to construction of Mid-Canada Line.

Appendix B: A Chronology of American Air and Ballistic Missile Defense Systems

9 November	DA publishes a policy directive for the AAA defense of CONUS, including provision for ARNG participation.
December	Second YF-102A delivered.
17 December	The first Nike-I-Ajax missile unit is moved on-site at Fort George G. Meade, Maryland: the 36th AAA Battalion, later to be redesignated 1st Battalion 562nd Artillery.
21 December	The first meeting of the Joint ADC-ARAACOM Planning and Coordination Committee results in the creation of a new, jointly approved objectives list.
24 December	USAF and United States Navy reach agreement on the seaward extension of radar for the contiguous system and Distant Early Warning (DEW) Line.
31 December	Phase-out of the 47 federalized ARNG AAA battalions assigned ARAACOM is complete.
	Ninety-one percent of ARAACOM units are on-site. Conversion to Nike-I will reduce the figure to 80 percent in the first quarter of 1954.

1954

	Tests in early months of the year indicate that YF-102 will be subsonic and will have a combat ceiling below 50,000 feet.
January	The Joint Strategic Plans Committee of the JCS is directed to prepare terms of reference for a joint air defense command.
11 January	USAF approves construction of five sea-based radar platforms known as "Texas Towers."
	USAF approves low altitude gap-filler radar program.
22 January	JCS agree to the establishment of a joint command for Continental Air Defense.
February	First flight of XF-104.
19 February	Air Force requirement for a two-place long-range jet interceptor outlined.
24 February	The President approves the recommendation of the National Security Council that a Distant Early Warning (DEW) Line be built.
March	All six Skysweeper battalions replacing the AW battalions are on-site.
25 March	ARNG on-site participation in AAA defense of CONUS is begun with deployment of Btry A, 245th AAA Bn (120-mm. gun) in New York City defense.
May	F-101 moneys delayed pending second flight test (expected in 1955); mass production postponed as a result of relaxation of tension following Korean armistice. "Fly-before-you-buy" policy instituted.
1 May	U.S.S.R. displays a jet bomber for the first time.
June	Following a controversy within the Air Force, decision to build the F-104 with a more powerful engine is made in mid-1954.
	Air Research and Development Command recommends the F-101 to fill USAF requirement for two-place long-range interceptor (stated on 19 February).
	263 F-94C's assigned to ADC.
2 June	The Canada–United States Military Study Group recommends that the two governments agree in principle to establishment of the DEW Line.

28 June	Raytheon is awarded a contract for design, development, and test of a complete Hawk weapon system.
1 August	Airborne early warning operations are begun off the West Coast.
2 August	JCS direct establishment of the Continental Air Defense Command (CONAD) as a joint command under the JCS.
September	52 out of 55 ADC squadrons equipped with all-weather interceptors; 38 of them have the F-86D.
1 September	HQ CONAD is established under command of General B. W. Chidlaw who is given operational control of ADC, ARAACOM, the Navy forces of the contiguous radar coverage system and augmentation forces of all services when made available during periods of emergency.
	NAVFORCONAD is established at Ent AFB, Colorado under command of RADM Albert K. Morehouse.
28 September	Development is initiated for a T-46 cluster warhead for Nike-I-B.
1 October	Major General Stanley R. Michelsen succeeds LT General Lewis as CG ARAACOM.
7 October	AFF indicates a requirement for a surface-to-air missile system capable of defeating a ballistic missile of all classes. The requirement will be restated by AFF successor CONARC on 12 November 1955.
8 October	9th Air Division is activated at Geiger Field, Washington, the 12th to be assigned to ADC.
8 November	Secretary of Army informs Secretary of Defense that studies performed in the Nike-I-B Program have concluded that the Nike-I System can be modified to control the Nike-I-B (Model 1810) missile at extended ranges in excess of 50 miles and up to 80,000 feet altitude without affecting the ability of the system to fire unmodified Nike-I missiles.
19 December	First flight of F-102.

1955

14 January	The first Nike-I-Hercules flight test missile is launched.
10 February	CoS Army directs CG, ARAACOM to initiate a study of possible substitution of civilian or reserve component personnel for military personnel.
March	BTL initiates a feasibility study for a weapon system to replace Nike-I and Nike-I-B about 1965. Emphasis is placed on defense against long-range ballistic missiles.
14 April	A Nike-I missile is accidentally launched by Btry C, 36th AAA Bn during an alert drill at Fort Meade, Maryland. Fragments of the missile fall in Barbersville, near Laurel, and on the Baltimore-Washington Parkway.
5 May	Agreement is reached with Canada reflecting establishment of the DEW Line in Canadian territory.
31 May	Eastern Army Antiaircraft Command is discontinued. Personnel are assigned the 1st AAA region.
	General Chidlaw retires. Major General Smith becomes acting Commander, ADC; LT General Michelsen becomes acting CINCONAD pending the arrival of CONAD and ADC designated Commander General Earl E. Partridge.
June	Construction begun on land portion of DEW Line.

Appendix B: A Chronology of American Air and Ballistic Missile Defense Systems

21 June	The Technical Advisory Panel on Aeronautics concludes that the existing antimissile program lacks cohesiveness and direction and recommends that a special high level task group be appointed and responsibility be vested in a single service with a higher level of support.
29 June	First successful Nike-I-B firing takes place at White Sands Proving Ground.
	Secretary of Defense states his conviction that the earliest practicable atomic capability for the Nike-I System can be achieved by priority development of the atomic warhead for Nike-I-B.
July	Army critically evaluates Project LAMPLIGHT, exhaustive study conducted by MIT, which omits the missile defense problem as "outside the LAMPLIGHT field of study" and "currently in the hands of a special committee of the USAF Scientific Advisors Board."
	ARAACOM initiates a program request to improve the AN/TPS-1D. From this came the AN/FPS-36, -54, -61, -69, and -71 series of radars.
5 July	Chief, R&D, DA directs Chief of Ordnance to modify the requirements of BTL study concerning weapon systems to replace Nike-I and Nike-I-B so as to focus on the ICBM as the prime target of the Nike-I-Zeus.
14 July	ARAACOM submits comments to DA on the feasibility of "integrating reserve troops with Regular Army troops in a dual (Nike-I) Battery."
16 July	CONARC in a letter to G-3, DA concurs with AA&GM School's objection to the 50 mile range limitation of Army SAM:
	(a) Maximum effective engagement of enemy aircraft.
	(b) Destruction of enemy aircraft carrying nuclear weapons at a safe distance from the defended area.
	(c) Improvement of antiaircraft effectiveness compatible with the increase in enemy aircraft speeds.
	(d) Exploitation of the flexibility of antimissile missile in the antiaircraft role.
	(e) Maximizing the surface-to-surface capability of Army antiaircraft guided missiles.
20 July	General Earle E. Partridge assumes command of CONAD and ADC.
August	ARAACOM submits to DA its own concept of military characteristics for an antimissile defense weapon.
16 August	The first HAWK missile is successfully fired at White Sands Proving Ground to determine flutter and drag characteristics of the missile airframe.
September	HQ 7th AAA Group is activated at Thule AFB, Greenland. It is assigned to First Army and attached to Northeast Air Command for operational control.
8 September	The 85th, 58th, and 37th Air Divisions are activated at Andrews AFB, Wright-Patterson AFB, and Truax Field, Wisconsin, respectively. These activations bring the total number of divisions assigned ADC to 15.
9 September	The number of Nike-I batteries deployed (136) equals the number of gun batteries (90-mm. and 120-mm.).
22 September	Nike-I becomes the dominant weapon of ARAACOM as conversion of the 602nd AAA Battalion of the Baltimore Defense increases Nike-I-l batteries to 140 and reduces gun batteries to 132.

8 October	The 20th Air Division is activated at Grandview AFB, Missouri, the 16th to be assigned ADC.
December	F-102A scheduled for production.
	DA authorizes the United States Army member of the Canadian–United States Permanent Joint Board on Defense to seek Canadian Army participation in the overall defense of Detroit. Under consideration is the relocation of two Nike-I batteries to Canadian sites, to be manned by Canadian personnel, in order to provide a balanced defense of Detroit.

1956

	Performance tests on lightweight, "ideal body" F-102A conducted in early 1956. F-102A becomes operational in mid-1956.
February	First flight of F-104A.
26 December	First flight of F-106A. The two-place F-106B first flies on 9 April 1958. In FY 1957, the F-106 goes into quantity production, while F-102 production is closed out.

Appendix C

A Chronology of Soviet Air and Ballistic Missile Defense

1941

First known Soviet Radar completed.

1943

Soviets receive significant information or samples concerning most of the operational radars in the United States and United Kingdom, including the U.S. SCR-584 fire control radar, which became the Soviet SON-2, the British "Elsie," a search light control and other U.S. types including the SCR-545, 527/627, 582/682, 602.

Development of RUS-2 radar.

1944

June	Reorganization of PVO Troops; Eastern and Western directorates established; Office of The Commander of Territorial PVO Troops abolished; supervision over the activities of the PVO fronts and zones, weapons planning and supply—transferred to the Red Army Commander of Artillery.
Spring	PVO Western and Eastern fronts eliminated, PVO Northern and Southern fronts established; improved control resulting.
	(Late) Soviet VRD3 (jet) bench testing begun.
	(Late) Capture of German jet engines.

1945

	Emphasis on Civil Defense lessens.
February	Stalin orders designs based on German jet engines.
8 May	Cancellation of Lend Lease Policy; decision reversed after strong protest by Soviets.
19 August	Recancellation of Lend Lease Policy—no reversal.
August–November	Flight tests of Me 262.
	Pre-prototype approval of native jet designs of 4 contenders.
October	Ground tests of YAK-15, wind tunnel testing.
December	Decision not to produce Me 262.

1946

Reorganization of armed forces—unified defense establishment under the Ministry of Armed Forces; previously had Commissariats. Dumbo, early warning radar, the first post–WWII system, quickly followed by a family of radars characterized by metric frequency, the use of Yagi antenna, goniometric techniques and nearly identical transmitters. The Ministry of the Communications Equipment Industry (MCEI) organized. Included production of radar, radio-engineering equipment, telephone and telegraph apparatus, electro-vacuum equipment, storage batteries and electro-carbon articles.

March	Aviation industry mission to Germany.
March–April	Validation of MiG-15 requirement.
2 April	Stalin confirms aviation ministry plan for jet development.
24 April	First flights of MiG-9/YAK-15.
18 August	SU-9 first flight.
19 August	Aviation day MiG/YAK prototypes fly at Tushino.
29 August	Stalin orders 20–30 jet aircraft in 80 days.
September	La-150 first flight.
September	British permit export of 10 Nene jet engines.
7 November–December	30 aircraft delivered for October Revolution Parade.

MiG-9 committed to production.

1947

25 February–May	State trials of YAK-15.
May	YAK-15 ordered to production with Lyulka RD10 engine.
March	Last of 25 Nene and 30 Derwent British jet engines received.
April	La-150 M first flight.
June	YAK-23 first flight.
2 July	MiG-15 predecessor flies.
August	YAK-15 U (tricycle gear version) passes state tests.
30 December	First flight of MiG-15.

1948

Subordination of National Air Defense Forces to the Artillery Commander of the Soviet Army eliminated.

June — Ministry of Armed Forces establishes a Chief Directorate of Air Defense and establishes National Air Defense Forces as a distinct type of troops. Civil Defense interests renewed; self-defense leaders reported in training. Plans emerge for training 4–5 million in Civil Defense.

Electronic experiments on the SA-1 for development of guidance subsystem.

Appendix C: A Chronology of Soviet Air and Ballistic Missile Defense

March	MiG-15 to production.
	Three designs of all-weather, radar-equipped, transsonic aircraft are unsuccessful, the SU-15, MiG I-320, and Lavochkin 200A.

1949

IZUMRUD AI radar modified for MiG-15.

German POWs report basement shelter construction program; basic radiofication of U.S.S.R. ordered, training of CD instructor(s).

MiG-15 bis modification with Soviet VK-1 engine.

Sukhoi design bureau closed; had begun SU-17 supersonic design.

Phase out of MiG-9 production.

1950

Industrial evacuation plans updated; call for "tens of thousands" of instructors.

Initiation of an Adcock-type radio direction finder; series provided HF/DF monitor coverage between 1.5 and 15 MHz.

January	MiG-17 first flight.
	Trials of 2-seat MiG-15 with AI radar.
February	Claim of Mach 1.0 for MiG-17.
	MiG-15 bis—to production with VK-1 and improved cannon.
November	German scientists tasked to study guidance problems of the SA-1.
1 November	First combat with F-51D Mustang in Korea.
8 November	First all-jet combat.

1951

Border Air Defense Line established; organizational part of the air defense system; Marshal of Aviation, K. A. Vershinin, named Commander of Border Air Defense Line Forces.

Token, V-beam radar, built by the Soviets; a major accomplishment; based on the U.S. AN/CPS-6 V-beam set, not released under the Lend Lease Policy but documented in the MIT Series reports.

SCAN ODD developed with German engineering assistance; the first Soviet radar with limited all-weather capability.

DOSAAF established.

Czechs and Polish licensed to manufacture MiG-15.

30 July	"Pre-project" approval of YAK-25 and MiG-19 design efforts.
	MiG-15 bis to Korea.
	Series production of MiG-17 as day interceptor.

1952

Colonel General N. N. Nagornyy named Commander of National Air Defense forces.

Production of a height finder, Patty Cake; not typical of Soviet Radars as it was an original design.

Early warning and surveillance radar on a bunkered building, GAGE; first static radar of significance employed by the Soviets; never achieving widespread deployment nor production in great numbers.

KRUG—the only Soviet ground-based Wallenweher wide aperture HF/DF system known to be in use; considered best of its kind; designed through German assistance.

Compulsory DOSAFF study circles begun; Civil Defense manuals published.

1 July	SA-1 prototype system tested.
November	SA-1 initial system test begun.

1953

Site construction for the SA-1 SAM system started; first site operation in 1954.

Antiaircraft General (Gritchin) made head of DOSAAF; 20-hour compulsory training program for DOSAAF members.

5 March	Stalin dies.
July	Sukhoi receives Hero of Soviet Labor; his bureau reinstated.

Border Air Defense Line Forces joined to National Air Defense Forces. Marshal Vershinin named Commander of National Air Defense Forces with Marshal of Artillery N. D. Yakovlev his first deputy.

1954

First Civil Defense publications mentioning atomic, bacteriological, and chemical weapons; Central Committee session of DOSAAF held, emphasizing its roles.

SCAN CAN deployment initiated; first Soviet AI system to use missile armament exclusively, developed from SCAN ODD.

May	Position of Commander-in-Chief of National Air Defense Forces established. Marshal of the Soviet Union, L. A. Govorov, named to the position.

1955

May Day—YAK-25 all-weather fighter and MiG-19 supersonic fighter are first observed.

First compulsory training program for adult population (10-hour); Tolstikov appointed Head of Civil Defense; Belov head of DOSAAF; beginning emphasis on using military as trainers and instructors.

Appendix D

Figures

D-1. Soviet and American Air Defense Systems

D-2. U.S. EW/GCI/ACO Radar

D-3. U.S. Fighter Aircraft Development

D-4. U.S. AAA and Surface Air Defense Missile Systems Chronology

D-5. U.S. Civil Defense Key Characteristics

D-6. Abbreviated Chronology USAD C^3

D-7. U.S. Air Defense Deployments by Year

D-8. Post-1954 Soviet Air Defense Organization

D-9. Soviet Aircraft Control and Warning Radar Development

D-10. Estimated Soviet Fighter Production 1946–1955

D-11. Soviet Fighter Prototype Maximum Speed

D-12. Development of Soviet Antiaircraft Artillery 1945–1960

D-13. U.S.S.R. Civil Defense Key Characteristics

D-14. Chronology of Soviet C^3 for Air Defense

D-15. Typical Soviet Air Defense District, 1955

Figure D-1. Soviet and American Air Defense Systems

Soviet and American Air Defense Systems

I. Early Warning and Target Acquisition Systems

II. Aircraft and Air-to-Air Missile Systems

III. Artillery and Surface-to-Air Missile Systems

IV. Civil Defense Systems

V. Command, Control, and Communications Systems

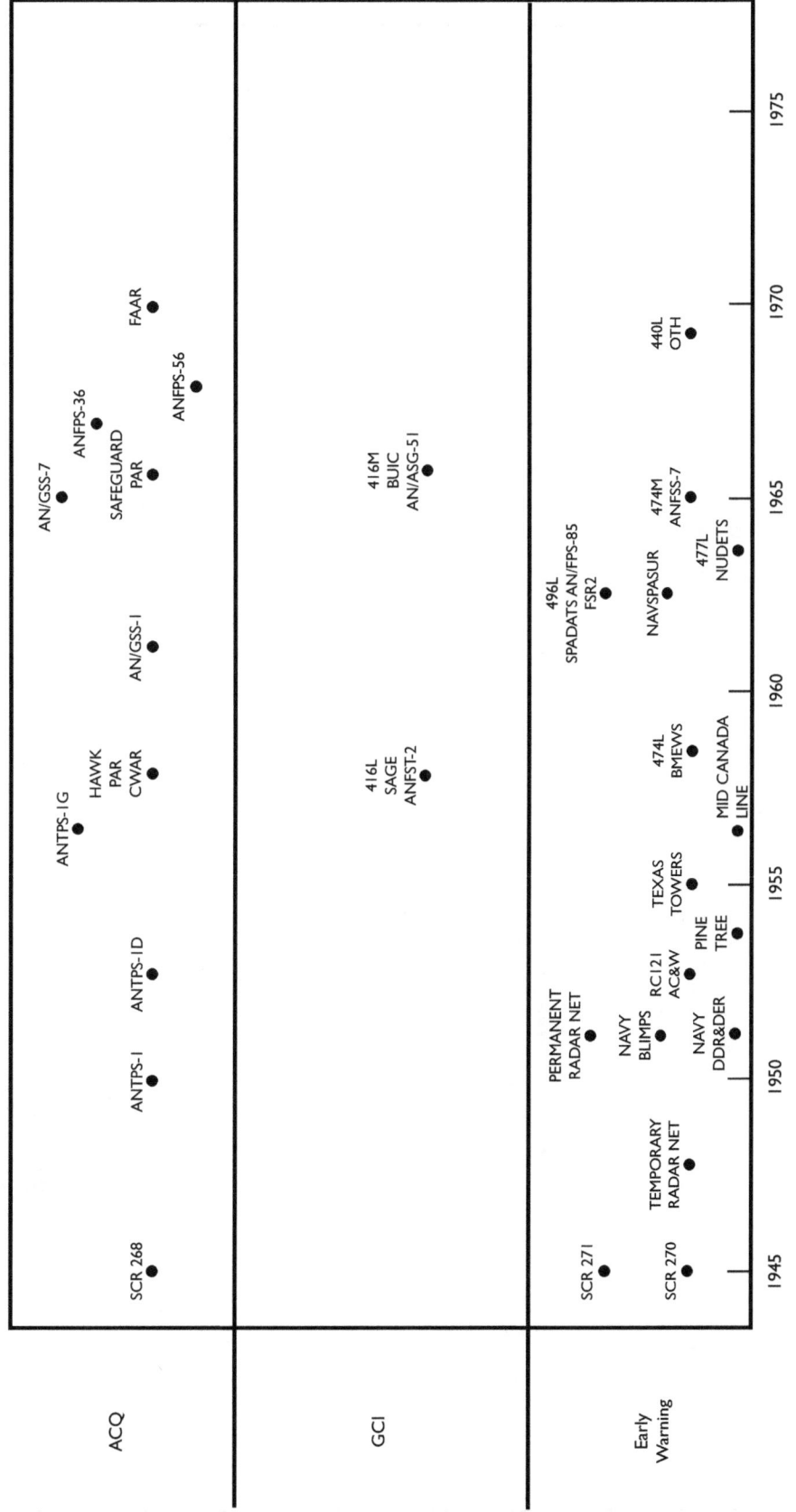

Figure D-2. U.S. EW/GCI/ACO Radar

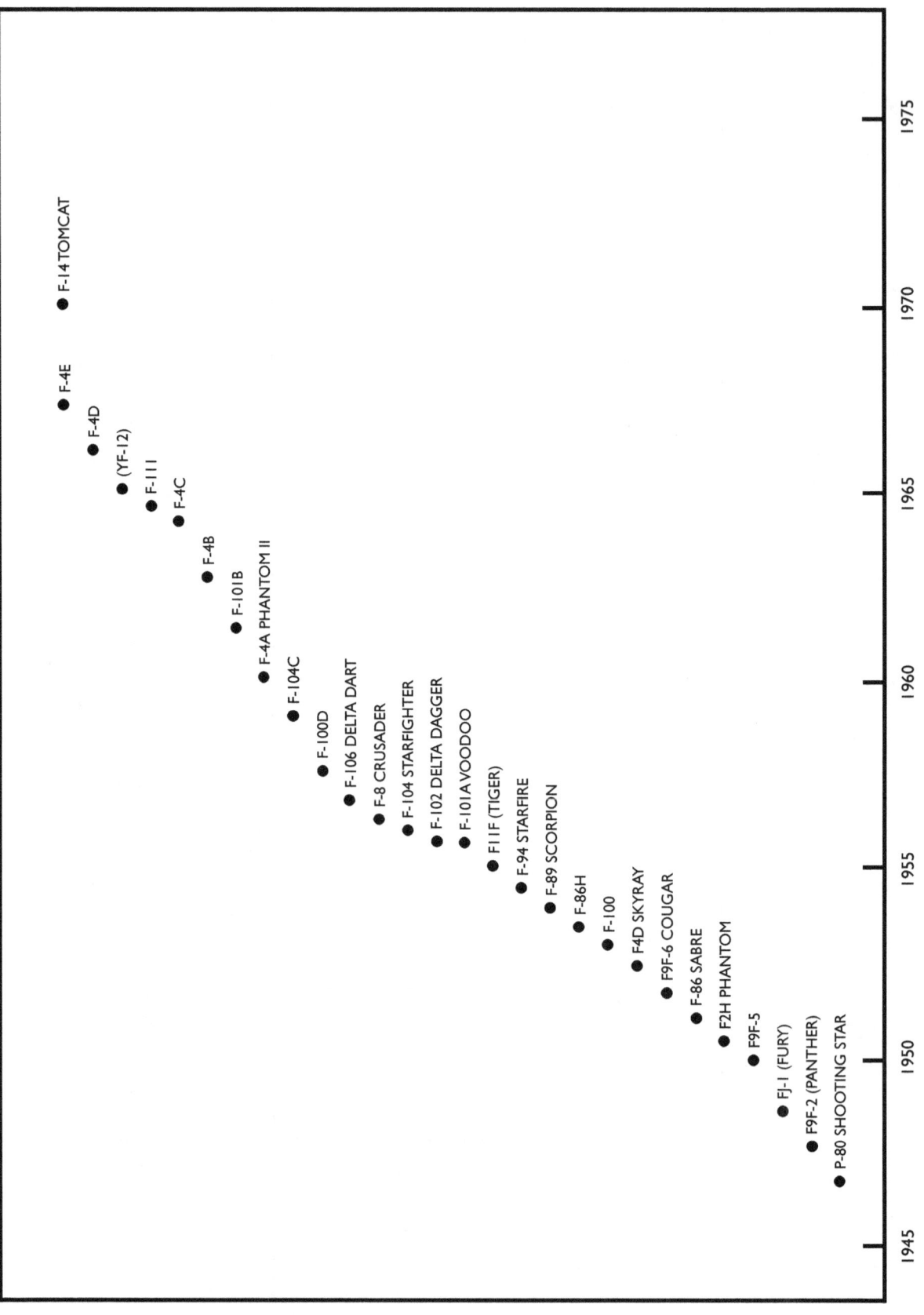

Figure D-3. U.S. Fighter Aircraft Development

Figure D-4. U.S. AAA and Surface Air Defense Missile Systems Chronology

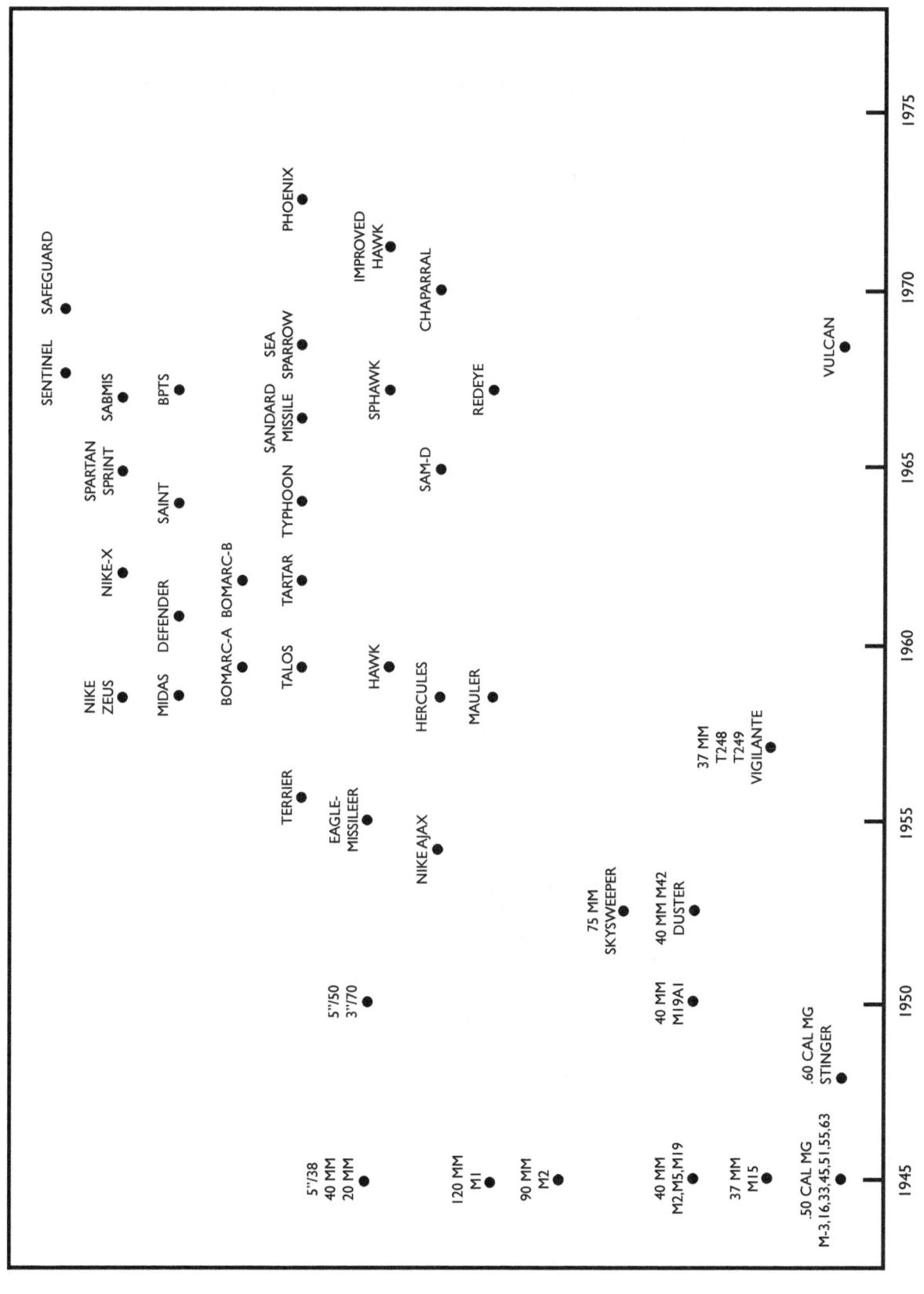

Figure D-5. U.S. Civil Defense Key Characteristics

1945–1950
- WARTIME OCD ABOLISHED
- WD STUDIES AND PLANS
- NSRB ACTIONS
- FWA RESPONSIBILITIES

1950–1955
- NSRB CD PLAN
- FCDA, OEM ESTABLISHED
- ODM RESPONSIBILITIES

1955–1960
- ODM, FCDA OCDM
- PL 85-606 INSTITUTED

1960–1965
- OCDM OEP
- CD TO SEC DEF
- ASD (CD) ESTABLISHED
- DAGR, DHEW RESPONSIBILITIES
- $250M CD APPROPRIATION
- OCD TO OSA
- CIV/MIL STRENGTHENED
- FALLOUT SHELTER PROGRAM

1965–1970
- PRESIDENTIAL SUPPORT
- CD WITH GEN NUC FORCES
- SHELTER PROGRAM CONTINUES

Post 1970
- MEASURED CD REDIRECTION
- CD REMAINS STATE ORIENTED
- CDPA ESTABLISHED
- ASSIST TO STATE AND LOCAL GOVERNMENTS

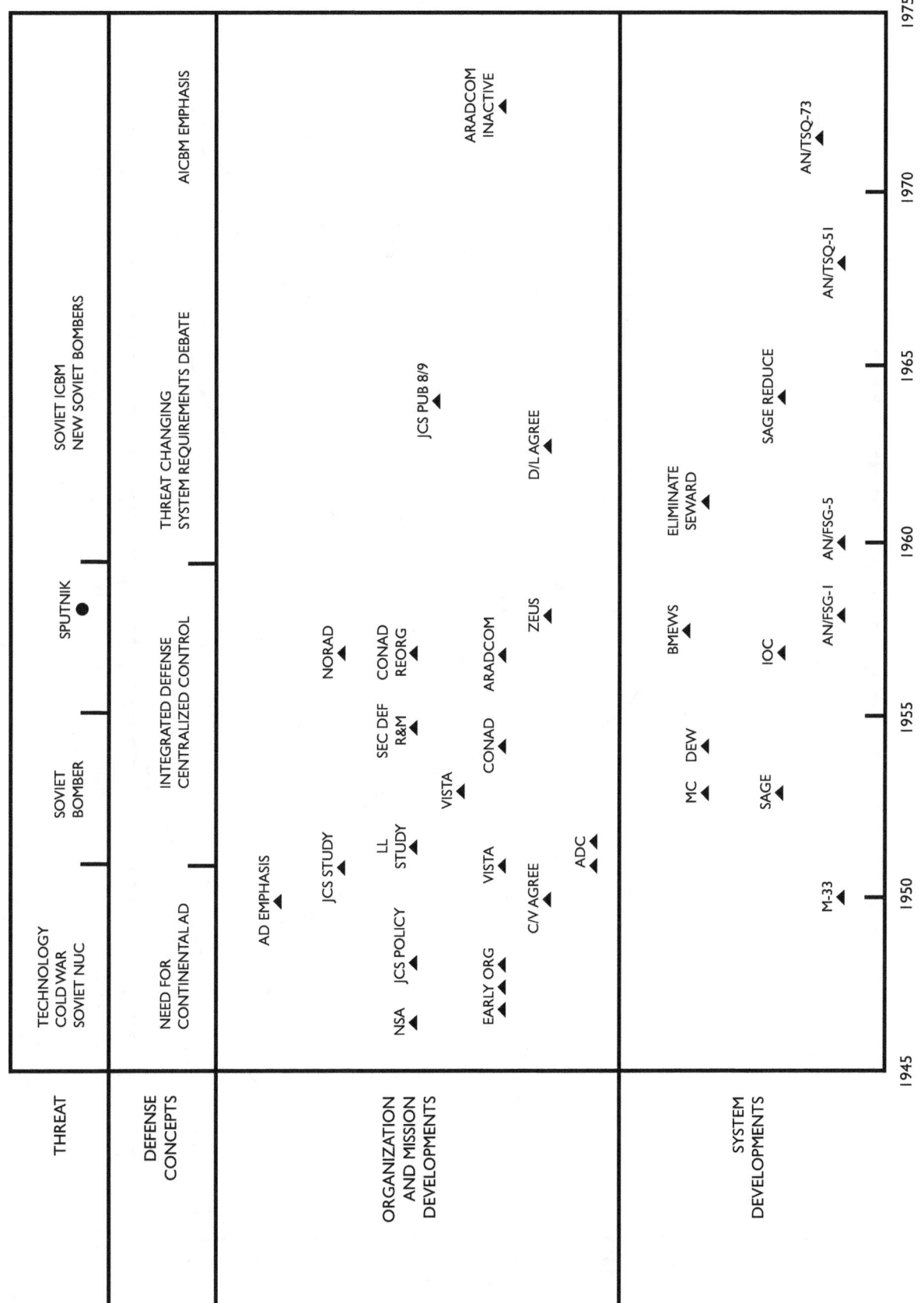

Figure D-6. Abbreviated Chronology USAD C³

Figure D-7. U.S. Air Defense Deployments by Year

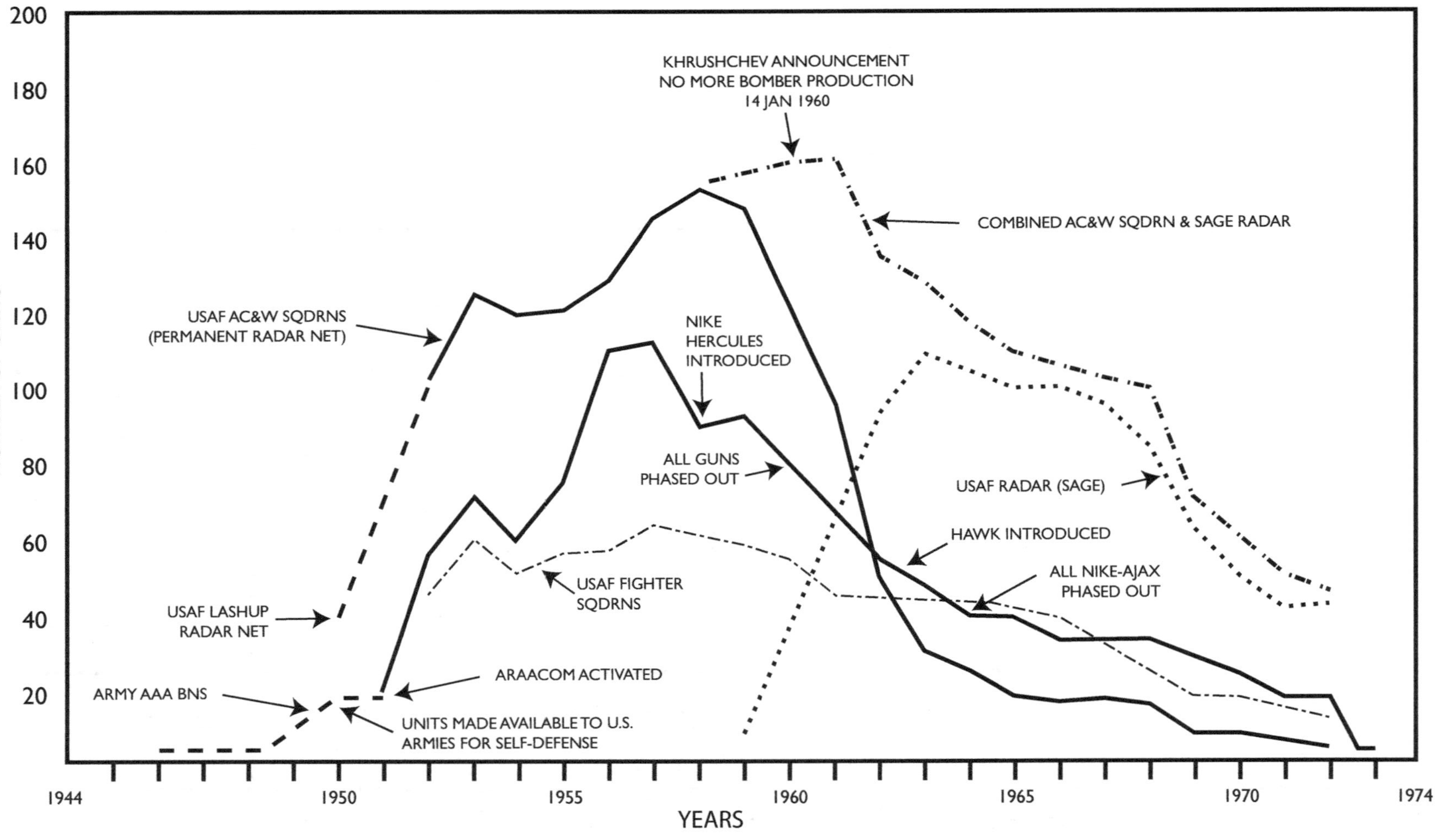

Figure D-8. Post-1954 Soviet Air Defense Organization

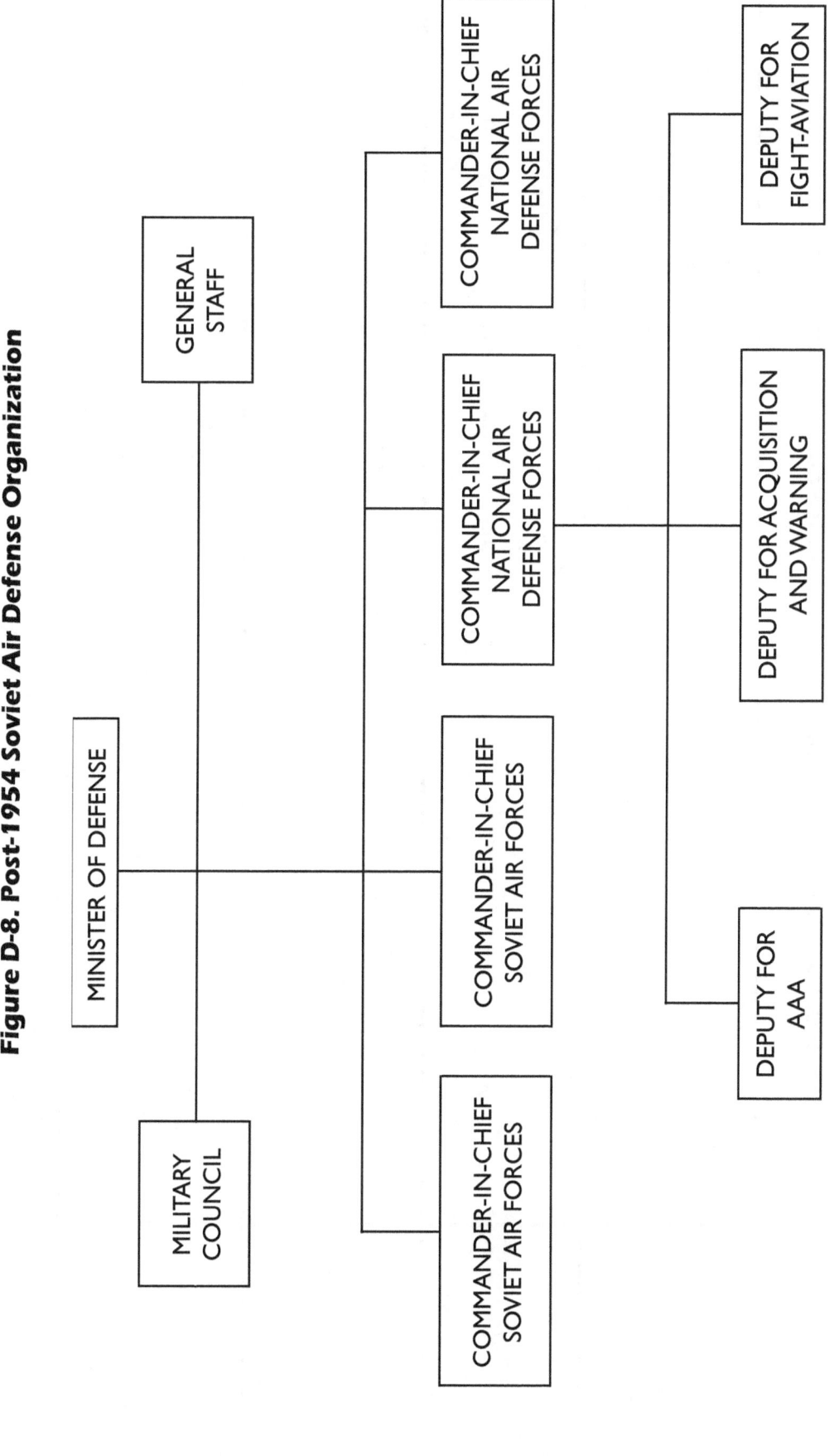

Figure D-9. Soviet Aircraft Control and Warning Radar Development

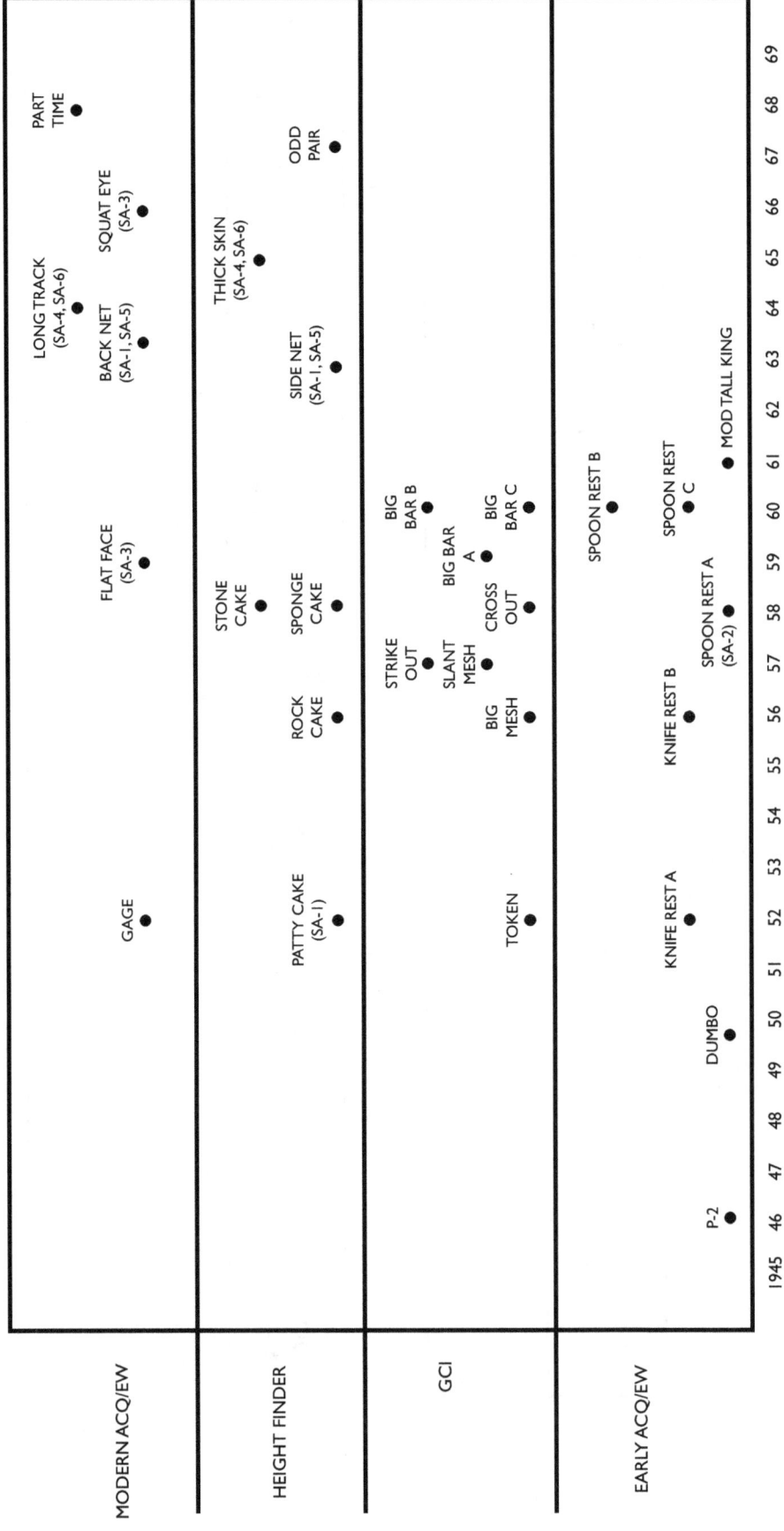

Figure D-10. Estimated Soviet Fighter Production 1946–1955

Designation	1946	1947	1948	1949	1950	1951	1952	1953	1954	1955	Total
Soviet NATO Propeller											
YAK-3	1400	300									1700
YAK-9 Frank	1300	650	650	300							2900
LA-7 Fin	1300	30									1330
LA-9/11 Fritz/Fang	15	700	1300	450	200	5					2670
Total Prop.	4015	1680	1950	750	200	5					8600
Jet											
YAK-15	15	250									265
MIG-9 Fargo	15	400	400								815
YAK-17 Feather		10	300	300							610
MIG-15 Fagot			60	850	2700	4200	3600	1100			12510
LA-15 Fantail			20	100							120
YAK-23 Flora				10	550	370					930
MIG-17 Fresco							400	3200	3500	2700	9800
MIG-19 Farmer									10	250	260
YAK-25 Flashlight									50	200	250
Total Jet (45)	30	660	780	1260	3250	4570	4000	4300	3560	3150	25560
Total Fighter	4045	2340	2730	2010	3450	4575	4000	4300	3560	3150	34160

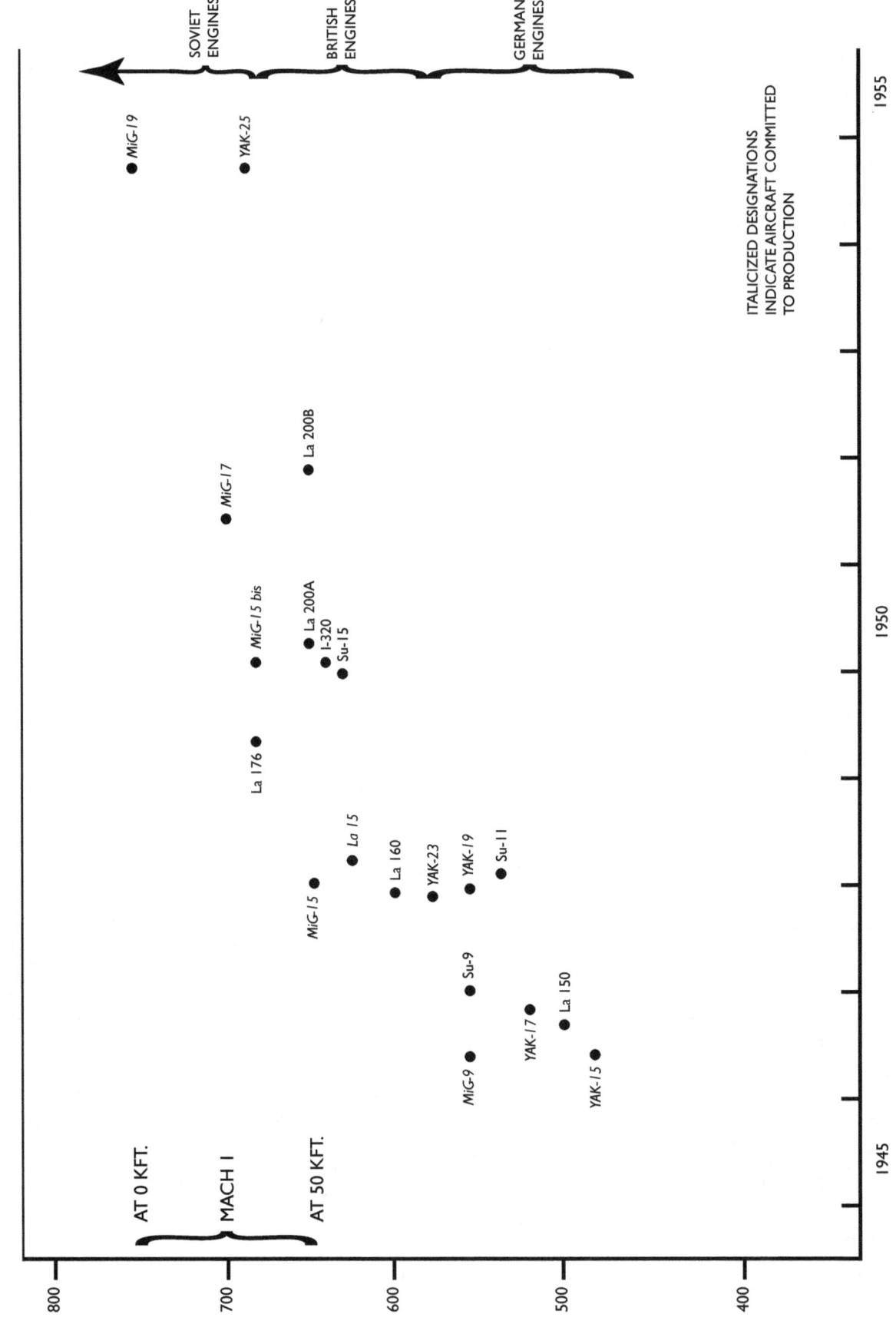

Figure D-12. Development of Soviet Antiaircraft Artillery 1945–1960

Caliber	Year of Introduction	Maximum Vertical Range (Ft)	Rate of Fire (Rds/min)
85 mm	1939	34,450	15–20
85 mm	1945	38,060	12–15
100 mm	1949	47,560	15
130 mm	1955	72,000	10–12

Figure D-13. U.S.S.R. Civil Defense Key Characteristics

1945–1960
- CD UNDER MINISTRY OF INTERNAL AFFAIRS (MVD)
- CD DIRECTED BY COL TOLSTIKOV
- CD ORGANIZED AROUND LOCAL AAA (MPVO)
- CD ORIENTED TOWARD CITY AND POINT DEFENSE
- ROLES AND FUNCTIONS EXECUTED BY COMPLEX OF CIVIL POLICE, FIREMEN, MUNICIPAL TEAMS AND PLANT TEAMS

1960–1972
- CD UNDER MINISTRY OF DEFENSE
- CD DIRECTED BY MARSHAL CHUIKOV WITH FIRST DEPUTY COL GEN TOLSTIKOV
- MILITARY INFRASTRUCTURE DEVELOPING THROUGHOUT CIVIL GOVERNMENT
- MILITARY CD OCS ESTABLISHED
- CD BECOMES BASIC ELEMENT OF SOVIET ARMED FORCES
- CD DEPUTIES PLACED ON MILITARY DISTRICT STAFFS
- MIL/CIV CD UNITS IN JOINT EXERCISES
- CD TRAINING TOWNS BUILT
- CD TRAINING PERVADES ENTIRE CIV/MIL STRUCTURE

Figure D-14. Chronology of Soviet C³ for Air Defense

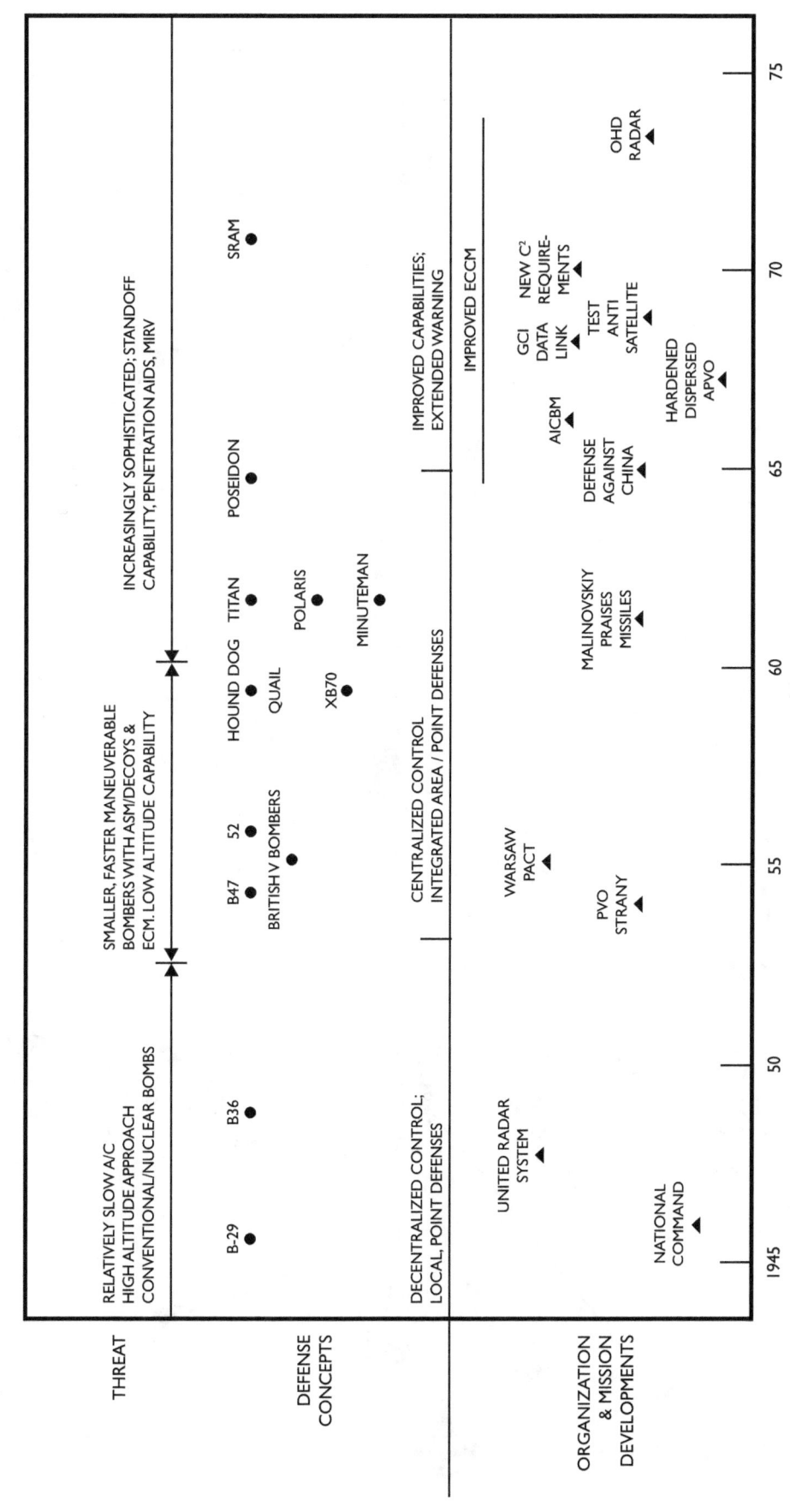

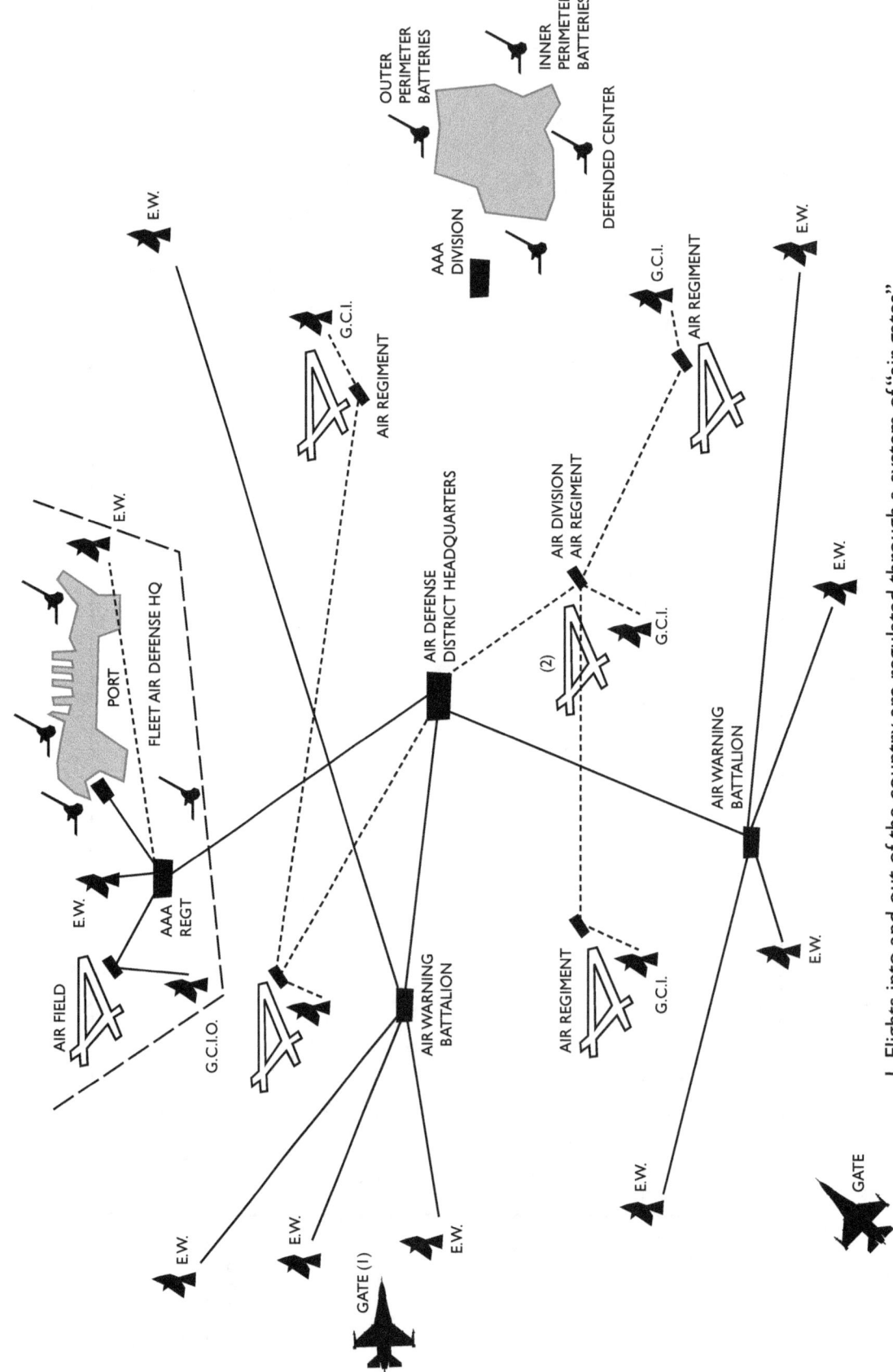

Figure D-15. Typical Soviet Air Defense District, 1955

1. Flights into and out of the country are regulated through a system of "air gates".
2. Each airfield defended normally by an independent AAA battalion.

Bibliography

Congressional Hearings and Reports, Government Contracts, U.S. Department of Defense Magazines and Periodicals

Congressional Hearings and Reports, Government Contracts, U.S. Department of Defense Magazines and Periodicals

AAF, "Roundup of Red Radars," *Intelligence Digest*, Volume 7, No. 8, January 1954.

AAF Statistical Digest, 1946.

"AA Situation in Soviet Zone of Germany," USAFE, *Intelligence Summary*, July 1953.

"Activation of New AAA Units," *The Coast Artillery Journal*, Volume 91, July–August 1948.

"Aerospace Force in the Sixties," *Air University Quarterly Review*, Volume XII, Winter and Spring, 1960–1961.

"Air Defense," *Bol'shaya Sovetskaya Entsiklopediya* (The Great Soviet Encyclopedia), 2nd edition, Volume 35, Moscow, 1955.

Air Materiel Command, *An Electronic Air Defense Environment for 1954*, McRee HQ, 15 December 1950.

Air Materiel Command, *Case History of the F-89 All-Weather Fighter Airplane (August 1945–January 1951)*, March 1952.

Air Materiel Command, *Development of Guided Missiles Through 1945*, Historical Study No. 237.

Air Materiel Command, *Development of Guided Missiles 1945–1950*, Historical Study No. 238.

"Air Warning System of the Soviet Union," *RCAF Intelligence Summary*, April 1955.

Annual Reports of the Secretary of Defense, 1948–1955.

Annual Reports of the Service Secretaries to the Secretary of Defense, U.S. Government Printing Office, Washington, D.C., 1948–1955.

Antiballistic Missile: Yes or No? For: Donald G. Brenna and Leon W. Johnson, Against: Jerome B. Wiesner and George S. McGovern, Introduction by: Hubert H. Humphrey, Epilogue by: William O. Douglas, Hill & Nang, New York, 1969.

Associated Universities, Inc., *Project East River*, New York, 1952.

Associated Universities, Inc., *1955 Review of the Report of Project East River*, New York, 1955.

Aviation Week, 1948–1955 issues.

"Bear Gives Reds a Longer Reach," *Air Intelligence Digest*, June 1955.

Bell Telephone Laboratories, Inc., *Antiaircraft Guided Missile System*, 15 July 1945.

Bell Telephone Laboratories, Inc., *Historical Summary of Nike-I Research and Development Program, July 1945–July 1951*.

Bell Telephone Laboratories, Inc., *Lokiya System Study*, 1 August 1954.

Bell Telephone Laboratories, Inc. and Douglas Aircraft Company, Inc., *Project Nike-I-History of Development*, New York, April 1954.

"Best Pictures to Date of Soviet V-Beam Radar," *Air Intelligence Digest*, March 1953.

"Bison, Badger Reveal Armament Development," *Air Intelligence Digest*, November 1954.

"Bison, Badger Reveal Electronics Progress," *Air Intelligence Digest*, November 1954.

Braddock, Dunn and McDonald, Inc., *Continuing Analysis of Strategic Defense Force (CASDET)*, 7 volumes in 3 parts, BDM/CS-15-69-0035, El Paso, Texas, 22 August 1969.

CIA, "Changing Soviet Civil Defense Concepts," Current Support Brief, 11 September 1962.

CIA, "Civil Defense in the U.S.S.R.," Economic Intelligence Report, November 1956.

CIA, *A Summary of Soviet Guided Missile Intelligence U.S./U.K.*, GM 4-52, 20 July 1953.

"Civil Defense of the U.S.S.R.," *Intelligence Review*, No. 209, October 1953.

"A Comparison of Soviet and U.S. Aircraft Production," *Air Intelligence Digest*, March 1949.

DIA, *Defensive Missile Systems (Trends) U.S.S.R.*, ST-CS-15-288-73, DIA Task No. T72-15-02, June 1973.

"Development Possibilities of Soviet Missiles," *Air Intelligence Digest*, October 1955.

DIA, DID, "A Decade of Soviet AC&W, Height Finder (HF) Radar Developments," Volume 1, No. 7–8, May–December 1963.

"DOSAAF Trains Soviet Civil Defense," *Air Intelligence Digest*, December 1953.

Ebenstadt Commission on Unification of the Armed Forces.

"Engine Development Projects in the U.S.S.R.," USAFE, *Air Intelligence Summary*, 1953.

"Estimate: By 30 June, Soviets Will Have Produced 40 Bisons," *Air Intelligence Digest*, June 1955.

"Estimate of Soviet Technical and Scientific Capabilities," *Intelligence Review*, No. 202, March 1953.

"Estimate of Soviet Technical and Scientific Capabilities," *Intelligence Review*, No. 203, April 1953.

Executive Office of the President, National Security Resources Board, *United States Civil Defense*, U.S. Government Printing Office, Washington, D.C., 1950.

Pyatdesyat Let Sovetskikh Vooruzhennykh Sil (50 Years of the Soviet Armed Forces), Voyenizdat, Moscow, 1967.

"First of the Many," *Air International*, November 1974.

Five Series of "Spotlight" Reports on Soviet Aircraft Designers, *Air Intelligence Digest*, 1950.

"Fly-By Highlights," *Air Intelligence Digest*, June 1955.

"From Cambodia to Cuba, the Ubiquitous MiG-17," *Air Enthusiast*, December 1972.

"Four Versions of Fresco," *Air Intelligence Digest*, December 1955.

"Further Data on New Soviet Medium AA Gun," Tactical and Technical Notes, *Intelligence Review*, No. 208, September 1953.

Georgia Institute of Technology Engineering Experiment Station, *Missile Catalog: A Compendium of Guided Missile and Seeker Information*, Research Project No. A-169, 1 April 1956.

"German-Designed Soviet Missiles," *Air Intelligence Digest*, December 1954.

Bibliography

Government Research Corporation, *Defense of the U.S. Against Attack by Aircraft and Missiles*, 1957.

Great Britain, Army, GHQ, AA Troops, *The Flying Bomb. The Defense of Antwerp and Brussels*, Printing and Stationery Service, 21 Army Group (British), May 1945.

"Ground Weapons Development in the U.S.S.R. in 1953," *Intelligence Review*, December 1953.

"How Far Can Bison (Type 37) Fly?," *Air Intelligence Digest*, October 1954.

"How Russia Stormed the Sonic Barrier," *Aviation Week*, 12 September 1955.

"How the Reds Build MiG-15s," *Air Intelligence Digest*, September 1952.

"How the Soviets Use Tactical Air Power," *Air Intelligence Digest*, April 1954.

"How U.S. and U.S.S.R. Aircraft Compare," *Air Intelligence Digest*, August 1953.

Hudson Institute, *Arms Control and Civil Defense*, edited by D. G. Brennan, Prepared for the U.S. Arms Control and Disarmament Agency, Harmon-On-The-Hudson, 1963.

Human Science Research, Inc., Civil Defense bibliography, January 1966, a compilation of reference relevant to the study of societal recovery from nuclear attack, McLean, Virginia, 1966.

"Impact of Nuclear Warfare," *Air Intelligence Digest*, January 1956.

"The Implications of the Soviet Air Defense Missile Program," ATC WIS, No. 6:54, 11 February 1954.

Institute for Research in Social Science, University of North Carolina, *The Soviet Aircraft Industry*, Chapel Hill, North Carolina, 1955.

International Business Machines Corporation, *The SAGE/Bomarc Air Defense Weapons System: An Illustrated Explanation of What it is and How it Works*, New York, 1959.

Johns Hopkins University, Operations Research Office, *Analysis of Military Assistance Programs*, 21 January 1958.

Johns Hopkins University, Operations Research Office, "Areas to be Defended Against Attack by Air," Stanford Research Institute, Washington, D.C., 1 December 1949.

Johns Hopkins University, Operations Research Office, "Areas to be Defended Against Attack by Air, Final Report," Stanford Research Institute, Washington, D.C., February 1950.

Johns Hopkins University, Operations Research Office, "Defense of the United States Against Attack by Aircraft and Missiles," Appendices G and H, "Weapons Studies-Part II," ORO-R17, 1955.

"Korea: Enemy Tactics," *Air Intelligence Digest*, December 1950.

"Last of the Lavochkins," *Flying Review International*, April 1968.

"Last of the Lavochkins—Part 2," *Flying Review International*, May 1968.

"Long-Range Missile Research in the U.S.S.R.," USAFE, *Intelligence Summary*, December 1953.

Los Angeles University of South California Department of Psychology, *Decision Strategies in AAW: I. Analyses of Air Threat Judgments and Weapons Assignments*, Principal Investigator: Joseph W. Rigney, Los Angeles, California, April 1966.

"Lyulka: A Soviet Pioneer," *Air Enthusiast*, November 1971.

McKinsey and Company, Inc., *Report on Non-Military Defense Organization Part I: A Framework for Improving Non-Military Defense Preparedness*, Washington, D.C., 31 December 1957.

McKinsey and Company, Inc., *Report on Non-Military Defense Organization Part II: Organization for Non-Military Defense Preparedness*, Washington, D.C., 21 March 1948.

McKinsey and Company, Inc., *Study of Civil Defense Reorganization*, Washington, D.C., 14 July 1961.

Memo(s) of MG H. R. Oldfield and others for G3, WD, Subject: AAA, cited in Greenfield, 27 September 1943.

"Malenkov: No. 1 Man in the U.S.S.R.," *Air Intelligence Digest*, April 1953.

"MiG-21: Air Superiority Soviet Style," *Air Enthusiast*, August 1971.

"MIKULIN Designed the Engine," *Air Intelligence Digest*, November 1954.

"Military Notes: U.S.S.R.," *Intelligence Review*, No. 209, October 1953.

"Missiles and Rockets," *Missiles and Rockets Eighth Annual World Missile/Space Encyclopedia*, Volume 15, July 1964.

"Missiles Around Moscow," *Air Intelligence Digest*, October 1955.

"More Punch in Soviet AA?," *Air Intelligence Digest*, March 1955.

"Moscow's AAA Defenses," *Air Intelligence Digest*, November 1951.

"The Moscow Military Supply Complex," *Intelligence Review*, No. 213, February–March 1954.

National Planning Association, Special Policy Committee on Non-Military Defense Planning, *A Program for the Non-Military Defense of the United States*, Washington, D.C., 9 May 1955.

"Newest Red Radar Resembles U.S. GCI," *Air Intelligence Digest*, July 1953.

"New Soviet AA Weapons," *Air Intelligence Digest*, October 1955.

Nike-I–Ajax Historical Monograph, AGG MA, 30 June 1959.

North America Air Defense Command, Office of Information, *The Aerospace Defense Story*, lecture, Colorado Springs, Colorado, 1962.

North America Air Defense Command, Office of Information, Direct of Command History, *Historical Summary, NORAD and CONAD*, Ent AFB, Colorado, December 1958.

North America Air Defense Command, Directorate of Command History, *Fifteen Years of Air Defense*, Ent AFB, Colorado, 1 December 1960.

North America Air Defense Command, *Operations of the Mid-Canada Line*, NORADM 55-7, 4 January 1962.

North America Air Defense Command, *Phase III: Sage/Missile Master Integration/ECM-ECCM Test (Deep River)*, Ent AFB, Colorado, 1963.

North America Air Defense Command, *Seventeen Years of Air Defense*, Historical Reference Paper No. 9, Ent AFB, Colorado, 1 June 1963.

Office of the White House, Executive Order 9562, 30 June 1945.

Office of the White House, Executive Order 10193 (15 F.R. 9031), 50 USCA APP 2153.

Office of the White House, Proclamation No. 2914, 15 F.R. 9029, 16 December 1950.

Ordinance Guided Missile and Rocket Programs Technical Report, Volume 2, 30 June 1955.

OSD Historian's Office, *History of Strategic Arms Competition Chronology U.S.*, Volume 1, October 1974, Volume 2, November 1974, Volume 3, December 1974.

OSD Historian's Office, U.S. Department of Defense, *History of Strategic Arms Competition (1945–1972) Chronology, U.S.S.R.*, Volume III, December 1974.

Bibliography

"Polikarpov: The Prolific Pioneer," *Flying Review International*, July 1968.

"Probable Guided Missile Sites Around Moscow," *Air Intelligence Brief*, No. 55-3, 30 August 1955.

Propaganda: Agitatsia, Leningrad, No. 18, quoted by Frederick C. Barghorn, *The Soviet Image of the United States*, Harcourt, Brace & Company, New York, 1950.

RAND, *Air Defense Study: Cost Methodology*, RM-1170, 2 September 1954.

RAND, "Recent Soviet Literature on Tactical Air Doctrine and Practice," S-1-71, 03164C, RP R25rm, 6336, July 1970.

RAND, *A Study of Non-Military Defense*, Report No. R-322, Santa Monica, California, 1958.

"Red AD Communications," *Air Intelligence Digest*, Volume 10:18–22, February 1957.

"Reds Latest AA Gun," *Air Intelligence Digest*, September 1954.

"Reds 7000-Pound-Threat Engine," *Air Intelligence Digest*, October 1954.

"Red War Ministry Journal Boosts Fighter Aviation," a condensation from "Military Thought" article, "Fighter Aviation in Modern War" by COL A. Volkov, *Air Intelligence Digest*, February 1953.

"Report on AAA Expansion," *The Coast Artillery Journal*, Volume 91, September–October 1948.

Research and Development Board, *Consolidated Technical Estimate*, 12 October 1950.

Rockefeller Brothers Fund, *International Security—The Military Aspect*, Special Studies Panel II Report, 1958.

Royal Institute of International Affairs, *Survey of International Affairs 1939–46*, Part III, "America, Britain, and Russia, 1941–46."

"Security Organs of the U.S.S.R. in Peacetime," *Intelligence Review*, No. 207, August 1953.

"Six Communist Fire Control Radars," *Air Intelligence Digest*, January 1954.

"Soviet AA Gunners' Training," *Air Intelligence Digest*, August 1955.

"Soviet Aerodynamics Research," *Air Intelligence Digest*, November 1955.

"Soviet Aircraft Armament," *Air Intelligence Digest*, November 1948.

"Soviet Air Defenses: How Good Are They?," *Air Intelligence Digest*, July 1954.

"Soviet Air Defenses: Role of AA Artillery," *Air Intelligence Digest*, July 1954.

"The Soviet Air Defense System: How Effective is it?," *Air Intelligence Digest*, March 1956.

"The Soviet Air Defense System: How it is Equipped," *Air Intelligence Digest*, March 1956.

"The Soviet Air Defense System: How it Operates," *Air Intelligence Digest*, March 1956.

"Soviets Air Order of Battle Enters New Stage," *Air Intelligence Digest*, October 1954.

"Soviet Air R&D," *Air Intelligence Digest*, September 1955.

"Soviet Air Shows," *Air Intelligence Digest*, October 1949.

"Soviet Air Tactics," *Air Intelligence Digest*, December 1949.

"Soviet Air Warning and Control of Interruption," Great Britain *Military Intelligence Report*, No. 83, 10 December 1952.

"Soviet Aviation Air Show: 1953," *Air Intelligence Digest*, November 1953.

"Soviet's 'Big Five' Aircraft Designers," *Air Intelligence Digest*, February 1954.

"Soviet Civil Defense: Policies and Priorities," Intelligence Memorandum, April 1967.

"Soviets Compress Aircraft Production Lead Times," an article on the series by MAJ George J. Keegan on "The Foundations of Red Air Power," *Air Intelligence Digest*, November 1955.

"The Soviet Concept of Active Air Defense," USAFE, *Intelligence Summary*, January 1954.

"The Soviets Copied the Derwent V Jet Engine," *Air Intelligence Digest*, March 1954.

"Soviet Electronic Countermeasures," *Air Intelligence Digest*, March 1955.

"Soviet Exploitation of Foreign Equipment," *Air Intelligence Digest*, November 1951.

"Soviet Guided Missiles Program," Joint British-U.S. Study of U.S.S.R.'s Guided Missile Program: A Survey Covering the Period from May 1945 to the Present, *Air Intelligence Digest*, July 1949.

"Soviet High-Thrust Engine?," *Air Intelligence Digest*, January 1954.

"Soviets Lead the World in Numbers of Aeronautical Engineers Trained," based on research by Mr. Nicholas DeWitt of Russian Research Center, Harvard University, *Air Intelligence Digest*, September 1955.

"Soviets Modernize Air Defenses," *Air Intelligence Digest*, August 1955.

"Soviets Modernize Naval Air Arm," *Air Intelligence Digest*, April 1955.

"Soviet Research and Development Centers," *Air Intelligence Digest*, May 1949.

"Soviet Scientific Developments," *Intelligence Review*, December 1953.

"Soviet Tactical Aviation-IV," *Air Intelligence Digest*, October 1955.

"Soviet Telecommunications," *Intelligence Review*, No. 83, 18 September 1947.

"Soviet Union Ranks in Aircraft Production Capacity," *Air Intelligence Digest*, October 1955.

Stanford Research Institute, *An Analysis of the U.S.-Soviet Strategic Interaction Process*, March 1967.

Stanford Research Institute, *Soviet Strategies, Objectives and Force Postures in Response to U.S. BMD, 1968–80*, March 1969.

Stockholm International Peace Research Institute, 1972.

"Three Soviet Air Force Academies," *Air Intelligence Digest*, June 1950.

"The Transient Glory of SAF Brass," *Air Intelligence Digest*, 1952.

"The Trend in Soviet AA Weapons," PACCOM-WID, *Air Intelligence Summary*, Volume 2–54, 8 January 1954.

"The 24th Tactical Air Army," *Air Intelligence Digest*, August 1953.

"Unification of the Soviet Military High Command," *Intelligence Review*, No. 213, February–March 1954.

"Unification Soviet Style: Military Power Held by Defense Ministry," *Air Intelligence Digest*, April 1953.

USAF Statistical Digest, 1947–1954.

"The Use of Radar in Soviet Antiaircraft Defense," Volume 7, No. 1, *Air Ministry Secret Intelligence Summary*, 1950.

U.S. Air Force, *Background Intelligence Data for Posture Statement on Strategic Initiatives*, AF/INAF, 3 January 1975.

Bibliography

U.S. Air Force, *Program and Manpower: Peacetime Planning Factors*, AFL 15-10, 2 February 1953.

U.S. Air Force, *Research and Development in the United States Air Force*, Report of a Special Committee of the Scientific Advisory Board to Chief of Staff, USAF, 21 September 1949.

U.S. Air Force, Air Defense Command, Historical Division, *Air Defense in Theory and Practice 1918–1945*, Denis Volan, Colorado Springs, Colorado, 1964.

U.S. Air Force, Air Defense Command, Directorate of Historical Services, *The Air Defense of Atomic Energy Installations, March 1946–December 1952*, Colorado Springs, Colorado, 5 August 1953.

U.S. Air Force, Air Defense Command, *The Air Defense of the U.S.: A Study of the ADC and its Predecessors Through June 1951*, Ent AFB, Colorado Springs, Colorado, 1952.

U.S. Air Force, Air Defense Command, *Air Defense Tactics-Techniques: A Stud of Air Defense Means and SOPs for Units Employed in Defense*, Ent AFB, Colorado, 1 July 1948.

U.S. Air Force, Air Defense Command, Historical Division, Office of Information, *A Chronology of Air Defense 1914–1961*, Historical Study No. 19, Ent AFB, Colorado.

U.S. Air Force, Air Defense Command, Historical Division, *The Development of Continental Air Defense to 1 September 1954*, USAF Historical Study No. 126, Maxwell AFB, Alabama.

U.S. Air Force, Air Defense Command, *Mutual Agreement for the Air Defense of the United States*, Ent AFB, Colorado, 15 July 1952.

U.S. Air Force, Air Defense Command, *Organization and Responsibility for Air Defense, March 1946–September 1955*, CONAD, ADC Historical Study No. 9.

U.S. Air Force, Air Defense Command, *Report of Conference: Improved Air Defense Systems Program*, 17–21 August 1953.

U.S. Air Force, Air Defense Command, Directorate of Historical Services, *Short History. A Decade of Continental Air Defense 1946–1956*.

U.S. Air Force, Air Defense Command, Historical Division, *United States Air Force Operations in the Korean Conflict 25 June–1 November 1950*, Historical Study No. 71, Maxwell AFB, Alabama, July 1952.

U.S. Air Force, Air Defense Command, Historical Division, *United States Air Force Operations in the Korean Conflict, 1 November 1950–30 June 1952*, Historical Study No. 72, Maxwell AFB, Alabama, 1953.

U.S. Air Force, Air Defense Command, Historical Division, *United States Air Force Operations in the Korean Conflict, 1 July 1952–27 July 1953*, Historical Study No. 73, Maxwell AFB, Alabama, 1953.

U.S. Air Force Air University Evaluation Staff, *Organization of the Air Defense Command*, Project No. AUIL-51-ES (AWC 5131), Maxwell AFB, Alabama, 10 December 1951.

U.S. Air Force Air University, *Fundamentals of Aerospace Weapons Systems*, U.S. Government Printing Office, Washington, D.C., May 1961.

U.S. Air Force Air University Chronology of World War II, *Development of Night Air Operations 1941–1952*, Historical Study No. 92, Maxwell AFB, Alabama.

U.S. Air Force Air University Libraries, *Air Defense, Air Tactics and Air Combat Tactics*, Maxwell AFB, Alabama, 10 September 1953.

U.S. Air Force Air University Libraries, *Air Defense Exercises of U.S. on the North American Continent*, Maxwell AFB, Alabama, 22 April 1957.

U.S. Air Force Air University Libraries, *Air Defense. The Role of the Air Force*, Maxwell AFB, Alabama, 8 March 1956.

U.S. Air Force Air University Libraries, *Air Base Defense*, Maxwell AFB, Alabama.

U.S. Air Force, Assistant Chief of Staff, Studies and Analysis, *Alternative Strategic Strategies*, prepared by MG Glenn A. Kent, Washington, D.C., 14 July 1969.

U.S. Adjutant General's Office, *Command and Staff Structure for an Arm Force in Air Defense of the U.S.*, Washington, D.C., 11 July 1950.

U.S. Army, *Field Manual 44-1: U.S. Army Air Defense Employment*, 1964.

U.S. Army Air Defense Command, "Chronology of Army Ballistic Missile Defense System Development and Deployment," Ent AFB, Colorado, Department of the Army, U.S. Army Air Defense Command, 15 May 1970.

U.S. Army, Air Defense Command, *Historical Data Book, Part I*, September 1969.

U.S. Army, Air Defense Command, *Report of Major Activities*.

U.S. Army Air Defense Panel, *Report of Army Air Defense Panel, 15 January 1949, to C of S, USA, Through Chief, Arm Field Forces*, Fort Monroe, Virginia, 1949.

U.S. Army Air Defense School, *Air Defense: An Historical Analysis*, Department of the Army, HQ, USAADS, Fort Bliss, Texas, June 1965.

U.S. Army Air Defense School, *Commanders Air Defense Information Book*, Fort Bliss, Texas.

U.S. Army Antiaircraft Command, *Antiaircraft Artillery in the Air Defense of the United States*, Ent AFB, Colorado, 12 December 1951.

U.S. Army, Army Ground Forces, Army Air Defense Panel, *Report of Army Air Defense Panel*, Volume III, 28 January 1949.

U.S. Army, The Artillery School, Antiaircraft Artillery and Guided Missiles Branch, Research and Analysis Department, *AAA Operational Difficulties World War II*, Technical Report No. 11, 15 June 1949.

U.S. Army Chief of Ordnance, "Letter to Bell Telephone Laboratories," 31 January 1945.

U.S. Army, Forces, Far East, Military Intelligence, *Homeland Defense Operations Record*, Japanese Monograph No. 157 (includes 157, 158, 159).

U.S. Army, Forces Far East, and Eighth U.S. Army (Rear), *Homeland Operations Record*, Japanese Monograph No. 17 (includes 17–20).

U.S. Army Ground Forces, Commanding General, "Letter to Chief of Staff, U.S. Army," 26 August 1946.

U.S. Army Safeguard System Command, "Chronology of the Development of Ballistic Missile Defense (1955 to the Present)," Department of the Army, U.S. Army Safeguard System Command, Huntsville, Alabama, 14 July 1970.

U.S. Army War College, *Air Defense Instruction at CSAWC and the Air WC*, a comparison prepared by COL P. H. Eubank, Carlisle Barracks, Pennsylvania, 24 February 1958.

U.S. Commission on Intergovernmental Relations, *A Staff Report on Civil Defense and Urban Vulnerability*, U.S. Government Printing Office, Washington, D.C., 1955.

U.S. Congress Joint Committee on Atomic Energy, *Civil Defense Against Atomic Attack*, Hearing, 81st Congress, 2nd Session, U.S. Government Printing Office, Washington, D.C., 1950.

U.S. Congress, *Investigation of the B-36 Bomber Program*, 81st Congress, 1st Session, 1949.

Bibliography

U.S. Congress, *National Aviation Policy*, Reprint of the Congressional Aviation Policy Board, 0th Congress, 2nd Session, Washington, D.C., 1948.

U.S. Congress, *The National Defense Program . . . Unification and Strategy*, 81st Congress, 1st Session, 1949.

U.S. Continental Air Defense Command, *The Air Defense of North America*, Ent AFB, Colorado, 7 February 1955.

U.S. Defense Civil Preparedness Agency, *Introduction to Civil Preparedness*, U.S. Government Printing Office, Washington, D.C., 1972.

U.S. Department of the Army, Air Defense Ad Hoc Committee, *CONUS Integrated Air and Missile Defense 1965–1970: A Study*, Washington, D.C., October 1959.

U.S. Department of the Army Assistant Chief of Staff, Intelligence, *Soviet Threat Relating to U.S. Army Air Defense Systems (Except Nike-I-X)-l964–1976*, Washington, D.C., 2 July 1964.

U.S. Department of the Army, DA Pamphlet 70-10, "Chronological History of Army Activities in the Missile/Satellite Field, 1943–1958," Department of the Army, Washington, D.C., 17 September 1958.

U.S. Department of the Army, *Civil Defense: 1960–1967, A Bibliographic Survey*, U.S. Government Printing Office, Washington, D.C., 1967.

U.S. Department of the Army General Staff, G-3, *Project Lineup*, Washington, D.C., 1955.

U.S. Department of the Army, *Nike-I Data Book*, January 1957.

U.S. Department of Defense, *Adjustment of Army/Air Force "Differences" in Air Defense*, Memo for the Chairman, JCS, Washington, D.C., 2 November 1956.

U.S. Department of Defense, *CONUS AD Program*, Memo for JCS, 19 June 1959.

U.S. Department of Defense, Office of Civil Defense, *Harbor Project*, Washington, D.C., 1963.

U.S. Department of Defense, Office of the General Council, A Report to the Secretary of Defense on the Organizational Questions Involved if Major Civil Defense Functions are Assigned to the Department of Defense, Washington, D.C., 10 June 1961.

U.S. Department of Defense, *Research Development Program*, November 1950.

U.S. Executive Office of the President, Office of Civil and Defense Mobilization, *Legislative History. Volume IV. Amendments to the Federal Civil Defense Act of 195*, Washington, D.C., 1991.

U.S. Federal Civil Defense Administration, *Annual Report*, 1951–1958.

U.S. Forces, European Theater of Operations, General Board, Antiaircraft Artillery Section, *Tactical Employment of Antiaircraft Units, Including Defense Against Pilotless Aircraft (V-1)*, Study No. 38, 1945.

U.S. General Accounting Office, "Activities and Status of Civil Defense in the U.S.," Report to the Congress on the Department of the Army by the Comptroller General of the U.S., Washington, D.C., 1971.

U.S. House of Representatives, Committee on Armed Services, *Amending the Federal Civil Defense Act of 1950, As Amended*, House Report No. 694 (to accompany H.R. 7576), 85th Congress, 1st Session, Washington, D.C., 5 July 1957.

U.S. House of Representatives, Committee on Armed Services, *Civil Defense Fallout Shelter Program*, Hearings before Subcommittee #3, 88th Congress, 1st Session pursuant to H.R. 3516, U.S. Government Printing Office, Washington, D.C., 1963.

U.S. House of Representatives, Committee on Armed Forces, *Civil Defense in Western Europe and the Soviet Union, Fifth Report*, 86th Congress, 1st Session, U.S. Government Printing Office, Washington, D.C., 1959.

U.S. House of Representatives, Committee of Conference, *Federal Civil Defense Act of 1950*, House Report No. 3235, 81st Congress, 2nd Session, Washington, D.C., 1951.

U.S. House of Representatives, Committee on Science and Astronautics, "A Chronology of Missile and Astronautic Events," 87th Congress, 1st Session, U.S. Government Printing Office, Washington, D.C., 1961.

U.S. House of Representatives, Hearing Before the Subcommittee of the Committee on Appropriations, 80th Congress, 1948–1949.

U.S. House of Representatives, Hearing on Research and Development, Government Operations Committee, 85th Congress, 2nd Session, 1958.

U.S. House of Representatives, Subcommittee on Military Operations of the Committee on Government Operations, *Analysis of Civil Defense Reorganization*, Reorganization Plan No. 1 of 1958, House Report No. 1874, 85th Congress, 2nd Session, Washington, D.C., 12 June 1958.

U.S. House of Representatives, Subcommittee on Military Operations of the Committee on Government Operations, *Atomic Shelter Programs*, House Report No. 2554, 85th Congress, 2nd Session, Washington, D.C., 12 August 1958.

U.S. House of Representatives, Subcommittee on Military Operations of the Committee on Government Operations, *Civil Defense for National Survival*, House Report No. 2946, 84th Congress, 2nd Session, Washington, D.C., 27 July 1956.

U.S. House of Representatives, Subcommittee on Military Operations of the Committee on Government Operations, *Hearings Civil Defense for National Survival*, 84th Congress, 2nd Session, Washington, D.C., 1956.

U.S. House of Representatives, Subcommittee on Military Operations of the Committee on Government Operations, *Status of Civil Defense Legislation*, House Report No. 829, 85th Congress, 1st Session, Washington, D.C., 22 July 1957.

U.S. House of Representatives, *Organization and Administration of the Military R&D Programs*, Hearings before a Subcommittee of Government Operations, 83rd Congress, 8–24 June 1954.

U.S. House of Representatives, *Organization and Management of Missile Programs*, Eleventh Report by the Committee on Government Operations, 86th Congress, 2 September 1959.

U.S. House of Representatives, *U.S. Defense Policies Since World War II*, Document No. 100, 85th Congress, 1st Session, 1957.

U.S. Joint Air Defense Board, *Doctrines and Procedures for Joint Air Defense: A Study*, Ent AFB, Colorado, 12 May 1954.

U.S. Joint Chiefs of Staff, Guided Missile Committee, *Guided Missile Syllabus*, Washington, D.C., 1946.

U.S. Joint Chiefs of Staff, Guided Missile Committee, Subcommittee No. 4, *Programs and Policies of the Services with Regard to Surface-to-Air Guided Missiles*, 14 August 1945.

U.S. Joint Chiefs of Staff, *Terms of Reference for CINCONAD*, Washington, D.C., 4 September 1956.

U.S. National Military Establishment, Office of the Secretary of Defense, *A Study of Civil Defense*, War Department, Civil Defense Board, "Bull Report," Washington, D.C., 1948.

U.S. National Military Establishment Office of Civil Defense Planning, *Civil Defense for National Security*, "Hopley Report," Washington, D.C., 1948.

Bibliography

U.S. National Security Resources Board, *United States Civil Defense*, NSRB Document 128, Washington, D.C., 1950.

U.S. Navy Secretary of the Navy Court of Inquiry, *Navy Court of Inquiry (in re: Pearl Harbor)*.

U.S. Office of Civil and Defense Mobilization, *Basic Report of Civil Defense and Defense Mobilization: Roles, Organization, and Programs*, For President John F. Kennedy, by Frank B. Ellis, Washington, D.C., February 1961.

U.S. Office of Civil and Defense Mobilization, *Federal Emergency Plan C: Working Draft*, Washington, D.C., 15 June 1961.

U.S. Office of Civil Defense Planning, *Civil Defense for National Security*, "Hopley Report," U.S. Government Printing Office, Washington, D.C., 1948.

U.S. Office of Defense Mobilization, *Report of the Gaither Committee*, The White House, 1957.

U.S. Office of Emergency Planning, *The National Plan for Emergency Preparedness*, Washington, D.C., 1963.

U.S. Office of Emergency Planning, *Report on the Evaluation of Exercise Spade Fork*, Washington, D.C., 21 December 1962.

U.S. President's Air Policy Commission, *Survival in the Air Age*, Summary of the Report of the President's Air Policy Commission, Finletter, Baker, Hoyt, et al., U.S. Government Printing Office, Washington, D.C., 1948.

U.S. President (Truman), *Unification of the Armed Forces of the United States*, Message from the President of the United States, H.D. 392, 79th Congress, 1st Session, U.S. Government Printing Office, Washington, D.C., 19 December 1945.

U.S. Senate Committee on Armed Services, *Civil Defense Program*, Hearing before the Civil Defense Task Force of the Preparedness Committee, 82nd Congress, 1st Session, U.S. Government Printing Office, Washington, D.C., 5 September 1951.

U.S. Senate Committee on Armed Services, *Hearings on the Federal Civil Defense Act of 1950*, 81st Congress, 2nd Session, Washington, D.C., 1950.

U.S. Senate Committee on Armed Services, "Study of Airpower: Hearings before the Subcommittee on the Air Force of the Committee on Armed Services," testimony of GEN Earle E. Partridge, CINCONAD, 84th Congress, Senate, 2nd Session, 16 April–1 June 1956.

U.S. Congressional Senate Subcommittee or Civil Defense of the Committee on Armed Services, Hearings on Operations and Policies of the Civil Defense Program, 84th Congress, 1st Session, Washington, D.C., 1955.

U.S. Senate, Subcommittee on Civil Defense of the Committee on Armed Services, *Interim Report on Civil Defense*, 84th Congress, 1st Session, Washington, D.C., 1955.

U.S. Strategic Bombing Survey, *The Effects of Atomic Bombs on Hiroshima and Nagasaki*, Washington, D.C., 1946.

U.S. Strategic Bombing Survey Chairman's Office, *Overall Report (European War)*, U.S. Government Printing Office, Washington, D.C., 30 September 1945.

U.S. Strategic Bombing Survey Military Analysis Division, *The Strategic Air Operations of Very Heavy Bombardment in the War Against Japan (XX Air Force)*, U.S. Government Printing Office, Washington, D.C., 1 September 1946.

U.S. War Department, Board of Officers, "Reorganization of the War Department and Related Matters," LG Alexander M. Patch, President, 18 October 1945.

U.S. War Department, Assistant Chief of Staff, G-2, German Military Document Series, RS-259, "Aviation and PVO," Peoples' Commissariat of Defense, 1938.

U.S. War Department, Assistant Chief of Staff, G-2, German Military Document Series, RS-158, "Communications in the Local Air Defense System," 1941.

U.S. War Department, Assistant Chief of Staff, G-2, German Military Document Series, RS-7, "Manual of the Soldier of VNOS," 1959.

U.S. War Department, Chief of Staff, G-2, German Military Document Series, RS-735, "Organization and Tactics of Local Air Defense," Directorate of Air Defense of the Red Army, 1940.

U.S. War Department, Assistant Chief of Staff, G-2, German Military Document Series, RS-37, "Temporary Instructions for the Air Defense of Troops," 1936.

U.S. War Department, "Circular No. 138," 14 May 1946.

U.S. War Department General Staff Office of the Provost Marshal General, *Defense Against Enemy Actions Directed at Civilians*, Study 3-B-1, Washington, D.C., 1946.

U.S. War Department, Memorandum(s) for CGs AGF, AAF, "Integration of AAA with AAF," 8 February 1943.

U.S. War Department, Office of the Provost Marshal General, "Defense Against Enemy Action Directed at Civilians," 30 April 1946.

U.S. War Department, OPD Memo for G-3, "Integration of AAA with AAF," 23 February 1943.

U.S. War Department Secretary of War, *Report of Pearl Harbor Board*, 1945.

"U.S.S.R. Air Defense System," *Air Intelligence Digest*, February 1950.

"U.S.S.R. Jet Development," *Air Intelligence Digest*, February 1949.

"What We Learned," *Air Intelligence Digest*, September–October 1953.

"Why Did Soviets Show Their New Bombers?," *Air Intelligence Digest*, November 1954.

WSEG, *The Continental Air Defense System*.

"Yakovlev's Lightweight—The YAK-23," *Air Enthusiast*, May 1973.

Author and Title

Adams, Benson D. *Ballistic Missile Defense*, American Elsevier Publishing Company, New York, 1971.

Ahnstrom, D. N. *The Complete Book of Jets and Rockets*, World Publishing Company, New York, 1957.

Akimov, N., et al. *Civil Defense*, National Technical Information Service, U.S. Department of Commerce, Springfield, Virginia, 1971. (Unclassified)

Alexander, Arthur. *Conversations on Soviet Aviation*, RAND Internal Note 21989, 22 February 1972.

Alexander, Arthur and Nelson, J. R. *Measuring Technical Change: Aircraft Turbine Engines*, RAND R-1017-ARPA/PR, June 1972.

Alexander, Arthur. *R&D in Soviet Aviation*, RAND R-589-PR, November 1970.

Alexander, Arthur. *Trip Report: 1973 Paris Air Show*, RAND Internal Note 22550-ARPA, July 1973.

Bibliography

Anderson, Dillon. "Selected Materials, Organizing for National Security," U.S. Senate, Committee on Government Operations, Subcommittee on National Policy Machinery, U.S. Government Printing Office, Washington, D.C., 1960.

Appleman, Roy E. "Okinawa, The Last Battle," U.S. Army in World War II: The War in the Pacific, Washington, D.C., Department of the Army, 1948.

Arnold, H. H. *Global Mission*, Harper & Row, New York, 1949.

Ashkerov, COL V. "Development of Air Defense Force Tactics During the Great Patriotic War," *PVO Herald*, (ACS/I Translation), April 1974.

Ashkerov, V. P., Zabelok, B. G., Kalugin, Ye. I., and Sherchenko, L. P. *Voyska Protivovozdushno Oboron Strany* (National Air Defense Forces), Moscow, 1960.

Barghoorn, Frederick C. *The Soviet Image of the United States*, Harcourt, Brace & Company, New York, 1950.

Barlow, E. J. *Active Air Defense of the U.S. 1954–1960*, RAND R-250, Santa Monica, California, 1 December 1953.

Barlow, E. J. *Contiguous Radar Coverage in the U.S. Air Defense Systems 1953–1960*, RAND RM-1077, Santa Monica, California, 1 May 1953.

Barnard, LTC Roy S. *The History of ARADCOM*, Volume 1, *The Gun Era 1950–1955*, HQ ARADCOM Historical Project, ARAD5M-1.

Batitskiy, P. "Development of the Tactics and Operational Art of the Country's Air Defense (PVO) Troops," *Voyennaya Mysl'* (Military Thought), No. 10, October 1967, (translated by Foreign Broadcast Information Service, 25 October 1968), FPD 0146/68. (Confidential/NOFORN)

Batitskiy, P. "The Soviet Armed Forces in the Defense of the Gains of the October Revolution—The National Air Defense Troops," *Voyenno-Istoricheskiy Zhurnal* (Military History Journal), No. 8, Moscow, August 1967.

Batitskiy, P. *Voyska Protivovozdushno Oboron Strany* (National Air Defense Forces), Voyenizdat, Moscow, 1968.

Batitskiy, P. "Worldwide Historical Victory," *Vestnik Protivovozdushnoy Oborony* (Air Defense Herald), No. 5, Moscow, 1970.

Baumbach, Werner. *The Life and Death of the Luftwaffe*, Coward-McCann, Inc., New York, 1960.

Bordeaux, T. A., et al. *Comparison of U.S. and U.S.S.R. Land-Based Air Defense Systems*, RDA-TR-5500-003, R&D Associates, May 1974.

Bottome, Edgar M. *The Missile Gap: A Study of the Formulation of Military and Political Policy*, Fairleigh Dickinson University Press, Rutherford, Pennsylvania, 1971.

Bridgman, Leonard, ed. *Jane's All the World's Aircraft, 1951–52*, McGraw-Hill Book, Company, Inc., New York, 1951.

Brodie, Bernard. *Strategy in the Missile Age*, RAND, Princeton University Press, Princeton, New Jersey, 1959.

Brown, Eunice H., et al. *Development and Testing of Rockets and Missiles at White Sands Proving Grounds*, Historical Information Branch, Information Office, U.S. Army, White Sands Missile Range, New Mexico, 1 October 1959.

Broybrook, Roy H. "Sukhoi's Fighters . . . The Fishpot and Fitter," *Flying Review International*, December 1963.

Bush, Vannevar. *Modern Arms and Free Men*, Simon & Schuster, 1949.

Byland, W. R. *History of Nike-I Project*, New York Ordnance District, 24 April 1954.

Chayes, Abraham and Weisner, Jerome B., eds. *ABM: An Evaluation of the Decision to Deploy an Antiballistic Missile System*, Harper & Row, New York, 1969.

Check, Gilbert John. *Defense of the Continental United States*, Carlisle Barracks, Pennsylvania, 11 March 1954.

Chesalov, A. "General Designer," *Aviatsiya i Kosmonavtika* (Aviation and Cosmonautics), No. 9, 1963.

Chidlaw, Benjamin Wiley. *Air Defense*, Carlisle Barracks, Pennsylvania, 25 March 1953.

Chidlaw, GEN B. W. *Air Defense*, Speech to NWC and ICAF, Fort McNair, Washington, D.C., 8 February 1954.

Chipman, William K. *Nonmilitary Defense for the United States—Strategic, Operational, Legal, and Constitutional Aspects*, National Security Studies Group, University of Wisconsin, Madison, Wisconsin, 1961.

Churchill, Winston. *Triumph and Tragedy*, Houghton Mifflin, Boston, Massachusetts, 1953.

Cibula, LTC Alvin M. *Antiaircraft Command and Center Study*, No. 26, Historical Section—Army Ground Forces, 1946.

Cobb, MAJ T. W. "Air Defense in the Soviet Union," *Air Defense Trends*, U.S. Army Air Defense School, Fort Bliss, Texas, June 1973.

Cole, J. P. and German, F. C. *A Geography of the U.S.S.R., The Background to Planned Economy*, 2nd edition, Butterworths, London, 1970.

Collier, Basil. *The Battle of Britain*, The MacMillan Company, New York, 1962.

Craven, Wesley F. and Cate, James L., eds. *The Army Air Force in WWII, The Pacific: Matterhorn to Nagasaki*, June 19 to August 1945, University of Chicago Press, Chicago, Illinois, 1953.

DeSeversky, Alexander P. *Air Power: Key to Survival*, Simon & Schuster, New York, 1950.

Dick, William White. *U.S. Army Air Defense Command*, USAWC Lectures 1962/63, Carlisle Barracks, Pennsylvania, 21 March 1963.

Digby, James F. *A Broader View of Some Air Defense Decisions: Notes for a Discussion*, RAND RM-3407 PR, Santa Monica, California, December 1962.

Dzhordzhadze, MG A. I. and Shesterin, COL F. "The Role of Historical Experience in Perfecting Antiaircraft Defense," *PVO Herald*, (ACS/I Translation), February 1972.

Dzhordzhadze, MG A. I. and Shesterin, COL F. "The Lessons of History and Improving Air Defense," *PVO Herald*, (ACS/I Translation), January 1972.

Egorov, P. T. *Civil Defense*, edited by Joanne S. Gailar, et al., U.S. Department of Commerce Technical Information Service, Springfield, Virginia, 1972.

Emme, Eugene M. *The Impact of Air Power*, D. Van Nostrand Company, Inc., Princeton, New Jersey, 1959.

Englebardt, Stanley L. *Strategic Defenses*, Crowell, New York, 1966.

Erickson, John. *The Soviet High Command, 1918–1941*, MacMillan and Company, Ltd., London, St. Martin's Press, New York, 1962.

Field, James A., Jr. *History of United States Naval Operations, Korea*, U.S. Government Printing Office, Washington, D.C., 1962.

Finletter, Thomas K. *Foreign Policy: The Next Phase*, Harper Brothers, New York, 1958.

Futrell, Robert Frank. *Ideas, Concepts, Doctrine: A History of Basic Thinking in the United States Air Force 1907–1964*, Volume 1, Aerospace Studies Institute, Air University, June 1971.

Futrell, Robert Frank. *The United States Air Force in Korea 1950–1953*, Duell, Sloan and Pearce, New York, 1961.

Gallagher, Matthew P. and Spielman, Karl F., Jr. *Soviet Decision-Making for Defense: A Critique of U.S. Perspectives on the Arms Race*, Praeger, New York, 1972.

Gallai, Mark L. *Ispytano v Nebe—Cherez Nevidnu u Barr'yeru* (Tested in the Sky—Through Unseen Barriers), Molodaya Grardiya, Moscow, 1965.

Garrett, Ralph L. *Civil Defense and the Public: An Overview of Public Attitude Studies*, (revised), Office of Civil Defense, Office of Secretary of the Army, Washington, D.C., 1971.

Garthoff, Raymond L. *Soviet Military Doctrine*, RAND, The Free Press, Glencoe, Illinois, 1953.

Garthoff, Raymond L. *Soviet Strategy in the Nuclear Age*, (revised edition), Praeger, New York, 1958.

Gatland, Kenneth W. *Development of the Guided Missile*, ILIFFE and Sons, Ltd., London, 1954.

Geiger, MAJ George J. "Roundup on Russian Jet Fighters," *Air Progress*, Fall 1960.

Gilpin, Robert. *American Scientists and Nuclear Weapon Policy,* Princeton, New Jersey, 1965.

Ginsburgh, Robert N. *U.S. Military Strategy in the Sixties*, W. W. Norton & Company, Inc., New York, 1965.

Goen, Richard L. *Analysis of National Entity Survival*, Stanford Research Institute, Menlo Park, California, 1967.

Goldberg, A. *A History of the U.S. Air Force 1907–1957*, D. Van Nostrand Company, Princeton, New Jersey, 1957.

Goure, Leon. *The Role of Civil Defense in Soviet Strategy*, Prepared for U.S. Air Force Project RAND, RAND 3703, Santa Monica, California, 1963.

Goure, Leon. *The Soviet Civil Defense Program*, RAND RM-2564, 1 August 1960.

Goure, Leon. *The Soviet Civil Defense Program: A Trip Report*, RAND RM-2684, 5 January 1961.

Goure, Leon. *Soviet Emergency Planning*, RAND P-4042, Santa Monica, California, 1969.

Golonne, N. N. *Views on Air Defense*, Gale and Polden, Ltd., New Jersey, Aldershot, England.

Grant, C. L. *The Development of Continental Air Defense to 1 September 1954*, SAF Historical Study No. 126, Maxwell AFB, Alabama, 1954.

Green, Constance McLaughlin, Thomson, Harry C., and Roots, Peter C. *The Ordnance Department: Planning Munitions for War. U.S. Arm in World War II: The Technical Services*, Office of the Chief of Military History, U.S. Department of the Army, Washington, D.C., 1955.

Green, William. "Billion Dollar Bomber, Parts I–III," *Air Enthusiast*, Serial July, August, September, October, 1971.

Green, William. "Mikoyan Quarter Century," *Flying Review International*, November 1965.

Green, William. "Sukhoi . . . Designer from the Shadows," *Flying Review International*, February 1966.

Greenfield, Kent R., Palmer, Robert R., and Wiley, Bell I. "The Army Ground Forces: The Organization of Ground Combat Troops," Historical Division, Department of the Army, Washington, D.C., 1947.

Gurevich, Mikhail I. "I Designed the MiG-15," *Aero Digest*, July 1951.

Hackett, Robert. *Strategic Defensive Forces*, USAWC Lectures, Carlisle Barracks, Pennsylvania, 16 March 1967.

Hammond, Paul Y. *The Cold War Years*, American Foreign Policy Since 1945, Harcourt, Brace & World, New York, 1969.

Hammond, Paul Y. *Organizing for Defense: The American Military Establishment in the Twentieth Century*, Princeton University Press, Princeton, New Jersey, 1961.

Harman, Alvin J. *Analysis of Aircraft Development*, RAND P-4820, March 1973.

Head, Richard G. and Rokke, Ervin J, eds. *American Defense Policy*, Third Edition, The Johns Hopkins University Press, Baltimore, Maryland, 1973.

Nowarra, Heinz J. and Duval, G. R. *Russian Civil and Military Aircraft: 1884–1969*, Harleyford, London, 1970.

Helfers, M. D. *The Employment of V-Weapons by the Germans During World War II*, Office of the Chief of Military History, U.S. Department of the Army, Washington, D.C., 31 May 1954.

Hesse, Herbert R. and Morgenthaler, George W. "Remarks on the Optimal Commitment of Defensive Interceptors and Surface to Air Missiles," Institute for Air Weapons Research, Chicago University, Chicago, Illinois, Report M576, 24 January 1958.

Holst, John J. and Schneider, William, Jr., eds. *Why ABM? Policy Issues in the Missile Defense Controversy*, Hudson Institute, Perqamon Press, New York, 1969.

Hopley, Russell James. *Civil Defense for National Security*, U.S. Industrial College of the Armed Forces, Washington, D.C., L49-70, 14 January 1949.

Huntington, Samuel P. *The Common Defense: Strategic Programs in National Politics*, Columbia University Press, New York, 1961.

Huzar, Elias. *The Purse and the Sword*, Cornell University Press, 1950.

Izmaylov, A. A. *Aviation and Astronautics in the U.S.S.R.* (Aviatsiya i Kosmonavtika SSSR), (N.A.S.A. Technical Translation F-13,142), Military Press, Moscow, 1965.

Jackson, Robert. *The Red Falcons: The Soviet Air Force in Action, 1919–1969*, Clifton Books, Brighton, England, 1970.

Jacobson, James W. *Civil Defense, 1962*, USAWC Lectures 1961/62, Carlisle Barracks, Pennsylvania, 16 March 1962.

Johnson, Ellis A. "Defense of the North American Continent," Speech at 5th Annual Symposium of the Defense Research Board of Canada at Ottawa, 30 November 1953.

Johnson, Robert Wells. *The North American Air Defense Dilemma—Is There a Solution?*, USAWC Student Thesis 60/01, Carlisle Barracks, Pennsylvania, 10 February 1961.

Jones, Robert H. *The Roads to Russia*, University of Oklahoma Press, Norman, Oklahoma, 1969.

Keller, K. T. "Letter to the SECDEF," 10 January 1951.

Kelley, Robert L. *Army Antiaircraft in Air Defense 1946–1954*, Historical Study No. 4, Directorate of Historical Services, HQ ADC, Colorado Springs, Colorado, 30 June 1954.

Kennan, George F. *American Diplomacy, 1900–1950*, University of Chicago Press, Chicago, Illinois, 1951.

Khrushchev, Nikita S. *Khrushchev Remembers: The Last Testament* (attributed—Strobe Talbott, translator and editor), Little, Brown, New York, 1974.

Bibliography

Kilmarx, Robert A. *A History of Soviet Air Power*, Praeger, New York, 1962.

Kintner, William Roscoe. *Peace and the Strategy Conflict*, Frederick A. Praeger, New York, 1967.

Kintner, William Roscoe. *The Prudent Case for Safeguard*, National Strategy Information Center, New York, 1969.

Kintner, William Roscoe. *Safeguard: Why the ABM Makes Sense*, Hawthorn Books, New York, 1969.

Kissinger, Henry A. *Nuclear Weapons and Foreign Policy*, Harper Brothers, New York, 1957.

Kolkowicz, Roman. *The Soviet Military and the Communist Party*, Princeton University Press, Princeton, New Jersey, 1967.

Kolodziej, Edward A. *The Uncommon Defense and Congress, 1945–63*, Columbus, Ohio, 1966.

Kramish, Arnold. *Atomic Energy in the Soviet Union*, Stanford University Press, 1950.

Krosnov, COL A. "The Evolution of Fighter Tactics," *PVO Herald*, February 1972.

Kuebel, Fletcher and Bailey, Charles W. *No High Ground*, Bantam, New York, 1960.

Kulikov, General of the Army V. "Antiaircraft Defense in the Defense of the Soviet Nation," *PVO Herald*, (ACS/I Translation), April 1973.

Lapp, Ralph. *The New Priesthood: The Scientific Elite and the Uses of Power*, Harper & Row, New York, 1965.

Larkins, James Randall. *The International Aspects of the Air Defense of the United States Against Attack by Hostile Aircraft*, Georgetown University, Washington, D.C., June 1959.

Lechy, William. "Diary of William Lechy," *The Lechy Papers*, Library of Congress, Washington, D.C.

Lee, Asher. *Air Power*, Praeger, New York, 1955.

Lee, Asher. *The Soviet Air and Rocket Forces*, Praeger, New York, 1959.

LeMay, Curtis E. "Address on U.S. Air Defense and Military Policy to the Air Power Council CONVAIR Management Club of Fort Worth," Office of Public Affairs, Department of Defense, Washington, D.C., 26 August 1960.

MacKintosh, J. M. *Strategy and Tactics of Soviet Foreign Policy*, Oxford University Press, London, 1962.

McGowan, Samuel B. *Bomber Defense Against Surface-to-Air Missiles*, Study Project 21-55A, Senior Observer Section, Mather AFB, Mather Field, California, 30 June 1955.

McMullen, R. F. *Air Defense and National Policy 1946–1950*, ADC Historical Study No. 22, 1965.

McMullen, R. F. *Air Defense and National Policy 1951–1957*, ADC Historical Study No. 24, 1965.

McMullen, R. F. "History of Air Defense Weapons 1946–1962," ADC Historical Study No. 14, Historical Division, Office of information, HQ ADC.

McMullen, R. F. *Interceptor Missiles in Air Defense 1944–1964*, ADC Historical Study No. 30, February 1965.

McMullen, Richard F. *An Overview of ADC Weapons*, Aerospace Defense Command History, Colorado Springs, Colorado, 1973.

McVeigh, D. R. *The Development of the Bomarc Guided Missile 1950–1953*, WADC, January 1956.

Mallan, Lloyd. *Peace is a Three-Edged Sword*, Prentice-Hall, Englewood Cliffs, New Jersey, 1964.

Malwad, N. *Civil Defense: As Annotated Bibliography 1960–1968*, Bhabha Atomic Research Centre, Trombay, India, 1970.

Marschak, Thomas, Glennan, Thomas K., Jr., and Summers, Robert. *A Strategy for R&D: Studies in the Microeconomics of Development*, New York, 1967.

Martin, Harold H. "Could We Beat Back an Air Attack on the U.S.?," *Saturday Evening Post*, 4 November 1950.

Martin, Thomas Lyle and Latham, Don C. *Strategy for Survival*, University of Arizona Press, Tucson, Arizona, 1963.

Maxam, William P. *Federal Civil Defense 1946–1963: A Study in Organization and Administration*, University Microfilms, Inc., Ann Arbor, Michigan, 1965.

Miller, Ed Mack. *Men of the Contrail Country*, Prentice Hall, Englewood Cliffs, New Jersey, 1963.

Millis, Walter, ed. *The Forrestal Diaries*, The Viking Press, New York, 1951.

Millis, Walter, Mansfield, Harvey C., and Stein, Harold. *Arms and the State: Civil Military Elements in National Policy*, Twentieth Century Fund, New York, 1950.

Mitchell, Donald W. *The Economics of National Security—Civil Defense: Planning for Survival and Recover*, ICAF, Washington, D.C., 1962.

Morenus, Richard. *DEW LINE: Distant Early Warning, The Miracle of America's First Line of Defense*, Rand McNally, New York, 1957.

Murdock, Clark A. *Defense Policy Formation: A Comparative Analysis of the McNamara Era*, State University of New York Press, Albany, New York, 1974.

Murphy, Charles H. *The Decision to Curtail Strategic Air Defense Programs in FY 1975: Rationale and Implications*, Congressional Research Service, U.S. Library of Congress, Washington, D.C., 15 April 1974.

Nemecek, Vaclav. "A Sukhoi Decade," *Flying Review International*, February 1966.

Nemecek, Vaclav. "A Sukhoi Decade, Part II: The Dry One's War," *Flying Review International*, May 1966.

Nemecek, Vaclav. "A Sukhoi Decade, Part III: Turbojets and Tribulations," *Flying Review International*, April 1966.

Newhouse, John. *Cold Dawn: The Story of SALT*, Holt, Rinehart and Winston, New York, 1973.

Palmer, Paul Carr. *Threat Ordering Criteria and Evaluation for An Antiballistic Missile Defense*, Thesis (MS), Naval PG School, Monterey, California, 1967.

Palmer, Robert R. *The Organization of Ground Combat Troops, United States Air Force in World War II*, Washington, D.C., 1947.

Partridge, Earle E. *CINCNORAD's Operational Concept for Control of Air Defense Weapons*, Speech given to the Armed Forces Policy Council, Colorado Springs, Colorado, 3 May 1956.

Partridge, Earle E. *Open Testimony Before the Armed Services Sub-Committee, 25 May 1956*, HQ Continental Air Defense Command, Ent Air Force Base, Colorado Springs, Colorado, 26 May 1956.

Perry, Robert. *Comparisons of Soviet and U.S. Technology*, RAND R-827-PR, June 1973.

Perry, Robert. *European and U.S. Aircraft Development Strategies*, RAND P-4748, December 1971.

Bibliography

Perry, Robert. *A Prototype Strategy for Aircraft Development*, RAND RM-5597-1-PR, July 1972.

Pile, Frederick A. *Ack-Ack*, George G. Harrap and Company, Ltd., London, 1949.

Ray, Thomas W. *A History of the DEW line, 1946–1964*, ADC Historical Study No. 31, June 1965.

Reamer, Edward D. and Rogers, Jack D. "A Method for Air Defense System Evaluation," Operations Research Office, Johns Hopkins University, Chevy Chase, Maryland, 30 June 1954.

Robertson, Bruce, ed. *United States Arm and Air Force Fighters 1916–1961*, Harleyford Publications, Ltd., Letchworth, Herts, England, 1961.

Roderick, Harry E. *Organizational and Functional Relationship of Air and Civil Defense*, AWC Thesis No. 1334, U.S. Air University, Maxwell AFB, March 1957.

Saville, MG G. P. *Air Force Weapons, Capabilities, and Developments*, Lectures to National War College, 15 February 1950.

Sanders, Ralph. *The Politics of Defense Analysis*, Dunellen, New York, 1973.

Sayer, A. P., comp. *The Second World War, 1939–1945, Army, Army Radar*, The War Office, Great Britain, 1950. (British-Restricted, U.S.-Confidential-Modified Handling Authorized)

Schilling, Warner R., Hammond, Paul Y., and Snyder, Glenn H. *Strategy, Politics and Defense Budgets*, Columbia University Press, New York, 1962.

Scott, William F. "Survival in the Nuclear Age: An Examination of a Soviet Concept," (Unpublished Ph.D. Dissertation), The George Washington University, Washington, D.C., 1974.

Semmens, Paul. "Preliminary Chronology, Blue Air Defense Systems, Strategic Air Defense History," Braddock, Dunn and McDonald, Inc., Colorado Springs, Colorado, 2 volumes-BDM/CS-85-74-1-0073, 25 November 1974.

Smith, William J. *Air Defense of the North American Continent*, AWC Thesis No. 1347, U.S. Air University, Maxwell AFB, June 1957.

Sokolov, V. L. *Soviet Use of German Science and Technology*, Research Program on the U.S.S.R., New York, 1955.

Sokolovsky, Marshal S. U. V. D. *Military Strategy*, Third Edition, (Harriet F. Scott, Translator), SRI Technical Note SSC-TN-8974-29, January 1971.

Solzhenitsyn, Alexander I. *The Gulag Archipelago: 1918–1956*, (Thomas P. Whitney, Translator), Harper & Row, New York, 1973.

Staudt, H. R. The Department of Defense Decision-Making Process, Unpublished M.I.T. Thesis, 1 May 1968.

Stanley, T. W. *American Defense and National Security*, Public Affairs Press, Washington, D.C., 1956.

Stockwell, Richard E. *Soviet Air Power*, Pageant, New York, 1956.

Stimson, Henry L. "The Decision to Use the Atomic Bomb," *Harper's Magazine*, February 1947.

Strickland, Donald A. *Scientists in Politics: The Atomic Scientists Movement 1945–1946*, Purdue University Studies, Lafayette, Indiana, 1968.

Sturm, Thomas A. *Organization and Responsibility for Air Defense, March 1946–September 1955*, Air Defense Command Study No. 9, U.S. Air Force, Air Defense Command.

Sturm, Thomas A., Volan, Denys, Billias, George, and Stevens, Howard. "The Air Defense of the United States: A Study of the Work of the Air Defense Command and its Predecessors through June 1951," Prepared by the Directorate of Historical Services, Office of the Air Adjutant General, HQ, ADC.

Taft, Robert A. *A Foreign Policy for Americans*, Doubleday & Company, New York, 1951.

Tammen, Ronald L. *MIRV and the Arms Race: An Interpretation of Defense Strategy*, Praeger, New York, 1973.

Terrett, Dulany. *The Signal Corps: The Emergency*, U.S. Army in World War II, The Technical Services, Office of the Chief of Military History, Department of the Army, Washington, D.C., 1956.

Thompson, George R. and Harris, Dixie R. *The Signal Corps: The Outcome*, U.S. Army in World War II, The Technical Services, Office of the Chief of Military History, Department of the Army, Washington, D.C., 1966.

Tikhomirov, V. I. and Paramonov, F. I. *Organization and Planning of Production at Aircraft Engine-Building Plants* Organizatsiya: Planirovaniye Proizvodstra na Aviadvigatele-Stroitel'nykh Zavodakh), (FTD Translation MT-24-499-73), Moscow, 1972.

Tokaev, G. A. *Betrayal of an Ideal*, (Alec Brown, Translator), Harvill Press, London, 1954.

Tokaev, G. A. *Comrade X*, (Alec Brown, Translator), Harvill Press, London, 1956.

Tokaev, G. A. *Soviet Imperialism*, Duckworth, London, 1954.

Tokaev, G. A. *Stalin Means War*, Weidenfeld & Nicholson, London, 1951.

Truman, Harry S. *Memoirs*, Garden City, New York, 1955.

Truman, Harry S. *Memoirs of Harry S. Truman II, Years of Trial and Hope*, Doubleday and Company, Garden City, New York, 1956.

Vandenberg, Arthur H. *The Private Papers of Senator Vandenberg*, Houghton Mifflin, Boston, Massachusetts, 1952.

Volan, Denys. *Air Defense in Theory and Practice 1918–1945*, Historical Division, Office of Information, HQ, ADC, 1964.

Weaver, Leon Hiram. *The Civil Defense Debate*, Social Science Research Bureau, Michigan State University, East Lansing, Michigan, 1967.

Welborn, M. C. *V-1 and V-2 Attacks Against the United Kingdom During WWII*, Technical Memorandum ORO-T-42, Operations Research Office, Johns Hopkins University, Washington, D.C., 1950.

Wesley, Frank Craven and Cate, James Lea, eds. "The Army Air Forces in World War II," *Men and Planes*, Volume VI, The University of Chicago Press, Chicago, Illinois, 1955.

Weyland, GEN O. P. "The First Jet Air War," *Air Intelligence Digest*, September–October 1953.

Wigley, Russell F. *History of the United States Army*, The MacMillan Company, New York, 1967.

Wigner, Eugene Paul, ed. *Who Speaks for Civil Defense?*, Scribner, New York, 1968.

Wilson, Charles E. *Continental Air Defense*, Memo to Secretary of the Air Force, U.S. Department of Defense, Washington, D.C., 21 June 1956.

Wohlstetter, Albert, et al. *U.S. Air Defense*, ORO Study R-17, Appendices D, E, F, N, 24 February 1958.

Wolfe, Thomas W. *Soviet Power and Europe 1945–1970*, The Johns Hopkins Press, 1970.

Wolfe, Thomas W. *Soviet Response to U.S. Military Policies and Problems*, RAND, RM-4798-PR, December 1965.

Yakimanskiy, N. and Gorbunov, V. "Certain Questions in the Development of the Theory of Operational Arts and Tactics of the National Air Defense Troops during the Postwar Period," *Voyenno Istoricheskiy Zhurnal* (Military History Journal), No. 3, Moscow, March 1973.

Yakovlev, Alexander S. *Fifty Years of Soviet Aircraft Construction*, (50 Let Sovetskogo Samoletostroeniya), (E. Vilim, Translator), N.A.S.A. Technical Translation, (Jerusalem, Israel Program for Scientific Translations), TTF-627, 1970.

Yakovlev, Alexander S. *Target of Life*, (Tsel' Zhizni), NTIS #AD674316, (1968 FTD Translation), Moscow, 1966.

Yarmolinsky, Adam. *The Military Establishment: Its Impacts on American Society*, Harper & Row, New York, 1971.

Zheltikov, COL. I. and Igolkin, COL V. *Certain Tendencies in the Development of Aircraft and Antirocket Defense, Voyennaya Mysl'* (Military Thought) April, 1965 (Translated by Foreign Documents Division, FPD 0146/68).

www.ingramcontent.com/pod-product-compliance
Lightning Source LLC
Chambersburg PA
CBHW080728230426
43665CB00020B/2654